# The Benevolent Deity

Errata: *The Benevolent Deity* by Robert J. Wilson

The following illustrations are photographs by Winfred E. A. Bernhard:

Cover and frontispiece (Portrait of Ebenezer Gay by John Hazlett)

Home of Ebenezer Gay, Hingham, Massachusetts

Exterior view of the Old Ship Church

"Wine Glass" Pulpit in Hingham's Old Ship Church

Title page of Ebenezer Gay's Dudleian Lecture on Natural Religion

Martin Gay (Portrait of son of Ebenezer Gay)

# The Benevolent Deity

## EBENEZER GAY AND THE RISE OF RATIONAL RELIGION IN NEW ENGLAND, 1696–1787

Robert J. Wilson III

UNIVERSITY OF PENNSYLVANIA PRESS
PHILADELPHIA

Frontispiece: Portrait of Ebenezer Gay, painted
between 1785 and 1786 by John Hazlitt (courtesy of
Mr. Ebenezer Gay of Hingham).

Library of Congress Cataloging in Publication Data

Wilson, Robert J. (Robert John), 1944–
    The Benevolent Deity: Ebenezer Gay and the rise
of rational religion in New England, 1696–1787

    Bibliography: p.
    Includes index.
    1. Gay, Ebenezer, 1696–1787.   2. Congregational
churches—Massachusetts—Clergy—Biography.
3. Massachusetts—Biography.   4. Arminianism—History—
18th century.   5. Rationalism—History—18th century.
6. Religious thought—New England.   I. Title.
BX7260.G279W54   1983      285.8'092'4 [B]      83-3657
ISBN 0-8122-7891-7

Printed in the United States of America

*For Audie*

# Contents

# Illustrations

# Prologue

The years following the Great Awakening in New England witnessed the commencement of a great theological struggle between the clerical champions of "Christian Liberty" and the defenders of "the good old Calvinistical Way." The adherents of "Christian Liberty," who were called Arminians by their opponents, were contending for the liberty of the mind and the soul to pursue truth and salvation free from prior restraint. During the 1750s, these Arminians openly challenged the assumptions of New England Calvinism that men and women were incapable of influencing their spiritual destiny. Their scholarly examination of biblical texts convinced them that there was no scriptural basis for the notion that salvation was limited in some foreordained way, or that the human race was totally depraved. Indeed, the Arminians believed that most men have, however obscured by Adam's Fall, a basic core of decency that, when properly developed, can merit approbation in the eyes of a benevolent and rational deity. Salvation, like temporal prosperity, was available to those with the moral and intellectual stamina to achieve it. Their orthodox opponents regarded the Arminian emphasis on human initiative as vain, presumptuous, and an implicit challenge to the necessity for the central event in Christianity—Christ's atonement on the cross.[1]

The Arminian movement may have arisen spontaneously as a reaction to a number of intellectual and social stimuli, but it took its shape as a major, quasi-denominational force in New England Congregationalism under the guidance of particular clergymen. Among these ministers, three have been most prominently associated with the movement. Jonathan Mayhew, minister at Boston's

West Church (1744–1766) became the outspoken, controversial publicist of this liberal theology. Charles Chauncy, minister at Boston's First Church (1727–1787) emerged as a discreet but powerful ally of the Arminians. The man more responsible than any other for sustaining and nourishing the Arminian movement, however, was the Reverend Ebenezer Gay, minister in Hingham's First Parish (1718–1787). The rationalist clergy, most of whom were at least a generation younger, turned increasingly to the old patriarch for intellectual definition and reassurance. Gay became, to use historian Alan Heimert's phrase, "the philosopher of Massachusetts rationalism."[2]

Despite his ubiquitous presence in the history of Arminianism, Gay has been something of a historical enigma. His role in the Arminian movement baffled nineteenth-century Unitarians, who had been told that he was an important figure in their history, without really being told why. In 1815, John Adams, who knew Gay quite well, responded to an inquiry by Jedidiah Morse, a zealous Calvinist minister, concerning the beginnings of Unitarianism: "I can testify as a witness to its old age. Sixty-five years ago my own minister, the Rev. Lemuel Briant; Dr. Jonathan Mayhew of the West Church in Boston; the Rev. Mr. Shute of Hingham; the Rev. John Brown of Cohasset; and perhaps equal to all, if not above all, the Rev. Mr. Gay of Hingham were Unitarians." This sense of Gay's importance in the development of liberal Christianity was shared by the great Unitarian preacher, Theodore Parker, who remarked to Sydney Howard Gay, a descendant, that "Your grandfather was the first Unitarian, & stood in the same relation to the Church of his day that I do to the Church of mine." Still, Parker could not define the nature of that relation. In 1910, the historian Samuel A. Eliot reported, with evident skepticism, that "Dr. Gay has often been called the father of American Unitarianism." This confusion has persisted until more recent times. Clifford K. Shipton, in his sketch on Gay in *Sibley's Harvard Graduates*, has written, "It is to the glory of New England that the ripples of this man's influence gradually spread to the far corners in spite of his way of calling attention to the most sacred canons of church and state." Shipton, however, failed to provide much evidence in support of his portrait of Gay as an influential and radical figure.[3]

Part of the confusion about Gay has to do with the imprecise understanding that nineteenth and even twentieth-century historians have had concerning the relationship between Arminianism and Unitarianism. The more fundamental reason for the uncertainty about Gay, however, is that, with the exception of twenty published sermons, his contributions to the Arminian movement were not public in nature. He disseminated his religious views by serving as teacher and sometimes paternal advisor to a host of younger ministers. His protégés included men such as Jonathan Mayhew and Simeon Howard, key figures in the transmission of the Arminian gospel. Gay worked tirelessly, though discreetly, to find pulpits for these young liberals, and he came promptly to their defense when they came under attack for their views. He assured them that they should indeed question the traditions of their fathers and that it was time to "Open [their] Eyes to the Light, and yield to the Evidence of Truth."[4]

Gay's long and fascinating intellectual odyssey began in the stimulating academic environment of early eighteenth-century Harvard. Europe's scientific revolution was breaking upon the "School of the Prophets" in full force. England's Dr. Samuel Clarke was showing the scholarly world the techniques of scriptural criticism and, by implication, encouraging students to divest themselves of all their doctrinal baggage when studying the Bible. Gay read Clarke eagerly and he also read the works of the physico-theologians, English and Scottish thinkers who inferred the attributes of God from the orderly and benign Newtonian universe. The scientific thought of the early Enlightenment seemed to Gay to mesh perfectly with an older, less controversial rational tradition. He found legitimation for the newer scholarship in the seventeenth-century works of Richard Baxter, Hugo Grotius, Archbishop John Tillotson, and that group of Restoration theologians who came to be known as the Cambridge Platonists. Gay emerged from Harvard with the conviction that every educated man should try to discover God's Truth for himself; that creeds and confessions were as irrelevant to the questing Christian as Aristotle had become for the natural philosophers. It was that empirical spirit that pushed Gay along from his close intellectual identification with Cotton Mather in 1718 to his association with William Hazlitt, an avowed Socinian preacher, in 1786.

Gay's Arminian theology was also a natural outgrowth of his social conservatism. He fervently believed that external conformity and obedience to authority formed the cement that held the religious and social hierarchy together. Therefore he preached the Law, encouraged good works, and tried to make his parish as inclusive as possible. When he advised a Hingham sailor to stay out of taverns, he was helping create a godly environment where that young man's soul might be saved. Gay instinctively opposed any socially disruptive or divisive forces. War, revolution, or the frenzied excesses of religious revivals were equally unsettling to him. He did not tell the lower orders of Hingham society that they were hopelessly depraved, nor did he encourage them to think that they were as sanctified as their pastor and the town's educated elite. Salvation, said Gay, was available to all, but "So far as a man's intellectual abilities and attainments are superior to others, he may, upon his receiving of grace, out-strip them . . . and be advanced to a higher form in the school of Christ."[5]

Ebenezer Gay shepherded his Hingham flock for the extraordinary period of sixty-nine years, during which time he became the living embodiment of the social, cultural, and intellectual character of that town. One cannot understand Gay without understanding Hingham. Consequently, this study has attempted to depict the evolving social, political, and economic life of eighteenth-century Hingham, from the time of Gay's settlement in 1718, through the Great Awakening, and into the post-Revolutionary era. Gay's world was not, however, circumscribed by Hingham's boundaries; indeed, by mid-century, he had emerged as the most influential minister on the South Shore. Therefore the eighteenth-century religious history of the coastal region between Boston and Plymouth forms another integral part of this study. Gay's ministry flourished in the distinctive theological and ecclesiastical climate of the South Shore, free from the social and religious pressures of Boston that inhibited Charles Chauncy and vexed Jonathan Mayhew. Indeed, Gay was able to fashion the Hingham Association of Ministers into a sort of Arminian haven where liberal clergymen could pursue their struggle for "Christian Liberty."[6]

Gay was a man who shunned public controversy, working behind the scenes whenever possible. Consequently, I have sometimes felt an almost palpable resistance to my attempt to draw aside the veil that Gay cast over his life. The attempt to resurrect his world has involved sustained digging into a widely dispersed body of correspondence, diaries, church records, and town records. One may only hope that the old patriarch's penchant for privacy has been successfully confounded, and that, in the process, a little more light has been shed on the history of rational religion in New England. Gay's pastoral life has been most fully illuminated by the enormous collection of manuscripts, including most of the Hingham First Church Records, housed at the Massachusetts Historical Society. I would especially like to thank the staff of the Society for their unfailing courtesy and efficiency. I am also in debt to Hingham Town Clerk John Studley and his staff for making the town records available to me, and for rendering many small kindnesses that facilitated my task.

I wish to extend my warmest thanks to those scholars at the University of Massachusetts who have read and criticized earlier drafts of this book with scrupulous care. I am indebted to Paul S. Boyer, Everett H. Emerson, Stephen W. Nissenbaum, and particularly to Winfred E. A. Bernhard. There are many other persons who have given me useful advice, insights, and access to documents. I am especially grateful to Robert C. Anderson, the Reverend Edward Atkinson, Cedric B. Cowing, William O. Gay, George E. Kirk, the Reverend Kenneth LaFleur, Julian Loring, the Reverend Paul R. Medling, John P. Richardson, the Reverend Donald F. Robinson, Kevin Sweeney, Patricia J. Tracy, James W. Wheaton, Conrad Wright, and my typist, Mrs. Eleanor Starzyk. I wish most particularly to thank Mr. Ebenezer Gay of Hingham, eighth in descent from the old patriarch, for his personal research, excellent advice, and friendship. If I have succeeded in putting some flesh on the dry bones of Parson Gay, it is very largely due to Mr. Gay's assistance. I owe my greatest debt to my wife, Audie Schwegman Wilson, who has contributed everything from editorial criticism and illustrations to our daily bread.

Finally, it has been my policy throughout the book to remain as faithful as possible to the spelling, punctuation, and capitalization in the eighteenth-century sources, both manuscript and printed.

# The Benevolent Deity

# CHAPTER I

# Dedham

Ebenezer Gay once observed that "the light of christian graces and virtues in them that are truly cloathed with it . . . rises in splendor, and goeth as gradually to such perfection, as that they shall shine forth as the sun in the kingdom of their Father." For the eighteenth-century Arminian clergy, this gradual unfolding of Light and Grace epitomized the ideal Christian life. Since Gay later came so dearly to value continuity and gradualism in both his spiritual and secular life, it would seem inappropriate to begin his story in a world of upheaval and turbulence. Fortunately we are spared this potentially jarring note, for Gay was born, August 15, 1696, in Dedham, a village whose collective temperament tended to be decidedly sober and measured.[1]

Ten years later, in the summer of 1706, we might imagine a traveler riding through Dedham on the Boston-Rhode Island Post Road. The rich farmland and luxuriant meadows that spread out on either side of the meandering Charles River contrasted vividly with the overcrowded streets and commercial bustle of Boston, just ten miles to the northeast. "Contentment" was the original name given to the community by its founders in 1635 and, to the casual observer, the peaceful, agricultural utopia implied in that name still persisted after seventy years. The traveler could see few signs of either the ostentatious wealth or the impoverishment that were becoming so evident in Boston. Dedham society was, in fact, in the process of change, but the alteration was still glacially slow and vigorously resisted. On the surface, a visitor would observe only a seventeenth-century, rural, Puritan community.[2]

The ride from Boston had been hot and dusty, and the

3

stranger might have felt the need to refresh himself. Seeing that Joshua Fisher's tavern was a bit crowded, he inquired about a quieter place, and was directed to Nathaniel Gay's ordinary, near the edge of the village center. He soon reined up in front of the well-built but modest single-bay dwelling that Nathaniel had erected in 1683. The traveler was greeted by Nathaniel's wife Lydia, a vigorous imposing woman of fifty-four, who apologized for her husband's absence. He was up on the roof of the schoolhouse making repairs to the chimney. Lydia felt that this was a bit risky for a sixty-three-year-old man, but Nathaniel had for years employed his considerable skills at carpentry to keep the Dedham school in good repair.[3]

Four of Nathaniel and Lydia's eight children still lived at home. Lydia relied increasingly on twelve-year-old Abigail for help with household chores, since the older daughter, Joanna, was soon to be married. The traveler next met Lydia's two youngest sons— Benjamin and Ebenezer. Benjamin, a robust and rather cocky lad of fifteen, might have spent the morning working on the few acres that would eventually, along with the house, constitute his inheritance. We might imagine that the youngest child, ten-year-old Ebenezer, had spent *his* morning diligently laboring with declension in his Latin accidence. Given Gay's later temperament, this is at least as likely a supposition as the alternative, that he was fishing over at Wigwam Pond. We do know that Nathaniel, quickly discerning the boy's intellectual promise, had early determined to devote the child of his old age to the ministry. The traveler would probably have beheld a slender, sandy-haired, rather precocious child; not particularly handsome but able to manage a most engaging smile.[4]

To the extent that Dedham in 1706 was still a tightly-knit community with commonly shared interests and values, the Gays were a family set slightly apart. Nathaniel Gay persistently exposed his children to influences from the world beyond Dedham. The very road on which they lived was an avenue of foreign intrusion into the village. Visitors such as our traveler would stop at one of the taverns or ordinaries such as Gay's, quaff a mug of flip, and bring news of the outer world. Young Ebenezer would hear reports of the grain shortage in Boston, rumors of projected expeditions against Quebec, or word of the Deerfield massacre. (Gay's horror of French Canada, which he later called "that land of heathenish darkness and popish superstition," stayed with him for the rest of his life.)[5]

Both of Gay's parents came from backgrounds that tended to make them a bit less parochial than many of their neighbors. Ebenezer's grandfather, John Gay, was one of the original proprietors of the Dedham grant. Sometime around 1636–37 he and his wife, the former widow Joanna Borden, moved from Watertown and settled on a twelve-acre homestead along the banks of the Charles, about one and one half miles north of the developing village center. John's physical distance from the town seemed to reflect his level of commitment to the community. For the next forty years he struggled to acquire an estate that would provide an adequate settlement for his five male heirs, and he soon managed to become the wealthiest landowner in Dedham. His wealth and seniority made him a figure of considerable influence, yet he served as selectman only once (1654) and held no other major town office. For John Gay, "Contentment" meant primarily the opportunity to acquire a landed estate with minimal interference.[6]

John's son Nathaniel involved himself in the welfare of the community to a greater extent than his father, though he too seemed to have little interest in the skirmishes and wrangles of local village politics. Nathaniel did move into the village center; he was chosen a trustee of the Dedham school; and he served several years as a tythingman, suggesting that the villagers confidently entrusted him with the guardianship of community and family morality. His skill as a carpenter, his competence as a surveyor, and his entrepreneurial talents were employed both for the profit of the town and of himself. Nathaniel, however, had spent a brief sojourn in the great world outside Dedham. In 1669, at the age of twenty-six, he went to live with a family in Charlestown (quite possibly the socially prominent Bunkers). After returning home a few years later, his ambitions for himself, and particularly for his offspring, seem to have focused on goals beyond the normal aspirations of a Dedham farmer.[7]

If John and Nathaniel Gay were not typical Dedham yeomen, neither was Ebenezer's maternal "grandfather," Eleazer Lusher. Lydia Gay had been raised in the Lusher household, but her real father was John Starr, an immigrant carpenter who wandered about the colony, apparently unable to ply his trade successfully. In her infancy, Lydia was entrusted to the care of her mother's sister, Mary Bunker Lusher, Eleazer's wife. Lusher was one of the major figures in the early history of the Bay Colony, and Lydia proudly transmitted the Lusher heritage to her sons. Eleazer Lusher was

the only citizen of seventeenth-century Dedham to achieve real distinction outside the context of the village. An active Dissenter in
England (possibly educated at Cambridge), Lusher arrived in Dedham in 1637 and quickly became a leader among the covenanting
saints who gathered the village church. Although Lusher served
Dedham for years as a selectman and town clerk (the latter from
1641 to 1663), he was better known as one of the leading magistrates of the colony. Serving on the Court of Assistants from 1662
to 1673, Lusher was, to use Kenneth Lockridge's description,
"a one-man ministry of all talents"—diplomat, judge, and, in
1671, collator of the laws of the colony. Edward Johnson in his
seventeenth-century *Wonder-Working Providence* included Eleazer
Lusher among the heroes of the New England Zion, "one of the
right stamp and pure mettle, a gratious, humble and heavenly
minded man." Later, when New Englanders began to grow less
confident in the success of their holy enterprise, this couplet went
about:

> When Lusher was in office, all things went well,
> But how they go since, it shames us to tell.[8]

The Lusher family heritage, Nathaniel's lively interest in education, their residence on the Post Road: these and other factors
combined to make Ebenezer and his brothers rather cosmopolitan
in their outlook. Lusher Gay, Ebenezer's second eldest brother
(b. 1685) was, in his maturity, a literate, well-informed man of affairs. No simple farmer, he became a large-scale land speculator,
dealt with men of the stature of William Bollan (the future colonial
agent), and died one of the wealthiest men in Dedham. Though he
was denied the Harvard education afforded his younger brother,
Lusher in later years became an ardent and devout bible scholar.
He frequently visited brother Ebenezer in Hingham to borrow
Hubbard's *Annotations* or Matthew Henry's *Commentaries*. This
pious and intellectually vigorous farmer eventually had the satisfaction of seeing two of his sons enter the ministry—a satisfaction
that was to be denied Ebenezer.[9]

The extent to which Nathaniel Gay's children held religious
and social values that diverged from those of the Dedham establishment became apparent as the new century progressed. In the
years from 1700 to 1740, whatever had remained of Dedham's corporate unity began to crumble under pressure from the outlying
areas. Historian Edward M. Cook has observed that, during this

period, "The Gay family was at the center of almost every dispute in Dedham." Nathaniel Gay had inherited from his father a great deal of land in that section of Dedham known as the "Clapboardtrees" (now Westwood). He used the inheritance to provide his two eldest sons, Nathaniel, Jr. and Lusher, with handsome farms. The Clapboardtrees region tended to be settled by other men like the Gays, land speculators and professional men who had closer ties to Boston than did the people of the village center. Nathaniel, Jr. and Lusher emerged as leaders in various attempts to wrest political control of Dedham's affairs from the town establishment. They were joined in their rebellion by their cousin John Gay, a tailor, and by their brother Benjamin, now the contentious and litigious owner of the Gay tavern (an ambitious expansion of his father's ordinary). Feelings became so heated at a town meeting in 1728 that John Gay took a poke at the moderator and Benjamin backed him up, musket in hand.[10]

The intellectual and social attitudes of the Gays and their neighbors were most clearly reflected in their struggle to establish their own church in the Clapboardtrees. Ebenezer, who by now was grown and well-established in his pulpit at Hingham, watched the efforts of his brothers with great interest. All of the boys had been reared on the learned, polished, and rational discourses of the Reverend Joseph Belcher. When Belcher died in 1723, the Dedham fathers called Samuel Dexter, a pious young clergyman whose preaching was more rough-edged than that of his predecessor, and whose soul-humbling Calvinist theology was far more uncompromising. The Gays had opposed Dexter's settlement from the start and, after losing that battle, indignantly withdrew from communion for several months. Matters came to a head in 1729 when Dexter apparently demanded that Sarah Gay (wife of cousin John) make a public declaration of her conversion experience before being admitted to full communion. The Gays were furious since this sort of performance had never been necessary under Pastor Belcher. They again withdrew from communion and began a campaign to establish a separate church in the Clapboardtrees. Despite Parson Dexter's earnest prayer that the Gays "may not be permitted to make any disturbance among us or Breaches upon us," they joined the other Clapboardtrees leaders in defiantly erecting a meetinghouse and engaging a minister whose preaching was more congenial. Dexter must often have felt beseiged by Gays on all sides, and never more so than in 1735 when an ecclesiastical council was called to deal with the Clapboardtrees schism. The council ruled in favor of the rebels, and the leading conciliar advocate of their cause was the Reverend Ebenezer Gay of Hingham.[11]

Clearly, Ebenezer Gay and his brothers were raised in such a way that they did not fully share the conservative, agrarian ideals of the Dedham establishment. This divergence, however, was a matter of degree, and it must not be assumed that young Ebenezer was in some sense impervious to the influence of his country surroundings. His immediate environment naturally reinforced the social institutions and hierarchical structure of the village. On a slight rise to the north of the Gays stood the meetinghouse, surrounded by the imposing houses of the town leaders. Immediately to the south and west, the Gay homestead was bounded by the burying ground. The somber graves of his grandsires and the other Dedham fathers lay within yards of the house. The most visible and formal expression of Dedham's social order could be observed at the meetinghouse on Sunday. Ebenezer entered the structure through three porches and three flights of stairs. Inside, the townspeople assumed their designated seats, which carefully reflected their sex, age, race, marital condition, and their spiritual or social eminence. The meetinghouse had a double run of galleries, the second tier of which had been built by Ebenezer's father in 1696. Ebenezer sat with the other boys in the short seats at the foot of the pulpit stairs. From that perspective, the Reverend Joseph Belcher must have appeared godlike in his raised pulpit.[12]

Since Nathaniel Gay had apparently devoted Ebenezer to the work of the ministry, it was natural that Pastor Belcher should supervise much of his preparation for Harvard. He provided a pastoral model for Gay that served the younger man in good stead for the rest of his long career. Belcher was a social conservative who tried (and failed) to revert to the practice of depending on voluntary contributions for his salary rather than a town tax, or "rate." In religious matters, however, he leaned toward the "liberal" camp of the day, since he supported John Leverett for the presidency of Harvard against the wishes of Increase and Cotton Mather. When Belcher took his master's degree at Harvard in 1692, he defended the proposition that the creation of the world can be proved on rational grounds; indeed, Belcher seemed to have no doubt that faith could be solidly grounded on "ratiocination."[13]

This erudite, rational divine was also a vigorous evangelical. Desperately concerned about a continuing decline in church membership, he did not allow strict Calvinist doctrine to intrude over-much into his efforts to bring his Dedham parish to Christ. In his sermons he urged the need for the kind of personal moral exertion that Reformed scholars called "preparation"; i.e., an attempt to make the soul presentable for God's electing grace. He exhorted his parishioners to "labor to have the righteousness of Christ imputed to them in order to their justification." Belcher believed in powerful preaching, and he often used his forensic gifts for the purpose of evangelizing the young people. Shortly before Ebenezer left for Harvard, Belcher preached a sermon to certain of the village youth who had been laboring under "convictions":

> Let me exhort and charge you to seek him presently, and not to sit down satisfied till you find him. And oh! that I knew what further argument to urge, that might possibly prevail with you to set about and persevere in this matter. God is my witness, I would do anything within my power, to bring you to a real interest in Jesus Christ.

It was quite possibly under this kind of preaching that young Gay first began to feel that God was working savingly upon his heart.[14]

Gay was fortunate in having Joseph Belcher as his guide and advisor in those early years. His good fortune was increased by the superior quality of the school that he attended. The Dedham free school, which his Grandfather Lusher had established, attracted a constant succession of young schoolmasters fresh from Harvard. This was, of course, true of other grammar schools as well, but Dedham, along with the towns of Hadley and Newbury, seemed especially prominent as a place of first employment for young Harvard pedagogues. In his last year at the Dedham grammar school, Gay came under the tutelage of Sir Elisha Callender (Harvard graduate scholars were then called "Sir"). Sir Callender was a Baptist; indeed he would become the most influential Baptist in the Bay Colony. Far from being an unlettered Anabaptist zealot (the Puritan stereotype of Baptists), Callender was a polished, refined young Harvard graduate, who would in eight years be ordained over the Baptist Church of Boston by the Mathers, father and son. Callender was, however, for all his "charitable and catholic Way of Thinking," an ardent Baptist. For one year, Ebenezer Gay learned Latin and Greek, construed and parsed, and reviewed Parson Belcher's sermons under the ferule of the eighteen-year-old Elisha Callender.[15]

The extent of Callender's influence on Gay is a matter of conjecture, but it must be noted that their accord on fundamental matters of pulpit style and even theology was nearly complete. Callender outlined his views on sermon delivery and pastoral politics to fellow Baptist John Comer at Newport:

> I must advise you to these things: 1. To studie well all your public discourses and look upon it your business to compose sermons in a handsome style and good method; 2. Carefully avoid all controversies in the pulpit.

If Callender imparted this same advice to young Gay, then it was scrupulously followed. One might also wonder if Gay were indebted to Callender in any way for his later anti-credalism. The belief that the Holy Scriptures were the only source of authority for the true Christian was fundamental to the Baptist tradition. As we shall see, Gay's suspicion of doctrinal authority came from many other sources, but Callender may have started him on the quest for "pure and undefil'd religion" at an early date.[16]

By the end of his grammar school years, Gay had a solid foundation in the classics. Given his later reputation at Harvard, it may be assumed that he easily mastered the *Sententiae Pueriles*, and that he translated the *Colloquies* of Erasmus, the *Metamorphoses* of Ovid, and even his New Testament Greek with facility. Nathaniel Gay spared no expense to prepare his son for Harvard; he may even have secured special tutoring for Ebenezer. Late in 1711, after Ebenezer had already been placed at Harvard, Nathaniel drew up his will. The document clearly reveals his anxiety and concern that Ebenezer be assured the financial means to continue "until the taking of his first Degree." The expenses were to be paid and discharged out of Nathaniel's estate, which would be managed by his son Benjamin. Lest Benjamin prove unsympathetic to this end, Nathaniel stressed at three separate points the importance of supporting Ebenezer at the college. He even stipulated that Benjamin should sell the lands of the estate if "the bringing up my son Ebenezer" should require it. Nathaniel Gay, Dedham husbandman, died on February 20, 1712, having insured that his son Ebenezer had been properly "fitted for the Universitie."[17]

# CHAPTER II

# Harvard

In the late spring of 1710, in the town of Dedham, a very earnest thirteen-year-old boy was hastily reviewing his Lily's Latin Grammar, and struggling with the syntactical complexities of New Testament Greek. At last, in early July, Ebenezer Gay set out in company with the Reverend Mr. Belcher for Cambridge. The journey was short, barely eight miles, and the prospect afforded by Cambridge Town was certainly not alien to Gay. He rode into a comfortably proportioned farm village, dominated but not overawed by the two college buildings, Old Harvard and Stoughton. The scene was not unlike Dedham, a superficial impression reinforced by the presence of the familiar Charles River, pursuing its tranquil course alongside the village.

Cambridge seemed the perfect setting for the contemplative life, but Harvard, despite outward appearances, was no peaceable kingdom. At the very time of Gay's arrival, a quiet but bitterly intense war was being waged at the college. The dimensions and ranks of the opposing sides were and are difficult to delineate. Nevertheless, the two camps were warring over real issues, even though those issues were not always clearly articulated. The conservative faction was championed by Increase Mather and, more centrally, by his son Cotton. In one sense, this was the popular party, supported by a majority of the members of the General Court, and by an increasing majority of the Boston clergymen. The conservatives feared that their beloved "school of the prophets" was becoming a school for heretics. This heresy was not so much defined in terms of theological deviance (although there were already mutterings about "Arminianism"), but rather as a fear that Harvard was no

11

longer defending the New England Way; that it was, in fact, becoming Anglicized. They complained that the scholars were studying the works of modern English liberals—Tillotson, Toland, Whitby—rather than the solid old Puritan divines such as Ames, Perkins, and Shepard. The free, "catholick," gentlemanly, and very English style of the Reverend Benjamin Colman of Brattle Street Church seemed the mode among many of the students. A Boston apothecary named John Checkley, just returned from several years in England, could be found at the college rather successfully pleading the cause of the Church of England. To the conservative faction, Harvard appeared to be producing future ministers who were latitudinarians at best, and who seemed to consider the old federal theology a bit outmoded. In 1717, the venerable Increase Mather came directly to the point, when he warned younger ministers against introducing innovations, "as long as there be any that are Conscientiously concerned to maintain the Old Religion of New-England."[1]

This general discontent with Harvard College was masterfully orchestrated by Cotton Mather. Mather was probably the most energetic and prolific scholar in eighteenth-century New England. He was also a vainglorious and rather paranoic man, who viewed John Leverett, the President of Harvard, as an interloper who had usurped the office that rightfully belonged to the Mathers. From 1707, the year of Leverett's appointment, until his death in 1724, Mather ceaselessly attempted to discredit his administration of the college. Whether the issue was lack of discipline or the composition of the Corporation (the college administration), whether the complaints came from Judge Samuel Sewall or the politician, Elisha Cooke, the source of the agitation could usually be traced to the restless pastor of Boston's Old North Church.

Despite the formidable opposition of Cotton Mather, President Leverett slowly established a firm base of support both within and without the college. His three principal allies in the Corporation were William Brattle, the minister of Cambridge, William's older brother Thomas, Treasurer of the Corporation, and Tutor Henry Flynt. Outside Cambridge, the President had strong support from clergymen, many of whom had been tutored by Leverett and William Brattle in the 1690s. Leverett could also look for backing from Governor Dudley and his Council. Thus, John Leverett was not without resources, as he waged a continual struggle against Mather, and a suspicious Board of Overseers.[2]

Leverett and Mather held sharply divergent views concerning Harvard's ultimate *raison d'être*. Mather wanted the institution to continue to function as an incubator for orthodox ministers who would strive to perpetuate the "New England Way," while Leverett had a more cosmopolitan vision of Harvard's educational goals. Although Cotton Mather and his supporters held the conservative ground in this dispute, it would be unjust to portray them as hopeless academic reactionaries. True, the Mather faction opposed the introduction of "Arminian" and "deistical" texts, but they fully supported the most exciting academic development of the period, the study of the new experimental philosophy. Harvard, by 1710, was no stranger to the empirical method, but it was only during the Leverett years that the religious, ethical, social, and humanistic implications of experimental science began to take hold.

Harvard educators had been sympathetic to the scientific method ever since, as Cotton Mather put it, "the great Lord Bacon show'd em the way to the Advancement of Learning." Harvard had, in a sense, accepted Baconian empirical technique before 1660, when the Copernican universe was allowed to displace the Ptolemaic system. Traditional, Aristotelian natural philosophy received a further jolt in 1686 when Charles Morton's up-to-date manual of science replaced the ancient, scholastic text of Magirus. A few years later, Tutor William Brattle introduced Harvard students to the highly mechanized universe of René Descartes. The consequence of all this was that Harvard College was well prepared to receive the two great giants of the early Enlightenment—Sir Isaac Newton and John Locke. Newton's discoveries and Locke's epistemology revitalized the already strong rationalist tradition at Harvard. The new disciples of Newton and Locke were not particularly concerned with abstract, metaphysical propositions; for them, "Reason" became the discipline of thinking, in a precise way, about the things that were real. The small college in Cambridge, then, was anything but a placid academic backwater. It was the scene of a fierce struggle between the Leverett and Mather factions that would intensify and very nearly pull the college apart; at the same time, the college was fully caught up in the excitement of the early English Enlightenment. Both these elements would be instrumental in helping to shape Gay's intellectual and political makeup.[3]

In the summer of 1710, however, Ebenezer Gay had only one overriding concern—passing his entrance examination. The questioning was conducted by the president and the three tutors. The atmosphere was polite, but no doubt intimidating for Gay, who really had no ancestral or immediate familial connections with the college. Gay found himself facing, in turn, Tutors Flynt, Whiting, and Remington, and the "Great Leverett" himself. Henry Flynt was only thirty-five at this time, affable, rather deaf, and a brilliant biblical scholar. He had not yet become the legendary, crusty old "Father Flynt," beloved and bedeviled by his successive classes of "wild colts." In 1710, the Mather faction felt that Flynt was altogether too fond of English liberal authors such as Tillotson, and they suspected him of Episcopal leanings. The second of the three tutors, Jonathan Remington, was, in contrast to Flynt, a rather severe, judgemental sort who had little tolerance for drinking, card playing, and the other corrupting activities in which his students engaged. A rather unimaginative man, the best advice he could impart to the graduating class of 1707 was "Get some Author's Scheme perfect." The third tutor was John Whiting, the man slated to be the mentor of the incoming freshman class. At that time, each Harvard class was put under the supervision of one tutor who guided them through their four years.[4]

Whiting, Remington, and even Flynt, were quite overshadowed by President Leverett. The complete English gentleman— tactful, articulate, elegant, mastering every situation with an easy grace, he was a man to whom one was instinctively deferential, and whose deportment "struck an Awe upon the Youth." His background as tutor, lawyer, judge, Councillor, and Speaker of the House had thoroughly prepared him for the demands of the Harvard presidency. A political conservative, Leverett loved ceremony and tradition, reviving many of the old formalities at Harvard. Gentleman that he was, he disliked the reformist zeal of the early Puritan authors, preferring and encouraging the study of English Latitudinarian divines.[5]

Gay apparently satisfied Leverett and Flynt that he could write and speak Latin *suo ut aiunt Marte* (without help), and that he had some facility in the Greek of the New Testament and Isocrates. He paid his quarter expenses, and made a copy of the college laws. Ebenezer apparently took this "covenant" with the college quite seriously, since he committed no recorded breach of discipline during the next four years. In the next step of the admission process, Gay was assigned to a chamber. The final step, and an important one, was the posting of his name in the buttery, a room where students could buy ale and bread. Gay paid the steward the customary shilling to have this service performed, only to be rather crushed when he discovered that he was ranked tenth out of the eleven entering students. This initial posting generally reflected one's social standing; then, during the next four years, it would be modified according to one's academic and moral performance. Given Ebenezer's modest background, his low position was not surprising, but, unfortunately for him, the Class of 1714 was inexplicably graduated in precisely the same position in which it was placed.[6]

Gay returned to Dedham, spending the remainder of the summer equipping himself for the ordeal to come. Properly outfitted by Nathaniel and Lydia, Ebenezer left the English-speaking world and, in the early fall of 1710, took up residence at Harvard College where Latin and the "learned tongues" held sway. For the next four years, most of the texts that Gay read were Latin texts; nearly all of the lectures were delivered in Latin; disputations, recitations, declamations, and compositions were composed and delivered in Latin. This syntactically tidy tongue was the perfect linguistic medium in which to study the orderly propositions of Petrus Ramus or the principles of Descartes. Ebenezer's freshman year, however, was primarily devoted to reading the ancients—Virgil and Cicero in Latin, Demosthenes and Isocrates in Greek. Gay's remarkable facility with classical languages soon became evident to his tutors. His mind, while not brilliant, was precise and meticulous, and he attacked Latin grammar, composition, and rhetoric with zeal. He even acquired a considerable competence in Hebrew, which was only taught sporadically and rather badly during his years at Harvard.[7]

The study of the learned tongues, though it dominated the freshman year, was only one element of the Harvard curriculum. Closely modeled on the medieval system, the course of study included the liberal arts of the trivium and quadrivium (music excepted), and the three philosophies—natural science, ethics, and metaphysics. Gay's introduction to philosophy began with Petrus Ramus's *Definitions*. Toward the latter part of the academic year, he began to engage in disputations. Every Monday and Tuesday morning, he undertook the defense or refutation of a Ramist proposition. The exercises were devised primarily to develop and refine the students' reasoning ability, and to assess the quality of their minds. A hopeful secondary effect, however, was that the Ramist system of logic would be assimilated by the student. Ramist logic was wholly orthodox, having been used by William Ames in his *Marrow of Christian Divinity*. Nevertheless, Ramus based his system on two fundamental assumptions that were congenial to Newtonian thought: (1) that creation is essentially orderly, and (2) that the human mind is put together in such a way that it corresponds to the structure of the world, and can therefore understand it. Thus the validity or invalidity of any proposition about the nature of things is self-evident to any intelligent man. The Ramist system, per se, may have seemed to Gay as it did to young Samuel Johnson at the Collegiate School in Saybrook, "a curious cobweb of distributions and definitions"; nevertheless, the system implied that the universe was constructed in an orderly, rational fashion, and that its principles could be discovered through the application of one's reason.[8]

Gay's early efforts at disputation were conducted under the guidance of Tutor John Whiting. Whiting, an ardent disciple of Locke, very probably acquainted his class with the *Essay on Human Understanding* (1690). If Ramus had implicit confidence in the capabilities of the human mind, Locke had an explicit faith in those powers. John Locke did not reason from a priori, scholastic postulates, however, but rather from the evidence of his own senses. Conservative Anglican though he was, in his *Essay* he challenged the value of tradition and revelation claiming "there is little need for revelation, God having furnished us with natural and surer means to arrive at a knowledge of them. For whatsoever truth we come to a clearer discovery of from the knowledge and contemplation of our own ideas, will always be certainer to us than those which are conveyed to us by traditional revelation." In short, religious truth could be perceived naturally; one could go very far in understanding the nature of the creator and his creation through the use of one's own rational faculties.[9]

During these early college years, Gay quite probably formed his conviction that Christianity was, in its essentials, a reasonable faith. As he and his fellow students explored the implications of the Lockean epistemology, they began to acquire that serene confidence in their faith that never deserted them. The existence of a benevolent creator appeared as self-evident as any logical proposition or geometric theorem. Confident in his own rational faculties, and armed with a classical education, Gay could study the Bible and the Christian tradition on his own terms. He should be able, with his own resources, to determine what was according to reason, above reason, or contrary to reason. Furthermore, he could apply the test of reason to his faith with the reassuring knowledge that he would not be carried too far into uncharted waters. Locke himself had epitomized the governing convictions of the period in the title of his book, *The Reasonableness of Christianity* (1695). Young Gay could fully embrace the teachings of Locke, and the science of Newton and Boyle, having been assured by these same gentlemen that the "New Learning" would only reinforce the fundamentals of revealed Christianity.[10]

Gay acquired a reputation for rigorous scholarship during his years at Harvard, but he was far from being a pale, ascetic pedant who rarely ventured forth from his chamber. He was, apparently, very much a social creature, witty, charming, and most amiable. Among his class friends could be numbered some of the most spirited and troublesome students at the college; yet Gay himself was never frivolous. He seemed to have moved quietly through Harvard with the same dignity, poise, and self-assurance that characterized his later years. Perhaps because of these traits, Gay was rapidly accepted by the upperclassmen, whom he tended to prefer to his own classmates.

Gay's class, the Class of 1714, was indeed rather lackluster. Of the ten other members, only Thomas Foxcroft approached Gay in intellectual stature and ability. Tom Foxcroft was wealthy, "polite and elegant," and strongly pro-Anglican at the time. He admired Gay, referring to him as "my worthy Brother," but the two were never too close; perhaps social barriers intervened. In any case, Gay seemed to prefer the company of lesser lights. These included John Brown, an earnest, pious, unexceptional student who later brought those same qualities into his ministry at Haverhill; Samuel Thaxter, Jr., a young man of limited ability, completely overshadowed by his dynamic father (the leading citizen of the town of Hingham); and Thaxter's roommate, Nehemiah Hobart, grandson of Hingham's first minister. Gay referred to Hobart as his "beloved Classmate" and found in him a companion with whom he could share his developing ideas, doubts, and anxieties. Eventually the two men would share the gospel ministry in the town of Hingham. Thaxter and Hobart were not the only members of Gay's class to come from Hingham—two cousins, Adam and Job Cushing, completed the roster. In fact, the most remarkable thing about the Class of 1714 was that four of its eleven members came from Hingham. Gay may have been a stranger to Hingham before entering Harvard, but he probably felt like a native son before he graduated.[11]

Most of Gay's lasting college acquaintances, with the notable exceptions of Hobart and Thaxter, came from the Class of 1713. He was quickly befriended by Perez Bradford, Stephen Williams, and Benjamin Crocker. Gay was particularly drawn to Williams, a promising young scholar from Deerfield who, at the age of ten, had witnessed the sudden and savage destruction of his town by the French and Indians. He and his family had been marched off to Canada in the dead of winter. At the outset, his mother faltered and was slain, but Stephen and the rest of the family survived. He spent nearly a year living among the French and the Abenaki Indians before he, his two brothers, and his father, the Reverend John Williams, were ransomed. Given this traumatic childhood, it is hardly surprising that Williams was less disposed than Gay to accept the rational, orderly universe of the Enlightenment. Indeed Williams became increasingly a defender of the old Puritan god, and would welcome the Awakening from his Longmeadow pulpit. Gay the Arminian and Williams the Calvinist were, however, both very much products of Leverett's Harvard, and would always be bound by the shared intellectual bonds of that experience.[12]

In his sophomore year, Gay began to breathe the free air of Harvard more vigorously. Like Leverett's Harvard itself, the year was an amalgam of things traditional and transitional. The daily routine of life at the college was now second nature. Gay was up at five A.M. for college prayers, followed by beer and bread for breakfast. For an hour after breakfast he studied the classical authors, mastering prose more difficult than that of Cicero and Virgil. At eight he listened to Tutor Whiting read and expound the *Metaphysics* of Burgerdicius, and, later in the year, Heereboord's *Meletemata Philosophica* (1659). Adrian Heereboord was a Dutch scholar and a disciple of Descartes; his *Meletemata* was the most popular compendium of ethics and metaphysics during Gay's years at Harvard. Heereboord organized his discussions of such topics as freedom of the will, the greatest good, and virtue, in a way that provided excellent grist for disputations.[13]

Morning lectures were followed by a rather formal dinner in the college hall. After dinner came the recreation hour, at which time Ebenezer could very likely be found in the Spencer Orchard, just north of Old Harvard, playing some form of football with Stephen Williams. Around two o'clock, Gay returned to the college hall where, in the presence of President Leverett, he would undertake to defend or negate, in Latin, a philosophical proposition—the defense of free will, perhaps, in Heereboordian terms. The ethical or metaphysical validity of the propositions disputed was less important than the skill and methodology of the disputer. These disputations were followed by "afternoon bever" (a snack), and a rather pleasant evening of study, recreation, smoking, and talking.[14]

Although the works of Newton, Locke, and their disciples were transforming Harvard during the Leverett years, the religious import of the "New Learning" was, at first, rather unclear. Neither tutors nor scholars suddenly rejected their Puritan heritage to become ardent followers of the proponents of natural religion. The catechistical instruction on Saturday morning still included orthodox religious works such as Johann Wollebius's *Abridgement of Christian Divinity* and Ames's *Medulla*. Even though the writings of Arminian Churchmen such as Daniel Whitby were available in the library, the students still most often consulted seventeenth century Puritans such as Perkins, Owens, or, Gay's favorite, Richard Baxter. Nevertheless, it was apparent to all that, somehow, the old order was passing.[15]

In 1712, Tutor John Whiting resigned his charge to accept a call to the ministry in Concord. Gay and his classmates were suddenly forced to change tutors in midstream, but the transition was probably a smooth one; the new man, Joseph Stevens, was also firmly in the Leverett camp. Stevens's "Tuition and care" of the Class of "14" were probably rather perfunctory, however, since he was actively campaigning for a pulpit in the Boston area. The formal inauguration of Joseph Stevens as a tutor of the college, January 29, 1712, afforded Gay a chance to witness one of those elaborate rituals in which President Leverett so delighted. The ceremony took place in Old Harvard Hall, with the President, Fellows, Masters, Bachelors of Arts, and undergraduates all seated according to their class rank. From his rather lowly perspective in the lower echelon of the sophomore class, Gay saw the entire college hierarchy arranged, from the lowermost freshman to Leverett's favorite, the brilliant Nathaniel Appleton, sitting foremost among the seniors.[16]

Before his sophomore year concluded, Gay was appointed waiter at the Fellows' table by the president and Tutor Stevens. This was the only financial assistance he received from the college, suggesting that his father's provisions for his maintenance at Harvard were adequate. Gay's fellow "Wait" was Benjamin Crocker, a junior sophister. Crocker was a pious and rather pedantic young man who worried about the spread of Arminianism and its pernicious effects, but Gay found him a congenial enough companion as they shared the slightly demeaning task of waiting on table.[17]

At the commencement of Gay's junior year, he began, in earnest, the study of natural philosophy. Now he would examine directly the fabric of the universe that so clearly proclaimed the divine hand. The principal textbook, Charles Morton's *Compendium Physicae*, was not exactly avant-garde, yet it did try to incorporate the Newtonian spirit within the framework of traditional scholarship. Although the junior sophisters continued their more traditional studies, the day was clearly carried by Newton, whom Cotton Mather that same year hailed as "the Perpetual Dictator of the Learned World in the Principles of Natural Philosophy."[18]

Fortunately, Gay's class had some excellent guides into the world of natural philosophy and mathematics. When they ventured into the library, they might chat with the new "Library-keeper," Thomas Robie, a brilliant young scientist who had just persuaded the Corporation to acquire and install an eight-foot telescope. Robie was soon joined by another very capable astronomer and mathematician named Edward Holyoke. Before the academic year was half over, Tutor Joseph Stevens received a call to settle at Charlestown as colleague to the Reverend Simon Bradstreet. Gay's class was once again forced to change tutors, for the third time in as many years, but the change was clearly for the better. On February 24, 1713, Stevens turned the class over to Edward Holyoke. Holyoke's specialty was mathematics and, for the first time, Harvard students began the serious study of algebra, trigonometry, and fluxions (calculus).[19]

Holyoke and Robie did not, of course, produce a class of dedicated empiricists. Gay and most of his classmates, while interested in the grand design of nature, were more interested in its Author. What did the study of mathematics, planetary motions, or the laws of gravity tell them about God and about man's relationship to God? These were the questions that most interested the sons of Harvard and, indeed, most interested the leading thinkers of the day. The answers, on the Continent, in England, and in the English colonies, were generally reassuring and hopeful. God did exist; he was benevolent, orderly, and rational, and had created man with the potential to also be benevolent, orderly, and rational. Every aspect of the New Learning seemed to elevate man and man's possibilities. What about the study of mathematics, for instance, that Tutor Holyoke was so earnestly promoting? Cotton Mather wondered "If the *Mathematicks*, which have in the two last Centuries had such wonderful Improvement, do for two hundred years more improve in proportion to the former, who can tell what Mankind may come to!"[20]

Most of the religious leaders of the day, from Benjamin Colman to Cotton Mather, saw Newtonian science as a powerful bulwark for revealed religion. Mather, particularly, was delighted that the abiding presence of God could be seen in the wonders of the visible world. He saw Newton principally as "the most victorious assertor of an infinite God, that hath appeared in the bright army of them that have driven the baffled herds of atheists away from the tents of humanity." It is true that, by 1710, Cotton Mather and others began to waver in their endorsement of reasonable religion; Mather was beginning to fear that his sovereign Lord was being chained to the principles governing a Newtonian world. For many of the students at Harvard, however, the mechanistic character of the universe was a testament to God's continuing presence and dominion. God is visible in nature—this proposition stood at the center of the new, enlightened theology. An English writer, the Reverend William Derham, best summarized this school of thought in 1713 when he published his *Physico-Theology*.[21]

Sir Isaac Newton continued to cast his shadow over Gay's senior year. Thomas Robie, the library-keeper, had begun his wide-ranging correspondence with William Derham. Edward Holyoke, Gay's tutor, ensconced himself one cold winter evening in the "turret" of the new Boston Town House to observe a lunar eclipse. Although the senior theses for the Class of 1714 have not survived, the "Quaestiones" that the students debated for their second degree reflect their continuing interest in science. Four of Gay's classmates, including Samuel Thaxter and Nehemiah Hobart, disputed questions dealing with physics, astronomy, and science generally.[22]

Gay's senior year had begun rather inauspiciously. In September, a severe case of the measles broke out and, by October 26, fifty of the scholars were laid low. Fortunately, as President Leverett put it, "It pleased Almighty God that this Sick proved not mortal to any, may it be so much more to the glory of ye divine goodness." Having survived this minor epidemic, Gay proceeded to prepare for the formal examination at the end of the term. The regular course work was over, and the senior year sped quickly by as the ordeal of "sitting solstices" loomed ever larger. Beginning June 10, the senior sophisters had to sit in the college hall each morning from nine to eleven and be examined "by all Comers." In practice, "all Comers" meant the members of the Board of Overseers. One day Gay and his fellows might have been visited by Judge Samuel Sewall, who would closely question them on a point in ethics, metaphysics, or theology. The next day William Brattle, Simon Bradstreet, Benjamin Colman, or John Leverett himself would question them, or perhaps they would ask Gay and John Brown to engage in a Latin disputation. This interrogation was Harvard's only formal examination, and a student's academic reputation rested largely on his performance here, and the recommendations of his tutor.[23]

Harvard and Cambridge now braced themselves for Commencement Day, a day that seemed to serve as New England's rite of spring. Lavish entertainment (financed by the graduating class), plentiful supplies of food and drink, and a generally festive mood marked the day. Sailors, hucksters, acrobats, ministers, and proud parents converged on the common. Presumably Lydia Gay was there, as were Ebenezer's brothers and sisters, but the seventh of July was not a day of unalloyed triumph for the young man. The day was oppressively hot, and the morning ceremonies in the meetinghouse were held up because of the late arrival of Governor Dudley whose "chariot" had broken down. The various dignitaries, including Judge Sewall and his son Joseph, Simon Bradstreet, and President Leverett, then assembled in the sweltering meetinghouse for the baccalaureate exercises. Thomas Foxcroft carried the day with a much applauded valedictory oration. Gay doubtless performed well in disputations on the senior theses, but the galling fact remained that he had graduated nearly at the bottom of his class. After the exercises were concluded, Foxcroft, Thaxter, and Hobart were honored with a visit from Judge Sewall, but if Sir Gay was in any way lionized, it was not generally noticed.[24]

There is no evidence that Ebenezer Gay ever seriously considered any vocation other than the ministry. Later that year, when he learned that his friend Stephen Williams had been called to the church in Longmeadow, he earnestly congratulated him on being "employed in yt high Service, ye Ministry of the Word." Gay now returned to Dedham to find employment and to begin his preparation for his second degree under the Reverend Joseph Belcher's tutelage. This was the usual course pursued by Harvard graduates preparing for the ministry. If they did not remain in residence at the college, they studied for their second degree under the direction of an established minister. The choice of a clerical mentor could be dictated by family ties, hometown relationships, recommendations from college officials, theological and intellectual affinity (an increasingly important factor after the Great Awakening) or economic necessity. The last arose from the candidate's need to support himself (if he had no fellowships) during this period of study. The customary recourse was teaching, and so, every year, Harvard graduates exchanged the amenities of Cambridge for the marginal and often lonely life of a village schoolmaster.[25]

On August 2, 1714, the Dedham selectmen appointed Sir Gay "to keep" the school. Although Gay quickly became impatient with the tedium of "ye Pedagogick Function," he was able to find relief from the boredom of drills in the Latin *Nomenclator* in the very congenial society of the Belcher household. One of the residents of the parsonage was Thomas Walter, Gay's predecessor at the Dedham school, who had apparently stayed on in Dedham, studying theology with Belcher. Walter was a brilliant, if somewhat erratic young man, who had graduated from Harvard in the previous year. He was the nephew of Cotton Mather and was credited by his contemporaries with all the genius and learning of his uncle. Gay was fascinated with the sharp wit and easy grace of "the Ingenious Walter." At the time, Walter was the object of his uncle's intense displeasure since the young man was openly supporting John Checkley and his pro-Anglican party.[26]

The young company that gathered under Joseph Belcher's roof also included another of Gay's friends from Harvard, Perez Bradford. The house was filled with theological controversy and political debate but both Thomas Walter and Bradford were even more interested in the Dedham parson's daughters. Although Ebenezer managed to resist the seductive charms of the Belcher beauties, he soon began to form his own attachment. Bradford had a sixteen-year-old sister back at his home in Duxbury. Jerusha Bradford was attractive, well-endowered, and a daughter of one of the first families of Old Plymouth. Gay found her irresistible, and may have commenced an active courtship even at this rather early date.[27]

Despite such pleasant diversions, this was a period of deep

uncertainty for Gay, as he began in earnest to prepare for his calling. The problems confronting "the sons of the prophets" were
formidable. The steady decline in church membership, which had
been a recognized problem for over fifty years, showed few signs of
abating. The various stratagems for responding to the crisis were
generating bitter hostility and suspicion among the New England
clergymen. Nearly fifteen years before, Benjamin Colman at Brattle
Street Church in Boston had stopped requiring the relation of
a conversion experience as a prerequisite for admission to full
membership. Solomon Stoddard, out in Northampton, went still
farther, construing the sacrament of the Lord's Supper as a con-
verting ordinance. Cotton Mather, horrified, had responded to all
this in 1705 with proposals for stronger ministerial associations to
deal with further unorthodox adventures, only to have Ipswich's
John Wise accuse him of raising the specter of presbyterianism.

The different responses to the problem of declining membership produced more than changes in admission standards and
forms of church government; some of the clergy were even beginning to tamper directly with doctrine. In their eagerness to evan-
gelize, many ministers were studiously ignoring the doctrine of
election, and were preaching a gospel message that stressed personal compliance. The charge of Arminianism was already being
leveled, and not without some warrant. Living in comparative isolation among the Indians on Martha's Vineyard, Experience Mayhew was wandering into an Arminian theology, asserting without
hesitation that men are "capable of acting as Free Agents." Mayhew
also believed that if the minds of the unconverted were reached,
their hearts would follow. Other clergymen, however, were preaching lively evangelical sermons calculated to produce emotional conversion experiences.[28]

By 1714 these differences in ministerial style and, to a lesser
degree, theology, had increased, and passions ran deeper. Many
of Gay's classmates began to take sides. In 1715 Benjamin Crocker,
Gay's fellow "Wait," expressed concern over "the Arminian & So-
cian Doctrine, of the pernicious tendency of its Spreading in Societies as it has." A few months later, Stephen Williams noted in his
diary that he had been at East Windsor to hear Timothy Edwards
(father of Jonathan) lecture on "an awakening subject . . . there was
an Extraordinary Stir among the people at East Windsor—many
that were crying what shall we do to be saved . . . Lord grant that
there may be such as these among us." In short, most of the major

theological and stylistic issues that split the New England clergy during the Great Awakening were matters of contention even before 1720. When, twenty years later, economic instability, the dangerous threat of itineracy, and a pinch of George Whitefield were added to the mixture, the inevitable explosion occurred.[29]

At the end of the fall term, Gay prepared to leave Dedham, and strike out for the remote world of the Connecticut River Valley. Stephen Williams had been the schoolmaster in the town of Hadley before he was called to the church at Longmeadow. It seems probable that, when the Hadley selectmen began casting about for a successor, Williams recommended his friend. Thus, in the winter of 1714, the Town of Hadley agreed with "Ebenezer Gay of Dedham" to keep the school for nine months at the rate of £26. The salary was hardly an inducement to travel to the edge of the civilized world, but the opportunities for a young Harvard graduate may have seemed greater than in the East.[30]

If Gay had expected Hadley to be a frontier settlement, he was quickly disabused. Soon after his arrival, he wrote to inform Stephen Williams that "I am engaged in ye Pedagogick Function in this Town, which may well be graced with the Epithet of Charming." The town was small and heading into decline, but still something of a center of learning and culture in the Valley. Gay's immediate predecessors at the school included not only Stephen Williams, but also Stephen's cousin Elisha, later to become rector of Yale College. Gay seemed to regard himself as an interloper of sorts, and he had a rather nervous sense of being on trial. After informing Williams that he had taken up his tutorial duties in Hadley, he wrote, "You, bearing a paternal respect for this School, Cannot welcome this news, knowing yt your Follower . . . is inpos mentis & Cordis to Come up to yᵉ Example Thou hast set him."[31]

Gay had come to Hadley to teach, but also to study theology. The foremost ecclesiastical figure in the Valley, Solomon Stoddard, lived just over the river in neighboring Northampton, and Gay became exposed to his teaching both indirectly, and, very probably, in the first person. The minister of Hadley, Isaac Chauncey, was a practical preacher who followed the Stoddardean gospel to the letter. He was clearly a Calvinist, who nonetheless believed that "Man's Nature is invested with those faculties of understanding and will, whereby he transcends the sensitive Creature and is allied to the Angels of Heaven." Chauncey's advice to young Harvard graduates like Gay, clearly caught up in their own scholarly world, was useful and sobering: "The great end of Preaching is to inform men's understandings, and to affect their Hearts; But high flown Expressions, that are unintelligible to the Vulgar, are so far from Reaching Men's Hearts, that they fly over their Heads."[32]

Throughout his ministry, Gay did retain the conviction that conversion was initially a rational process, a matter of intellectual assent, and only then followed by the more intuitive response of the affections. His sermons were invariably tailored to meet the level of his listeners, plain and practical exhortations to repentance and reformation. Gay's nine months in Hadley did not turn him into a Stoddardean Calvinist, but probably did confirm him in his preference for an authoritarian ministry, and liberal standards for admission to church membership. He certainly shared Isaac Chauncey's belief that "the design of the Gospel is to promote obedience." He also agreed with Chauncey's basically Arminian proposition that "If Persons are acquainted with the Principles of Religion, Entertain the Doctrines of the Gospel as Articles of their Creed, and Live Moral and Religious Lives, they are Visible Saints."[33]

The opportunity for Gay to study and exchange views with Isaac Chauncey, and possibly Solomon Stoddard and William Williams of Hatfield, did not really mitigate the tedium of teaching, and a growing sense of isolation. The schoolhouse, which faced on "the broad street" of the town, was constantly filled with droning recitations from the Primer, the Bible, a catechism, or Lily's Latin Grammar. The village, which had once seemed so charming to him, now seemed more like a prison. He expressed his despondency in a rather amusing letter to Stephen Williams, written only six months after his arrival:

> I have often read the Poets Elegies of Solitude: Blessed Solitude! first state of human kind, &c. . . . and by their sounding words & Charming notes my soul was Captivated to a belief that what they said of it was true: but now, I am ready to think that y$^e$ Encomiums are nothing but the Chimaeras of Poetic Brains.[34]

He went on lamenting that "I have been swallowed up by y$^e$ . . . saturnine humour, Melancholly, for want of Company: My quondam Acquaintance have wholly forgotten me." But he continued that he recently was reassured by some letters from his classmates that he was indeed remembered, and that most of his friends were sharing the same miserable fate. Nehemiah Hobart was keeping school at Eastham, Job Cushing at Hingham, and Benjamin Crocker at Yarmouth. Crocker wrote that "he is almost killed with keeping school. It seems all our Class are become Pedagogues, even Thaxter who keeps at Weymouth." Parson Chauncey reminded Gay that schoolmasters had a grave spiritual responsibility, but even this failed to convince the young man of the relevance of his profession.[35]

If Gay had expected any calls to settle in the Connecticut Valley, he was disappointed. Consequently, in the fall of 1715 he left the "solitude" of Hadley and returned to Dedham. By the winter of 1716, however, he once again found himself employed as a schoolmaster, this time in the town of Ipswich. Two years before, that town had voted to establish a free school for teaching both grammar and English scholars. In February of 1716, a committee of the town was charged with appointment of the school's first master, and the choice fell upon Ebenezer Gay. Gay was to keep the school for one year, and was instructed to perfect the young scholars "in y$^r$ reading & to instruct y$^m$ in writing & Cyphering." The tedium of the task was not relieved by the physical setting. The town had voted to convert the old watch-house from its previous use to a grammar school. The watch-house was located in the center of town on the common, but it was a dark, rather grim place nearly eighty years old. Part of the task of the conversion doubtless fell to Gay.[36]

One of the advantages of the Hadley school for Gay had been proximity to the great Solomon Stoddard. Now, in Ipswich, he had the good fortune to have as a neighbor the Reverend John Wise, minister in Ipswich's "Chebacco" parish. When Gay came to Ipswich in 1716, Wise's influence and reputation were nearing their zenith. Stephen Williams, that same year, noted in his diary that "When I have been with Mr. Wise & other great Scholars I have been ready to conclude I am Such a poor creature." During Gay's year at Ipswich, Wise was busy preparing his best known treatise, *A Vindication of the Government of New England Churches*. The *Vindication* was written principally to express Wise's views on church-state relations and congregational autonomy, but it also reveals just how far the trend toward rationalism, natural religion, and Arminianism had proceeded during Gay's formative years. Wise had an exalted view of man as a "Creature which God has made and furnished essentially with many Enobling Immunities, which render him the most August Animal in the World . . . whatever has happened since his Creation, he remains at the upper-end of Nature, and as such is a Creature of a very Noble Character."[37]

Forty-three years later, the echoes of Wise's rational theology reverberated in Gay's famous Dudleian lecture on natural religion. Wise believed that all men had intuitive rational truth in their soul. In 1716 he forthrightly proclaimed that by the law of nature man had "an Original Liberty Instampt upon his Rational Nature." In 1759, Gay told his Harvard audience the same thing, declaring a little more succinctly that *Men are a Law unto Themselves.* Again, in balancing the respective merits of reason and revelation in his Dudleian lecture, Gay praised the Bible because "'tis there we learn the Religion of Nature in its greatest Purity,"; or, as Wise put it in 1716, "Revelation is Nature's Law in a fairer and brighter edition."[38]

John Wise was not alone in his rationalistic humanism. As has been suggested, the scientific spirit of the early Enlightenment had captured the imagination of everyone from Colman to Mather. They had caught a vision of man's possibilities that forever banished the "total depravity" of the Calvinistic Reformed tradition. Whether they shared that vision from the pulpit was another question; but when Cotton Mather, that champion of orthodoxy, exclaimed, "O my Soul, what a wondrous Being art thou! How capable of astonishing Improvement!"—one can easily sense the change in the wind. Mather agreed totally with Wise when, in 1711, he wrote in his diary quite simply that "the voice of Reason is the Voice of God." In the next decade, the works of the English rationalists began to have a significant impact on the development of the liberal religious tradition in New England, but by 1717 an indigenous tradition was already well underway.[39]

In the winter of 1717, Gay left the school at Ipswich, and returned to Cambridge. He was now prepared to take his second degree, having only to preach a trial sermon, hand in a synopsis of Arts, and respond to a *Quaestio.* The trial sermon was referred to as "commonplace," and the name is particularly apt for Gay's first recorded attempt at preaching. The theme was a standard exhortation to repent. Although there "was once a gracious Correspondence between God and Man," sin has "rendered men most unlike to god. God and Man are now Separated, Not as to the essential but as to y^e gracious presence of God." Gay did not depict this separation as an awful, unbridgeable chasm. Rather he suggested that men could, through their own initiative, move some distance toward effecting a reconciliation. "Let us," he said, "labour to renew Our acquaintance with god."[40]

Commencement day for Sir Gay finally arrived. After the morning ceremonies for the Bachelors were completed, Gay and his fellow inceptors (M.A. candidates) gathered for the afternoon ceremonies. They were all prepared to reply to a question that had been arranged and printed beforehand. These *Quaestiones* were often quite representative of a candidate's concerns and feelings about broad philosophical issues. Most of Gay's classmates were on hand to receive the second degree. The temper of the Class of 1714 was probably best expressed by Job Cushing's affirmative response to the *Quaestio*: "An Virtus consistat in Mediocritate?" Gay's *Quaestio* has been described by Clifford K. Shipton as "curious." Roughly translated from the Latin, the question asks "whether a particular place and condition is assigned by God immediately after death to each human soul according to whether they behaved well or badly in the present world?" "Affirmat respondens Ebenezer Gay." Gay had an abiding concern about order and rank that apparently extended even to the hereafter. Rather than a simple relegation to heaven or hell, Gay seemed to be envisioning souls individually arranged by degree: a sort of eternal social stratification where rank depended not on wealth or eminence, but on moral virtue. Even though social order and the old hierarchy seemed to be crumbling away in New England, surely God maintained stability and order in the world beyond.[41]

The years of preparation and study were now over. Gay had completed his philosophical and theological training for the ministry, and had been granted his Master's degree. At the age of twenty-one, he was ready to join the ranks of the Levites in New England. This circumspect young Dedhamite had managed to maneuver through the treacherous political waters of Leverett's Harvard without being too openly associated with any faction. Perry Miller has placed Gay in the ranks of the Leverett party, along with John Barnard, Edward Holyoke, Nathaniel Appleton, and Edward Wigglesworth. Given Gay's subsequent liberal behavior, this seems logical enough, yet it does not square with the facts. All the evidence from the period suggests that Gay associated himself with men of an orthodox, moderate Calvinist stripe. Indeed, if he leaned toward any "camp," it was that of the Mathers. When Gay was settled over the church at Hingham, he was attended at his ordination, not by Leverett supporters such as Benjamin Colman,

Benjamin Wadsworth, or young Nathaniel Appleton, but rather by Cotton Mather and his rigidly orthodox disciple, Joseph Sewall.[42]

Ebenezer Gay, in later life, became an ardent champion of the ideas that he first encountered at Leverett's Harvard. He may not have fully embraced the theological implications of the New Learning at that time; later reading in the works of the great English rationalists convinced him of the validity of rational theology. The challenge that Newton and Locke posed to the Calvinist Reformed tradition must, however, have seemed clear to a student of Gay's ability. Tradition, though, had been important in Dedham. Had he no obligation to try to preserve the legacy of his grandfather, Eleazer Lusher, in a period of social and cultural transition? That is certainly what Cotton Mather was trying desperately to do. Yet Gay was irresistibly drawn toward what seemed to be true, and he felt that the insights of Newton and Locke were leading him closer to the truth about his Creator and His will. John Leverett's Harvard left its mark on Gay, even if he was not in the first rank of the young liberals of the day. Leverett, after all, was hardly a fanatical deist, nor were any of Gay's tutors. More important than any particular books on the shelves was the atmosphere of free inquiry that Leverett encouraged. As Benjamin Colman so aptly put it in 1712, "No place of education can boast a more free air than our little college may."[43]

# CHAPTER III

# Hingham:
# The Early Years

On June 11, 1718, a trim, elegant barge was rowed through the morning fog on Hingham Bay. The barge was headed eastward, quickly passing Grape Island as its pilot steered toward a small harbor. This singular vessel, known as the "Castle barge," was carrying four of the Bay Colony's most prominent citizens to witness an ordination in the South Shore town of Hingham. Later that day, Ebenezer Gay, not yet twenty-two years of age, would officially commence his lifelong ministry in that town. The forthcoming ordination, however, was only one of the topics being discussed by the convivial company aboard the barge. The group's host was the Attorney-General of Massachusetts, the honorable Paul Dudley, son of the former Royal Governor. Dudley's guests were the Reverend Dr. Cotton Mather, and two of Mather's most faithful disciples, Joseph Sewall and Thomas Prince, the young ministers of Boston's Old South Church.[1]

Cotton Mather was in excellent spirits as he chatted with Dudley. God seemed at last to be smiling on the Mathers. When the barge was rowed out of Boston Harbor, they left behind a town in which nearly every church was, or soon would be, pastored by young Mather men, stout champions of the Covenant. Even old Increase Mather felt his hopes for a revived orthodox clergy rising, declaring "I shall leave ministers in Boston, who, I trust, will defend the Churches, when I shall Sleep with my Fathers." Nearly triumphant in Boston, Cotton Mather was now preparing a major assault on Harvard College with the help of Paul Dudley, a former enemy of the Mathers. The haughty, aristocratic Dudley had joined the Mather camp after the Leverett administration humiliated his

31

family by rejecting the nomination of his brother William as Treasurer of the college. Thus, Mather was being rowed to the Hingham ordination, as he noted in his diary, in "good Company"—the
Attorney-General, a powerful new ally; Thomas Prince, Mather's
brilliant young alter ego; and Joseph Sewall, a serious, capable
young man, whose orthodox mind was utterly untroubled by the
new spirit of scientific inquiry.[2]

Why was this impressive delegation from Boston traveling to
the ordination of a young country parson? The presence of a
Dudley, a Mather, and a Sewall at this event surely had implications
for Gay's early ministry, though one can only speculate about the
precise motives for their presence. Certainly their visit suggests, at
least, that Gay's star was already on the rise. Gay's "high reputation
for scholarship" may have already impressed the Mathers, and Cotton's presence in Hingham may have been his way of lending his
*imprimatur* to Gay's ordination. It would then follow that Mather
perceived Gay as being in the mainstream of the rising tide of
orthodoxy, a supposition that Gay's early ministry does little to
contradict.[3]

The Castle barge, with its august company, rounded Crow
Point and headed into Hingham Harbor. On the port side, the
snug harbor was bounded by a long peninsula, the outer extremity
of which was called "World's End." The crew rowed the barge past
three small islands, an occasional fishing boat, and finally prepared
to dock near a substantial tide-water gristmill which, with its dam
and wharf, separated the harbor from a large mill-pond beyond.
The barge was secured and the Honorable Paul Dudley gracefully
disembarked to greet the welcoming delegation. The official greet-
ers, which included most of Hingham's ruling hierarchy, were led
by the town's veteran representative to the General Court, the energetic Colonel Samuel Thaxter. The whole company then proceeded up the town street, a wide thoroughfare that was divided
along its entire length by the "Town Brook." The visitors were entertained briefly at the handsome old home of Colonel Thaxter,
eventually meeting with the ordination council, and the nervous
young candidate himself.[4]

Ebenezer Gay was about to be ordained pastor over a parish
with a very singular history. The development of Gay's theology
and ministerial style cannot be fully understood outside the context
of the social, cultural, and religious milieu of Hingham. Collec-
tively, Hingham had a temperament and personality that was quite

distinctive, and over the years Gay virtually became the visible embodiment of that special character. Thus, the story of the circumstances that helped shape that character must be told before proceeding further.

In the seventeenth century, the town of Hingham was on the periphery of the Massachusetts Bay Colony, both in a geographic and religious sense. Hingham is located on Massachusetts' South Shore, and was originally bounded by Weymouth on the west and Scituate on the south and east. The town almost seemed to be a buffer zone between New Plymouth and Massachusetts. The early tendency of the town's leaders to defy the General Court was probably reinforced by this geographical proximity to Plymouth Colony.[5]

If one had been able to view Hingham from the air in 1718, four major areas of settlement would have been discerned. At the harbor and immediately to the west lay the old town, the center of community activity and the most heavily populated area. A somewhat higher elevation, called the Lower Plain, rose from the town and continued half a mile or more inland. Another population cluster had gathered on this plain and was centered about the militia training field (this area was later called Hingham Centre). A third and slightly higher elevation known as Glad Tiding Plain succeeded the Lower Plain and supported that part of the town called South Hingham. The original Hingham grant also included what later became the town of Cohasset (set off in 1770), an area always distinct from Hingham proper, with its own harbor, separated from Hingham Town by three to four miles of rugged, wooded terrain (see Appendix 2-A). As the town grew, each of the smaller population centers became more self-consciously autonomous. Hingham has a diverse topography consisting of several prominent hills, numerous ponds (which have supported some light industry from the seventeenth century on), swampy areas, and rocky, arid terrain. Nevertheless, much of the land was arable, and when Gay assumed his pastoral duties in 1718, Hingham's economy was still essentially agricultural.[6]

By 1633, a small farming community had already begun to flourish around the harbor. These original planters, about eighteen families in all, had come from England's West Country—Devon, Dorset, and Somerset—and they called their settlement Bare Cove. They had emigrated from an agricultural region that had been relatively unaffected by the more radical Puritan elements of the English Reformation. However, in that same year, 1633, the vanguard of a well organized group of immigrants from Hingham, a town in England's Norfolk County, joined the Bare Cove settlers. During the next five years, these new arrivals gradually increased their numbers until, after seven shiploads, they dominated the community. Unlike the agrarian West Countrymen, these later settlers were predominantly weavers and artisans from East Anglia. They had left England partly because of economic depression, but principally in order to preserve their dissenting Puritan community, the integrity of which was being threatened by Archbishop Laud and his drive for uniformity.[7]

Most of the East Anglians had been members of the parish of St. Andrew's in old Hingham. Their pastor, Robert Peck, was a vigorous leader and a defiant nonconformist. The polity of Peck's church was clearly presbyterian, though it was that type of presbyterianism that vested a great deal of autonomy in individual churches. In the early 1630s, St. Andrew's leaders had decided to emigrate, and by 1635, enough had settled in Bare Cove to cause the town to be incorporated under the name of Hingham. The final impetus toward migration occurred when Matthew Wren, a zealous Anglo-Catholic, was appointed Bishop of Norwich in 1635. Wren's new church policies quickly made life intolerable for Peck and his followers and, in March of 1638, the visible church of old Hingham decamped for new Hingham aboard the *Diligent*. Peck served as Teacher of the new church for about three years, when he was persuaded to return to his living at St. Andrew's. With the arrival of the *Diligent*, the character of Hingham changed decisively. The East Anglian population was now in the majority, and the leaders of the old Hingham community were elected to nearly all the town and provincial posts. The West Countrymen were being displaced by a cohesive and resolute group of settlers from Norfolk.[8]

In 1635, Peter Hobart came from Haverhill in Norfolk to join his family in new Hingham, and to organize a church. Hobart was a devoted follower of Robert Peck, and a graduate of Magdalene College at Cambridge. Having left behind, as Cotton Mather put it, a "Cloud of prelatical impositions and persecutions," Hobart became Hingham's first minister and immediately began to shape the new church according to his highly independent, presbyterian vision. Under Hobart's strong-willed leadership, the old parish of

St. Andrew's reconstituted itself in Massachusetts. Hobart and his church eventually came into what seemed an inevitable conflict, both with their West Country neighbors and with the authorities of the Bay Colony. Hingham had grown rapidly, and by 1640 had a population of about seven hundred. Hobart became the central figure of authority in this sizable town since, as in old England, the church and the town became virtually one. In Hobart's church, power did not lie in the congregation, but rather in the consistory, a ruling presbytery composed of the minister, the elders, and the two deacons. This system was clearly at loggerheads with the developing "Congregational Way" espoused by Governor John Winthrop and the other magistrates of the Bay. Winthrop characterized Hobart as a man who "being of a Presbyterial spirit, did manage all affairs without the church's advice."[9]

Peter Hobart and his followers came into open conflict with both their adversaries, West Countrymen and Bay Colony magistrates, in 1645. This "sad unbrotherly contention" erupted when a Lieutenant Anthony Eames was elected captain of the "trained band," Hingham's local militia. Eames was the most prominent of the West Countrymen, and the only one to have kept an important official position. Apparently determined to purge the town of all West Country influence, the East Anglian leaders arranged for the militia band to hold a second election, at which they succeeded in choosing one of their own for the captaincy. Eames refused to go quietly, however, and enlisted the support of the Boston magistrates, who upheld the legitimacy of the first election. The irascible Peter Hobart then tried to have Eames excommunicated from the Hingham church, and fired off a petition to Boston, signed by his family and seventy-seven of his East Anglian supporters, complaining "of their liberties infringed." John Winthrop, on his part, was determined to quelch this "slighting of authority" in Hingham, but Hobart resisted the authority of the Boston rulers with the provocative reminder that they "were but as a corporation in England."[10]

Hobart was deliberately aligning himself with the presbyterian Parliament in England, while leading his Hingham parish into a state of ecclesiastical secession from Winthrop's congregational establishment. He apparently supported the 1645 petition of Dr. Robert Child, which openly challenged the religious intolerance of the Puritan authorities. Hobart was widely known for his inclusive attitude toward infant baptism. Throughout his ministry he baptized the infants of Anglicans and even those of nonchurch members. Parents who were not members of the established church, for whatever reason, brought their children to be baptized, some coming from towns as far distant as Lynn.[11]

After this protracted and largely successful struggle with the West Countrymen and the General Court, the Hingham leaders came to value stability and order above all else. By the 1650s, the ethnic conflict was over. Perhaps 60 percent of the West Countrymen had left town, and most of the remainder had been assimilated into the Norfolk families. Indeed, during Gay's early ministry, the only West Country descendant of any prominence was Thomas Andrews, the town treasurer. The families that remained in Hingham became increasingly inbred. By 1680, two clans, the Beal-Hobarts and the Lincolns, comprised one-quarter of the town population. The town became a very close-knit community peopled by well-rooted and extended patriarchal families. As the number of families declined, a strong ruling oligarchy emerged, bent on preserving what might be called the "Hingham way."[12]

By 1680 the members of the *ancien régime* were rapidly dying, the fierce old loyalties were weakening, and at the same time the more remote areas of the town were beginning to grow. The ethnic conflicts had been replaced by geographical ones. There seemed to be a general sense that a new start was needed and that the symbol of this rebirth should be a new meetinghouse. Consequently, in 1681, the town built a handsome structure (forty-five feet by fifty-five with posts twenty feet high) that has since become known as the Old Ship Church. The new meetinghouse was a conservative response to developing sectional pressures. The intent seemed to be to dissipate the drive to establish new parishes in South Hingham or Cohasset by erecting a new, more commodious meeting place. As it was, the residents of "the plains" (Hingham Centre and South Hingham) were dissatisfied that the new meetinghouse was not more centrally located. The inhabitants of "the plains" were (and would remain) a minority, but they were disproportionately wealthy, owning much of the best farmland. Tradition and the majority prevailed, however, and the new building was erected only slightly south of the old meetinghouse.[13]

Having completed the meetinghouse, the town next assigned eight men the formidable task of seating it. The result was an extraordinarily intricate tapestry of social precedence in which the old guard and the newer leaders, learned men and wealthy men, "the plains" and "the towne" were dexterously interwoven. One's social standing in Hingham was immediately indicated by the row of seats one occupied on the floor and in the gallery. Wealth was far from being the principal determinant of rank, yet the seating pattern was so arranged that the average town assessment rate for the occupants of each row gently declined along with the general social status of that row. Although the meetinghouse seating assignments did not include the entire population of Hingham, they did reflect Hingham's basic social structure in 1681. The seating chart and assessment rates suggest a town in which, though there was no great disparity of wealth, social distinctions were nonetheless carefully observed. Hingham, like Gay's boyhood home of Dedham, had developed that blend of "hierarchy and collectivism" (to borrow Kenneth Lockridge's phrase) that so often characterized a stable and conservative community.[14]

Ebenezer Gay, then, inherited a very conservative parish, and a church accustomed to a presbyterian style of governance. The latter was largely the contribution of the fiery Peter Hobart, but if Hobart set the ecclesiastical tone of the parish, his successor, John Norton, was chiefly responsible for shaping a theological framework for the church. Norton provided an important, if undramatic link, between Hobart, the tempestuous English presbyterian, and Gay, the rational Massachusetts Arminian. At the height of the militia controversy, Edward Johnson had written of Hobart:

Oh Hubbard! why do'st leave thy native soils?

Is't not to War 'mongst Christ's true worthies here . . .

Norton, on the other hand, was the son of one of Christ's true worthies, the Reverend John Norton of Ipswich, author of *The Orthodox Evangelist* (1653). During the younger Norton's ministry (1678–1716), the citizens of Hingham began to perceive their minister as a mediator of controversy, rather than a fomenter of same.[15]

Norton was the first minister to preach in Hingham's Old Ship Church, and he provided a theological foundation on which Gay could safely erect his Arminian edifice. Norton's deviations from orthodoxy were ever so slight, but nonetheless significant. His theology echoed that of his orthodox father. They both had a profound sense of God's total sovereignty, they both preached man's depravity and unconditional election, yet the younger Norton suggested that fallen man was not completely without light: "Our case is bad; yet not desperate." There is a vestigial moral sense to which God can and does appeal in persuading men to accept salvation.

In 1716, Norton the younger declared that even the pagans responded to the moral law which "is written in the hearts or natures of all the children of men." In order to prove this he listed analogous strictures to each of the ten commandments, culled from the writings of Sophocles, Homer, Pythagoras, and Menander. "God's law," said Norton, "is nature's law." Norton, however tentatively, began to understand redemption in a more anthropocentric way, and he also began to broaden the franchise of salvation. Perhaps more important than his mildly liberal theology, Norton left Gay a legacy of toleration. Well before the Massachusetts Charter of 1691 which provided for liberty of conscience, Norton was stressing the importance of spiritual independence. He declared that "none can command the conscience and heart but God: man can reach to the outward man, they cannot command man's heart and will."[16]

Norton's surviving sermons reveal a man who preached to his Hingham flock with wit, grace, eloquence, and moving imagery. When he died in October of 1716, the town and parish felt keenly the loss of a "rare man" and they proceeded with great deliberation to secure a successor. In March of 1717, the town voted on terms of settlement. They decided on an annual salary of £110, plus an additional £200 for initial expenses. These were rather attractive terms, which suggest that the leaders of the church were not bargain hunting. The quality of the men invited to preach confirms this view. Before the church and parish settled on Gay, they had already extended invitations to Samuel Fiske and Thomas Prince. Fiske, who had been highly recommended by the Harvard College authorities, was called by a vote of 105 in his favor, but refused the call on the grounds that it was not unanimous. The next invitation to settle was unanimously extended to the scholarly Thomas Prince, but that cosmopolitan young man evidently considered the Hingham parish a bit too rustic and elected to remain in Boston.[17]

In the fall of 1717, Ebenezer Gay came down from Cambridge to preach in Hingham. Gay was probably familiar with the town since, as has been noted, two of his closest friends at college were Samuel Thaxter, Jr., the son of Colonel Thaxter, Hingham's leading citizen, and Nehemiah Hobart, the grandson of the great Reverend Peter. Gay's preaching was well received (his first sermon was a jeremiad) and he returned to Cambridge to take his second degree and await further developments. In early December, three of Hingham's town leaders came up to the college to invite Gay to "preach with us four sabbaths upon probation in order to a settlement." Gay's probationary period seems to have been a complete success. His personality, pulpit style, and theology were perfectly suited to Hingham. Indeed, the month of December had not yet ended before a town meeting assembled for the purpose of extending a call. On December 30, 1717, "the Church did separate themselves from the Congregation and by a unanimous vote did approve of and call Mr. Ebenezer Gay to be the Pastor of the Church of Hingham." The "Congregation" (the town, in effect) concurred unanimously, and both groups ceremoniously appointed a delegation "to acquaint the said Mr. Gay with their proceedings." [18]

In addition to the formal delegations, the town also appointed a committee to do the real work of negotiating with Gay, and to inquire "what his principles are concerning church discipline." The Hingham leaders were apparently satisfied with Gay's theology, and were now turning to the clearly more important business of ascertaining his views on church order and moral rectitude. The composition of this rather important committee reveals something about the dynamics of Hingham's political and social structure in 1718. The average age of the seven-member committee was fifty, and three had been assigned seats when the Ship Church was built in 1681. They were all men concerned with preserving Hingham's distinctive traditions, and they were all political and/or religious leaders. The head of the committee was Colonel Samuel Thaxter, whose pre-eminence has already been described. The other members included Deacon Peter Jacob, who was also a selectman; Deacon Benjamin Lincoln who was also town treasurer; and Captain John Norton, town clerk and son of the former minister. [19]

The list at once suggests the general congruity in Hingham between religious and secular leadership, but the committee was also balanced in a variety of less apparent ways. Each geographic section of town was represented, with the exception of Cohasset, which was in a state of virtual rebellion at the time. Most of the important Hingham clans were represented, from the increasingly influential Lincoln family to the declining but still powerful Beal-Hobarts. Finally, the occupation of each of these men suggests the diverse economic interests of the Hingham oligarchy. The list includes two "gentleman-traders," a clothier-fuller, a tailor, a mariner, a "malster," and one sturdy yeoman. [20]

Young Mr. Gay of Dedham apparently satisfied this formidable committee that he could indeed fill the shoes of Norton and Hobart. The apparent ease with which Gay sailed through all potential opposition to his settlement in Hingham indicates that those qualities of leadership that marked his later ministry were already well-developed. In addition, Gay's gift for political and theological accommodation probably served him well. Some years later, he advised a nephew who was being ordained, that ministers ought, "without entrenching on Christian sincerity, to differ from themselves, that they may agree with others." Thus, having gained the complete support of the community, Gay awaited the day of his ordination.[21]

The ordination council was largely a sympathetic one. Gay had invited his old mentor and spiritual father, the Reverend Joseph Belcher of Dedham, to preach the sermon. Another of Gay's former teachers, the Reverend John Danforth, had journeyed from his Dorchester parish for the service. The other three participants were neighboring ministers. The first was the venerable Zechariah Whitman, minister in Hull, the center of the local ministerial association. The second was Nathaniel Pitcher, a quiet liberal from First Scituate. Finally, and most importantly, there was the Reverend Nathaniel Eels, minister of the Second Church in Scituate. Eels was a muscular, energetic man of forty, with piercing black eyes and heavy brows. He was clearly the arbiter of ecclesiastical authority on the South Shore from Braintree to Pembroke. Like the rest of the council, Eels was a moderate Calvinist, which is to say that he tended to emphasize the importance of ethical responsibility in the process of salvation, but would furiously resent being labeled an Arminian.[22]

At the ordination service, Joseph Belcher adjured Gay to "Make full proof of thy ministry." John Danforth then gave the charge, Eels extended the right hand of fellowship, and Whitman and Pitcher laid on hands. The party then descended the meeting-house hill, crossed over Broad Bridge and returned to the Thaxter mansion, where Colonel Samuel had expended £15 on a handsome entertainment. The following morning Cotton Mather and his friends boarded the Castle-barge and returned to Boston. Ebenezer Gay was fairly launched on his long ministry in Hingham.[23]

Gay's settlement in Hingham was greeted with general approbation, but it was also clear that his success would depend upon the fulfillment of the ordination charge to make full proof of his ministry. Some of the feelings and expectations were conveyed in a letter from the Reverend Jedidiah Andrews (a former Hinghamite and now a Presbyterian minister in Philadelphia) to his brother

Thomas, one of Gay's examiners. He wrote that "The news of the happy settlement of the town, after the loss of that rare man Mr. Norton, in another that they are pleased with, exceedingly rejoices me." He then inquired whether Gay attended to "the instructing and diligent catechising of the youth? I've often thought the decay of religion in New England has been much owing to Minister's leaving the most important matter very much to schoolmasters who did it to the halves." Gay later exchanged several very cordial letters with the resolutely Calvinist Reverend Andrews, and he did personally attend to the duty of catechising the youth.[24]

One of Gay's very few surviving manuscript sermons dates from this early period, and it was preached at a "publick Catechising" in Hingham and later at Pembroke. The sermon improved a passage from the book of Romans, a book that contained the heart of Gay's essentially Pauline theology. He praised Paul's Epistle to the Romans "for the Excellency & Sublimity of the Matters treated," and warmly agreed with those who called it "the most divine Epistle of the most holy Apostle." The tone of the sermon was evangelical, urging his young listeners actively to seek a reconciliation with a clearly benevolent deity. In ripe Enlightenment language, he declared that "Our wise Creator made the pursuit of Happiness a deep Principle in Mans Nature." He declared that true felicity could be achieved only through "Justification & eternal Salvation," and these were "the Portion of Such and only of Such as are in Christ Jesus." This simple and steadfast adherence to the *kerygma*, the essential Gospel message, was the wellspring of Gay's ministry and theology. In his published sermons, he cloaked it in enlightened, rationalistic prose, and in later years defended its "Arminian" tone against his Calvinistic opponents. But, whatever the prevailing theological winds, Gay preached one central story to the people of Hingham for sixty-nine years—Christ crucified.[25]

Immediately after the town extended its call, the Reverend Mr. Gay began discharging the duties of his pastoral office. Early in 1718, he commenced recording births, marriages, deaths, and church admissions in his meticulous and precise way. Through wars, pestilence, earthquakes and revolution he entered "The Names of those who have been admitted to full communion since my ordination," from 1718 until 1787. In 1743, he expanded his list of deaths to include "Negros, Mulattos, and Indians," separately entered under the rubric "The death of Blacks." The quality of Gay's vital records has attracted some of the best early demographers, including Edward Wigglesworth, William Godwin, and even Thomas Malthus.[26]

Gay included another category of church members in his records, which he styled "adult persons that have been baptized since my ordination." He commenced this practice on April 5, 1718, when he baptized twenty-year-old Susannah Stoel, a young wife who had just moved to Hingham from Scituate. Susannah, who previously had no church connection, then owned the covenant, and was admitted to the Ship Church as a half-way member. Ten years later, she became a member in full communion. Gay was using the half-way covenant as an evangelical tool for bringing the unchurched into God's kingdom. This practice, with its Arminian implications, was not new. Simon Bradstreet's church in Charlestown had been bringing in outsiders under half-way status since the 1670s. Although only sixty-one adults were baptized during Gay's ministry, their presence suggests that he envisioned a more inclusive Christian community than simply the visibly regenerate and their children. At the very least, these new Christians would pledge themselves to lead godly, virtuous lives. Later, largely at Gay's discretion, they might be admitted to full communion. Gay always believed that salvation was a matter of degree. In point of fact, eighteen of the sixty-one adults were later admitted to full membership, including four blacks.[27]

In 1768, fifty years after his ordination, Gay informed the Reverend Ezra Stiles that he had introduced the half-way covenant in Hingham. Unfortunately, Gay did not keep a separate list of covenant owners except for the baptized adults mentioned above. The latter list, however, does substantially confirm Gay's assertion, and also suggests that he introduced the half-way covenant at the outset of his ministry. In Hingham, since the days of the presbyterian Hobart, the church had been viewed as an instrument designed to maintain the piety of the whole community. Both Peter Hobart and John Norton had baptized children more or less promiscuously. Consequently, when Gay introduced the half-way covenant to Hingham, it was not a liberal innovation but rather a conservative reform. By asking that parents at least "own the covenant" before their children could be baptized, Gay was emphasizing the importance of individual, ethical responsibility. He may also have hoped that adoption of the half-way covenant would bind the citizens of Hingham closer to the church.[28]

Gay did not, however, attempt to steer the Old Ship Church

into the mainstream of orthodox congregational polity. For instance, in 1768, and probably fifty years before, Gay followed the practice of requiring no "relation." This painless procedure for admission to full communion was probably another inheritance from Norton and Hobart, rather than a Colmanesque innovation brought in by Gay. One has the feeling that the relation of a radical conversion experience in early eighteenth-century Hingham would have been a source of acute discomfort for all concerned. Gay's actual admission procedure, judging by Ezra Stiles's brief description, seems to have corresponded exactly with that practiced at Boston's West Church in the late 1740s. The candidate would inform Gay that he thought it his "duty to join with the Church in full Communion." Gay would then announce the candidate's intention to the church. There followed a fortnight's interval during which Gay and the deacons would inquire into the character of the proposed member. Finally on the first Sunday of the month, "Sacrament Day," the candidate would be presented to the church. He would stand facing Gay, while the latter proposed some basic essentials for the candidate's assent such as a "belief of the Scriptures as the word of God" and a "belief in Christ." The candidate would then affirm the propositions (in Boston's West Church he was spared the necessity of any vocal utterance by merely giving a nod) and the church would approve his request for membership. This system clearly left the matter of admission to full communion to the discretion of the minister, and Gay exercised this authority in true Stoddardean fashion. He once advised a younger minister: "Use aright the Keys of the Kingdom of Heaven; opening the Door of Entrance into Christian Communion . . . to the duly qualified; and shutting it against the profane and unworthy."[29]

Gay settled easily into the presbyterian mold of the Hingham pastorate. He had a certain magisterial style that inspired deference, even as a young man. In order to catch a glimpse of Gay in the pulpit in his early years, one might try to envision the scene on a Lord's Day morning in March 1720. A day of fasting had been proclaimed, and Gay's text was suited to the occasion. Thomas Joy, the sexton, had finished ringing the bell (surely with exuberance) and Gay ascended the large pulpit to begin the order of worship. He was twenty-four years old, slightly above average height, with light sandy hair and an extraordinary face. His head was rather large, his eyes were narrowish and coldly gray, but his most striking feature was an enormously wide mouth that was located nearly at

the bottom of his face with very little chin beneath. With this unusual countenance, Gay could assume expressions that were fright-
eningly forbidding or radiant with benevolence.[30]

Gay's text on this morning was taken from the ninth chapter
of Ezekiel, which describes the prophet's vision of the slaughter of
the guilty. All those in Jerusalem who did not visibly have the
Lord's mark upon them were to be slain, beginning at the sanctuary. We do not know how Gay improved the text, but it would be
difficult to imagine anything other than a thundering, Calvinistic
jeremiad, and Gay was quite capable of delivering one. He believed
that "An Ambassador of Christ ought to deliver his important Mes-
sages in a lively manner with an agreeable Fervour." The minister
should "speak sometimes in the thundering accents of the Law's
threatenings, & sometimes in the sweet strains of Gospel-promises."
Too much inflamed pulpit oratory, however, was undesirable since
it might obscure the message.[31]

Gay's insistence on clothing his weekly sermons "in a plain
Country-Dress" arose from a quite deliberate determination not to
separate himself from his parish. Because of the increasing lack of
deference toward the clergy encountered in many early eighteenth-
century New England towns, ministers were seeking security by
emphasizing their clerical and professional distinctiveness, rather
than relying on the questionable loyalty of their parish. They saw
themselves more and more as a special class of Levites, the sole
custodians of religious life in the community. To a certain extent
Gay shared this view, and indeed, in presbyterian Hingham it was
no novelty. He insisted that men should "set a high value" on ministers, "and pay a deference to them." He declared that if the
preacher "be not, as well as his Pulpit, somewhat elevated above
the lowest station, few will mind his words or obey them." Indeed
Gay made it clear that clergymen stood somewhere between the angels and the generality of mankind. Nevertheless, while Gay expected the deference due his station, he very wisely refused to
claim especial sanctity because of his clerical ordination. In his first
published sermon, significantly titled *Ministers Are Men of Like Passions with Others*, he stressed the importance of "self-acquaintance"
for ministers, and suggested that the "weak and depraved Nature"
of clergymen was a positive advantage. Since ministers had the same
"vitiated Nature" as all men, they could reach others on their own
level. Because of this attitude, which was probably both sincere and
strategic, Gay succeeded in firmly identifying himself with the laity.

Consequently, during the awakening, he easily retained the loyalty of his parish, unlike so many of his fellow Levites. He shrewdly observed that those "who deify Ministers one day, are apt to vilify them the next, often they who Cry Hosanna, soon change their note, & say Crucify, Crucify."[32]

In the first decade of his pastorate, Ebenezer Gay ministered in the spirit of Boston's Benjamin Colman. Like Colman, he had an easy, tolerant, catholic style, and he was fundamentally orthodox. He rigorously avoided "the offensive peculiarities of . . . party" in favor of "the more weighty things in which we are all agreed." Gay felt that it ill-behooved Harvard gentlemen to engage in doctrinal disputation in full view of their parish flock. Furthermore, he had little interest in dogmatic theology or abstract reflection; he believed that God had constituted him "Overseer" of his Hingham parish, and he devoted most of his energy to shepherding his flock. He later urged a young minister at an ordination "As constrained by the Love of Christ, feed his Sheep, and feed his lambs. In doing which, with tender Care and unwearied Diligence, the whole Business of the Pastoral Office consisteth."[33]

Finally, like Colman, Gay was an evangelical who felt no hesitancy in vigorously trying to reach the unchurched. His introduction of the Half-Way Covenant to Hingham, the frequency with which he baptized adults, and his "preaching up" the "Terrors of the Law," all reflect his evangelical style. In his early years he declared that the only value of preaching moral duty was to show "Sinners that they are dead Men, being condemned already." Then, "groaning under the pangs of the New-birth," men are prepared "for a work of the gospel" through which "a saving Change is wrought in the Soul." Gay's record of admission to full communion indicates that he had three special "harvests" of sinners—in 1719, 1723, and after the earthquake of 1727. (See Appendix 1.) As any evangelical pastor would, he worried about his inability to bring more males into the fold. To that end he insisted that the explication of the gospel be "adapted to the lowest Capacity. . . . In this way the believing Wife (who is not allowed to speak in the Church) may gain the unbelieving Husband, whom the Preacher cannot."[34]

The members of Hingham's First Parish responded warmly to this young evangelist. The harmony between pastor and people was reflected in the financial generosity of the parish. Gay never had occasion to complain that the Levite had been forsaken. Inflationary pressures beginning in the 1720s debased the worth of his £110 settlement, so in 1727 the Parish Committee responded by establishing a monthly lecture. The money Gay received for preaching the monthly lecture operated as a sort of "cost-of-living" salary adjustment, beginning at £80 and gradually increasing to £170 by 1741. In addition to the regular support of the parish, Gay's ministry was partially subsidized by private individuals. In 1731, James Lincoln, a prosperous farmer in West Hingham, died and left Gay a legacy of £110. At the time Gay was heard to remark that "Tho' this was so considerable a Gift; yet it was not near so much as the Deceased had given him [Gay] in his Life time." Gay also received a substantial portion of his support in "country pay" (pay in kind), and once again Hingham seems to have been faithful and conscientious. The Parish records contain none of the pathetic pleas for more firewood that so many clergymen were forced to make. Indeed, by 1728, Gay felt moved to congratulate his parish: "I speak it to your praise, that I have not been necessitated to ask for any maintenance; but what ye have done towards it, ye have done of your own accord." His expectations grew so high that one small deviation in performance prompted the following terse and rather autocratic note to the Parish Committee: "I call your attention to the salt marsh hay delivered to me. It is poor in quality and short in quantity, and I don't expect to have to speak of this a second time." [35]

Since, from the outset of his ministry, Gay was relatively free from financial anxiety, he quickly turned his attention to marriage and child-rearing. In 1719 he journeyed to Duxbury and asked that rather austere worthy, Lieutenant Samuel Bradford, for the hand of his daughter Jerusha in marriage. Ebenezer Gay and Jerusha Bradford were married on November 3, 1719, in a union that elevated both the social and economic position of the new minister. Jerusha was quite overshadowed by her husband, and is nearly invisible in the family papers. She apparently had great reserves of "patience and fortitude" which were often needed during the remaining sixty-four years of her life. She ran the enormous Gay household with quiet efficiency, and entertained their numerous guests with her "accustomed kindness & Civility." [36]

Ebenezer and Jerusha at first lived in the house of Captain John Norton, the town clerk and son of Gay's predecessor. In 1721 Captain Norton died suddenly, his widow remarried two years later, and the old Norton home seems to have been left more or less in the charge of the Gays. By 1727 Gay had four children—Samuel

(1721), Abigail (1722), Calvin (1724), and Martin (1726). Gay did not name his male children capriciously, but invested each name with some special religious significance. Samuel, the first-born, was clearly intended to be given to the service of the Lord, as was the biblical Samuel. The name also, happily, identified the child with his grandfather Bradford. Martin and Calvin suggest Gay's self-conscious identification with the broad Reformation tradition. With less profound implications, Gay named a later son Jotham for the biblical king of Israel whose mother was Jerusha. This rapidly expanding clan was further augmented when Gay acquired a servant, "Maria, a mulattoe woman."[37]

The Gay family was beginning to strain the limited capacity of the small, rather antiquated Norton house and, in 1727, Gay moved to correct matters. Adjoining the Norton property, there was an elevated 6½ acre lot fronting on Town Street, which had lain vacant since the old Loring tavern burned down eighty years before. Gay purchased the land from John Langlee, "Shipwright," for £120 "current money." Probably in the following year, Gay built the handsome dwelling that so perfectly expressed his personality. The house was a 2½ story, rectangular, pitched-roof affair, somewhat large for the period, but not ostentatiously so. Though it was painted a rather austere blue-gray on the outside, the interior was lively and colorful. Someone (Jerusha?) adorned the cream colored walls of the family sitting room with a free hand vine design, very like eighteenth-century crewelwork. The woodwork, fireplace wall, and the wainscott (added later) were all painted a light green. The whole effect suggested that nature's god in all his vibrancy was very much alive in the Gay house. The domestic hierarchy was also subtly reflected in the interior decoration. The mouldings in the parlor and master bedchamber were more elaborate than those in the sitting room or other bedrooms. Finally, despite the pressing need for space, the house clearly revolved around Gay and his needs. In addition to the master bedchamber and the parlor, the parson also had a study and, possibly, yet another room for receiving parishioners. Thus three, and perhaps even four rooms of the parsonage were set aside for Gay and his clerical responsibilities.[38]

Although Ebenezer Gay's early ministry in Hingham was largely successful, it was less than a clerical paradise on earth. For one thing, even as he was being ordained, one geographical third of his parish was in the process of secession. From the time of Hingham's first settlement, one could easily foresee that if the section known as Conohasset (Cohasset) should ever attract enough settlers, it would eventually separate from the mother town. For five years prior to Gay's settlement, the Cohasset villagers had been struggling to form a separate parish. The dispute had been protracted and quite bitter at points. The basic point at issue was, characteristically for Hingham, whether Cohasset should have fiscal autonomy. The Hingham leaders were perfectly willing to let that remote settlement have their own church and minister, but they wanted the control of the purse strings to remain on Town Street. The Cohasset villagers finally took their case to the General Court, which decided in their favor, despite intense opposition from the Hingham town leaders. By the time Gay began preaching, the secession of Cohasset as a parish was a *fait accompli*. On December 12, 1721, the Cohasset Church was organized as the Church of the Second Parish in Hingham.[39]

Gay was not devastated by the loss of Cohasset. The constituent members included only the eight signers of the covenant, their wives, and one additional male. Furthermore, the organizers selected Gay's "beloved classmate" and close friend, Nehemiah Hobart, as their minister. Hobart, under Gay's influence, was an evangelical preacher who was continually questioning and modifying his theological views. Although his parish tended to remain conservative, Hobart's theology had apparently evolved so much before his death in 1740 that Jacob Flint (Cohasset's fifth minister) felt justified in characterizing him as anti-Trinitarian.[40]

The First Church leaders graciously permitted Gay to attend Hobart's ordination, where he made "the first prayer." Although they had lost some important revenue, these leaders could well afford to be tolerant, since the Second Church remained very much under their control. Nehemiah Hobart was the first of the neighboring ministers to enter wholeheartedly into the theological orbit of Ebenezer Gay, and the First Parish had other ties with Cohasset as well. The leading spirit behind the organization of the Cohasset parish, and their first deacon, was John Jacob, the wealthiest land owner in Hingham. John's brother was Peter Jacob, the prosperous owner of a fulling mill, who was a deacon of the First Church. Deacon Peter Jacob, in his turn, was quite devoted to Gay. Thus, the Cohasset church became a sort of fiefdom of the Jacob family and, through them, a satellite of Gay's church. The feudal relationship was cemented when Nehemiah Hobart married one of Deacon

Peter Jacob's daughters, and named his first child John Jacob Hobart.[41]

The secession of the Cohasset parish provides, in some respects, an illustrtion of how the Hingham oligarchy managed to assimilate inevitable changes with a minimum of disruption. Gay became an integral part of that oligarchy, and to understand his life and ministry fully in the period from 1720 to 1740, one must have at least a summary grasp of the social and economic climate of Hingham during those years. Beginning about the time of Gay's ministry, this peaceable kingdom, like many of its sisters, began experiencing all sorts of strains and stresses. Rapid population growth, accompanied by an increasingly unequal distribution of wealth, threatened Hingham's delicate social balance. In 1723, the town very reluctantly elected two tythingmen. The office had been vacant for some time, and the Hingham leaders had previously rejected the notion that official guardians of morality were needed in their town. During the 1720s and 1730s a variety of new regulations and ordinances were passed. Drinking had become a problem and in 1728 the town voted "to have but three Taverns." In 1732 strict curfews were passed "to prevent Disorder in the Night by Indians, Negroes & Mullatoe Servants or Any Other Irregular persons." By that same year the level of pauperization had increased to the point that the town voted, after much debate, "that there should be a house Erected & set up near to the stock for employing the Poor and Correcting the disorderly."[42]

In addition to these more obvious signs of discord and disorder, political discontent was growing. The oligarchy had tried to balance the various sectional interests of the town, but real political power was becoming concentrated among a few men. Just a little west of Parson Gay's residence on Town Street was the home of Colonel Samuel Thaxter. Out of a total of sixty-three town meetings held in the 1720s, Colonel Thaxter was chosen moderator on twenty-five occasions. Immediately west of the Thaxter residence was the home of Lieutenant Thomas Andrews, the town treasurer, and just west of Andrews was the residence of Benjamin Lincoln, town clerk. This triumvirate, Thaxter-Andrews-Lincoln, with Gay as a silent fourth partner, dominated town government.[43]

In 1727, the year of the great earthquake, the control of the "Town Street" ruling clique was challenged by the powerful Cushing clan, which had long dominated South Hingham. Their leader was a thirty-one-year-old farmer and mill owner named Abel Cushing. The attack centered on the First Church, that symbol of community cohesion which, like the town, was also dominated by Colonel Thaxter and Deacon Benjamin Lincoln. Less than six years after the Cohasset secession, Cushing and the South Hinghamites were also preparing to withdraw. They objected to the distance (which was really not very far for most of them) and to the lack of space in the meeting house. On November 27, their agent, one Jonathan Farrow, prayed that the First Precinct would allow the "Great Plain" (South Hingham) "something to enable them to carry on the preaching of the gospel among them." The petition was voted down.[44]

The influential Captain Thomas Loring, who lived in Hingham Centre just between the two factions, assumed the role of mediator between the upstart Cushing and the intractable old Colonel Thaxter. On December 28, he appointed a committee that rather desperately attempted "to make more room in the meeting house by putting the seats nearer together." This was quickly found to be unworkable. Finally, in the midst of all this political and terrestrial upheaval, two members of the old triumvirate, Benjamin Lincoln and Thomas Andrews, died, within two days of each other.[45]

At this point, the fundamentally conservative character of Hingham reasserted itself. There was no political revolution, no church schism, but compromise and adjustment. The number of selectmen was increased from three to five and, thereafter, each section of the town received representation. This included not only Hingham's major divisions—the old town, South Hingham, and Cohasset, but also smaller yet equally distinct sections such as West Hingham, Hingham Centre, and Rocky Nook. Access to office remained restricted, but political influence was more evenly distributed among the old families. Between 1718 and 1740, the Beals, the Cushings, and the Lincolns filled 53 percent of all the selectmen's annual terms, but at least the Beals and the Cushings represented outlying areas. Abel Cushing, the principal dissident, was elected to the first of his thirteen terms as selectman, while Colonel Thaxter continued to hold precedence in town and church meeting. Benjamin Lincoln was replaced as town clerk and selectman by his son, Colonel Benjamin Lincoln, and Lieutenant Thomas Andrews was replaced as town treasurer by his son, Thomas Andrews. Not even the names had changed.[46]

The church responded to the dissent with the same sort of

compromise and accommodation. The number of church assessors was increased from three to four so that the outlying areas would usually be assessed by one of their own. Finally, in the 1731–33 period, the Ship Church itself was enlarged and renewed. Fourteen feet were added on the east side, and the aging building received new clapboarding, new windows, a new bell and "Bellfrey." The South Hingham faction was mollified and, for some time, there would be no further divisions in Hingham.[47]

The tensions and upheaval that threatened Hingham's stability in the 1720s provided an excellent chance for Gay to exercise and develop his pastoral talents. He tried a little of everything. Sometimes he preached in the calm, rational spirit of Archbishop Tillotson and the Latitudinarians, telling his flock that "we have a Hell to avoid, and a Heaven to obtain," the latter obviously being in their best interest. On other occasions the pulpit shook with Calvinist jeremiads.[48]

The ambiguities in Gay's sermons during these years reflect not only uncertainty over pastoral tactics and strategy, but also an intellectual caution and uncertainty over the relation of his Puritan heritage to the age of Newton and Locke. At Harvard, Gay had been caught up in the exciting discovery of man's enormous potential, yet he felt that as man was exalted, he must not be allowed to eclipse the glory and sovereignty of God. As one of Gay's favorite authors, Richard Baxter, put it, "If you discover an error to an injudicious man he reeleth into the contrary error, and it is hard to stop him in the middle verity." Gay was not an injudicious man, and he *was* determined to stop in the middle verity. He shared Benjamin Colman's belief that "God deals with us as with rational creatures." Nevertheless, for Gay, this rational godly light was very dim, indeed nearly vestigial. God used this badly corrupted moral sense to prompt his elect to seek salvation. The light of natural reason could lead men only to the point of conversion, after which they would have a truer sense of the nature of God.[49]

Gay's first published sermon clearly reflects the unfocused theology of this period. The sermon, *Ministers Are Men of Like Passions with Others*, was delivered in 1725 at the ordination of Joseph Green over a newly gathered church in Barnstable. This was an important first effort for Gay, who was eager to establish his intellectual reputation generally, and among the Mather faction particularly. Joseph Green, the ordination candidate, had a reputation as "a Superior Scholar," and was a great personal favorite of Cotton

Mather. Eight days after the sermon was delivered, Gay anxiously sent a copy to Green hoping that he would undertake "the Trouble of Supervising it & Correcting of it." He added that "Mr. [Benjamin] Eliot hath promised me to inspect it as it shall come out of the Press." Gay even persuaded his classmate, Thomas Foxcroft, now minister of Boston's First Church, to write an introduction to the sermon. Foxcroft obliged by praising this "Sheaf of First Fruits from my worthy Brother" and assuring the readers that the sermon would promote "the Designs of the Evangelical Ministry." By "Evangelical," Foxcroft meant those ministers who preached redemption through Christ crucified, as opposed to "those *unevangelical* and (pretended) *rational* Christians, whether Preachers or Professors, whose favourite topick is the Religion of Nature." Gay was fully in accord with Foxcroft in promoting a Christocentric, evangelical ministry. He asserted that "The Contempt of the glorious Gospel is doubtless the most provoking Evil of the Times." Furthermore, he declared that the light of natural reason "is so universally obscured by the prevalence of moral corruption, that those places may well be called regions of darkness, where the light of the glorious gospel doth not shine."[50]

*Like Passions*, which the conservative Foxcroft so warmly endorsed, contains remarks that reflect nearly every basic assumption of post-Awakening Arminianism. A belief in the essential benevolence of God, an Arminian postulate, was expressed throughout the sermon as Gay frequently referred to "the Wisdom and the Goodness of the God of Nature." Gay's lifelong stress on the right of private judgement made its first public appearance as he warned the Barnstable congregation not to "believe whatever their Teachers say, & practice what they bid them do, without examining whether they speak according to the Law & the Testimony." Gay himself certainly ignored the Calvinist doctrine of election when he affirmed that men could be saved "by the Help of Divine Grace (which is offered to all)." Though God's grace was essential to salvation, the opportunity to respond to the gospel message was not, in Gay's view, limited to a few.[51]

The road to salvation, as Gay preached it, involved the sort of moral exertion stressed in the old Reformation concept called "preparation." Expressed in the most fundamental way, preparation involved making the soul presentable for the visitation of God's electing grace. In Gay's ministry, however, preparation itself became the mechanism of salvation. He always stressed the importance of a sanctifying obedience to the Law, while he de-emphasized the centrality of the conversion experience. Though he often expressed a dim view of human nature, he believed that the potential for true virtue lay within us all. If men and women "would but wash off the dirt, which blinds the Eyes of natural Reason," they would understand their proper duty. With his passion for education, Gay quite naturally invoked the metaphor of the Law as a schoolmaster who prepared "the Church for the University of the Gospel." Even after entering the university, believers would continue the process of sanctification, proceeding "from one degree of Grace to another, until they arrive to the perfection of Holiness." [52]

For all its Arminian tone, Gay's first published sermon is nowhere explicitly anti-Calvinistic. Indeed, the one author that Gay specifically cited in his sermon was John Edwards of Cambridge University (1637–1716). Edwards was an Anglican Calvinist and a fire-breathing controversialist who had vigorously attacked John Locke as well as the leading English Arminians, defending election and original sin with his last breath. The fact that Gay read and admired this orthodox Calvinist, however, simply reflects the very catholic literary taste of the New England ministers in the 1720s. Questions of theology and doctrine took a back seat to the more pressing strategic question of the survival of the church. Except in a very few cases, the theology of most New England ministers was largely undifferentiated; indeed a sort of amiable confusion seemed to prevail. The future liberal, Ebenezer Gay, could quote from John Edwards; and the future conservative, Ebenezer Parkman of Westboro, could read *The Religion of Nature Delineated* by the English rationalist, William Wollaston, and "take it to be a very excellent piece." [53]

This sort of catholicity was not characteristic of all parts of the Commonwealth. In the Connecticut River Valley, for instance, there was a heightened sensitivity to any preaching that smacked of Arminianism. This was due in part to the defections of some of the tutors at Yale College to Anglicanism. In the Valley, the early battle against Arminianism was directed against Episcopacy. The Valley's resistance to liberal heresy was also due to the enormous influence of Solomon Stoddard who continued to remain a firm Calvinist. Although Stoddard, like Gay, was an ardent evangelical who believed in the principle of preparation, he nevertheless clung rigidly to the belief that the actual conversion experience occurred in a given moment and only through God's unconditional grace. Ten years removed from Stoddard's influence, Gay was already losing sight of that crucial point. The Connecticut Valley ministry in the 1720s, with some exceptions, remained faithful to the Stoddardean Calvinist tradition.[54]

The ministers of eastern Massachusetts were slower in responding to the doctrinal threat of Arminianism. The religious leaders of Boston, and of the North and South Shores, were urbane, catholic gentlemen who were far more concerned with ecclesiastical disorder than with subtle doctrinal deviance. This attitude was equally characteristic of old Plymouth whose tradition of mild toleration was well established. Cotton Mather tried mightily to become the arbiter of orthodoxy, but his personal eccentricities and obsessions prevented him from becoming an East Coast Stoddard. Finally, the considerable influence exercised by the wealthy laity tended to inhibit all but the strongest of Mather's clerical apostles from delivering unadulterated Calvinist sermons. Unlike their Connecticut Valley counterparts, many of the leading citizens in the Boston area were either Anglicans or, as the Reverend Peter Clark of Salem Village put it, "[they] indulge a secret opinion of their own sufficiency, and power to repent and turn to God when they please." Not surprisingly, the clergy frequently ignored the advice given some years before by Increase Mather: not to avoid "such things as may be offensive to some of the Wealthiest people in the Town."[55]

In this rather loose theological climate, Gay's first published sermon was well received. His particular writing style also tended to draw attention away from any suspicious theological content. Foxcroft was clearly impressed with his classmate's flawless scholarship and genteel style. Gay's published sermons always *sounded* solid and respectable, even when he was asserting the most baldly Arminian proposition. Furthermore, he usually added some rather heavy-handed humor that may have dulled the reader's critical faculties. This humor usually took the form of puns that were uniformly dreadful. In concluding the ordination sermon for Joseph Green, Gay said, "We trust that he will be a JOSEPH unto his Brethren. . . . The Lord make him a fruitful Bough . . . and always GREEN."[56]

If *Ministers Are Men of Like Passions* prefigured Gay's later Arminianism, his second published sermon, a thundering jeremiad, revealed his strong Calvinist roots. Late on the night of October 29, 1727, Gay's friend and neighbor, the Reverend Nehemiah Hobart of Cohasset, nervously recorded that "about 40 minutes after 10 in the night happened the most general and most violent shock of an earthquake that has been known amongst us. It lasted two or three minutes and several times in the night after were heard some distant rumblings." Gay, like scores of other New England ministers, wasted no time on improving this dreadful providence to the terrified citizens of Hingham. Here was proof at last that the almighty God was indeed imminent and quite ready to smite New England for its iniquity. As Gay told his flock after one of several earthquake jeremiads, "I thought it meet to stir you up," and he had considerable success. In 1728, thirty-four people were admitted to full communion, compared with nine the year before and, alas, six the year after (see Appendix 1). Although the response to Gay's best evangelical efforts was impressive, he was clearly dissatisfied, and chided his congregation: "to our shame & sorrow it must be said, there hath not been that noise & shaking among the dry bones here, which there hath been in other places under the late awful Dispensations." Distressed at the transience of this brief awakening, he complained that "they flag; Their dread of God's Wrath, and concern for their Souls abate."[57]

The earthquake of 1727 may not have appreciably rattled the dry bones at Hingham, but it did evoke the full power of Gay's evangelical oratory. He combined two of his new monthly lectures delivered in this vein, and published them together as *A Discourse on the Transcendent Glory of the Gospel* and *A Pillar of Salt, to Season a Corrupt Age* (the latter title is quintessential Gay). In these sermons, Gay tried Solomon Stoddard's formula—"powerful preaching" and a vigorous presentation of the gospel—to continue the work of conversion begun by the earthquake. In the dedication to the *Transcendent Glory* he rather wistfully expressed his hope:

> The voice of God, which is full of majesty, from the deep places of the earth, hath awakened many to give the more earnest heed to his sweet and gracious voice, speaking from heaven in the gospel of Christ; and by the latter more than the former, is their conversion (which we hope is real) effected.

Throughout the *Transcendent Glory* sermon, Gay stressed God's mercy rather than his wrath, declaring that "All the Terrors on

Mount Sinai will not drive a Sinner out of his Natural Estate, home unto Christ. There must be a Hope set before him."[58]

The "Hope," however, failed to drive most of the sinners out of their natural estate, and Gay decided to resort to the "Terrors." In the second sermon, *A Pillar of Salt*, he pulled out all the rhetorical stops, challenging the hesitant:

> Will you still linger, when the Clouds of God's Displeasure are visibly hanging over our Heads, ready to burst with Thunder and Lightening; and the Earth under us is sensibly heaving to vomit Fire and Brimstone, to consume us?

He vividly compared Hingham with Sodom (admittedly a strained comparison), painting a terrifying picture of impending destruction, and empathetically describing how those "poor tormented wretches in Sodom did run screaming about, when the showers of flaming brimstone came down upon them, and their bodies were so many blazing torches."[59]

*A Pillar of Salt* was a model of Reformed theology. In one sentence, Gay summarized the essentials of New England Calvinism, declaring that "God's electing Love, Covenant-faithfulness, almighty Power, and Christ's continual Intercession shall prevent the total Defection of the Saints." The fundamental nature of man, which he had described in such exalted terms three years before, now became "a Fountain of moral defilements." As long as men continued "in the Corrupt State of Nature, they are mystically in Sodom," unable to escape the "gross Pollution which they are wallowing in," full of "spiritual Putrefaction." Although this was a less than sanguine characterization of human nature, it should be remembered that Gay's purpose was clearly to "stir them up." Thus, the sermon need not be viewed as a headlong plunge back into the dark waters of Calvinism, but rather as a plea for resolute action, calling upon the resources of the human will to avoid the temptation of looking back, as Lot's wife did.[60]

The year 1728, the tenth year of Gay's ministry, was a very full one for him. He was conducting a revival, helping to adjust the dispute with South Hingham, and vigorously moving to establish a reputation in Boston. He was also a helpless witness to the slow death of his second child, six-year-old Abigail. In the midst of all this, he was invited to preach a sermon before the Honourable Artillery-Company in Boston. The sermon, entitled *Zechariah's Vi-*

*sion of Christ's Martial Glory*, was undeniably the worst of any of Gay's published works. It is full of military ardor, with Gay urging "The reviving of the Military Spirit, which hath for so many years languished among us," and challenging his listeners to "willingly go Forth to War, whenever ye shall be called thereto." The good soldier should look for his example to Christ, whom Gay depicted in vivid red, awash in the blood of his enemies, "the head of all the Train-bands of Heaven." Christ was the supreme commander, astride a horse "the glory of whose nostrils is terrible." If the image of glorious nostrils did not rivet the attention of the soldiers, surely they were captivated by Gay's description of their heavenly allies, the "Angelick-Artillery, the Celestial Cavalcade." Bewailing the lax military discipline and rampant immorality of the soldiers, Gay suggested that at the very least, "Good Behaviour" should prevail "in the Camp, because of the Angels." [61]

The sheer banality of this sermon is hard to explain. Perhaps Gay was trying too hard to please his chief patron, the militant Colonel Samuel Thaxter, or perhaps his mind was simply elsewhere. In any case, one has the feeling that his heart was not in it. Gay was fundamentally a man of "pacifick disposition" and not a warrior. In *Zechariah's Vision*, only one sentence foreshadows his later views: "It should not be your Sport and Pastime, to kill Men whom ye ought to love." [62]

Gay's published sermons, even this last, extended his reputation into the most fashionable circles. He soon attracted the notice of the Royal Governor, William Burnet, a handsome, highly literate man who was the son of the learned Gilbert Burnet, Bishop of Salisbury. William Burnet was well-versed in English rational theology and was himself the very essence of genteel catholicity. Once when consulted about whether to have grace before or after meat, he replied, "Anyway, or no way, as you please." This elegant gentleman reportedly told an acquaintance that "among the clergy of Massachusetts, Mr. Bradstreet of Charlestown, and Mr. Gay of Hingham had the most erudition." This, if it is true, was high praise for a young country parson. Gay later repaid it, after a fashion, by diligently wading through all three volumes of the elder Burnet's *History of the Reformation*. [63]

Governor Burnet's opinion of Gay's scholarly attainments was widely shared and, by 1730, Harvard candidates for the ministry were already seeking him out. Thus, at the age of thirty-three, Gay began the most important undertaking of his long career—the education of a host of young liberal ministers who insured, as Clifford Shipton has put it, "that the ripple of this man's influence gradually spread to the far corners [of New England]." In November of 1729, the first student known to have read theology with Gay arrived in Hingham. His name was Daniel Rogers, and he was the son of Gay's predecessor at the Ipswich grammar school. At his commencement Rogers had argued against the proposition that justification by faith alone abrogates the necessity for good works. This response to the "Quaestio" suggests that Rogers may have been a budding Arminian, and a glance at his later career does nothing to contradict that notion. Like so many of those who subsequently came under Gay's tutelage, Rogers became a virtual carbon copy of the master, theologically, politically, and socially. He was settled at Littleton where he became known, like Gay, as "a very rational and learned divine . . . and a complete gentleman in his manners." Like Gay, he was a socially active minister who became known for his facility at adjusting ecclesiastical disputes. Like Gay, he vigorously opposed the Great Awakening, became a Loyalist in the Revolution, was harassed by a Whig mob and faced them down with courage and dignity. Obviously, this close parallel suggests that these were two men of very similar temperament, yet one cannot discount Gay's intellectual and personal influence on the younger man. As George Willis Cooke, the Unitarian historian, has written, Gay was "a man of strong, original, vigorous nature, a born leader of men, and one who impressed his own character upon those with whom he came into contact."[64]

In 1730, the ambitious Hingham parson took advantage of another opportunity to enhance his already growing prestige. Governor Burnet had died in 1729, literally driven to an early grave by his battles with the General Court, and Jonathan Belcher had been appointed to the post. Gay wasted no time ingratiating himself with this new administration, publishing a sermon delivered at his monthly lecture, "on Occasion of the Arrival of His Excellency Jonathan Belcher, Esq." The sermon was entitled *The Duty of People to Pray for and Praise their Rulers*, and its political implications would have delighted even the most despotic Stuart monarch.[65]

Like the deity he worshipped, Gay envisioned the perfect ruler as a benevolent patriarch. Indeed, rulers "are stiled Gods, not only in respect of their Dignity, but because they resemble him in their extensive Beneficence. . . . Rulers are political Fathers of their People." In Gay's conservative view, the stability of the government rested entirely with these minor deities: "They are the Pillars of the Commonwealth, the main Supporters of it, without which the Fabrick would unavoidably sink." If a ruler should prove incompetent or wicked, well, "People receive some Good from their Government, at least in comparison of the Mischiefs they would suffer from Anarchy, or a total want of Government." Invoking the lessons of Old Testament history, Gay insisted that introspection, not resistance, should be the popular response to oppressive government. A bad ruler was merely the instrument of God's judgement, therefore "People should take to themselves their share of the blame of the Mis-Conduct and Mal-Administration of the Government over them, and not impute it all to their Rulers."[66]

Jonathan Belcher was presumably gratified by the sentiments expressed in this sermon, particularly by Gay's description of the new governor as "the light of the Morning, when the Sun riseth after a darksome night." In any case, Belcher became quite favorably disposed toward Gay, an attitude that was also fostered by the presence of Colonel Samuel Thaxter on the Governor's Council. In 1732, chiefly through Thaxter's influence, a rather special invitation was extended to Gay, which he readily accepted. Belcher was preparing to go to Maine to confer with the Indians who were becoming increasingly militant over a number of grievances. It would appear that only three Dissenting ministers were asked to accompany the Governor. Gay was one; Nathaniel Eels, still the leading minister on the South Shore, was another; and Mather Byles, the highly refined young minister of Boston's new Hollis St. Church, was the third.[67]

Governor Belcher, "attended by a Quorum of His Majesty's Council, and a Number of the Members of the House of Representatives and other Gentlemen," set out for Maine in H.M.S. Scarboro. They arrived at an island near Falmouth in Casco Bay where a large tent was erected to receive the various sachems and sagamores. The precise role that Gay and his fellow divines played in the expedition is unclear. Belcher clearly wanted to lure the Indians away from French Catholicism, but he was promoting (at least publicly) Anglican missionaries for the purpose. In any case, it was a most entertaining sort of junket for Gay, and a socially productive one. He probably listened with fascination and amusement as Governor Belcher attempted to convince Loron, a Penobscot chieftain, of the superior merits of English Christianity:

> If you have a mind to understand the true English Religion, it shall cost you nothing; and when you understand it you will certainly know, that you are cheated, when your Sins are Pretended to be pardon'd for Skins.

Here was Reformed theology truly stripped to the essentials.[68]

At the beginning of the 1730s, Ebenezer Gay could not really be called an Arminian. He was a superb Biblical scholar, an excellent teacher, and a Harvard gentleman. He cherished Hingham's presbyterian traditions, and was clearly devoted to the principle of an inclusive rather than an exclusive church. He was an active, practical pastor, an evangelical who preached Christ crucified. For all these reasons, Gay was not inclined to stress man's inability in the attainment of salvation. The doctrines of Calvinist orthodoxy in no way suited his rational temper, yet he could see no value in openly challenging them. One might be tempted to call Gay a moderate Calvinist at this point, but perhaps a more accurate term would be "empty Calvinist." He continued occasionally to invoke the language of Calvinist orthodoxy, but he preached a message that increasingly bore little or no relationship to Calvinism.

(*Top*) The home of the Reverend Ebenezer Gay, Hingham, Massachusetts (from a photograph by the United States View Co., Cambridgeport, Massachusetts, ca. 1870). (*Bottom*) The two-and-one-half-story house built by Ebenezer Gay between 1727 and 1728, Hingham, Massachusetts.

A view of Hingham's Old Ship Church (1681) from the burial ground hill in the rear.

The "wine glass" pulpit in Hingham's Old Ship Church, installed in 1755.

## CHAPTER IV

# The Great Noise About Arminianism

On September 17, 1735, the Reverend Nehemiah Hobart left his Cohasset parish and rode into Hingham town to participate in the centennial observances of the First Parish. He noted in his journal that the Reverend Mr. Gay "gave an excellent sermon" from the text "for we are strangers before thee and sojourners as were all our fathers." In this sermon, Gay was not only helping the people of this conservative town to reaffirm their own separate identity, but he was also happily merging his own life and ministry into that identity. Gay was nearly forty. His seventeen-year ministry in Hingham had been, on the whole, attended with success. His circumstances were prosperous, and this in turn enhanced his prestige. Gay once observed, with a clear insight into what would come to be called the Protestant Ethic, that "How highly soever the affected Poverty of mendicant Friers hath been . . . reverenced among the Papists; yet experience sheweth that the poverty of Protestant Ministers is that for which their Persons are often despised."[1]

Temporal prosperity continued to attend Gay in the 1730s, due to the unfailing generosity of his parish and his own natural ability in business matters. The legacy of a parishioner had left him with a small interest in the gristmill at the Town Cove. Gay then purchased more stock in the mill, until by 1737 he owned nearly a half interest in the mill and its dam privileges. Parson Gay had joined Colonel Thaxter as one of the leading investors in the harbor area. He then turned to expanding his own homestead. In 1740 he bought the adjoining eight-acre Norton estate from the grandson of the former minister for £600. Three years later, he sold the dwelling house, together with 1½ acres to one Elisha

Leavitt. Gay retained the remaining land which increased his home lot to thirteen acres. This handsome little farm provided the family with a steady source of produce and salt marsh hay. A large part of the responsibility for plowing and cultivating the land was assumed by Jerusha Gay's brother-in-law, Peter Lane, a substantial farmer who lived just a bit to the west on Town Street.[2]

The growth of Gay's real estate was proportionately related to the growth of his family. He firmly believed that ministers should have "something of a worldly Estate to transmit to their Posterity." That posterity was already straining his resources. Ebenezer and Jerusha had been fruitful, and they multiplied almost on a biennial basis. By the time of his centennial sermon in 1735, there were seven children, ranging from fourteen-year-old Samuel to the infant Jerusha. Samuel was ready to enter Harvard College, having been prepared under the expert tutelage of his father and the Hingham schoolmaster, Cornelius Nye.[3]

Ebenezer Gay, in short, had good reason for celebrating on the occasion of Hingham's centennial. He had harvested sixteen souls that year; he was becoming financially sound; his family was growing and in health; and his beloved Samuel was preparing for the high call of the ministry. Forces were already in motion, however, that would seriously disturb his intellectual and spiritual complacency. Within ten years this man who so hated doctrinal controversy would find himself among the religious leaders who preached a "new body of divinity" called Arminianism.[4]

The old controversy about Arminianism had lain dormant since the Anglican defections at Yale in the early 1720s. In 1726, Cotton Mather commented on the apparent theological uniformity: "I cannot learn, That among all the Pastors of Two Hundred Churches, there is one Arminian; much less an Arian, or a Gentilist [i.e., a pagan]." Then, with almost no prelude, the battles erupted again in 1733–34. As Jonathan Edwards in Northampton put it, "About this time, began the great noise that was in this part of the country about Arminianism." The concern was not confined to the Connecticut River Valley, however. In 1734, the Reverend John White of Gloucester helped generate much of the furor with a vivid depiction of "the Arminian Scheme" in his *New England's Lamentations*. When White and Edwards raised the hue and cry about Arminianism, they were not, as some scholars have argued, worrying solely, or even primarily, about the spread of Anglicanism and the activities of the S.P.G. missionaries. Instead, they were concerned, as White said, about "Our Young Men."[5]

In increasing numbers, Harvard was graduating ministers who preached a humanistic moralism that bore little resemblance to the old orthodoxy. John White's lament was not a perfunctory jeremiad, but rather a response to specific incidents. The first major confrontation had occurred in August of 1733 in the frontier parish of North Yarmouth, Maine. On that occasion, an ecclesiastical council had been called by the congregation and the local clergy to investigate the "rank Arminianism" of the Reverend Ammi Ruhammah Cutter. This was really the first of the "Arminian heresy" trials, and the ecclesiastical council, having performed a very distasteful task, concluded the proceedings with a warning. Within two years, however, Cutter's intransigently Arminian views (and personality) had led to his dismissal. At the same time, the new minister at Marlborough, Benjamin Kent, was strongly suspected of entertaining Arminian views, and down at Eastham, the doctrinal errors of the controversial Reverend Samuel Osborn were beginning to supplant his previous moral indiscretions as an issue.[6]

Jonathan Edwards, like John White, had particular people in mind when he sounded the general alarm about Arminianism in the Valley. Edwards was beginning to suspect that some of the ministers in the Hampshire Association were not altogether orthodox, particularly the Reverend William Rand of Sunderland. Edwards's older colleague, Stephen Williams of Longmeadow, shared his suspicions, having heard that Rand "has advanced some new notions as to the doctrines of justification." The Connecticut Valley ministry was still feeling the impact of the Anglican defections at Yale. Consequently, they had become quite adept at sniffing out Arminians. Coupled with this Anglican-Arminian phobia, was the vigorous persistence of Stoddardean Calvinism, championed by Stoddard's grandson, Edwards, and the indefatigable zeal of the powerful Williams clan.[7]

In 1734, a moderately liberal young Harvard man named Robert Breck wandered into Connecticut and immediately began to antagonize the forces of orthodoxy. He first attempted to settle at Windham. However, after a few provocative remarks such as "the Heathen that liv'd up to the Light of Nature should be saved," Breck found himself in deep trouble with his neighbor, the Reverend Thomas Clap. Such observations may have gone unchallenged in Cambridge, but they were quite unacceptable to Yale conservatives. Hastily departing Windham, Breck responded to a call from Springfield, Massachusetts, and promptly met a challenge from the conservative Hampshire Association. Breck's rather dubious conduct as an undergraduate, together with his fuzzy liberalism, made him easy prey for Edwards and the Williamses. During the bitter and protracted controversy, William Rand of Sunderland, and Gay's former teacher, Isaac Chauncey of Hadley, opposed the attempts of the other ministers to make the Hampshire Association the arbiter of orthodoxy. The liberal supporters of Breck stressed the threat to congregational autonomy raised by the Hampshire Association. In defense of that autonomy, the Springfield Church defied the local association and ordained Breck with a ministerial council characterized by a Hampshire minister as being "fetch'd from very remote Parts of the Country." Mr. Breck's conduct throughout this unpleasant affair was rather disingenuous. Under all sorts of pressure, including arrest and detention, Breck recanted and publicly subscribed to all five points of the Synod of Dort. This putative change of heart convinced absolutely no one, but it did facilitate the ordination, and Breck lived to preach his mild Arminianism another day.[8]

The sudden concern over the doctrinal laxity in the younger New England clergymen is not surprising. If, as Perry Miller and Conrad Wright have argued, a hitherto latent Arminianism was gradually emerging from the ambiguities of covenant theology, there had to come a point when orthodox ministers began to perceive the danger. It was during the early 1730s when the vanguard of the identifiably Arminian clergy came of age. Of the sixty New England ministers that Wright has classified as Arminian, only three were born before 1700. This post-1700 generation of clergymen were less and less disposed to maintain the old Puritan balance between human initiative and total subjection to the Divine will.[9]

The younger ministers were being taught principally by the men of Gay's generation, the most influential of these preceptors being Edward Wigglesworth, Hollis Professor of Divinity at Harvard. Wigglesworth, together with influential ministers such as Nathaniel Appleton and Gay, were not exactly well-springs of pure Calvinism. At Leverett's Harvard these three had been exposed to Newton and Locke, to the physico-theologians, to the new Biblical criticism of Dr. Samuel Clarke, and to the mild Arminianism of leading Anglican theologians such as Tillotson and Whitby. They acquired a great faith in reason and free inquiry, perhaps epitomized by Daniel Whitby's assertion that "we should call no man guide or master upon earth, no Father, no Church, no Council." This contact with the moderate rationalism of the early Enlightenment forever separated Gay and many of his clerical contemporaries from the old faith of New England; yet they maintained a firm though intellectually rather shallow allegiance to that world. They would not openly disavow their Puritan inheritance, fearing the disruptive consequences of such a repudiation. For all these reasons, men such as Gay, Wigglesworth, and Appleton were ill-suited to pass on the torch of Puritan orthodoxy. Their free, catholic, and often skeptical approach to theology was a necessary, intermediate step between the "preparationist," sacramental Puritanism of the late seventeenth century, and the brazen Arminianism of young Harvard heretics like Ammi Cutter and Benjamin Kent.[10]

Younger ministers were being influenced not only by their "free and catholick" mentors, but also by an influx of Arminian and even deistical books—"corrupt books" John White called them—which encouraged the younger men in their conceits by "exalting and extolling *free Will* and *self Sufficiency*." If the testimony of several writers of that time may be credited, the impact of English rational thought was profound, even in those pre-Awakening days. Samuel Johnson, the Anglican apostate at Yale, later attributed his rejection of traditional Puritanism to the influence of the library sent to Yale in 1714 by Connecticut's London agent, Jeremiah Dummer. Johnson may not have fully understood the implications of the "New Learning," but he found himself "emerging out of the glimmer of twilight into the full sunshine of open day." By 1723, Harvard had a similar "Satan's bookshelf" that included Samuel Clarke's *Scripture Doctrine of the Trinity* (1719); the fifth edition of Clarke's *Discourses on the Being and Attributes of God* (1719); three volumes of Archbishop John Tillotson's *Works* (1720); and Daniel Whitby's *Whole Duty of Man* (1712). Rationalists and Latitudinarians, albeit staunch Christians, these authors began to form an essential part of the Harvard intellectual milieu as early as Gay's student days.[11]

By the 1730s, newer and more radical authors were coming to the fore. Some of the new writers were Arians, Socinians, and militant deists. The age of science and reason was finally coming into direct conflict with Christian revelation. As early as 1696, a rather facile Irish writer named John Toland had shocked the Anglican establishment with the publication of his *Christianity Not Mysterious*. Toland effectively exploited the ideas of his friend John Locke, declaring that nothing in Christianity was unreasonable or supernatural. In 1730, Matthew Tindal, a skillful controversialist at Oxford, amplified Toland's conclusions in *Christianity as Old as the Creation*, proclaiming that nature and reason revealed God perfectly, and that revelation, therefore, was quite unnecessary. Indeed, said Tindal, anyone who felt a need for supernatural revelation was displaying contempt for the perfection of God's handiwork. Tindal was joined in his sensational critiques of Christianity by other clever writers such as Thomas Woolston and Thomas Chubb, the latter a journeyman glovemaker. These deists did not offer a coherent philosophical system in place of orthodox Christianity, but instead delighted in exposing its logical inconsistencies. In England, this deistic assault reached its peak in the late 1720s and early 1730s; within a few years, the shock waves reached the colonies.[12]

In New England, these "corrupt Books" apparently had a varied and enthusiastic readership. Early in 1740, the Reverend Benjamin Colman wrote to a fellow clergyman about the presence of these books at Harvard: "I truly wish many of our *modern & new Books* had never *arrived* or been read there; & particularly such as *Mr. Chubb*. . . . These corrupt our young Men's Judgement & Style too." The fastidious Reverend Colman may have been disturbed by the inferior writing style of Thomas Chubb, but to the Reverend Samuel Moody, a bluff old evangelist on the Maine frontier, the "Writings of such as are called Free-Thinkers" could easily tempt the unwary to perdition. Moody, like Colman, attested to their general availability: "About this Time, I went into a Stationer's Shop, as I used frequently to do; and there I espy'd some of the *Arminian Books*; such as I had read but too much in; and the Bookseller told me, of what esteem they were in *England*." By 1739, even the Reverend Ebenezer Parkman of Westboro, that most circumspect of moderate Calvinists, had begun reading Thomas Chubb's deist tract, *The True Gospel*.[13]

The arguments of the English deists and Arminians had about them a common-sense quality that raised serious doubts among some clergymen whose own theology was pragmatic and uncomplicated. Thus the Reverend Samuel Moody wrote: "I must acknowledge, with grief of Soul, that by reading *Arminian Books* . . . I came to be so stumbled at the *Doctrine of Election*, that I could not hear it preached without being very uneasy." Moody's uneasiness was widely shared. He settled his anxiety by resolving to "lie at the foot of the divine Sovereignty, putting my Mouth in the Dust," but this self-abasement did not come so easily to the rational gentlemen of Leverett's Harvard.[14]

Gay and many of his fellow moderates were less upset by the Arminianism of the English liberals than by the extension of that Arminianism into deism. It was as though they suddenly realized how close to the deistic abyss they themselves had been treading. The writings of Tindal and Chubb caused many clergymen to view New England's budding Arminianism with alarm. Homegrown heretics such as Ammi Cutter, Benjamin Kent, or Robert Breck seemed solidly orthodox when contrasted with the English deists; but, if those Arminians were allowed to continue unchallenged, New England would surely be infected with Arianism, Socinianism, deism, or worse. Clearly the time had come to draw the line.

As early as 1730, that line was drawn by the Reverend John Bulkley of Colchester, Connecticut. In that year, Bulkley published a sermon entitled *The Usefulness of Reveal'd Religion, to Preserve and Improve that which is Natural*. The sermon was both a hymn of praise to "the works of God in Creation," and a strong repudiation of the deists' attack on the Bible. Bulkley warmly defended the importance of "Divine Revelation" (i.e., the Bible), but he did so on the grounds that it improved our understanding of "the sincere and pure dictates of Nature." Bulkley, then, insisted that reason and revelation were inseparable, but he *began* with reason and "Natural Light." For Bulkley, Christianity was "no other than Natural Religion reinforced, and improved by Divine Revelation." In 1730 this was, as Bulkley recognized, "a somewhat untrodden Path," but during the next twenty years, Gay and most of his fellow Arminians would staunchly defend Bulkley's "reason *and* revelation" position. This *via media* enabled the New England Arminians to reject the intellectual lure of deism. They were able to pray with the Reverend Israel Loring of Sudbury: "when Atheism and Deism break in upon us, as a raging Sea, Say then Hitherto shall you Come and no farther."[15]

As the controversy over Arminianism in the 1730s dissipated the theological fog of the previous decade, various clerical factions began to take shape. By 1735 many clergymen, distressed by the frank Arminianism of recent Harvard graduates, and humbled by the surprising religious revival in Northampton, were moving away from rational preaching and back toward a more emotional faith. On the East Coast, Gay's classmate Thomas Foxcroft, at Boston's First Church, was the principal leader of these forces. Laymen, as well as ministers, became more sensitive to any preaching that had even the slightest Arminian savor. This suspicious atmosphere was reflected in the correspondence of an elderly parishioner in Framingham who worried about "those loose & Licentious Doctrines which I fear are Lurking & only wait for opportunity to appear Barefaced." In this conservative tide, the men who did continue to preach a rational, humanistic gospel did so with a necessarily firmer commitment. The challenge of the English deists, the impact of Jonathan Edwards's revived Calvinism, the heresy trials of Cutter, Breck and Kent—all these factors caused the Arminian-leaning clergy to think through their position more carefully, and to prepare to defend it. During these years, Ebenezer Gay began to drift slowly into the Arminian camp.[16]

Although Gay later demonstrated a thorough familiarity with the eighteenth-century English liberals, he came into the Arminian fold through an older (and more respectable) tradition of religious liberalism. To begin with, Gay was a "Baxterian," a useful term that Caleb Gannett, one of Gay's students, later used to describe himself. Richard Baxter (1615–91) was evidently a figure of major importance for Gay, both as a pastoral model and as a source of legitimation. Gay quoted Baxter extensively, and possessed a copy of Edmund Calamy's 1713 *Abridgement of Mr. Baxter's History of His life and Times*. Baxter, like Gay, was an ardent scholar, a rational expositor of scripture, and an enemy to dogmatic, sectarian theology. During the Protectorate, Baxter had been summoned to London to help settle "the fundamentals of religion." His critics contended that what Baxter had proposed as fundamentals "might be subscribed by a Papist or Socinian," to which Baxter replied, "So much the better, and so much the fitter it is to be the matter of concord." Like Baxter, Gay frequently expressed his frustration with ministers whose sermons dealt with partisan, controversial matters, rather than "the more mighty things in which we are all agreed."[17]

Gay's Baxterianism was not confined to a pragmatic approach to theology, but also extended into the realm of pastoral relations. His sense of the vital importance of clerical responsibility in maintaining social order corresponded closely with Baxter's. Richard

Baxter tried to create a climate where men would be forced "to learn the word of God and to walk orderly and quietly . . . till they are brought to a voluntary, personal profession of Christianity." Here was Gay's approach exactly. First one must create an orderly, outwardly religious environment (a concept reinforced since Baxter's day by Lockean psychology); in this socially stable atmosphere, men would be encouraged to live righteously, read the Bible, and finally make a voluntary profession of faith. In this conversion morphology, external piety precedes inward conversion. Gay, like Baxter, was prepared to use rigorous means to bring men into the church and to keep them out of the taverns, but their profession of faith must ultimately be voluntary—a matter of private, rational assent.[18]

Richard Baxter was a rationalist, but he was no Arminian, despite the charges of his arch-Calvinist enemies. However, the principal philosophic source for Ebenezer Gay's humanistic theology was provided by a man who was an Arminian in the most literal sense—Hugo Grotius. Grotius (1583–1645) was a Dutch jurist, politician, and theologian who had studied under Arminius at Leiden, and who suffered imprisonment and exile because of his support of the Arminian party. His influence on Gay was profound. Gay carefully read Grotius's *The Truth of the Christian Religion* (a sort of Dutch *Pilgrim's Progress* published in 1622) and his *On the Law of War and Peace* (1625). Gay's copy of the former work, acquired in 1731, included a four page note which he had extracted "From ye Life of H.G. as drawn up by ye Translator of his Rights of War & Peace."[19]

Grotius's influence on Gay came during the latter's formative years, providing an enduring philosophical framework for some of Gay's deepest feelings about society and religion. In some cases, Gay borrowed quite directly from Grotius. In his first published sermon, Gay's concept of the Law as a schoolmaster preparing the Church for the gospel surely echoes Grotius's assertion that "the law is a tutor to lead us to Christ." This parallel might be dismissed as the coincidental use of a common metaphor were it not for the fact that other sentences and passages from Grotius's works occur frequently in Gay's sermons. Gay was indebted to Grotius for theological, political, and sociological insights. He marked a passage from the introduction to his copy of *The Truth of the Christian Religion* (1729 ed.) in which Grotius's translator asks "How is it that the Generality of Christians in one Country are Zealous for Calvinism, and in another Country as Zealous for Arminianism? . . . because they are the established Doctrines of the Places they live in." Gay shared the optimistic belief of Grotius and his translator that if each man would rely on scripture rather than man-made rules of faith, and be "permitted quietly to enjoy his own Opinion, the Foundation of all Divisions would be taken away at once." This can help explain how a man like Gay, who was so fearful of discord in his parish, could steadfastly support the right of private judgement in the interpretation of the scriptures. Gay sincerely believed that rational men (men of some intelligence who could control their baser emotions) who read the Bible without sectarian bias would be in fundamental agreement on the basic questions of religion. Furthermore, Gay never seemed to doubt that right reason and God's written revelation pointed to the same ecclesiastical and theological structure that existed in Hingham.[20]

Among all Grotius's works, his brilliant treatise on international law, *On the Law of War and Peace*, seems to have had the most direct influence on Gay's social and political views. Grotius applied the New Testament teaching on nonresistance to the obligations of subjects toward their rulers. Harking back to the example of the early Christian churches, he advocated absolute submission to rulers, even though a ruler be wicked and tyrannical. This was Gay's position precisely, and he forcibly expressed his views in his 1730 sermon—*The Duty of People to Pray for and Praise Their Rulers*. In Gay's sermon, however, he pictured this submission principally as a natural and proper response to the god-like beneficence of the royal governor. Grotius, though, based his principle of nonresistance on the broader Christian tradition of pacifism. Once the argument is put on that plane, then one must deal not only with the question of political nonresistance of subjects, but also with the moral problems created by war. Grotius was not an extreme pacifist, and he believed that citizens ought normally to obey their rulers in time of war. Nevertheless he vigorously supported the right of conscientious objection when, in the well-informed opinion of an individual, he believed a given war to be unjust. Here, of course, is the classic example of the conflict between obedience to God and to the state, and Grotius clearly taught that obedience to God and Reason should take precedence.[21]

Gay carefully pondered the arguments of Grotius concerning war and the proper ordering of society, assimilated them, and expressed them in a remarkable sermon delivered in 1738.

He preached the sermon in the Old Ship Church on May 16, a "Training-Day," before four local militia companies. Entitled *Well-Accomplish'd Soldiers, a Glory to Their King, and a Defence to Their Country*, the sermon immediately invites comparison with his last military oration, *Zechariah's Vision*, delivered ten years before. At first glance, the two sermons seem alike, both being attempts to inspire military ardor, competence, and preparedness. A closer reading, however, reveals just how far Gay had come in ten years. In contrast to the uninspired, militaristic cant of *Zechariah's Vision*, *Well-Accomplish'd Soldiers* provides a thoughtful, mature discussion of the moral problems and responsibilities engendered by war. By 1738, Gay clearly felt sufficiently confident and secure to raise some unsettling questions about the morality of war, and to do it before old Colonel Thaxter and the local military establishment.

*Well-Accomplish'd Soldiers* does not preach pacifism, but rather advocates a sort of situational ethic based on the rational judgement of each soldier. Unabashedly citing "Heathen Moralists" and "Pagan Philosophers," Gay demonstrated that "war in some cases, and with some restrictions, is lawful and expedient, the Light of Reason and of Scripture plainly discovers." He based this tepid endorsement of the propriety of some wars on "The Law of Self-preservation which is the Law of God and Nature." Having admitted the occasional necessity for war, however, Gay went on to emphasize the ethical responsibility (or right of private judgement) that every soldier must assume in time of war. The passage is one of Gay's most eloquent and, when read from a religious perspective, consummately Arminian:

> Soldiers are to fight as rational and moral agents, and not go forth to the war, as the horse, which hath no understanding rusheth into the battle. . . . I cannot think, but that soldiers, who are pressed into a war, should be convinced of the lawfulness of it: and should not be obliged to engage in it, on a blind presumption that there are good reasons for it, though they must not know them. All that are killed by them in an unjust war, are murdered.

These are strong words, and they urge a rational resistance to the will of the state, a position that seems diametrically opposed to Gay's social conservatism. The following observation, taken from Hugo Grotius's *On the Law of War and Peace*, strongly suggests Gay's source of inspiration: ". . . if a war is unjust there is no disobedience in avoiding it. Moreover, disobedience in things of this kind, by its very nature, is a lesser evil than manslaughter, especially than the slaughter of many innocent men."[22]

In addition to providing a thoughtful discussion of ethical behavior in war-time, *Well-Accomplish'd Soldiers* also affords a revealing glimpse into the social and religious ideas that Gay held in the late 1730s. Gay did not provide these insights inadvertently, but instead used this military sermon very deliberately as a platform for expounding his social philosophy. For instance: "Good Order is the Beauty and Strength of an Army, as well as of any other Society: And it consists in the prudent Conduct of Officers, and obsequious Carriage of Soldiers." Again we encounter Gay's concern with social hierarchy and subordination. Gay expressed delight with the way in which the militia embodied the idea of "The Great Chain of Being." In this, the military followed natural law since "All his [God's] Creatures are ranged by him in a goodly and convenient Order." He even advised the militia commanders as to the best way to engage "the dutiful respects" of their subordinates, thus revealing something of his own pastoral style. He suggested, for instance, that the men would be more impressed "by a grave Deportment, a steady Conduct, and singular Expertness," rather than "by a strutting Gate, big Looks, and domineering Words." Finally, Gay's description of the way in which a good soldier acquired martial skill sounded remarkably like the way in which the Arminian ministry viewed the attainment of Grace. He told the militiamen that "Military Skill is to be obtain'd from the Lord of Hosts, in the use of proper Means; and not to be expected by extraordinary instruction or immediate Infusion . . . it is an acquired Endowment. By Study and Exercise, Men are to learn War." Ebenezer Gay would not trust the defense of the town of Hingham to "antinomian" soldiers.[23]

If *Well-Accomplish'd Soldiers* advanced some unconventional notions about military service, it reflected Gay's general frame of mind in the late 1730s. He was becoming increasingly impatient with the general hue and cry against Arminianism. Gay's former college tutor, Edward Holyoke, had once characterized another minister as being "too much of a gentleman, and of too catholic a temper, to cram his principles down another man's throat." That description perfectly fitted Gay who, as a true son of John Leverett's Harvard and as a good latitudinarian, much preferred to dwell on "the more mighty things in which we are all agreed." Like so many of his colleagues, he was uncomfortable with doctrinaire Calvinism for intellectual as well as practical reasons. He came increasingly to resent those orthodox clergy and laymen who demanded conformity to their notion of strict Calvinism. Gay would have agreed completely with the Reverend Benjamin Doolittle who, in 1739, angrily declared, "I am no papist to make either Calvin or Arminius my pope to determine articles of faith for me."[24]

At first Gay's annoyance was directed less toward the "orthodox" critics than toward those brash clergymen who were, in effect, letting the Arminian cat out of the bag. In 1735 he had an opportunity to express his disapproval when he responded to an invitation from the Marlborough Association to join in an ecclesiastical council called to deal with the troublesome Reverend Benjamin Kent. Settled in Marlborough in 1733, young Kent had quickly alienated members of his congregation as well as the neighboring clergy. His combative personality (which was to serve him well in his subsequent legal career) and his apparent propensity for resorting to "profane and filthy expressions" formed the core of the problem. Some members of his church, however, soon charged that not only was Kent temperamentally unsuited for the ministry, but that he was a "profest Arminian" as well.[25]

Gay arrived in Marlborough late in January of 1735 in company with old Colonel Samuel Thaxter (even at this late date, Gay apparently still moved in the shadow of this influential magistrate). Not surprisingly, Gay agreed with the other council members that Kent's erratic behavior was an embarrassment to the dignity of their profession. He was equally unsettled, however, by Kent's candid disavowal of much of the Westminster Assembly's Catechism and his insistence that election was conditional "on the foresight of good works." Gay may well have felt that such an open challenge to Calvinist orthodoxy was unnecessary and irresponsible. Consequently, he set his hand to the unanimous decision of the council that Kent be suspended, though he probably did so with a troubled conscience. Within a month Gay found himself sitting on another ecclesiastical council, this time in his home town of Dedham. Here he cheerfully lent what assistance he could to his brother Lusher, his cousin John, and their "Clapboard-trees" neighbors as they struggled to separate themselves from Dedham's First Parish and from the rigorous Calvinist preaching of Samuel Dexter. Having aided his family in their little rebellion, Gay even put forward one of his theology students, Nicholas Loring, as a candidate for the new Clapboard-trees pulpit.[26]

Gay was not the only future liberal who was jolted out of his theological complacency during the Arminian scare of the 1730s. The controversy also had a catalytic effect on the Reverend Charles Chauncy, the young man who would soon emerge as the leader of the forces opposed to "revival" Calvinism. In 1735 Chauncy had been for eight years Thomas Foxcroft's loyal assistant at Boston's First Church. Like his seniors, Gay and Foxcroft, he was quite consciously committed to the defense of the Puritan Way, combining a great confidence in man's reason and understanding with a strong evangelical piety. Also, more like Gay and less like Foxcroft, Chauncy was beginning to grow uneasy over the increased stridency of those ministers and laymen who demanded allegiance to strict Calvinist orthodoxy. Gay and Chauncy would soon join forces for the first time in the defense of the Arminian heretic, Samuel Osborn.[27]

Gay's involvement in the Osborn affair began in 1738, a very difficult year for the Hingham parson. On July 3, his fifth son and namesake died exactly one year and four months after his birth, probably from a diphtheria epidemic that Gay and young Dr. Ezekiel Hersey had been battling for two years. The disease apparently ravaged the entire Gay household, and the parson himself was seriously ill during much of the summer. By September, Gay had so much recovered his health that he embarked, in company with his neighbor, the Reverend William Smith of Weymouth, on a journey to Yale College. The purpose of this expedition is unclear, though there exists the possibility that Gay may have been assisting a faction that wanted to preserve and increase the Arminian domination of the Yale Board of Trustees. We do know that Gay maintained a close liaison with Connecticut Arminians in the post-Awakening years.[28]

Even as Parsons Gay and Smith were returning home from their New Haven expedition, events were taking place on Cape Cod that would embroil Gay deeper in the Arminian controversy. An ecclesiastical council, convened at Eastham, had taken evidence that would lead within a month to the dismissal of the Reverend Samuel Osborn from the Second Parish of that town. Osborn was an Irishman who had been preaching in Eastham for twenty years. During that period, Osborn had been repeatedly attacked and maligned by one Nathaniel Stone, a neighboring minister, who had charged Osborn with everything from incompetence to immorality (laying particular stress on the latter). Finally, during the furor over Arminianism, Stone discovered Osborn's Achilles' Heel—his highly unorthodox theology. In June 1738, a council was called to examine the charges of several members of Osborn's church that he was "venting erroneous doctrines." The council, which Osborn invariably referred to as "that Antinomian Council at Eastham," quickly discovered that they did indeed have a genuine Arminian heretic on their hands. Osborn was charged with "venting" essentially the same errors that Benjamin Kent had preached three years before. He denied the sufficiency of Christ's atonement. He denied the doctrine of unconditional election. He declared that "men can do that upon the doing of which they shall certainly be saved." This last affirmation carried Osborn even further beyond the pale than Kent; indeed, most moderate Arminians would have disagreed, believing that man is ultimately justified by faith alone. To Osborn, however, the truth of the gospel seemed self-evident and, he asked contemptuously, "are we justified because we believe what we can't help believing?" Osborn was an extreme Arminian, believing in the natural ability of man to meet the legal requirements for salvation, and despising creeds and confessions, holding the scriptures to be "a sufficient Directory." [29]

The Eastham Council, not surprisingly, found Osborn guilty as charged, and he was expelled from his pulpit. Osborn, however, defiantly continued to preach in his home, and appealed the decision of the council to the ministers in Boston. Benjamin Colman clearly wished to avoid entanglement with Osborn, but over at the First Church, the ailing Thomas Foxcroft (perhaps through Chauncy's influence) was interested. Foxcroft dispatched a team of ministers to confer with the former council and with the members of Osborn's church in order to determine if a second council was justified. With the exception of Salem's Benjamin Prescott, the entire team consisted of ministers from the South Shore: Ebenezer Gay, Nathaniel Eels of South Scituate, John Hancock, Jr., of Braintree First, and Daniel Lewis of Pembroke. Nathaniel Eels, the leader of the group and senior minister on the South Shore, set the tone. He was a pragmatic, moderate Calvinist and a strong defender of ministerial authority. The same might be said for his colleagues, none of whom had been pleased to see a minister of twenty years standing ejected from his pulpit for theological deviations. It is quite possible that, at this point, Eels and company did not fully appreciate the extent of Osborn's deviations. In any case, the investigating team agreed to the need for a second council. Shortly thereafter, Osborn attended a meeting at the Reverend Nathaniel

Appleton's home in Cambridge where Gay and some others urged a second, expeditious hearing. Following that meeting, Gay and John Hancock, Jr. set out in the snowy December weather for Lexington to consult with the influential Reverend John Hancock, Sr., who was keenly interested in the matter. Clearly there was a great deal of discussion among the leading ministers of the colony concerning the proper disposition of the Osborn case. The result of all these meetings appears to have been a quiet decision to abandon Osborn to his fate, precisely what Benjamin Colman wanted to do in the first place. This reversal of support may have been a consequence of Osborn's increasingly noisy Arminianism, but whatever their reason, Osborn's fellow ministers treated him shabbily.[30]

Still confident of support, Samuel Osborn invited an enormous council of representatives from thirty-two churches to convene at Eastham. As Osborn put it, "great Provision was made," but on the appointed day, "there did not come one Man of them; nor any Word from any of them, giving the Reason why they Fail'd." "Abus'd and disappointed," Osborn set out on a four hundred mile journey, visiting each minister of his council and asking the reason for their absence, but he "could get no satisfactory Answer." Sadder but wiser, Osborn now secured promises in writing from each of the pastors that they would come to Eastham on another day. Osborn dejectedly recorded the results of this second attempt: "The Day being come, they fail'd again; none of them appearing, save Mr. Prescot and Mr. Gay, having no delegates with them." Two lone ministers, Ebenezer Gay and Benjamin Prescott, had honored their written promise.[31]

Throughout the entire episode, Gay appears to have been particularly eager to see Osborn vindicated. That impression is reinforced by his rather lonely presence at Osborn's "council" at Eastham, probably without the approval of Colonel Thaxter. In June 1740, Gay took advantage of another opportunity to demonstrate his support of Osborn. The latter, still pressing his case in Boston, had, after some reverses, secured a supportive statement signed by eleven ministers. This statement was issued on the eve of George Whitefield's arrival in Boston, and it inevitably constituted a theo-political statement on the part of the signers. The first name on the list was Ebenezer Gay; it was followed by the names of such revival opposers as Charles Chauncy, Samuel Mather, Benjamin Prescott, and Peter Clark. Not only was Gay the first signatory, but he was also quite possibly the author of the statement. The syntax, phraseology, and somewhat archaic tone, as well as the wry pleas for tolerance and the familiar impatience with doctrinal arguments, all argue for Gay's authorship.[32]

In this declaration of support, the signers denounced the "hard Measures" Osborn received from the council that condemned him, and lamented the failure of their colleagues "to forward another Hearing of his Cause, which he seasonably claim'd as his just Right." The statement then turned from procedural questions to the charges of doctrinal error laid against Osborn. The most damaging of the charges concerned Osborn's affirmation of four articles that included such baldly Arminian propositions as "men's obedience is a cause of their justification." Concerning the four censured articles, the ministers declared "We can't find that the said Articles necessarily couch or include any dangerous Errors, But that taking them with a christian, candid and charitable Construction, to us it appears, they well accord with the Truths laid down in the Gospel." The importance of a "charitable Construction" was reiterated since "without it some of Mr. Osborn's Expressions might appear inaccurate and erroneous." (Surely this is Gay's gentle irony.) In the statement's conclusion, Gay, Chauncy, et al. laid their fingers directly on the issue that was causing increasing dissension among clergy and laity, and they parenthetically summarized the classic Arminian position on justification:

> We are humbly of the Opinion, That the most of the Disputes, which have taken up much of the Zeal of Christians, and upon which they have broke Charity one with another, which refer to Men's Power, and the Causes of Justification (whilst on all Hands they have agreed in ascribing their Justification to what Christ has done and suffered as the meritorious Cause thereof, and the Ability they have to perform good Works, to the Assistance of the Spirit of Grace) have been a Disservice to Christianity.[33]

Gay, Chauncy, and the other ministers who supported Samuel Osborn quite rightly saw the question of "Men's Power" in the process of salvation as an increasingly divisive issue. To Gay man's natural ability to perform good works was a gift from God and he was obligated to use that gift in assisting the spirit of Grace. Man could accept or reject God's offer of salvation. This proposition was increasingly self-evident to the enlightened minister of Hingham's First Church, and did not derogate one whit from God's sovereignty. Others, of course, believed that it did, and tirelessly pointed out the

vanity and presumption of the Arminians. John White, the minister at Gloucester, wrote in his *New England's Lamentations* (1734)
that "According to the Arminian Scheme, Faith is the Cause, at
least the Antecedent of Election; whereas according to the Gospel
'tis the Effect or Fruit. For this is their Opinion, that such as believe,
and persevere in Faith and Obedience, are elected to Salvation,
which may rather be called Postdestination than Predestination."
White then criticized the sheer effrontery of these Arminians for
attempting to place their own will before the will of God. The truth
that the Arminians refused to confront, said White, was that "some
are chosen to Salvation, others are left. . . . We may well with the
Apostle Paul cry out, O the depth! These are Acts of Sovereignty,
beyond our Comprehension."[34]

The preaching of God's sovereignty was a rebuke to those
men who were caught up in the self-confident, rational, humanistic spirit of the Enlightenment. In 1736, the Reverend William
Cooper warned Robert Breck at the latter's ordination to "Guard
especially against those fashionable, but dangerous opinions of the
present day, that derogate from the *sovereignty of God*." The growing revival party took great delight in exposing the Arminian drift
in New England preaching, and they exhibited a very thorough
understanding of just what Arminianism was and what kind of a
challenge it posed to Calvinist orthodoxy (witness *New England's
Lamentations*). As early as 1733, Benjamin Kent, while denying that
he was an Arminian, observed that "Freewill & Universal redemption, are the two corner stones of Arminianism." Many of the converts to experimental religion understood the Arminian mind,
because they too had drifted away from their Calvinist moorings;
their testimonials must have been galling to the "free and catholick" ministers. Samuel Moody, out on the Maine frontier, acknowledged that he had been "mightily pleased in reading what so much
exalts man, and nourishes the natural bent and bias we have to set
up Self, and a dreadful lothness to be at God's disposal." Down at
Yale College, David Brainerd, the future missionary to the Indians,
confessed, "I could not bear, that it should be wholly at God's Pleasure, to save or damn me, just as he would."[35]

Unlike Brainerd, who would ecstatically acknowledge God's
awful and mysterious sovereignty, Gay never could tolerate the
idea of a capricious Lord. His life to date had been largely an attempt to find and maintain order in his church, his society, and in
the universe. He was not a radical humanist, nor did he deny Di-

vine Grace offered through the death and resurrection of Christ as the meritorious cause of man's salvation. Nevertheless, all his careful study, from Ramus, Wollebius, and Baxter, through the Latitudinarians and Grotius, had convinced him that God was fundamentally benevolent, and that His universe was orderly and rational. For Gay, the reasonable nature of the old federal theology (when its Calvinist elements were ignored) comported well with the world of Locke and Newton. This Puritan rationalism had been reinforced by his tutors at Harvard, and by his various early mentors—Jonathan Belcher, John Danforth, Simon Bradstreet, and Cotton Mather himself. Isaac Chauncey, the minister of Hadley during Gay's tenure as schoolmaster in that town, had described the way to salvation thus: "Comply with the Terms of the Gospel, and you are made for Time and Eternity." No mystery here; nothing incomprehensible or irrational. Man was guided, as the great Archbishop Tillotson had put it, by "a plain moral precept of eternal obligation" in a universe of "fixed and immutable nature."[36]

In 1735, Gay's dear friend from college days, the Reverend Stephen Williams of Longmeadow, wrote in his diary, "I desire to bow myself before ye Lord with utmost humility—acknowledging I am vile, worthless—Sinful, Exposed to ye Divine wrath." It was all very well for Stephen to feel that way, and the widening theological differences between the two men certainly caused no rift in their friendship. Nevertheless, none of Gay's surviving writings ever approach that tone of self-abasement. He seemed temperamentally incapable of it. Perhaps Gay realized that Williams and men like him were really more faithful to the tradition of the Puritan fathers, and that he, Gay, must now quietly part company with the Old Calvinists. He could not reject the new humanism of the age, and plunge men back into total depravity and total reliance on God's good pleasure.[37]

## CHAPTER V

# The Great Awakening:
# The Noisy Passions
# A-Float

The stormy years of New England's Great Awakening opened happily enough for Gay. On a fair, pleasant day in late August of 1740, he and Jerusha had traveled to Cambridge for the Harvard Commencement. His eldest son, Samuel, at the age of nineteen, was concluding a distinguished undergraduate career. Unlike his father, who had received no financial support from the college, Samuel had been a Hollis scholar for two years, in addition to being voted portions of "Col. Fitch's Legacy," "Rev. Gibb's Donation," and the "Benjamin Browne gift." Samuel's commencement, however, was a rather bittersweet occasion for his father, since the younger Gay had chosen to follow the call of Aesculapius rather than that of Christ. Gay was disappointed, but had resolved that if his son was to be a physician, he should have the best possible training. Consequently, within a short time, Samuel Gay was in Chelsea, England, studying medicine.[1]

If Parson Gay felt a bit let down by his eldest son, he found a source of consolation in his nephew and namesake. Ebenezer Gay, Jr. was the second son of Lusher Gay, our Ebenezer's pious brother. Perhaps his name shaped his destiny, for he was far more like his uncle Ebenezer than any of the Hingham minister's own children. Young Ebenezer became noted for his "superior learning," his "cool and penetrating judgement," his dry wit, and his pulpit eloquence (in which he somewhat surpassed his uncle). Indeed, he even had the great misfortune of bearing a marked physical resemblance to his uncle. At the time of Samuel Gay's commencement, young Ebenezer was in residence as a Hopkins Fellow. He had been graduated in 1737, and had studied theology with the Reverend John Taylor of Milton, a gentle, scholarly clergyman and a good friend of Uncle Ebenezer. Now, at the age of twenty-two, young Ebenezer was preparing for his second degree, and preaching occasionally at his home church in Dedham's "Clapboard-trees" Parish. The elder Gay had been trying, unsuccessfully, to put his nephew forward as a candidate for the Cohasset pulpit, which was then vacant.[2]

Gay had taken great pride in the achievements of his son and nephew at Harvard. The Gay family was now "established" at the college. Ebenezer was also doing his best to establish the Gay family back in Hingham, and was succeeding almost too well. In addition to Samuel, the clan in 1740 included three boys—Calvin (16), Martin (14), Jotham (7)—and four girls—Abigail (11), Celia (9), Jerusha (5), and Persis (1). Jerusha Gay, Sr., now forty-two, would shortly be pregnant once again, this time with their last child, the frail Joanna. Fortunately, Parson Gay's financial resources continued to grow apace, and the church assessors remained faithful. They increased the appropriation for Gay's monthly lecture by £10 each year, so that he could cope with the inflationary pressures of that period.[3]

By 1740, Gay's position in Hingham's First Parish seemed more secure than ever. After the death of old Colonel Samuel Thaxter in November, Gay became the unchallenged patriarch of his congregation. He may not have been universally beloved, but no documentary record of opposition from this period has survived. Two years before, in 1738, certain residents of South Hingham had renewed their petition to be set off as a separate parish, but this in no way reflected any dissatisfaction with Gay. The three deacons of the church were now all men of Gay's generation and quite loyal to him. Deacon Solomon Cushing, tanner, and Deacon Thomas Andrews, Town Treasurer and landed gentleman, were two of the five wealthiest men in Hingham and both carried considerable political clout. Gay leaned heavily on both men, but particularly on Cushing, the brother of his college classmate, the Reverend Job Cushing of Shrewsbury.[4]

By 1740 Gay had ministered in Hingham for a sufficiently long time to become something of an institution. His personal traits and eccentricities, his pastoral style, and his preaching were already beginning to coalesce into the Parson Gay of Hingham folklore. This fund of anecdotes, apocryphal stories, and reminiscences are a very mixed blessing to historians. They illuminate several facets of his life-style and temperament but, like the fables of Parson Weems, they tend to acquire a reality of their own that sometimes impedes an accurate understanding of the man.

Some of these tales, as transmitted by nineteenth-century antiquarians, describe the life at the parsonage. According to one tradition, Gay's water well was the result of divine intervention. He had been having great difficulty in locating any reservoir of water beneath his homestead. For some time, work had been in progress on a well just in front of the house, with no results. The parson, however, with the confidence of Moses in the Wilderness, began praying that the workers might strike water. He concluded his supplications by preaching a sermon from the text, "Spring up, O well, sing ye unto it." Gay then exhorted the workmen to take heart and dig a little deeper, and lo—they found water. The story points up Gay's penchant for selecting "appropriate" texts, his good humor, which frequently found its way into the pulpit, and the deep reverence and even awe in which he was held by many of his parishioners.[5]

During the course of this rather pleasant interlude on the eve of the Awakening, Gay lost a very dear friend. In May of 1740, Nehemiah Hobart, Gay's classmate and the minister of the Cohasset Parish, died after a severe epileptic seizure. Two years before, Hobart had recorded in his journal: "Several epileptic fits taken at Mr. Gay's while at dinner and held all the afternoon and fore part of the night, very much lost." He went on to describe how Gay had tenderly cared for him through the night, the next day, and the following night. Whenever one is tempted to view Gay as an autocratic, bloodless rationalist, one is reminded of Gay the pastor, a deeply compassionate, very loving man, to whom others responded in kind.[6]

At about the time that Gay lost his old friend Hobart, he acquired an excellent, if somewhat eccentric new neighbor, in the person of one Cornelius Nye. Gay had probably known Nye at Harvard, and, during Gay's first year in the ministry, Nye also came to Hingham to keep the school for one year. Either he found Hingham particularly congenial, or other prospects failed to open up, for the one year lengthened into sixteen. He and Gay worked as a team, cultivating the minds of the more promising young men of Hingham. By 1739, however, Nye had grown bored with teaching, and he purchased the old Langlee property that adjoined Gay's lot on the east, with the intention of opening a tavern. By 1744, Nye was in business, and his establishment probably helped accommodate the growing number of ministers and other dignitaries that came to Hingham to consult with Gay. Poor Cornelius apparently became the chief recipient of Gay's often withering sarcasm. One story describes Nye's anxiety over a reception to be given for the Governor and Council. He asked Gay if it was probable that his scholarly ability would be recognized in such august company. Gay replied, "Say nothing whatever about it, and I am sure His Honor will never suspect it."[7]

All things considered, Gay was well-prepared in 1740 to weather the coming storm. Financially, socially, politically, and theologically, Gay and Hingham had formed a harmonious union. Gay not only drew comfort from his relations with the town, but also from his rapport with the neighboring ministers. Along the South Shore of Massachusetts Bay, from Dorchester to South Scituate (later to Pembroke and even Kingston), like-minded ministers were beginning to form a powerful association. The South Shore ministers of this period tended to be tolerant, moderate Calvinists with presbyterian views on the proper mode of church government. Like Gay, they were inclined to be socially conservative, antienthusiastic, cautious, personally genial and urbane. They generally preferred inclusive parish churches, rather than exclusive congregational churches. This preference was reflected in the requirements for membership in their churches—i.e., a knowledgeable profession of faith, a godly walk, and regular attendance on the sacraments. Furthermore, in order to preserve tranquility in their parishes, these clergymen frequently exercised near autocratic authority.[8]

The South Shore ministry, it would appear, continued to adhere to its distinctive presbyterian tradition. Gay cheerfully accepted and even augmented that tradition, which blended nicely with his Matherian devotion to synodical church government and ministerial authority. At ordination services Gay frequently spoke of the importance of "Presbyterian Ordination," and, on one occasion, he extended the right hand of fellowship to a new minister in Marshfield "in the Name of the Presbyters here present." In 1741, John Fowle, Cohasset's new minister, was ordained "by the solemn Imposition of the hands of the Presbytery according to the direction of the Gospel." The term "Presbytery" seemed to connote a consociated, regional church establishment that had a sacerdotal understanding of the ministry. The frequent use of words like "presbyter" and even "bishop" in South Shore ordination sermons suggests that here were ministers who were quite jealous of their authority, both individual and collective.[9]

In the years immediately preceding the Awakening, the South Shore ministers were beginning to meet and act in concert with greater regularity. The idea of an active clerical association in the region was not new. Sometime in the late seventeenth century, as the spirit of consociationism grew, the South Shore ministers formed the Weymouth Association, following the recent example of the ministers of Boston. By subscribing to Cotton Mather's Proposals of 1705, they indicated their support for greater ecclesiastical authority and diminished congregational power. The Proposals were defeated in the legislature, however, and the Weymouth Association faded from view. However, by 1722, there were two Associations in the region south of Boston. The one to which Gay probably belonged was the Hull Association, the apparent successor to the old Weymouth Association. The second clerical association was called the Plymouth Association, which included most of the towns in the westerly part of the Old Colony.[10]

The formation of the Hull Association paralleled the attempts of the South Shore, in the 1720s, to establish an identity independent of Boston to the north, and old Plymouth to the south. On two occasions, in 1726 and in 1730, the General Court debated the wisdom of creating a new county composed of the towns of Hingham, Braintree, Weymouth, Hull, Scituate, Abington, and (in 1730) Hanover. In fact, Colonel Samuel Thaxter was using all his influence to make Hingham the "shire town" of this proposed new county. The projected county was not to be, but the efforts of both the civil and religious leaders of the South Shore reflect the region's growth as a distinct social, economic, and religious entity. The Hull Association, however, seems to have foundered. This may have been due to the transcendent influence of Nathaniel Eels, who ministered on the southern boundary of the Hull Association. Eels's South Scituate Parish was, in fact, a part of the Plymouth Association, and he emerged as a leading mediator of ecclesiastical affairs in the Old Colony. However, he turned his face north just as frequently, tending to dominate clerical politics on the South Shore as well. Accordingly, when disputes arose, it fell to Eels to assemble a council and settle the matter, and the Hull Association fell into disuse.[11]

Sometime during the 1730s, the South Shore ministers association was revitalized, in part because of the intervention of the Reverend John Hancock of Lexington. Hancock was one of the senior ministers of the province (he had settled in Lexington in 1698), and his strong will was felt in regions far beyond Middlesex County. Since 1704, his name had been associated with proposals to strengthen church government. He held a magnified view of the importance of the clerical office that very nearly approached the episcopal; indeed, he became known as "Bishop" Hancock. In 1726, the Bishop had managed to place his eldest son, John Jr., in the vacant pulpit of Braintree's First Church. Three years later, the elder Hancock's influence on the South Shore was further extended when his pupil and son-in-law, Jonathan Bowman, was installed at Dorchester. Gay and his fellow ministers were certainly not insensitive to the old man's wishes. It may be recalled that Gay made a special point of riding to Lexington to consult with him in the midst of the Osborn affair. In 1739, the Reverend William Smith of Weymouth good-naturedly acknowledged old Hancock's weight in local affairs, when he wrote to Gay that "according to the bishop's desire which you know passes for a positive command with me, his unworthy Curate, I now send you word that the ministers' meeting is to be at Brother Bowman's next Tuesday."[12]

The continuing vitality of the revived association was due principally to the combined efforts of John Hancock, Jr., William Smith, and Gay. The success of the younger Hancock in Braintree was something of a surprise. One Boston minister expressed the general opinion when he wrote that at the very least Hancock "could make a very handsome bow, and if the first did not Suit, He'd Bow Lower a Second time." Gradually, however, during his eighteen-year tenure in the Braintree pulpit, Hancock came into his own. He formed a close friendship with Gay, which was probably cemented by his marriage in 1733 to Mary Hawke Thaxter, the widow of Gay's classmate, Samuel Thaxter, Jr. (Gay had always admired Mary, once declaring that she had a "happy firmness of Mind, not very common to her Sex.") Hancock became an excellent minister in his own parish, and he also emerged as a central figure in the Association. During the Awakening, he became known as the scourge of itinerants, penning savage indictments of Gilbert Tennent and others. At his untimely death in 1744, Gay said that the "associated Pastors of the Vicinity will weep. . . . Few Brethren in the Ministry have liv'd together in greater Unity than we . . . and under God, it hath seem'd to be very much owing to Mr. Hancock's excellent Spirit, and earnest Care to keep up ministerial Communion, and preserve brotherly love." Hancock, in Gay's view, clearly played a primary role on shaping a strong South Shore association.[13]

William Smith gave the association a center, which was in fact its old home—Weymouth. Smith was settled over Weymouth's First Church in 1734, and he quickly settled down to a life resembling that of an English country vicar. He seemed generally more interested in the art of grafting fruit trees and the fine points of animal husbandry than in the fine points of theology. Consequently, this genial young man offended no one, and soon became a sort of general secretary for what was now, once again, called the Weymouth Association. Gay was delighted to have Smith as a neighbor. The latter frequently became Gay's traveling companion when ecclesiastical councils were called, and the two men exchanged pulpits with great regularity. Smith, in his turn, was quite impressed with Gay's biblical scholarship, and circulated the Hingham minister's sermons among his colleagues. On one occasion, when informing Gay of a forthcoming association meeting, Smith wrote, "you are Desired to be as a Lovely Song unto us,"—a metaphor that clearly suggests how much Gay's personality overshadowed his physiognomy.[14]

The Weymouth Association provided an institutional framework in which Gay could quietly extend his influence. After the death of John Hancock, Jr. in 1744, Gay became the leading figure among the associated pastors. Advancing age was beginning to diminish the influence of Nathaniel Eels, and in any case, he was not a member of the Association. Because of his growing dominance of the Weymouth Association (soon re-named the Hingham Association), Ebenezer Gay would shortly become the most important minister on the South Shore.

For some years prior to 1740, New Englanders had heard reports about the religious revivals and stirrings in the Middle Colonies. A new religious excitement had seized the Presbyterians in New York and New Jersey, encouraged by ministers such as Jonathan Dickinson, Ebenezer Pemberton, and William Tennent, Sr. and his sons. Expectation ran high in New England and the field was white for harvest when, on September 14, 1740, the Reverend

George Whitefield sailed into Newport, Rhode Island. Charles Chauncy later maintained that this day marked the commencement of New England's "Time of Troubles," and he was probably not far wrong. Whitefield was a twenty-six-year-old evangelical Calvinist from England, and a close associate of the Wesleys. He had wandered about England, preaching to the multitudes in the open air. In 1739, he brought his charismatic preaching to the colonies, for the purpose of raising funds for an orphanage to be built in Bethesda, Georgia. After preaching in Newport for two days, he arrived in Boston, preceded by a publicity barrage that any modern evangelist would envy. The town was his. He dined with Governor Belcher, and was enthusiastically endorsed by the Reverends Thomas Foxcroft, Benjamin Colman, Joshua Gee, and most of the rest of Boston's religious establishment. Whitefield preached to audiences that numbered in the thousands, creating something approaching mass hysteria in some of the churches. He preached on the Boston Common, in the fields, and in the Harvard Yard. On this last occasion, two of the faces in the crowd belonged to Ebenezer Gay, Jr. and a young freshman named Jonathan Mayhew who became "inflamed with the Love of Christ." George Whitefield had undeniably ravished Boston and, sometime after his departure, Timothy Cutler, the unsympathetic rector of Christ Church, summarized his view of the social upheaval occasioned by Whitefield in a letter to a friend: "Our presses are for ever teeming with books, and our women with bastards." [15]

During his first tour of New England, George Whitefield did not personally visit the South Shore or old Plymouth Colony. The task of extending the great work to southeastern Massachusetts fell to the second of the Grand Itinerants, the Reverend Gilbert Tennent, a Presbyterian minister from New Brunswick, New Jersey. Tennent and his two brothers had been trained for the ministry by their father, William Tennent, Sr., a graduate of the University of Edinburgh and the founder of the "Log College," a seminary that produced well-educated, pietistic Presbyterian ministers (the antecedent of Princeton College). Whitefield, after leaving New England, met Gilbert Tennent at Staten Island and, after some vigorous persuasion, convinced him that he was the man to keep the evangelical fires burning in Boston. Accordingly, Tennent arrived in Boston in December of 1740 and commenced a punishing schedule of preaching in the midst of an unusually severe New England winter. [16]

Unlike Whitefield, Tennent received a decidedly mixed reception. Descriptions of his preaching style vary widely, according to the sympathies of the observer. An outraged Timothy Cutler related how "people wallowed in snow, night and day, for the benefit of his beastly brayings." To balance this, we have the sympathetic account of the Reverend Thomas Prince: "He seemed to have no regard to please the eyes of his hearers with agreeable gestures, nor their ears with delivery, nor their fancy with language; but to aim directly at their consciences, to lay open their ruinous delusions . . . and drive them out of every deceitful refuge wherein they made themselves easy." Prince's impressions are probably closer to the mark than Cutler's. Having long been faced with the infuriating complacency of Scotch-Irish Presbyterians in his own parish, Tennent tried to overcome the "presumptuous Security" of his hearers. He strove to put his listeners under "convictions"—to show them, to their terror and dismay, that they were not Christians after all, and that they had urgent need to repent. He apparently did this less with histrionic bombast than with a searching, earnest, compelling exposition of scripture, a style employed by the best revivalists from Edwards, through Finney, to Graham. Stripped of an occasional ranting tendency, his preaching was precisely the sort that Ebenezer Gay was continually recommending to younger ministers. This may help explain why Gay welcomed Gilbert Tennent into the pulpit of the Ship Church.[17]

In the early stages of the Great Awakening, Gay was as sanguine as most of his colleagues. He may not have been as euphoric as Benjamin Colman or Thomas Foxcroft, but he was hopeful that this was a true work of the Holy Spirit. In the course of his twenty-three year ministry, Gay had experienced times of special grace, and had reaped the spiritual harvest, so at first he tended to take this new revival in stride; indeed, he intended to exploit it as fully as possible. He was somewhat disturbed by the growing number of itinerants, and the excesses in Boston, but his basic attitude was that "This precious Season of Grace calls for peculiar Watchfulness and Diligence, that none under preparatory Convictions, may fall short of saving Conversion."[18]

In early March of 1741, an exhausted Gilbert Tennent was slowly proceeding from town to town along the South Shore. Gay and his deacons invited him to stop in Hingham and deliver the Thursday lectures. Gay was anxious to reinvigorate the church in Hingham, and Tennent seemed perfect for the purpose. He was well-educated (a *sine qua non* for Gay), and he had allied himself with the New England Presbyterians, a group whose theology and polity were nearly at one with Hingham's religious heritage. Gay even agreed with Tennent when the latter complained about the soul-deadening effects of an unconverted ministry. Within the year, Gay was stressing the importance of "sanctifying Grace" for a "valid and useful ministry." Graceless, unconverted men, he declared, "are a Stench to the Nostrils of His Holiness."[19]

John Hancock of Braintree, who was far more nervous than Gay about the potential consequences of Tennent's visit to the South Shore, left this slightly biased account of the evangelist's progress: Traveling in "Pomp and Grandeur," Tennent "came eating and drinking, galloping over the Country with his *Congregatio de propoganda*, &c. . . . with a Troop of 20 or 30 Horse, entering into other Men's Labours, and devouring their Livings." Tennent and his entourage arrived in Hingham on March 5. He preached his first sermon from the text "Awake, thou that sleepest, and arise from the dead, and Christ shall give thee light." This was followed later in the evening by a sermon on the classic regeneration text: "Except a man be born again, he cannot see the kingdom of God." No contemporary description of Tennent's impact on the gathering at the Old Ship has survived, but the Reverend Nathaniel Leonard recorded his impressions of Tennent's visit to Plymouth a few days later:

> All Persons were put upon examining themselves, warned against trusting in their own Righteousness, and resting in the Form of Godliness, without the Power, &c. These things, together with pathetical Invitations to Sinners to come and embrace the LORD JESUS CHRIST as offered in the Gospel, made a wonderful Impression on the Minds of all Sorts of People at the first.[20]

One month to the day after Gilbert Tennent's departure from Hingham, two young men, both twenty years old, were admitted to full communion. Presumably, Tennent's eloquence had awakened their sleeping souls; they were put under "convictions"; they repented; they joined the community of saints at Hingham. The one, John Thaxter, was a member of the highest echelon of Hingham society. The grandson of old Colonel Samuel, John (Harvard, 1741) would shortly inherit much of his grandfather's wealth, social and political influence, and even his military rank. The other young man, Noah Ripley, was the son of a poor cooper in Hingham

Centre. Shortly after his conversion, Noah left Hingham to seek his fortune in Woodstock, Connecticut. The spirit of God's grace was beginning to move in Hingham, touching rich and poor alike.[21]

The conversions of Thaxter and Ripley marked the commencement of the Great Awakening in Hingham, or at least of a somewhat heightened sensibility to the promptings of the Spirit. After Tennent's lecture, the revival in Hingham proceeded largely under Gay's careful control and direction. Things did not get out of hand. Sixteen souls followed the two young men into full communion in 1741, and, in 1742, twenty-seven new communicants swelled the membership rolls (see Appendix 1). Hingham had waded into the waters of the Awakening, but only up to her knees. When contrasted with comparably sized towns in southeastern Massachusetts such as Plymouth (84 admissions in 1741–42, Hingham had 45) and Middleborough (174 admissions in 1741–44, Hingham had 76), the revival in Hingham seems to have been a rather modest affair. The majority of those admitted to full membership in 1741–42 were not single, young people such as Thaxter and Ripley. Instead, 73 percent of those admitted were married and their average age was 31.7 years. Sixteen men and women (out of forty-five) were admitted as couples, a customary practice with Gay. At one point, two sisters, Lydia and Mary Lane, fifteen and nineteen years old respectively, and their sixteen-year-old cousin Irene Lane (Gay's niece), were admitted together. These were the only admissions during the height of the revival that were even slightly unusual, and even in this instance there were numerous precedents during non-revival periods. In short, the Awakening in Hingham was, in most respects, business as usual—just more of it.[22]

Gay was determined to encourage a more experimental piety in his parish, but he would not admit ranting enthusiasts into the church who would disturb the peace of his "family." He declared that ministers "are constituted Rulers over God's Household, and Obedience to them is plainly required. . . . Waving all Dispute about the immediate Receivers of Ecclesiastical Authority from the Head of the Church, this is without Controversy; that it belongs to the Ministers of Christ to exert it. Whoever be the first Recipient of the Keys of the Kingdom of Heaven, the Stewards of Christ's family should turn 'em." Gay had no intention of surrendering those keys to anyone else.[23]

The particular character of the revival in Hingham can be understood more completely by looking at some of the social and economic forces that were affecting the town in the early 1740s. The Great Awakening has been linked by scholars (with varying degrees of success) with economic uncertainty resulting from the decline in foreign trade, shortage of specie, and the suppression of the Land Bank; with population growth resulting in a shortage of arable land and subsequent social dislocation; and even with epidemiological causes. Without going so far as to interpret the Awakening as being wholly the result of deeply rooted socioeconomic forces, one can surely maintain that these forces created a climate of uncertainty in which evangelical Calvinism would thrive. Most of these potentially disruptive forces were present in Hingham in the early 1740s, and a firm hand on the helm of the Old Ship was clearly required.[24]

Between the years 1711 and 1749, the population of Hingham increased at an estimated rate of 1.7 percent per year. The growth in population was closely correlated with an increasingly unequal distribution of wealth. During these years, a clearly defined upper class was beginning to emerge. By 1741, despite the characteristic conservatism of Hingham's leading families, this growing inequity was beginning to be perceived and resented. In July of that year, a special town meeting was called by "19 of the inhabitants" to express their concern over the fencing and enclosures that were encroaching on that symbol of community—the common lands. The names of these nineteen disgruntled citizens were not recorded, with the exception of their leader, that inveterate rebel, Abel Cushing. However, the legality of the whole meeting was protested by twenty-five men whose names *were* recorded, including ten current or former selectmen, the town treasurer and clerk, all three First Church deacons, and the two wealthiest men in town. Nevertheless, despite the opposition of such men as Deacon Thomas Andrews, Captain John Jacob, and Benjamin Lincoln, the town voted to prosecute anyone who "shall presume to fence or make encroachments on said lands."[25]

The pressures of population growth, land shortage, and increasing economic inequality were certainly present in Hingham in the early 1740s. The level of social and economic frustration, however, was mitigated by the increasing availability of employment in nonagricultural pursuits. Hingham's fishing and shipbuilding industries and the size of its commercial fleet were just beginning their rapid expansion (an economic transformation that

TABLE 1. Average Age of Males and Percentage of Females Admitted per Decade to Hingham First Church from 1720–1759

| Decade of Admission | Total Admissions | Average Age of Males | Percentage of Females |
|---|---|---|---|
| 1720–29 | 112 | 32.6 | 53% |
| 1730–39 | 91 | 33.3 | 58% |
| 1740–49 | 116 | 31.2 | 67% |
| 1750–59 | 75 | 30.2 | 63% |

SOURCE: Ebenezer Gay, "Record of Births, Marriages, Deaths, and Admissions, 1718–1786" (Hingham Church Records). Note: The decrease in total admissions after 1750 is due, in part, to the formation of Hingham's Third (South) Parish.

is more fully described in Chapter 8). Daniel Scott Smith, as a result of his demographic analysis of marriage patterns in Hingham, has suggested that the amount of available farmland began to decrease significantly at about this time. As much of the excess farm labor was absorbed by the growing mercantile economy, the age of economic maturity in Hingham gradually dropped. If one then accepts the argument of historian Philip Greven, that the age of economic maturity should correspond with the age of conversion (full church membership signifying a social coming of age), one would expect a gradual long-term drop in the average age of admission to the church. This proved to be precisely the case (see Table 1). Furthermore, this gradual decline in age operated independently of the Awakening. As Table 2 suggests, there was no precipitous drop in the age of conversion during the Awakening years. Hingham's young men did not need Gay's church as an escape from economic disappointment.[26]

One of the more striking statistics of the Hingham Awakening is the sudden decline in the percentage of male converts. The situation was precisely reversed in towns such as Plymouth or Middleborough where New Light preachers kept the evangelical fires blazing. In the Old Colony, so many males were added to the membership rolls that the normal female majorities were reduced, in some cases, to sexual parity. The Reverend Peter Thacher of Middleborough, pleasantly surprised, noted that: "the Grace of God has surprisingly seized and subdued the hardiest men, and more Males have been added here than of the tenderer sex." Cedric B.

TABLE 2. Average Age and Percentage of Males Admitted to
Hingham First Church from 1738–1745

| Year of Admission | Total Admissions | Average Age of Males | Percentage of Males |
|---|---|---|---|
| 1738 | 11 | 37.4 | 55% |
| 1739 | 5 | 32.0 | 40% |
| 1740 | 8 | 30.8 | 50% |
| 1741 | 18 | 30.8 | 45% |
| 1742 | 27 | 33.3 | 30% |
| 1743 | 14 | 32.0 | 21% |
| 1744 | 17 | 25.8 | 35% |
| 1745 | 10 | 30.6 | 30% |

SOURCE: Ebenezer Gay, "Record of Births, Marriages, Deaths, and Admissions,
1718–1786" (Hingham Church Records).

Cowing, in an article called "Sex and Preaching in the Great
Awakening," has argued that the "Terrors of the Law," as they were
mercilessly expounded by evangelical Calvinists, profoundly affected males. The awful truths of God's word, when preached by
ministers such as Jonathan Edwards or Eleazer Wheelock, pierced
the indifference of even the most phlegmatic men, arousing, in
turn, anger, fear, conviction of sin, total psychological collapse and
submission, and finally the great joy of the new birth. The fact that
the revival in Hingham did not seize and subdue the men suggests,
again, that Gay refused to allow the New Light to ravish his parish.
Although he was capable of powerful preaching, he would not, and
probably could not, embrace the fervent Calvinistic rhetoric of the
more successful evangelists. Once, in describing evangelical techniques, Gay said that sinners should not be "meerly affrighted or
forced, but charm'd into a Surrender to the Lord."[27]

The church membership statistics, however, reveal more than
Gay's inability to bring males into the flock; they also show a positive and dramatic increase in the number of female converts. In
this respect, Gay's revival ministry closely resembles that of the
English Methodist, John Wesley, whose Arminian preaching was
attracting far more females than males in these years. Perhaps
the elements of Gay's Arminian gospel were more attractive to the
women of the period than the Calvinistic demand for total submission to a harsh, sovereign, and patriarchal god. In any case, as

Table 1 shows, after the Great Awakening women continued their 60 plus percent preponderance in admissions to full communion. This certainly reflects a declining religiosity among Hingham males, but it may also be related, in subtle ways, to Gay's increasingly Arminian ministry.[28]

While Gay was endeavoring to encourage and yet control the revival in Hingham, his nephew and namesake was struggling to cope with a much more volatile situation in the Connecticut Valley town of Suffield. Young Ebenezer had been called by the Suffield church in November 1741. The town's former minister, Ebenezer Devotion, had died in April of 1741, leaving the flock exposed to the New Light wolves in territory that was generally supportive of the Awakening. Within three months of Devotion's death, a neighboring minister noted "strange & unusual things in Suffield," including the reception of ninety-five new members into the church by the Reverend Jonathan Edwards, an outsider from Northampton. The passions of the town had been inflamed by several prominent evangelists, including George Whitefield, Edwards, Joseph Bellamy, and Samuel Buell. The people of Suffield were said to be given to "Raptures and violent Emotions of the Affections, and a vehement Zeal." To make matters worse, in 1740 the General Court had authorized the formation of a new parish in the west part of town and, although the new parish was not yet settled, it formed the center of most of the New Light activity.[29]

Young Gay was not altogether unsuited to his new parish. He could paint terrifying pictures of damnation in his sermons, and he may have fallen under Whitefield's influence at Harvard. He apparently had been recommended to the town both by his uncle's old friend, the Reverend Stephen Williams of Longmeadow, and by his brother-in-law, the Reverend John Ballantine of Westfield. Despite these credentials, he had received a rough reception from the more boisterous elements in the West Parish faction. Young Gay expressed his anxiety about the growing turmoil in Suffield in a letter to Stephen Williams. In the event uncle Ebenezer was unable to come to the ordination service, he asked Williams to prepare a sermon, hoping that he would be less controversial than, for instance, Jonathan Edwards or a more radical New Light. Gay wrote, "A middle way I have often heard you plead for as safest— And I believe a Discourse from you w$^d$ be taken well f$^{rm}$ all sides."[30]

Due to the severity of the season, young Gay had just about given up hope that his uncle would attempt the long, overland journey to the Connecticut River Valley. He needn't have worried, however, since the Hingham parson had no intention of allowing anything to interfere with this trip. Gay quickly gathered up a small delegation consisting of his friend and neighbor, Elisha Leavitt, and Deacon Solomon Cushing. These three shortly joined forces with two of the Dedham clan—Gay's brother Lusher, and Eliphalet Pond, the son of Gay's oldest sister. On January 11, 1742, a cold, miserable day, the five men arrived in Suffield. The following day Stephen Williams arrived and rejoiced to see his "ancient friend." Gay was equally pleased, later writing to Williams that it was "a pleasure to me to renew old acquaintance, this was one great comfort of my journey." Williams doubtless conveyed his careful appraisal of the situation to the Hingham minister. Although Williams was a firm supporter of the revival, the situation in Suffield disturbed him. After talking with some of the Suffield men, he concluded that they "seem to have religion at heart—but I fear ye zeal boils over." By the following day then, Gay had a very clear sense of the situation that his nephew had to face in Suffield.[31]

The ordination sermon, which he entitled *Ministers' Insufficiency for Their Important and Difficult Work*, was not unremittingly critical of the revival. Indeed, he warmly praised "the great Things which have been of late done among this people." He told his nephew that "The LORD of the Harvest sends you to labour in a Field, that is white already to Harvest." (The younger Gay, incidentally, took this hint and, in the following month, admitted over forty souls into church membership.) Yet he carefully reminded his listeners that a lasting and true conversion was not possible without a rational obedience to God's Law, and he stressed the necessary union between the Covenant of Grace and the Covenant of Works (the Law).[32]

Although he was not yet prepared to damn the Awakening in its entirety, Gay showed no hesitation in attacking lay exhorters and enthusiastic itinerants. Indeed, five months before Chauncy entered the lists with his important sermon, *Enthusiasm Described and Caution'd Against*, Gay was describing and cautioning against enthusiasts with might and main. Indeed, one might suggest that the entire ordination sermon was fashioned for the purpose of excoriating radical New Lights. The basic theme, implied in the title, might be restated thus—If Harvard-trained ministers, after diligent study and preparation are unprepared for their high calling, how much more inadequate are these rambling illiterates?[33]

Gay characteristically focused his opposition to the revivalists on their lack of proper training. After all, he said, "The Toil of the Brain is harder to endure than the Sweat of the Face." He berated the foolishness of those who "have not by diligent Study acquir'd some tolerable Accomplishments for so weighty and difficult a Service . . . whatever Pretences they make to immediate Impulses and extraordinary Assistances from the Spirit of God." Gay perceived an assault on the high, professional standards of the ministry. He hoped that these deluded fanatics would tire of "the silly satisfaction of hearing themselves, and seeing others crowd to hear them talk in Publick," and that they would cease their attempts "to intrude themselves unqualified into the sacred, tremendous Office." In the midst of all this spiritual turmoil, he could easily understand how a young minister might be tempted to think "that unpremeditated Sermons, deliver'd with much Noise and Fervour, tended most to Edification, and that the chief part of a Minister's Work was the Labour of the Lungs. But, though rambling Discourse sometimes take exceedingly with the injudicious, yet Ministers should not on that Account remit of their Studies."[34]

Gay insisted that an intellectually sound sermon need not be dry and passionless. Every minister should always strive for "fervent, powerful preaching," but that is different from using "artful or apish Gestures, extraordinary Emotions, and vehement accents to strike the Senses and Imaginations of People, without informing their Judgements." Then, in Chauncyesque fashion, Gay declared that New Light preaching merely "set the noisy Passions a-float to the drowning of a rational edifying Attention; whereby Preaching is made the *acting of a Part*, and an Ordinance of Christ is turn'd into a theatrical Amusement." He summed up his indictment of the itinerants and lay exhorters with a strikingly apt quotation from scripture:

> To many a one, who is now A-Days eager to run before GOD sends him, it may be said as it was to Ahimoaz by Joab, 2 Sam, 18–22, "Wherefore wilt thou run, my Son, seeing that thou hast no Tidings ready?"

From Gay's perspective, this expressed the whole matter in a nutshell.[35]

The elder Gay remained in Suffield long enough to preach two lectures for his nephew, and, on January 19, in near blizzard conditions, he and his party set out for Springfield and then home.

Shortly after his return to the coast, Gay traveled to Boston to wish godspeed to his eldest son, Samuel, who was embarking on a voyage to England where he would study medicine. Upon returning home, Gay found the revival sweeping the South Shore, and he soon became engaged in the pleasant task of carefully reaping the harvest in Hingham. He wrote a note to Stephen Williams that caused the latter to rejoice that "religion is reviving on that Side ye country." Gay's correspondence also reflects his continuing anxiety about his nephew's welfare. He wrote young Ebenezer that he was quite worried about "the growing disorders & difficulties in your Parish." With an informality and tenderness that he rarely used when writing to his own children, Gay told his nephew "Did I live nearer to you, my Concern for y$^r$ Welfare & peace Could not be greater than it is, and all the benefit you would have by my Conversation, would be to know more of that hearty affection which at this distance I bear towards you." [36]

In the summer of 1742, Gay's hostility toward the Awakening intensified rapidly, as he watched his nephew's trial by fire in Suffield. His growing revulsion was compounded as he began to read and hear about the antics of James Davenport in Boston. Unquestionably the most frenzied of the Grand Itinerants, Davenport had thoroughly disturbed the equilibrium of that town. The *Boston Evening-Post* described him

> returning from the Common after his first preaching, with a large Mob at his Heels, singing all the Way thro' the Streets, he with his Hands extended, his Head thrown back, and his Eyes staring up to Heaven, attended with so much Disorder, that they look'd more like a Company of Bacchanalians after a mad Frolick, then sober Christians who had been worshipping God. . . .

Davenport greatly embarrassed many supporters of the Awakening, and enraged its opponents. He denounced ministers such as Benjamin Colman and Charles Chauncy by name, damning them as unconverted. He was utter anathema to a man like Gay, the incarnation of every evil that Gay had condemned at his nephew's ordination. After the summer of 1742, Gay and many other moderates like him began to swell the ranks of the revival opponents. [37]

Meanwhile, the attacks on the younger Gay were increasing in frequency and boldness. He had to endure continuous interference and disruption from Suffield's West Parish, which still had no settled minister. His clerical authority was being challenged so effectively that he even felt obliged to allow the extremely zealous itinerant, Benjamin Pomeroy, to preach several times from his pulpit. The young man was becoming desperate, and his uncle wrote him a letter urging moderation and perseverance. In this letter, written in December 1742, we have the clearest indication of the elder Gay's changing perceptions of the revival. He wrote, "The Times are perillous. The *Glorious Day* (as many term it) is not all day—'tis awfully Clouded & Darkened—and the *Glorious Work* (which many speak of with entire satisfaction & Joy) appears to me now as Chang'd into a ruinous War, and a pious heart will tremble for the Ark of God." Aware of his nephew's delicate situation, Gay's advice was to "be as slow to deal with offenders in a way of publick Discipline, as a good Conscience will Let you be, for you are aware of the danger even when there is great Need of it."[38]

Back in Hingham, Parson Gay's changing attitude toward the Awakening was mirrored not only in his response to his nephew's tribulations, but also by the books he was reading. In June 1741, clearly caught up in the excitement of "the Glorious Work," he began studying *A Serious Call to a Devout and Holy Life*, a 1728 work by William Law, one of England's most forcible opponents of Lockean rationalism. Law had clashed frequently with that arch-rationalist Matthew Tindal, and had vigorously argued against the importance of human reason. He was, in fact, a rather profound mystic and believer in the inner light, who influenced both Whitefield and Wesley. In 1741, then, Gay may have been flirting with New Light mysticism, but the divisiveness and disruption caused by the revival soon made him question its authenticity. By late 1742, he was reading the works of Lord Edward Herbert of Cherbury (1583–1648), one of the Cambridge Platonists. Herbert had rejected all revelation, believing that unassisted reason could discover the five axioms that supported all religions: (1) There is a God. (2) He ought to be worshiped. (3) Virtue and piety are an essential part of worship. (4) Man should repent of his sins. (5) There are rewards and punishments in a future life. Gay was not as extreme a rationalist as that, but Lord Herbert may have helped lead him from the frightening intellectual abyss that Law's mysticism represented, back to the solid, comfortable ground of reason.[39]

By the end of 1742, the revival on the South Shore was slowing down, but the ruptures and rancor that followed in its wake were just beginning. Gay summarized the situation in Hingham in a letter to his nephew: "We are in this Parish free from Strife at present, tho' the Itch after new things, and new Preachers of 'em is still lurking in some among us." The spiritual needs of the small group of New Light dissidents in Hingham were apparently being met by the Reverend James Bayley, minister in Weymouth's South Parish. Bayley was a man of about Gay's age, who had been settled in Weymouth for nearly twenty years. In 1741, about the time that Gay was reading Law and allowing Tennent to preach from his pulpit, James Bayley had received "a gracious turn . . . from the most High." The experience transformed Bayley into what Clifford Shipton has called a "quiet New-Light." He was not quiet enough for Gay, however, who did not appreciate Bayley's habit of preaching "publickly & from house to house," particularly when the latter wandered across the Weymouth line into South Hingham. With the territorial jealousy of any devoted parish minister, Gay wrote his nephew that "Baily some times Comes into our Borders, and preaches in private houses—I don't hear of any notable Effects." In the years following the Awakening, Bayley allied himself with the ministers of the Plymouth Association, the champions of neo-Calvinism on the South Shore.[40]

By the beginning of 1743 the threat that the Awakening posed to good order and unity in the churches was manifest to most thoughtful men. Itinerancy, lay exhorting, censoriousness, church divisions, unruly behavior during worship services, in short, all the socially disruptive elements of the revival, caused many besides Gay to "tremble for the Ark of God." There was a rebellious, leveling spirit abroad in the land that seemed to conservatives to threaten the entire social and economic order in New England. The authority of the educated clergy was being openly defied. Farmers and mechanics were charged with neglecting their families and their work to spend all their time attending lectures and revival meetings. This state of affairs predictably left the radical pro-revivalists unmoved, and caused the members of the growing opposition to become, as one Maine minister put it, "exceeding virulent and mad." The major change caused by the excesses, however, was among that large body of moderates who supported the revival. Men like Benjamin Colman and Thomas Foxcroft, not convinced that church disorder was a necessary concomitant of a glorious work of God, became increasingly alienated. Even such a bulwark of the revival as Jonathan Edwards was forced to remind the New Lights that "Order is one of the most necessary of all external means of the spiritual good of God's Church."[41]

# CHAPTER VI

# The Great Awakening: The Captain Kept His Place

Every year a large number of ministers gathered in Boston on the day that counselors were elected to the General Assembly. By the 1740s, this convention had long since become formalized. Two ministers were chosen in advance—one to deliver the Election Sermon on the opening day of the legislature, the other to address the ministers directly on the following day. The convention also took up a collection, usually for the support of missionary work. In 1743, the Annual Convention became a political arena as Charles Chauncy led the Old Light troops into battle. The forces opposing the Awakening had never been so spirited or so organized. Their rallying cry had been succinctly expressed by Robert Breck of Springfield a few months before, when he wrote that "all New Light is almost extinct—and God grant that all New Light may be, entirely that the Old, the true Gospel Light, may Shine forth the more gloriously and victoriously!"[1]

During the pre-convention maneuvering, Chauncy had firm and crucial support from members of the South Shore delegation. Gay was present but was characteristically circumspect, giving place to the more vocal John Hancock of Braintree, and to Nathaniel Eels. The convention was apparently not well-attended, facilitating matters for Chauncy and the Old Lights. The tone of the gathering was set by Nathaniel Appleton of Cambridge who delivered the Election Sermon. Appleton systematically condemned itinerancy, lay exhorters, immediate revelation, and the need for dramatic conversion experiences. He further warned the New Lights against "speaking too slightly of good works," although he did chide the opposers for denying that there had been "a glorious work of God in the land of late." At the conclusion of this keynote sermon, the convention elected Nathaniel Eels moderator, and then chose a committee to draft a testimony concerning those matters "of a dangerous tendency" which Appleton had enumerated.[2]

The committee, which included such vigorous opposers as John Hancock of Braintree and Benjamin Prescott of Salem, drafted a testimony that essentially restated Appleton's sermon, but went even further in its indictment of the Awakening. The testimony declared that such New Light doctrines as "sanctification is no evidence of justification" were of a piece "with other Antinomian and Familistical errors" [the Familists were a seventeenth-century sect which held that all religion consisted in the exercise of love]. The committee also condemned those who presumed to denounce their ministers as "Pharisees, Arminians, blind and unconverted, &c., when their doctrines are agreeable to the gospel and their lives to their Christian profession." Their final draft was such an unsparing condemnation of the revival that some of the moderates objected. At the insistence of Joseph Sewall, a final article was added which noted that "where there is any special Revival of pure Religion in any Parts of our Land, at this Time, we would give unto God all the Glory." Even this rather weak attestation was hotly debated, though the convention adopted it by a small majority. The adoption of this article was the only setback for the Chauncy forces. After Chauncy himself delivered the Convention Sermon, the entire testimony was adopted, though not without the protests of Boston's Second Church minister Joshua Gee, the outmaneuvered leader of the pro-Awakening men. The members of the Chauncy faction wisely decided not to advertise their rather small numbers and rejected a proposal to sign their names to the document. The tenuousness of their victory was underscored when Nathaniel Eels informed the convention that he could not subscribe the testimony personally, but would only do so as moderator. John Hancock was puzzled and somewhat indignant at Eels's stance, remarking that Eels was "the most famous of any in these parts for a steady opposer of the very errors and disorders mentioned in the Testimony."[3]

By pushing through such a complete condemnation of the Awakening, Chauncy, Hancock, et al. had somewhat overreached themselves. Even before the Convention Testimony was published, the Reverend Joshua Gee, Chauncy's chief opponent at that assembly, was busily organizing another convention to counteract the results of the first. With the support of influential Boston ministers such as Foxcroft, Prince, Sewall, and Colman, Gee extended an invitation to all ministers who were "persuaded there has been of late a happy revival of religion" to gather in Boston during the July 7 Harvard Commencement.[4]

This second convention was well-attended; perhaps as many as ninety clergymen were present, and many more sent written attestations. The meeting was far more moderate and less rancorous than the Annual Convention had been. The ministers present acknowledged and condemned all the "errors and disorders" that attended the Awakening, but they steadfastly affirmed that there had been a "remarkable revival of religion in many parts of the land, through an uncommon divine influence; after a long time of great decay and deadness." Interestingly, they warned certain ministers against being "led into, or fixed in, Arminian tenets, under the pretence of opposing Antinomian errors." The *Testimony and Advice* which they drafted could, with good conscience, be signed by any moderate supporter of the revival, and so it was. There were sixty-eight signatories in all, including Nathaniel Eels. Nearly every minister in the Plymouth Association subscribed to the paper. Even some ministers in Gay's immediate neighborhood—not only his New Light neighbor, James Bayley of South Weymouth, but Benjamin Bass of Hanover, Ezra Carpenter of Hull, and John Fowle of Cohasset—felt that this second testimony represented their views fairly and so endorsed it. The two revival testimonies concerning the Great Awakening provided, in a broad way, the first public delineation of the New Light and Old Light factions, and Gay's failure to sign the second testimony proclaimed him unmistakably as a Chauncy man.[5]

In September of 1743, all the ministers of New England had an opportunity to affirm publicly their opposition to the Awakening. In that month, Charles Chauncy brought out his *Seasonable Thoughts* and thereby, as Perry Miller has put it, "exploded his biggest bomb, a major work in American Literature or in the century." Chauncy devoted much of the book to indignant recitations of the various ecclesiastical and social disorders that followed in the wake of the revivalists. More importantly, however, he struck the intellectual keynote of the growing opposition to the Awakening—a vigorous reaffirmation of Puritan rationalism as refined and reinforced by the eighteenth-century Enlightenment. Responding directly to

Jonathan Edwards's emphasis on the centrality of heightened emotions (or "affections," as Edwards more profoundly understood them), Chauncy responded: "There is the Religion of the *Understanding* and *Judgement*, and *Will*, as well as of the *Affections*; and if little Account is made of the *former*, while great Stress is laid upon the *latter*, it can't be but People should run into Disorders."[6]

These sentiments were shared by a great number of those who composed the clerical and secular establishment of the day. Seven hundred and forty-one of them, in a list headed by Governor William Shirley, subscribed for *Seasonable Thoughts* before it went to press. This list was published along with the book, and it quickly became a sort of *Who's Who* of revival opposers. Normally, the eclectic reading habits of the New England clergy make it difficult for the historian to correlate possession of a particular book with the owner's endorsement of the views expressed therein. In this instance, however, since not a single radical New Light appears on the list, one can say with some certainty that subscription implied approval. This is not to suggest that all the subscribers were proto-Arminians or virulent opposers like Chauncy; some were moderate Calvinists who still thought that the Awakening, purged of its excesses, was a work of God. At the moment, however, all the subscribers were quite unhappy with itinerancy, lay exhorting, and the general disruption of order in the parish, and they cheered Chauncy on as he flailed away at those evils. Ebenezer Gay subscribed, as did several of his kin—his brother Lusher Gay; Lusher's son, the embattled Reverend Ebenezer Gay of Suffield; his son-in-law, the Reverend John Ballantine of Westfield; and Jerusha Gay's brother, Gamaliel Bradford of Duxbury.[7]

The South Shore, with remarkable solidarity, publicly declared its dissatisfaction with the Awakening by the subscription of fifteen ministers from Dorchester to Kingston. On the other hand, not a single member of the Plymouth Association affixed his name. The South Shore was emerging from the Awakening with a religious character, rooted in historical, economic, and geographic causes, that differed markedly from the Old Colony. The South Shore ministers were generally more "presbyterian" and authoritarian than their fellow clergymen in old Plymouth; for those reasons, and others, they were also far less receptive to the experimentalism of the New Lights. Opposition to the Awakening was generally stronger on the upper South Shore, lessening in force as one moved down the coast toward Plymouth.

Among the ministers who subscribed to *Seasonable Thoughts,* only four names from the South Shore were absent. Two of these men, James Bayley of Weymouth and Samuel Veazie of Duxbury, were unabashed New Lights. The other two, Samuel Brown of Abington and Ezra Carpenter of Hull, were in such deep trouble with their congregations that they may not have dared to risk the consequences of subscription. The ecclesiastical fragmentation that Gay and his colleagues feared was now becoming a reality on the South Shore. Long-standing local quarrels, dissatisfaction with an autocratic minister, financial problems, and old antagonisms now became merged with attitudes toward the revival. Any minister who had expressed an opinion about the Awakening was now vulnerable, as his local foes focused their opposition on revival-related issues. The Great Awakening also led to the disappearance of the comfortable religious consensus that had characterized the South Shore ministry. As the parsons argued among themselves, a loss of respect for clerical authority inevitably followed, and the spirit of Separation stalked the land.[8]

The first major ecclesiastical rebellion on the South Shore occurred in the small and rather poor town of Hull, which lay almost due north of Hingham on the narrow peninsula that encloses Hingham Bay. Itinerant New Lights had preached in Hull with impunity and with a great measure of success. They encouraged a substantial faction in the church to charge their minister, the Reverend Ezra Carpenter, with failure to preach the doctrines of grace. This was another way of saying that they believed their pastor was an Arminian. Carpenter, "a rational preacher of the Gospel," was, in fact, leaning in that direction. He also happened to be a capable pastor who had toiled patiently in that rather unstable little community for twenty years, earning Ebenezer Gay's respect and friendship along the way. On December 12, 1743, the "dissatisfied" brethren sent messengers to a meeting at Carpenter's house where they presented him with a document that charged him with fifteen doctrinal errors. They also requested an ecclesiastical council and submitted their choices for members—Peter Thacher of Middleborough, Nathaniel Leonard of Plymouth, and John Porter of Bridgewater—three of the leading New Light evangelists in the Plymouth Association. The Hull separatists clearly understood who their friends were. In order to balance the council, Carpenter and his supporters chose Gay, Nathaniel Eels, and one of the ministers from Boston's Old South to complete the roster.[9]

The custom of going out of the neighborhood to invite ministers who were likely to support a particular faction began, as we
have seen, in the mid-1730s; by the end of 1743, in the bitter aftermath of the Awakening, the practice was in common use. Most
ministers were no longer invited to serve on ecclesiastical councils
in order to render disinterested judgements, but were chosen instead because of their identification with a particular religious
party. After some further maneuvering among Carpenter and his
opponents at Hull, a council of five churches met in late February 1744. The final invitations were extended to Gay and Eels,
Thacher and Porter, and, a new fifth member, John Hancock of
Braintree. The addition of Hancock weighted the council in favor
of Carpenter and his adherents. The council declared that all the
charges brought against Carpenter "were groundless; and advis'd
the Separatists to acknowledge their Misconduct to their Reverend
Pastor and the Church, and to return . . . and so prevent an Ecclesiastical Procedure against them." The dissenters, however, were
not intimidated, and the strife in Hull continued until 1746, when
Gay, Eels, and three other ministers were invited to another council. All this second council could do was acknowledge the hopeless-
ness of the situation and acquiesce in recommending Carpenter's
dismissal. Gay was furious at this intimidation of a competent gospel minister with whom he had worked for twenty years. The Hull-
ites eventually called the Reverend Samuel Veazie, a New Light
minister who had been dismissed, after a protracted dispute, from
his church in Duxbury.[10]

Gay watched in frustration as Ezra Carpenter wandered
about the South Shore for six years trying to find a living. Finally, in
1753, Carpenter learned that Keene and Swanzey, two New Hampshire towns, were searching for a minister. Both towns had been
burned to the ground by the Indians in 1747, and were now being
resettled. Carpenter decided to try his fortunes there and accordingly accepted a call to minister to both Keene and Swanzey, as they
had temporarily united in one church. His ordination sermon was
delivered by none other than Ebenezer Gay who, in one of those
acts of personal loyalty typical of the man, had made the long
and hazardous journey to the New Hampshire frontier. Gay's trip
might be seen as an act of expiation for his failure to save his old
friend from the inflammatory and schismatic politics of the New
Lights. He spoke bitterly of how Carpenter "by the infelicity of the
late Times, was constrained to ask a Dismission from the Church in

Hull." Then, addressing Carpenter directly, he said that "it was grievous unto me . . . to part with your Neighborhood; You have been a Comfort to me, in the intimate, unbroken Friendship that hath subsisted betwixt us."[11]

In the summer of 1744, while the Hull controversy was at its height, Gay became even more deeply involved in the New Light/Old Light controversy. Strife had erupted in the town of Abington, just southwest of Hingham. The Reverend Samuel Brown, the quick-tempered patriarch of the Abinigton church, was under attack by what he called a "Sect yt has Sprung up among us Called New Lights." The dissatisfied brethren were unhappy with Brown's doctrinal views as well as his conduct of the pastoral office. The errors in doctrine which were charged to Brown suggest that he was a rational preacher with, as a town historian put it, "an inclination to Arminianism." He was accused of preaching: "That there is no Spirituall or Mysterall Interpretation to some verses in the Scripture"; "That you Make no Clear Distinction between ye Law & ye Gospell." If Brown had been, like Gay, more adept at pastoral relations, his doctrinal errors might have been overlooked. The people of Abington, however, had endured thirty-two years of "arbitrariness in church . . . government," and their more serious allegations reflected their discontent. They charged Brown, for instance, with "neglecting to Visit & Examine [his] Flock."[12]

Brown and the dissenters were unable to resolve their difficulties amicably, and so, at a church meeting on August 31, 1744, all parties agreed to join in calling a council. Once again, as in the Hull case, both parties insisted on inviting ministers who would support their respective positions. Brown and his followers, who comprised a majority, invited Gay, Eels, and William Smith of Weymouth. The aggrieved brethren selected three moderate pro-revivalists: Habijah Weld of Attleborough, Elias Haven of Wrentham, and John Cotton of Halifax. Gay and Eels prevailed and Samuel Brown was cleared of all charges, but this did nothing to restore peace to the parish. The embittered Brown soon signed a testimony that condemned George Whitefield, and then began systematically to take disciplinary action against his opposers. He told them, "I have been as a Father to this Town," and he asked the leader of the opposition (which from 1744 to 1749 had become a majority) "To Consider the Case of Corah, & whether you are not Guilty of yᵉ Same Sin . . . and whether you may not Expect Something of the like punishment to light upon you." (Korah was a Levite who rebelled against the authority of Moses, and who, as punishment, was swallowed up by the earth together with all his followers.) Brown was eventually brought down by this sort of arrogance. He died in 1749 while arranging financial terms for his resignation.[13]

Gay was becoming more and more despondent as established ministers like Carpenter and Brown were deposed by militant New Light factions. How long could he prevent the storm that raged on every side of his parish from washing into Hingham and swamping the Old Ship? In the midst of all these troubles, in early May 1744, Gay was shocked to learn of the death of John Hancock. Along with Gay and William Smith, Hancock had been instrumental in reviving the old Weymouth Association. In his vigorous denunciation of itinerancy and enthusiasm, Hancock had served as the cutting edge of the South Shore's opposition to the revival; now, at the age of forty-two, he was suddenly gone. Gay was asked to preach the funeral sermon, which he titled *The Untimely Death of a Man of God Lamented*. After a moving eulogy for Hancock, Gay expressed his darkened mood when he said, "Several burning and shining Lights in the spiritual Candlesticks, have lately been put out by Death: Others are clouded with Affliction, and Cover'd with Reproach." Nevertheless, Gay told the Braintree congregation that they should rejoice in the legacy of Hancock: "As a wise and skillful Pilot hath he steer'd you a right and safe Course, in the late troubled sea of Ecclesiastical Affairs; . . . so that you have escaped the Errors and Enthusiasm which some, and the Infidelity and Indifferency in Matters of Religion, which others have fallen into." This was clearly the sort of encomium that Gay hoped could justly be applied to his own ministry. Three months after Hancock's death, Gay rode to Dedham for another funeral. Lydia Lusher Gay, the matriarch of the clan, had expired at the age of ninety-two. Although the great age to which his mother lived prefigured Gay's own longevity, he never seemed to take heart from her example. He always expected that, like Hancock, he would be struck down in his prime.[14]

Although by late 1744 the fires of the Great Awakening were flickering out, the destruction of church order, discipline, and unity that they left were becoming increasingly apparent. Those who had opposed the Awakening almost from its inception surveyed the ruins with a grim I-told-you-so attitude. Baffled by the extent and intensity of this religious upheaval, they looked for scapegoats and found them among the more incendiary itinerants. After the publication of his journals, George Whitefield, the Grand

Itinerant himself, became the particular object of their wrath. Whitefield's candor had surprised and alienated many of his former supporters. He had, for instance, written in his Journal: "I am persuaded, the generality of preachers talk of an unknown and unfelt Christ. The reason why congregations have been so dead, is because they had dead men preaching to them." After lamenting the state of the unconverted ministers in New England, he went on to attack both Harvard and Yale, writing "As for the Universities, I believe it may be said, their Light is become Darkness, Darkness that may be felt." This was too much, even for a solid Old Calvinist such as Edward Holyoke, Gay's former tutor and now president of Harvard College. Holyoke's objections, however, were feeble when compared to the blast delivered from the South Shore by Samuel Niles. The seventy-year-old parson from South Braintree was no liberal; indeed he was the most rigid Calvinist in the region. Still, after reading Whitefield's remarks, he asked "What can be the Design of this Gentleman in publishing such Representations of our Colleges, unless it be to induce us to content ourselves with illiterate and enthusiastic Exhorters, whom he or his Friends have set up, 'till we can be supplied from *England, Scotland, Ireland, the Orphan-House in Georgia*, or the Shepherd's Tent?" [15]

On October 19, 1744, the object of this growing resentment arrived at York, Maine for his second preaching tour of New England. George Whitefield's return visit to Massachusetts had its bright moments, but on the whole the trip was a disappointment to the young evangelist. He was not in good health, and his reception in Boston was, in several quarters, cooler than the fall weather. The newspapers were full of criticism from both clergy and laity. He was charged, as usual, with encouraging enthusiasm, separatism, itinerancy, and general spiritual disorder. Gradually, the attacks focused on the question of Whitefield's authority and legitimacy. By what right, his detractors asked, did he presume to come into an established parish and preach as though the local inhabitants were pagans who had never heard the Christan gospel?

The anti-Whitefield sentiment took its most effective form in a series of testimonies from several ministerial associations that condemned him. The publication of these testimonies was coordinated to give the impression of a growing and irresistible tide of revulsion against Whitefield. There can be little doubt that the mastermind behind this campaign was the junior minister at Boston's First Church, Charles Chauncy. The opposition commenced in December 1744, when two associations in Essex County wrote a letter to "the Associated Ministers of Boston and Charlestown" asking the latter, for the good of the Commonwealth, to refuse Whitefield admission to their pulpits. To this letter was appended the decision of the influential Cambridge Association to refuse Whitefield permission to preach in their churches. This rebuke from Nathaniel Appleton, the highly respected minister at Cambridge, was a major blow to Whitefield and his supporters. Appleton was the embodiment of catholic toleration and usually preserved perfect neutrality in controversial matters. These anti-Whitefield resolutions were quickly followed by the opposition's major assault on the evangelist—*The Testimony of Harvard College, against George Whitefield.* Before the Harvard Testimony appeared, however, the Grand Itinerant set out on a preaching tour of the South Shore.[16]

Whitefield had engaged to preach for Gay's New Light neighbor, the Reverend James Bayley of South Weymouth. He set out from Boston in a fierce snowstorm, spent the night in Milton, and rode on through bitterly cold weather to arrive in Weymouth on December 22. That evening the evangelist wrote in his journal: "When I came to Weymouth found Yesterday's violent storm made people think that I would not come. The congregation was small, but there seemed to be a very considerable melting and moving among them." One can easily imagine Gay's agitation at the prospect of Whitefield melting even a small crowd at his very doorstep. Whitefield then passed precipitately through Gay's Hingham and Eels's Scituate on his way to the next friendly haven, the Duxbury parish of New Light minister Samuel Veazie. Nathaniel Eels eventually explained, in a published letter to his South Scituate congregation, the reasons why he (and Gay) had refused to invite Whitefield to preach. He criticized the evangelist for "representing the Pastors of these Churches to be Men of no Grace" and for "countenancing and encouraging Separations and Separatists from our Churches." Eels's principal objection, however, as one might expect from a minister schooled in the presbyterian tradition of the South Shore, was that Whitefield simply had no authority or right "to turn a vagrant Preacher, and to ramble about the World." If Whitefield had been granted this authority, Eels challenged him to "tell by whom; whether by any Bishop of the Church of England; or by any Presbytery, among the Dissenters in England, Scotland, or anywhere else." Eels also advanced the rather labored theory that Whitefield was an agent of subversion for the Anglicans:

"Doth he not design hereby to weaken these Churches, and to fill up the Church of England with Members that are grieved with our Ministers for indulging him in his Irregularities?"[17]

Gay's opposition to Whitefield was every bit as determined as that of Nathaniel Eels, but one oral tradition indicates that the evangelist very nearly received an invitation to preach in Hingham. The tale was related in 1880 by the eighty-one-year-old Reverend Calvin Lincoln, sixth minister of Hingham's First Parish. No contemporary documents have been found that substantiate the story, but, at the very least, it appears to reflect Gay's attitude toward Whitefield with some fidelity. According to Lincoln, "Many of the prominent people of Hingham" wanted to hear Whitefield speak and "for this purpose a committee was chosen by the citizens to obtain the consent and cooperation of their pastor." Again, there is no other evidence to suggest that the New Light was breaking in upon the Hingham oligarchy; more probably, they simply had a natural curiosity to hear one of the great orators of the age. After all, Gay had permitted Gilbert Tennent, that Son of Thunder, the use of his pulpit three years before. During those intervening years, however, Gay had seen the religious consensus and social stability of the South Shore seriously jeopardized, and he was now in no mood to play with fire. Consequently, Lincoln goes on, having learned of the committee's impending visit, Gay "received his visitors very kindly at the parsonage and entertained them in a most agreeable way by giving a description of his voyage across the Atlantic. He told them how the captain kept his place, the mate kept his place, and the crew kept their place, and the ship was safely navigated to her port of destination. The committee took in the meaning of their pastor's remarks and went away without even referring to the object of their visit." We do know that George Whitefield did not preach in Hingham, and that Gay, that benevolent autocrat, remained undisputed captain of the Old Ship.[18]

While George Whitefield was itinerating on the South Shore, Harvard College unleashed its *Testimony* against him. Although the authors of the *Harvard Testimony* repeated all the now familiar litany of charges, most of their rancor was directed at Whitefield's anti-intellectualism. The testimony was not the impressive, scholarly defense of the primacy of Reason that one might have expected; instead its tone was waspish and condescending. The authors quickly asserted that "it is most evident that he [Whitefield] hath not any superior Talent at instructing the Mind, or showing the Force and Energy of those Arguments for a religious Life, which are directed to in the everlasting Gospel." Imagine then, the supreme arrogance "that such a young Man as he should take upon him to tell what Books we shou'd allow our Pupils to read." The testimony then directly cited Whitefield's condemnation of Yale and Harvard in his *Journal*, and declared "What a deplorable State of Immorality and Irreligion has he hereby represented *Us* to be in! And as this is a most wicked and libellous Falshood (at least as to our College) as such we charge it upon him." [19]

The vindictive tone of Harvard's testimony against Whitefield did little to diffuse its impact. Charles Chauncy decided that the appearance of the Testimony should be closely followed by another denunciation. To that end, he dashed off a quick note to Ebenezer Gay. This note suggests that Chauncy had now come to regard Gay as his chief lieutenant on the South Shore. Chauncy had apparently urged his boyhood friend, the Reverend John Taylor of Milton, to propose a convening of the Weymouth Association for the first Wednesday in January 1745. This having been settled, Chauncy informed Gay that "You are desired to engage the Gentlemen your way to be there without fail." He added in a postscript, "The College Testimony will be out next Tuesday." Gay's response reflected the urgency and bustle that Whitefield's presence had ignited among the anti-revivalists of the South Shore. After receiving Chauncy's note, Gay immediately forwarded it to William Smith of Weymouth with this scribbled notation:

> Mr. Smith, I this Minute received this Letter and transmit it to you in a hurry—believing we had best agree to Mr. Taillor's & Bow [Jonathan Bowman of Dorchester] appointment off the Association Meeting—I will send to the men beyond me—and you will to those your Way—that there may be no mistake.
>
> your Serv'     E. Gay[20]

Gay and Smith raised the hue and cry as they were bid, and so, on January 15, twelve ministers braved the winter weather to gather at William Smith's parsonage in Weymouth, the old center of the association. Daniel Perkins and John Angier, two lonely Old Lights from Plymouth County, came all the way from Bridgewater. This was not a gathering of religious liberals. Two of the gentlemen present, Samuel Dunbar of Stoughton and Samuel Niles of Braintree, were as rigorous Calvinists as might be found in New England. The rest were more moderate, but they were all Old

Lights—men who viewed religious fervor with suspicion when it threatened the good order of their parish. Like Gay, many of those present were proud of their scholarship, and seethed at Whitefield's attack on Harvard. The result of their deliberation was published as *The Sentiments and Resolutions of an Association of Ministers (convened at Weymouth, Jan. 15, 1744/5).*[21]

The Weymouth Testimony was more restrained and dignified in tone than the Harvard Testimony, though it followed the same line of attack: "Having read the Testimony of the Reverend Honoured President, Professors and Tutors of Harvard College; and the Testimonies of three Associations of worthy Ministers; we declare our Concurrence with them in the Articles exhibited against Mr. Whitefield." The South Shore ministers were particularly concerned about Whitefield's emphasis on visible conversion and gathered communions of saints. They had already witnessed the disruptive effects that bands of New Light zealots had wreaked on the delicate social balance of their parishes. They wrote that "people think, and are perhaps taught to think, that few or none are saints, but those who follow him and his cause. What must be the effect of this, but to raise the most virulent enmity and malice in the hearts of his followers, against those who are called opposers?" The testimony then drew up a sweeping indictment of Whitefield that pithily summed up the entire campaign against him: "We must therefore bear our *strongest Testimony* against his Enthusiastick *Spirit*, because we judge it to be the *grand Source* of the *Uncharitableness, Errors, Divisions* and *Confusions* of these Times."[22]

The Weymouth Testimony also contained something that all the previous testimonies lacked—a spirited defense of the essential role of reason in preaching and in understanding the gospel. The somewhat gratuitous inclusion of this section immediately suggests Ebenezer Gay's influence. Stylistically and substantively, the passage is pure Gay, anticipating his later discourses on reason and revelation:

> Here we would also take Notice of the Manner in which the Gentleman has disparag'd *Humane Reason* and *Rational Preaching*. For tho' we all allow that *Reason* is not sufficient to conduct us to Duty and Happiness without *Revelation*, and the *Assistances of God's Spirit*; yet how can we possibly judge of any Revelation without the proper Use of our *Reason*? We judge it to be one of the distinguishing Glories of Christianity, that it is a *Reasonable Service.*[23]

The publication of *The Sentiments and Resolutions* marked the beginning of a new era in the religious history of the South Shore. In the past, local clergy had preserved ecclesiastical harmony in the region through informal cooperation. They had been generally guided in their affairs by Nathaniel Eels and, to a lesser extent, Samuel Niles. The pressures of the Great Awakening, however, seemed to require a stronger and more formal arrangement, if clerical authority were not to be despised. For this purpose, the old Weymouth Association had been reinvigorated, largely through the efforts of John Hancock, Jr. and Ebenezer Gay. Just as the revival seemed to be gasping its last, George Whitefield's visit to the South Shore threatened a new outburst of enthusiasm and disorder, and the Association eagerly joined Charles Chauncy's anti-Whitefield campaign. The twelve ministers who gathered in Weymouth shared remarkably similar views on ecclesiastical questions, though their theologies differed markedly. After the publication of the testimony, the power of the Weymouth Association grew steadily. Following the death of Nathaniel Eels in 1750, Gay became the dominant force in the association; the theological differences, after some major battles, began to disappear, and the association acquired a philosophical as well as a political unity.

The New Light had failed to break in appreciably upon Hingham during the Awakening years, but the peace and good order of the town and church was nevertheless rent by a nasty and divisive power struggle. By the end of 1746, most of the residents of South Hingham had split off from the First Church, built their own meetinghouse, been granted a separate parish and precinct, and settled a new minister. A discerning contemporary, observing the splitting off of Hingham's Third (South) Parish, decided that "Religion had nothing to do in the Case." Indeed, the separation seems to have been rooted primarily in the economic and social skirmishing of the Hingham oligarchy. Although the Awakening did provide an atmosphere of general ecclesiastical confusion that facilitated the schismatic enterprise of the South Hinghamites, no evidence has yet come to light to suggest that anyone was dissatisfied with the style or content of Ebenezer Gay's ministry. That Gay was able to retain the support and even affection of all factions during this bitter and protracted struggle is an impressive testament to his pastoral skill.[24]

The leader of the South Hingham secession movement, forty-six-year-old Abel Cushing, was no less ambitious than when he led the "rebellion" of 1727. He and his younger brother Theophilus dominated the economic life of South Hingham. Abel operated a fulling mill, Theophilus ran a sawmill and a gristmill, and they both held over one hundred and fifty acres of land, five times the average in South Hingham. Consequently, the Cushing brothers felt ready and able to challenge the old Lincoln-Thaxter-Andrews oligarchy, which still made most of the important political and economic decisions in Hingham. The Cushing brothers were clearly pushing to obtain for South Hingham the same sort of financial and political independence that the Cohasset Parish enjoyed, but they faced serious obstacles. For one thing, the south part of Hingham, unlike Cohasset, was not separated from Hingham Town by any major natural divisions (see Appendix 2-A). Furthermore, Glad Tidings Plain, which formed the population center for South Hingham, was situated barely two miles from the Old Ship meeting-house, making it difficult to plead the hardships of distance as a cause for separation. Finally, the population growth of South Hingham did not begin to match that of Cohasset, and the area's material prosperity was fairly well limited to the Cushings. Nevertheless, for reasons of pride and economic self-interest, the Cushing brothers were prepared to fight for a separate parish, a separate precinct, and even a separate township.[25]

After some preliminary skirmishes, Abel and Theophilus Cushing opened their campaign with an audacious act. On June 22, 1742, they raised a meetinghouse on land owned by Theophilus, very near his house. The Cushings and their supporters had asked permission of no one, perhaps assuming that, when presented with this *fait accompli*, the other town leaders would have no choice but to yield to their request for a separate parish. If this was their hope, they were quickly disabused. Abel Cushing, who had served as town moderator on seven different occasions since 1741, suddenly found himself on the periphery of town politics. The rest of the Hingham oligarchy were enraged at this act of defiance and, led by Town Clerk Benjamin Lincoln, Esq., they bitterly opposed each petition of South Hingham for separation. Lincoln was supported in his opposition by Jacob Cushing, a cousin of the two rebels who lived in Hingham Centre, the traditional buffer zone between the Town and the Plain. Jacob Cushing was a very influential magistrate who, from 1737 to 1758, served for fourteen years as Hingham's Representative to the General Court. He owned and operated a sawmill at what would later be called Triphammer Pond in South Hingham, thus rivaling the business interests of his cousins, Abel and Theophilus. Furthermore, he lived within the area that the brothers wished to have included in the new parish. A proud and independent man, Jacob had no desire to lend his financial support to his cousins' private fief and parish church.[26]

Throughout the winter of 1743–44, the South Hinghamites petitioned the town meeting to be set off as a separate parish and they were consistently rebuffed. In May, when the Cushing brothers defined the boundaries that they wished to claim for their parish, the appalled town leaders angrily pointed out that their claims "included more than half the lands of the whole parish." The South Hingham faction now concluded, if they had not already done so, that the Town would never accede to their demands. Consequently, they gathered sixty signatures and took their petition for a separate parish to the Great and General Court. The Hingham selectmen met this new escalation by immediately dispatching Jacob Cushing, Benjamin Lincoln, and Dr. Ezekiel Hersey to oppose the petition in Boston. Jacob Cushing put his case to his old legislative associates with great energy, and the investigative committee proved sympathetic to his arguments. They denied the South Hingham petition, noting that "the Boundary that they pray for, will have much the larger part of the Parish set off to them." The committee did, however, allow the remittance of taxes for individuals who wished to support a separate preacher in South Hingham, and, in October 1743, the assessors of the First Church dutifully remitted £25 to the South Hingham petitioners. The General Court, however, had not reckoned with the dogged persistence of Abel and Theophilus Cushing, who resubmitted their petition the following year. This time the committee relented and, in March 1745, voted to grant the petition for separation to the South Hinghamites.[27]

The Cushing brothers immediately followed up their victory by introducing another petition to the General Court for a separate *precinct*. This was really the heart of the matter, since it put the raising and distribution of taxes for their church entirely under the control of the South Hinghamites. The First Parish would permanently lose about one-fifth of its income, so once again Jacob Cushing, Benjamin Lincoln, and Benjamin Loring were sent to Boston to fight the Cushing brothers. They lost, tried again in 1746, and lost again. The Cushings had triumphed, although the dispute dragged on for years with acrimonious quarreling over the location of the boundary line between the two precincts. Abel Cushing was especially clever at devising ways to further antagonize the leaders of the First Parish. In January 1747, for instance, he and two other gentlemen were appointed a committee "to request of the first Church in Hingham some part of the Furniture of their Communion table provided the reverend Mr. Gay shall think proper to advise to it." Predictably, the committee reported twelve days later "on the question of communion furniture that Mr. Gay did not advise to it." By this time, Gay was probably a bit surprised that Cushing did not ask for the table and plate as well.[28]

Parson Gay dealt with this secessionist crisis in his parish with all the skill of a consummate politician. The Hingham minister carefully followed the advice he had dispensed to his nephew out in Suffield, which could be summarized as "Go slow." Although Gay's interests clearly lay with the Town faction, he refused to become openly involved in the quarrel. John Gorham Palfrey, the nineteenth-century historian, described Gay at the end of his ministry as "having been the bond of union from a time to which the memory of scarcely any living could ran back." By the early 1740s, one could argue that Gay had already assumed his role as the living symbol of Hingham's essential unity. Therefore, during the controversy, he wisely adopted the elevated posture of spiritual leader of the flock, saddened by the civil strife in the parish, but unwilling to intervene. This policy was epitomized in a letter that Gay sent to the newly gathered South Hingham Church late in 1746. He had been invited to attend the ordination of their new minister, and he wrote to decline the invitation. The letter is a marvel of tact and more than a bit disingenuous; it shows Gay the great pacificator at his best, and for that reason merits full quotation:

> Beloved Brethren
> I Communicated to the Chh under my pastoral Care the Letter you Sent to us desiring our Presence & Assistance at the Ordination you are preceding to. By withholding their Vote of Compliance with your Request, the greater part of the Brethren by far signified their unwillingness to grant it; whence and by what I can since learn 'tis plain to me, that I cannot attend the Ordination of your Minister as a Delegate from this Church, it being the mind of the generality of them not to Send any. I am Sorry that Matters are So Circumstanced betwixt you & your Brethren Here, that they are not free to Countenance and assist you more in the Settlement of the Gospel Ministry

amongst you. I meddle not with what has been in Controversy between you & Them being of a Civil Nature, Therefore shall be ready to Serve you all I can in your Religious Affairs & Interests, as a Christian Neighbor & Gospel Minister, Tho I now may Not in the particular you have desired as the Messenger of a Church (than which an Elder in an Ecclesiastical Council is Nothing more). Since the Important Affair before you may be as well Managed without us as with us, I pray you to be Content that the Church Should not be Active in it, & Explicitly encouraging of it, Since they have not Sufficient Light therefore.

I believe it Seems hard to you to be Refused what you have asked of your Mother Church, whose breasts you have Sucked. But you know it has been a Day of Temptation and provocation in the Town. And Angry Resentments (whether Just or unjust) are not wont soon to be quite laid aside, after the Strife between Contending parties is at an end, and the Conquered when they Submit are not presently So loving friends, as afterwards they sometimes prove. If you patiently & Silently pass over the Conduct of the Church toward you, I hope there will be a comfortable harmony of affections between you & us.

On the walls of a new Meetinghouse were once engraven these words: *Build not for faction nor a Party, But for promoting faith & Repentance in Communion with all that Love our Lord Jesus Christ in Sincerity.* May this be verified in the House ye have Erected for divine Worship! I wish you God's presence in it at all Times, and Especially on the Morrow at the Ordination of a Pastor over you, & I pray God to make him a great Blessing to you & to your children.

I am your Sincere & Affectionate
friend & late unworthy Pastor
E Gay[29]

Gay's policy of moderation and conciliation brought its rewards. Another minister might have been sorely vexed at having lost two-thirds of his parish (Cohasset and South Hingham) in twenty-eight years, but Gay, whatever his private reaction, yielded gracefully. Consequently, he retained his influence in South Hingham, as he had done in Cohasset. In fact, the Cushing brothers, with characteristic impudence, attempted to steal him away from the First Church! In one of its first actions, the new parish chose the Cushing brothers and one Thomas Wilder "a Committee for to treat with the Rev. Mr. Gay and give him the offer of the parish for to settle amongst them." The founders of Hingham's Third Parish clearly remained devoted to their former pastor. Gay was also quickly reassured, if he ever had any doubts, that he had not nursed a brood of New Lights in South Hingham. The church covenant that the South Hinghamites adopted was quite sober and rational in tone, as this excerpt suggests: "We declare our serious belief of the Christian religion, as it is taught in the Bible, which we take for a perfect rule of faith, worship, and manners." The most gratifying result of the South Hingham secession for Gay, however, was their choice of a minister. In Daniel Shute, Gay found that he had not lost a parish, but that he had gained another son.[30]

Daniel Shute graduated from Harvard in 1743 after a distinguished undergraduate career. When he took his second degree, he upheld the affirmative of the *Quaestio* (translated): "Whether the mind of Christ was rational before it entered his human body?" This was an interesting proposition that could have afforded Shute the opportunity to discuss the rational character of the godhead, though unfortunately we can never know just how he handled the question. By June 1746, the twenty-four-year-old scholar from Malden was preaching in the South Parish, and three months later he happily accepted a unanimous call to settle there. Shute may have been anxious to settle in Hingham in order to work and study with Gay. The attraction was certainly not the paltry salary of £40 per year which the Cushings were offering. As Shute later noted, however, "When I was about to Settle in the Ministry . . . I took but very little Care about my Temporal Interests."[31]

As we have seen, the First Church refused to permit Gay to attend Shute's ordination, making relations between the two men initially awkward. They quickly got over this embarrassment, however, and soon became the best of friends. As an early historian of Hingham put it, Shute and "his venerated friend, Dr. Gay, . . . in whose footsteps he delighted to tread" enjoyed "a friendly intercourse during their long and useful ministries." Indeed, Daniel Shute almost literally became Ebenezer Gay's *alter ego*; their personalities and theology meshed perfectly. Shute believed, like Gay, in the importance of privately examining the scriptures. He forcefully expressed this belief in one of his ordination sermons:

> The greater your attention to the gospel is, the less will you be in danger of being misled by the scholastic distinctions and wild notions of imperfect and fanatic men. With a mind divested of prepossessions, open to the admissions of the evidence of truth, and removed from a servile dependence on the decisions of the GREAT and GOOD, you ought assiduously to search out the good and acceptable and perfect will of God.

This vigorous defense of the right of private judgement became, in the post-Awakening years, an almost formulaic expression
of theological liberation for the rationalist, anti-Calvinist, Liberal
ministry. Clifford Shipton's assessment of Shute as an "extreme Arminian" may be a bit exaggerated, but Shute was clearly a full-
fledged member of the fraternity.[32]

By his own testimony, Daniel Shute acknowledged Gay as a
principal influence in the development of his theological views. Indeed, he came to regard the older man, quite self-consciously, as a
father figure. Gay returned the affection. Shute had arrived in
Hingham just after the untimely death of Gay's eldest son, Samuel.
This may have had some bearing on Gay's paternal affection for
Shute. Gay exchanged pulpits with Shute far more often than with
any other minister. He delighted in the younger man's wit and his
scholarly, inquisitive mind. Heretofore Gay's most intimate friend
among the local ministers had been William Smith, the gentle,
rather deliberate pastor of Weymouth's First Church. Shute provided Gay with faster intellectual company, and gradually supplanted Smith as Gay's partner in traveling to ecclesiastical councils
and conventions. Daniel Shute's arrival in Hingham also heralded
the change that would, in the late 1740s and early 1750s, transform
the old Weymouth Association from a group of Old Light, moderate Calvinists into a society of young Arminians who looked to Gay
as their spiritual leader.[33]

Thus it happened that, after a bitter, rancorous struggle, the
First Parish in Hingham was split asunder in the midst of the Great
Awakening. The two principal results of this power struggle among
the Hingham oligarchs were distinctly (and happily for Gay) non-
radical. The first was the emergence of a little church in South
Hingham that bore an extraordinary resemblance to its mother.
The second was the reproduction of Ebenezer Gay, in the person
of Daniel Shute. In a less conservative town than Hingham and
with a less flexible minister than Gay, the church split could have
ended in major religious and social upheaval.

By 1745, the fervor and excitement of the Great Awakening
had dissipated. The average layman was now more interested
in Colonel William Pepperrell's expedition to Louisbourg than in
George Whitefield's itinerations. After all the noisy passions had
subsided, however, it became clear that even the appearance of religious unity among New England Puritans was a thing of the past.

One broad faction emerged as a direct outgrowth of the revival; at various times it was composed of neo-Calvinists, Edwardseans, New Divinity men, Hopkinsians, Separates, Separate-Baptists, and Baptists. These were the men and women who were shaken to the core by a highly emotional encounter with the incomprehensible sovereignty of the Lord of Creation. The emergence of the Liberal-Arminian wing of Puritanism was more indirect. As we have seen, Charles Chauncy had assembled a well-organized faction of opponents to the revival in order to seize control of the Annual Convention in 1743. The religious opinions of this party were quite diverse, ranging from strict Calvinism, through moderate Calvinism to full-fledged Arminianism. They could all be properly called Old Lights, however, meaning that they were opposed to the means of the revivalists and to the latter's claims to immediate inspiration. The old Weymouth Association on the South Shore was composed of just this sort of Old Light mix. After witnessing the parish rebellions in Hull, Abington, and even Hingham, the South Shore ministers united in nearly unanimous opposition to Whitefield and the revivalists. As Gay said in 1745, all they wanted was "Security, Liberty and Tranquility, in an evil, very unsettled World."[34]

The Awakening had a further effect, however, on men like Gay who were already tending towards Arminianism. Gay had no solid commitment to Calvinistic orthodoxy; he detested creeds and tried to remain determinedly open to truth and, as he (rather ironically) put it, "new light." Like his Puritan ancestors, Gay began to define much of his theology by what he renounced and found unacceptable. If, for instance, the practice of undiluted Calvinism seemed to lead to the intolerable zealotry and enthusiasm of the New Lights, then he wanted no part of it. The Great Awakening had sent things out of control, and men had to re-exert control over their lives through the efforts of their own will. Reason must govern the unruly passions; strict moral standards must be observed; men must tap their god-given potential for good. In short, unlike many of his contemporaries, Gay did not separate opposition to the revival from opposition to the Calvinism of the revivalists. The Great Awakening was over and the Arminian Awakening was about to begin.[35]

# CHAPTER VII

# Pure and Undefiled Religion

Early in May of 1745, Jerusha Gay ushered two visitors from Boston into the parlor of the parsonage. The two men, a Mr. Clap and a Major Little, introduced themselves to Parson Gay and promptly informed him that the lower house of the General Court had selected him to deliver the Election Sermon later that month. Gay, for once, was taken completely by surprise, having apparently been a last-minute choice for the honor. The hard feelings that the Great Awakening had engendered among the Boston clergymen still lingered, and so the members of the General Court thought it prudent to look out of town for less controversial speakers. The political reasons for his choice were unimportant to Gay; he welcomed the opportunity and immediately set about preparing his sermon.[1]

The Election Sermon was always delivered on the last Wednesday in May, the day on which the members of the newly elected House of Representatives assembled in Boston to be sworn in. This event, one of the last vestiges of John Winthrop's Holy Commonwealth, was one of the few occasions at which the clergy could speak out directly on political issues. The speaker generally described the character of good rulers and the principles of good government, as envisioned in the covenant theology of New England Puritanism. During the eighteenth century, the ministers began to incorporate the concepts of the early Enlightenment into their lectures, and the Election Sermon became a major source for the dissemination of political ideas. By May 29, Ebenezer Gay was fully prepared to perform his role as spiritual advisor to the state.[2]

Election Day was a great festive occasion in colonial Boston.

All slaves and apprentices were given a holiday, and Bacchus held court on Boston Common. In 1745, the sun was shining and the air was clear and cool; it was, as a local observer put it, "a fine, fair day." When the inauguration ceremonies in the Town House (later called the "Old State House") were concluded, a great procession began to form at the west entrance. The Royal Governor, William Shirley, emerged, accompanied by his Councillors and the members of the Great and General Court. They proceeded across Church Square, between two lines of the scarlet-coated First Corps of Cadets, to the old brick meetinghouse of Boston's First Church. A large congregation, including most of the ministers of the province, had already assembled inside. At the proper time, Ebenezer Gay solemnly ascended the steps to the pulpit of his old friends, Thomas Foxcroft and Charles Chauncy, and began—"May it please your Excellency." One can't help sharing Gay's elation at this moment. The son of Nathaniel Gay, the Dedham carpenter, had come a long way.[3]

Gay began his sermon with his usual felicitous habit of comparing the royal governor with God, symbolized in this instance by the sun. A good ruler such as Governor Shirley was like that blazing orb, "bearing the Image of God's Authority, and shining with the Rays of his Majesty." Gay, however, was not quite ready to totally deify William Shirley, acknowledging, with sound astronomical erudition, that even the "Sun hath its Spots." The obligatory flattery concluded, Gay quickly turned to a candid and shrewd appraisal of the problems that faced the province in 1745, and some of the ways in which the administration might cope with them.[4]

Gay had always regarded any campaign against the French and the "papal tyranny" as a just war, and so he lavished praise on the "brave General" who had just taken the Grand Battery, one of Louisbourg's principal defenses. He tempered his encomiums, however, with gloomy but accurate reflections on the effect this "expensive War" would have on the province, which "hath very feeble Sinews to support it." The war had created a temporary prosperity, but Gay recognized that this was only a bubble floating on a very uncertain economic sea. All of the North American colonies were mired in an economic recession caused principally by the War of the Austrian Succession. "The Channels of Trade," as Gay put it, "are in a Manner shut up." This situation was exacerbated, in Gay's view, by Governor Shirley's decision to continue the supply of

paper money, a policy that fiscal conservatives considered inflationary. Gay, like many of his clerical colleagues, tended to be a hard-
money man, since he received a fixed salary and suffered from
the vicissitudes of currency fluctuation. Accordingly, he warned
the governor of the evil consequences "that are fear'd, from the
continually sinking Credit of our Medium of Exchange, which is
converted into an Instrument of Injustice." Gay urged Shirley to
intercede with England for more support for the war "lest the
Province, curtail'd in its Bounds, impoverish'd with War, and sunk
under a Load of Debt, should be quite discouraged from attempting any further Service for the Crown beyond what plain Duty ex-
acts." More help from His Majesty's government might avert the
need for "a heavy Yoke of Taxes," and thus "complaining in our
Streets will be prevented."[5]

After lecturing Governor Shirley and the magistrates on their
responsibilities to their subjects, Gay turned to the "Duty of an
Obliged People." He asked his listeners to obey their superiors in
all things and not to "admit the jealousies which envious, self-
designing men are always ready to propagate, nor join in the clam-
ors of the uneasy malcontents." Gay was clearly more vexed over
the "uneasy malcontents" than he was over the war, the economy,
or any of the other issues he addressed. The authority of ministers
and magistrates, the properly constituted rulers of society, had
been challenged by itinerant preachers and unruly congregations.
Close friends and associates in his professional fraternity had suddenly been ousted from pulpits that they had expected to occupy
for life. Although Gay had responded to the Awakening with moderation and political flexibility, he had clearly been infuriated by
the ecclesiastical rebels. The rational, likeable, urbane minister of
Hingham's First Parish had become an implacable foe of the New
Lights, and this Election Sermon marked the opening phase of his
retaliation.[6]

Gay told his audience:

> Not only are our temporal Affairs perplex'd, but our Religion, and
> the Ministry thereof, and Means of Education, are at present under
> a Cloud: . . . Will our Rulers, as far as their Authority and Influence
> will reach, preserve them from being corrupted with Errors,
> darkened with Ignorance and Sin, aspers'd and blacken'd with foul
> Slanders, unjust Reproaches, and for Want of outward Means of
> Support, reduc'd to so low and despicable a state.

He then seemed to hint that the General Court should enact the kind of anti-revival legislation that Connecticut had adopted, starting with a ban on itinerancy. "Far be it from our Rulers to espouse a Party in Religion," he declared, "But let them own and promote the great and substantial Things in which pure and undefil'd Religion consists, and by their Example teach People to go in the Footsteps of the Flock . . . and adhere to the Ministry which the Gospel ordains." Despite his genuine aversion to factions, Gay was nevertheless speaking for a religious party. Phrases such as "pure and undefil'd Religion" were becoming code words for Liberal-rational-Arminian religion. Gay was not only requesting the government to support the Old Light clerical establishment: he was also, in effect, asking the magistrates to "own and promote" a liberal, enlightened faith.[7]

The choice of Ebenezer Gay to deliver the 1745 Election Sermon was, in fact, a formal acknowledgement of his emergence as one of the leading ministers in the province. The sermon itself exposed him to an even wider audience; it must have been well received, since Gay was invited back to Boston within two months to deliver the Thursday Lecture. Judging by his text, he probably preached a sermon of thanksgiving (Massachusetts was ringing with them) for the surrender of Louisbourg. The Election Sermon also established him unequivocally in the minds of many as an opponent of the Awakening and the New Light movement which it spawned. He would now be called on with increasing frequency to help adjudicate church disputes that involved the "uneasy malcontents" of the New Light party, or challenges to "pure and undefil'd religion." Gay was temperamentally well-equipped to play the role of arbiter and diplomat, having a great store of what the Romans called *dignitas*, that quality which immediately commanded the respect of all parties. His "grave Deportment" was leavened by a dry wit and a genuine passion for conciliation, both of which tended to disarm potential adversaries.[8]

Shortly after returning home, Gay had an opportunity to strike a blow at the New Lights and the threat they seemed to pose to the established ministry. He entered into the struggle between the Reverend Thaddeus Maccarty and that good man's church and parish in Kingston, a coastal town just north of Plymouth. In most of the church controversies that arose during and after the Great Awakening, one can find local, non-doctrinal issues underlying the dispute. The Maccarty case, however, was fought almost entirely on the question of opposition to or support for Whitefield revivalism. Young Maccarty was a moderate Calvinist who had been settled over the Kingston Parish in November 1742 with the blessings of Scituate's Nathaniel Eels, the South Shore patriarch. Kingston had managed to resist the great tide of revivalism that swept through most of Plymouth County, and the church leaders had been anxious to secure a minister who would continue to hold the revival at bay. Maccarty, at first, seemed to be the man. True, he had signed the pro-revival testimony of 1743 but, as we have seen, this was a very moderate document that any but the most inveterate opposers were happy to sign. He even subscribed to the Old Light bible—Chauncy's *Seasonable Thoughts*. Nevertheless, Maccarty suddenly found himself on a collision course with the town establishment over George Whitefield's second visit to New England in 1744–45.[9]

Maccarty had apparently grown increasingly frustrated over his inability to awaken the sinners in Kingston to the perilous state of their souls. During Whitefield's visit, Maccarty went to hear him on three or four occasions, not to invite him to preach in Kingston, but simply, it appeared, to observe his evangelistic technique. Whatever his motive, these visits were not appreciated by many of his people, who subjected him to verbal abuse and petty harassment. Maccarty, unfortunately, lost his temper, and pastor-parish relations quickly deteriorated. About that time, early in 1745, the pro-revival clerical majority in Plymouth County convened at Taunton and published a pro-Whitefield testimony, explaining their reasons for admitting him into their pulpits. This action was taken in direct response to the anti-Whitefield resolutions that Chauncy and Gay had been promoting. Although Maccarty did not attend the Taunton Convention, he did send them a letter of support, which was worse. The letter, which warmly endorsed Whitefield, was published, and Maccarty fell utterly from grace. He was now completely at odds with the Kingston town and church establishment, and all parties agreed on the need for an ecclesiastical council.[10]

Thaddeus Maccarty had such pathetically little support that he was forced to agree to a council consisting "wholly of opposers . . . looking to them as just & impartial men that would consider both sides of the Question." The "just & impartial men" were Daniel Perkins and John Angier, two implacable Old Lights from Bridgewater, and Ebenezer Gay, who was out for New Light blood. Gay clearly saw Maccarty as a defector who was corrupting a town that had previously been undefiled by the New Light. After hearing all parties, the council drew up a humiliating confession for Maccarty to sign, in which he was required to ask the forgiveness of "my Aggrieved Brethren" and to give them "the strongest Assurance that can be desired that it should be my care not to offend them by encouraging any Itinerant Ministers and Exhorters among them, or by promoting an Enthusiastick turn of mind which is prejudicial to Religion, and has been in part at least productive of unchristian Divisions and Separations in the Land." Maccarty, to his credit, refused to sign the confession and gracefully withdrew from the Kingston church. Less than a year later, he was happily settled in the pulpit of the Worcester Church.[11]

Since Thaddeus Maccarty had lost his pulpit because of his sympathy for Whitefield, one might expect his successor to be an anti-revival man, and so he was. On September 12, 1746, the former minister of Sunderland, forty-six-year-old William Rand, was installed in the Kingston ministry. Rand had graduated from Harvard with Charles Chauncy in "*the* Class" of 1721, and the two remained lifelong friends. Three years later, in 1724, Rand had brought his rational, tolerant, scholarly preaching to Sunderland, a small village on the Connecticut River. By the 1730s, Rand was causing concern among the more conservative ministers in the Hampshire Association. Stephen Williams of Longmeadow and Jonathan Edwards of Northampton both suspected him of Arminianism. Neither the Valley revivals nor the Awakening caused Rand to cease urging his Sunderland congregation to discard their doctrinal (read Calvinist) baggage and search out scriptural truths for themselves. Rand's sermons, though they were "pleasing to judicious and discerning . . . hearers," did not sit well with the large number of New Lights in his congregation. Nevertheless, he did not moderate his opposition to the Awakening, and, early in 1745, he was directing the Hampshire County forces in Chauncy's anti-Whitefield campaign. On July 25, 1745, Rand was dismissed from his pulpit and, within two months, the Old Light from Sunderland was settled in Kingston to replace the unfortunate Maccarty.[12]

The Kingston controversy affords the first glimpse of the religious party lines that hardened so quickly in the aftermath of the Awakening. These factions, as we have seen, had been aligning themselves since the early 1730s, but now they were out in the open and increasingly militant. Old-style moderates who tried to maintain the Puritan balance between Calvinism and humanism were becoming a minority. As the great disputes over original sin and free will developed, these factional alignments were increasingly defined by their theological postures. In the early post-Awakening years, however, the great dividing line was one's attitude toward revivalism. Maccarty was ousted from Kingston principally because he was perceived as pro-revival and Rand was brought in because he was an opposer.

After 1745, membership in ministerial associations began to be determined less by geography and more by clerical politics. For example, the Plymouth Association was dominated by the New Lights, so William Rand joined the Weymouth Association, even though his Kingston parish was barely six miles from Plymouth. Rand became very active in the association, frequently delivering the brief lectures that opened their meetings. In William Rand, Gay had a staunch ally deep in Plymouth County. The scales were balanced, however, since James Bayley, the New Light minister in Weymouth's South Parish, was resolutely attached to the Plymouth Association. Although there were moderates in both associations, the two groups drifted in perceptibly different directions during the years between 1745 and 1770. Ebenezer Gay and his Arminian protégés and allies came to dominate the Weymouth-Hingham Association, whereas the Plymouth Association was the home of New Lights such as John Porter, Josiah Crocker, Sylvanus Conant, and at least one New Divinity (extreme Calvinist) man, Chandler Robbins of Plymouth. Thus we find William Rand delivering a lecture in Hingham in which he declared "I shall show the folly & madness of an Intemperate Zeal in matters of Religion," while the members of the Plymouth Association were debating "Whether an unregenerate Man can do anything directly or indirectly toward his Regeneration in any Sense whatever." On the South Shore, the ministers were damning the New Light, while in Plymouth County their colleagues were anathematizing Arminians.[13]

The growth of religious parties among clerics and laity in the post-Awakening years was accompanied by the widening theological schism between Arminians and Calvinists. The arguments over the mechanics of conversion and ecclesiastical order were soon overshadowed (though never supplanted) by debates over some of the great questions of Reformation theology—justification by faith, freedom of the will, original sin, and the doctrines of grace. They all asked essentially the same question—Does man have an active or a passive role in God's great plan of redemption? The orthodox Calvinists believed that man was totally depraved and incapable of influencing the destiny of his soul. The Arminian party believed that, through his God-given rational faculties (enfeebled though they were) man could come to understand what God expected of him, and could then, *if* he so desired, work toward his salvation by striving to live according to Christian ethical and moral standards.

The Arminian ministers, unlike the Calvinists, felt no obligation to defend any particular orthodox scheme. Indeed, they openly denounced all creeds and dogmas as man-made corruptions of the true gospel. Approaching the scriptures in the enlightened, empirical spirit of Locke and Newton, Gay and his friends eagerly subjected the Bible to their own "scientific," analytical techniques. They were attempting to get at the historical truth of the gospel, and to return to the practices of primitive Christianity. Applying their reason, their linguistic skills, and the techniques of historical criticism, they carefully scrutinized the New Testament gospels and epistles. Every true minister of the gospel, according to Gay, "searches impartially after Truth," wherever that search might lead; and the only source of truth was "Scripture itself—the Standard of Truth, and Measure of Duty." Therefore, Gay urged his colleagues to *"Preach the Word*—the Gospel, the Word of Truth; that People may be taught as the Truth is in JESUS; rather than as it is in the Writings of any Men, how renowned soever for Orthodoxy, or admired for Learning." Their task was to purge the church of the corrupting influences of the Calvinists, whom Gay rather tauntingly compared with "the *Gnostics*, *Nicolaitans*, and many other impure Heretics, with whose monstrous Opinions the christian Church was early infected."[14]

This bold, empirical, enlightened spirit, which blossomed in New England in the post-Awakening years, received its intellectual nourishment from the works of liberal Anglican clergymen. The most influential among these was Dr. Samuel Clarke (1675–1729), a towering figure among the eighteenth-century rational divines. He was one of the Latitudinarians, the philosophic successors of the Cambridge Platonists, who strove to pursue a middle course between the High Churchmen and the deists. Clarke's contribution to the development of rational-Arminian religion was twofold. The first was his proclamation, in *The Being and Attributes of God* (1704), that the Lord of Creation was fundamentally benevolent. Clarke was the first fully to develop the proposition—soon to become a commonplace in eighteenth century thought—that the harmony, order, and beauty of the universe argued inescapably for a creator who was wise and beneficent. God was just and rational, and, if one behaved, there was nothing to fear. Clarke's vision of the benevolent deity became central to Arminian thought. One could hardly rely on moral virtue for one's salvation, if God was irrational and capricious.[15]

Samuel Clarke's second legacy to rational religion was even more important. In 1712, he published *The Scripture-Doctrine of the Trinity*, a scholarly and nondogmatic examination of one of the most sacred pillars of the Athanasian and Nicene creeds. In his investigation, Clarke used all the techniques of scriptural criticism available, comparing and examining every relevant New Testament text, paraphrasing, and investigating the earliest patristic writings on the subject. It was a pioneer work. Clarke was not championing a clear, alternative, anti-Trinitarian point of view such as Arianism or Socinianism; he simply wanted to peel away all creeds and traditions in order to get back to the scriptural truth as the primitive Christians understood it. As it turned out, Clarke could find no scriptural proof for making Christ consubstantial with the Father, and orthodoxy was confounded; but Clarke's empirical spirit and methodology were more important than his conclusions. He earnestly believed that "The peace and unity of the Church can be assured but two ways: either by that of charity, and allowing learned men a liberty of examining things, which is the Protestant and Christian method; or by introducing with force an universal ignorance, which is the method of Popery."[16]

Samuel Clarke's works had an immense influence on New England ministers, both directly and indirectly. Charles Chauncy frequently cited Clarke as a source, and Jonathan Mayhew, the most outspoken Arminian in the mid-eighteenth century, considered him an "admirable writer." Clarke's liberal spirit and techniques of scriptural criticism were adopted by a group of rationalist clergymen in England, most of whom were forced to leave their Church of England pulpits. These liberal dissenters, whose ranks included John Taylor (1694–1761), George Benson (1699–1762), and James Foster (1697–1753), were the men principally responsible for spreading Clarke's message to the colonies. They were all men of Gay's generation and, like him, had gradually come to doubt the reasonableness of orthodox formulations. Among these three Clarkite liberals, John Taylor was the most widely read in New England.[17]

Taylor, a minister in Norwich, became intrigued with Samuel Clarke's methodology, and applied it to an examination of that great bulwark of Calvinism, the doctrine of original sin. The result was a superb controversial piece called *The Scripture-Doctrine of Original Sin* (London, 1738). Taylor criticized, with devastating effectiveness, the arguments that supported the concept of inherent sinfulness, and, in the post-Awakening decade, his works became the rallying point for the Arminian movement in New England. Ministers such as Gay, Chauncy, and Jonathan Mayhew, who were vigorously preaching the importance of moral endeavor, could no longer tolerate the doctrine of original sin; it had become equally obnoxious to many of the wealthy merchants and aspiring entrepreneurs in their congregations. By 1751, Daniel Gookin, a Boston bookseller, was trumpeting Taylor's *Scripture-Doctrine* at the head of a list of advertisements for Arminian books. One can hardly say whether the liberal clergy were more impressed by Taylor's attack on original sin, or by the Clarkite technique that he employed. Nearly forty years later, when Charles Chauncy published his universalist tract, *Salvation of All Men*, he acknowledged his "obligations to the writings of the late reverend Dr. *John Taylor* of *Norwich*." Chauncy disagreed with some of Taylor's views on original sin, but he declared that it was Taylor's "*example* and *recommendation* that put me upon studying the *scriptures* in that *free, impartial,* and *diligent* manner, which led me into these sentiments." Taylor's *Scripture-Doctrine of Original Sin* quickly became a staple in the education of rational divines, and was still being recommended to Harvard divinity students by Professor Henry Ware as late as 1806.[18]

The works of Clarke, Taylor, and the other English liberal theologians articulated and legitimatized (in the eyes of some) the growing confidence, in mid-eighteenth-century New England, that men were really capable of pleasing God. The growing Arminian movement best expressed what the modern church historian, C. C. Goen, has called "a mood of rising confidence in man's ability to gain some purchase on the divine favor by human endeavor." In 1743 William Balch, an Essex County minister, had apparently decided, in the spirit of John Taylor, to meet head-on the doctrinal questions of election and original sin. He asserted that a determinedly wicked man cannot be saved and, according to his opponents, he declared that "Man by Nature is more inclined to Virtue than Vice." Despite the efforts of John White and other conservatives to convict him, Balch was vindicated by a council in 1744. However, in 1746, some other North Shore Calvinists re-examined Balch's testimony at the 1744 council and declared that Balch had given "Works" too prominent a part "in Man's Justification." Balch made a vigorous reply to this attack. Consequently, by the time Ebenezer Gay delivered the Annual Convention Sermon in 1746, all the "Doctrines of Grace," the mainstays of Calvinism, were being hotly debated in the immediate context of the Balch affair.[19]

Gay did not need the Balch controversy to remind him of the schismatic forces at work in post-Awakening New England. Even as he prepared his Convention sermon, two of his neighboring colleagues, Ezra Carpenter of Hull and Samuel Brown of Abington, were engaged in losing battles with their congregations, having been charged with the same doctrinal offenses as Balch. Gay was distressed by the rapid development of "Party-Spirit" and he vigorously condemned "such intemperate Zeal, and satyrical Violence, as hath brought much Smoke and Darkness into the Sanctuary." At the convention, Gay planned to use his talent for healing and conciliation in order to help clear away that smoke and darkness. His sermon was entitled *The True Spirit of a Gospel Minister Represented and Urged*. The "True Spirit" embodied Gay's conception of the ministry—strong, well-educated pastors who ministered to their flock in a practical, simple, and noncontroversial way. Although he intended his sermon to be an appeal for reconciliation, Gay could not resist confronting the two major causes of religious controversy in 1746: first, the continued activity of New Light exhorters and the growth of the separatist movement, and second, the growing resistance to Calvinist orthodoxy and its doctrines of grace, epitomized in the Balch controversy.[20]

As Gay had anticipated, passions were running high at the convention; indeed, there had not been a peaceful conclave since Charles Chauncy had engineered the Old Light coup at the 1743 convention. This particular gathering was distinguished by its designation as the "Anniversary Convention." Presumably, the ministers were commemorating that occasion when, one hundred years before, Richard Mather, John Cotton, and other Puritan divines gathered in Cambridge to prepare a "Platform" of church discipline. Significantly, the Cambridge Platform was a conservative document that responded to the threats posed by Antinomianism and other forms of congregational extremism. The Cambridge

Platform channeled the structure of church government in Massachusetts toward greater authoritarianism: more power was vested
in the ministry; a greater emphasis was placed on outward morality.
Gay's "centennial" sermon suggests that he clearly understood the
parallel.[21]

Gay addressed his principal concern, the restoration of peace
and unity to the churches of the Commonwealth, with an eloquence that surpassed any of his other sermons. He was fifty years
old, in the prime of his ministry, and fully conscious of the importance of his effort. Consequently, he pulled out all the rhetorical
stops. He reminded his audience that by "disagreeing in Opinion
concerning some Appearance of Religion, and Methods of promoting it, we grew strange to one another, left off associating together
as before, and shunned a Communication of ministerial Labours."
He urged that his colleagues not allow mere strategic differences to
keep them from taking "sweet Counsel together." "*Let us be* like-
minded," he insisted, "or people are apt to say, *lo here is Christ, or
there*! In this or the other Set of Principles, in this or the other Way
of Worship." Reflecting on the Awakening, or as he called it "the
late *Provocation*, the Day of Temptation," Gay paraphrased the passage from 1 Kings 19:11–12:

> The Lord is not in the Wind of boisterous Passion; nor in the Earth-
> quake of intestine Jars and destructive Schisms; but *in the small voice*
> of Dove-like Simplicity, Innocence, Meekness, Lowliness and Love.[22]

As the last passage suggests, Gay placed most of the blame for
the recent religious and social upheaval on the New Light preachers and exhorters. Whenever these "zealous Advocates for Grace"
entered a community, they tended "to undermine, or impair practical Christianity." Furthermore, these ranting enthusiasts were totally unprepared for the high calling of the gospel ministry. For all
his popular condescension, Gay had long regarded ministers as a
highly professional group, elevated by their education and their
sacerdotal office above the congregation. He now reiterated those
views in the most emphatic way: "A vain Pretence to the Holy
Spirit's making [ministers] fit for this Office without proper Education, and painful Study, is not encouraged by this Discourse." Ministers, he warned, cannot attain "the *excellent Spirit* which has been
describ'd, unless they do come out of the *Schools of the Prophets*, furnished with competent Knowledge" and all the "Advantages of a
liberal Education." He defended Harvard, and even Yale, by af-

firming that "Happy is our land in Regard of the Seminaries of Learning, planted in it." He then went on to express his contempt for untrained lay exhorters in his usual way, by damning them with a text from scripture:

> When God shall cause the *unclean Spirit* to pass out of the Land, and any such person shall yet presume to Prophesy, . . . [he] shall confess, as in Zech. 13. 5. "I am no Prophet, I am an Husbandman; for Men taught me to keep Cattle from my youth."

What could convey more incisively Gay's sense of the vast social and professional gulf that separated him from lay preachers and evangelists?[23]

Gay condemned the New Lights and Separatists not only for their lack of a gentlemanly education, but for their intolerance. As the Arminian movement grew, the "orthodox" party (neo-Calvinists and, increasingly, Old Light Calvinists) began refashioning their church covenants into confessions of faith designed to weed out heretics. This was anathema to Gay. He had long been opposed to creeds, and the recent scholarship of John Taylor and the other Clarkites had strongly reinforced his tendency to rely only on Holy Writ for spiritual guidance. So, for the first time, Gay began to crusade openly for the "right of private judgement." He asserted that a truly meek and humble minister "Usurps not a Dominion over the Faith and Consciences of any, by urging his private Opinion as the Doctrine and Law of *Christ*, and imperiously obtruding his Sense of Scripture, for Scripture itself." This ringing defense of intellectual liberty in matters of faith, however, looked back to Richard Baxter rather than forward to Thomas Jefferson. Gay was speaking here as a latitudinarian trying to preserve the old religious establishment through accommodation rather than confrontation. The forces of religious pluralism, unleashed in the Awakening, had shattered the Puritan synthesis, and Gay instinctively understood that toleration was the only way to prevent a further hardening of the schisms.[24]

Despite his pleas for unity, Gay was clearly partisan. He was not interested in protecting New Light ministers from persecution (indeed, as we have seen in the Maccarty case, he eagerly joined in), but he was always ready to defend any clergyman who was charged with preaching Arminianism. Gay could see nothing wrong with ministers who preached righteousness and the law. He fervently believed that external conformity and obedience was the cement that held the religious and social hierarchy together, and the havoc wrought by the Awakening did little to disabuse him. So, he enthusiastically helped launch the Arminian counterattack when he told the assembled clergymen that no minister should ever permit himself "to call *Good Works* abominable, which he is to affirm constantly, that they who have believed in God, ought to maintain."[25]

Ebenezer Gay not only defended the so-called Arminian clergy in his 1746 Convention Sermon, but in a very real sense, he cast his lot with them. He not only vindicated the right of William Balch and others to question the Calvinist doctrine of original sin, he joined them in rejecting it. In a sense, this was nothing new. For years, Gay's preaching had implied that man was an effective agent in securing his own salvation. He had preached this *de facto* Arminianism in an intellectual climate that did not demand a rigorous adherence to the Calvinist creed. The Awakening, however, had changed all that, and in the polarized atmosphere of 1746, Gay felt obliged openly to disavow any allegiance to the Calvinist scheme with its obnoxious representation of men wallowing in sin and guilt, unable to lift a finger to better their condition. In one remarkable passage, he very deliberately restated the doctrines of grace in Arminian terms:

> A pure Spirit is cautelous against the Abuse of the *Doctrines of Grace*, understanding and explaining them as Doctrines according to Godliness, and designed to promote universal Holiness. . . . *Election of Grace*, thro' Sanctification of the Spirit unto Obedience: To the Means, as well as to the End. . . . *Redemption* from the Curse of the Law, as a special Engagement to keep the Commandments of God. . . . *Effectual Vocation* to be unto Holiness, and the Operations of the divine Spirit therein, as not excluding humane endeavours after Grace, or superceding all use of our enfeebled Faculties in the Work of it. . . . *Justifying Faith* as receiving whole Christ, not dividing his Offices, nor substituting his Obedience in the Place of ours. . . . *Perseverance* in Grace, to be accomplished in a way of continual Circumspection, and dutiful Diligence, working out our Salvation with Fear and Trembling.[26]

This whole passage, which was an unabashed and eloquent affirmation of the Arminian gospel, seems a bit jarring in a sermon that had been intended to reconcile contending clerical factions. Nevertheless, the neo-Calvinists and Old Lights failed to raise a fuss. Perhaps the content of the message was overshadowed by Gay's temperate, restrained style of delivery; perhaps the assembled ministers were so anxious for an end to controversy that they only heard his plea for unity; or perhaps the New Lights had given up on the Annual Convention, conceding the ground to Chauncy and his followers. Whatever the reason, one of the clerics present was able to remark, with an almost audible sigh of relief, "A peaceable meeting. Blessed be God!" The conventioneers then took up the offering that Gay urged "for the Relief of necessitous Souls," collected £232, and went home. Whether Gay realized it or not, as his chaise rattled down Orange Street and out the Boston Neck, his Convention Sermon marked a clear and critical juncture in his career. He had broken ranks with moderate Calvinist opposers, such as his friend and neighbor Nathaniel Eels, and joined the Arminians. In fact, in the eyes of many contemporaries and later historians, he would become known as the father of New England Arminianism.[27]

Much of the anger and frustration that Gay expressed in his Convention Sermon was occasioned by the unsettled state of church affairs in Hingham in 1746. The bitter fight over the secession of the South Hingham Church, described in Chapter 5, was just drawing to a close. In addition to those troublesome people in "The Plain," Gay was worried about the future stability and direction of the Cohasset Church. John Fowle, the minister of that church, was apparently in the midst of a nervous breakdown that was rendering him increasingly "peevish and irregular." Fowle was no Arminian, but he had firmly aligned himself with the Old Lights, and had subscribed the anti-Whitefield Weymouth Testimony. After a rocky five-year tenure in Cohasset, he was now determined to resign, and he wrote to William Smith of Weymouth, secretary of the Association, requesting that the area ministers sanction his resignation and move expeditiously to replace him. Fowle expressed his fear that, if the members of the Cohasset Church were left to their own devices, "many of em should be strongly inclined to settle a New Light Minister." The prospect of Hingham's Second Parish (Cohasset) falling to the New Lights was extremely alarming both to Gay and to Nathaniel Eels of Scituate. Despite all the efforts of these two men, the New Light faction in neighboring Hull was about to turn out the Reverend Ezra Carpenter for preaching Arminian doctrines. Now Cohasset appeared to be tottering. Gay needed a vigorous young minister who would move to restore order and reason in the Second Parish, and so he turned to his friends at Harvard College.[28]

Scattered bits of evidence exist which, in their cumulative force, suggest that Gay had a regular connection with Harvard that helped him recruit ministers of the right stripe for placement in South Shore pulpits. These contacts probably included Edward Holyoke, Gay's old tutor and now president of the college, as well as his good friend Nathaniel Appleton, who had been minister at Cambridge since 1717. At some point, perhaps through Appleton, Gay became acquainted with a circle of high-mettled young liberals whose wit, scholarship, and heterodoxy had caused something of a stir in Boston. The group included Lemuel Briant (class of 1739), John Brown (1741), Gad Hitchcock (1743), and Jonathan Mayhew (1744). All of these men, except Mayhew, were eventually settled on the South Shore, eagerly joining Gay's enlightened circle of ministers. In 1747, however, Gay clearly wanted young Mayhew to occupy the Cohasset pulpit, strongly recommending him to Deacon John Jacob, the patriarch of the Second Parish. Accordingly, the small country church in Cohasset extended its invitation to Jonathan Mayhew to occupy the pulpit of their handsome new meetinghouse.[29]

Jonathan Mayhew was soon to become the most outspoken and prominent advocate of enlightened, rational, Arminian Christianity in New England. Gay may have been more instrumental in formulating and exploring the new Arminian theology, but Mayhew was its publicist; he grabbed the headlines. His fame spread still further in the 1750s when he began his lifelong struggle against the Church of England, and what he perceived as the threat of Episcopal tyranny in the colonies. His eloquent condemnations of the Anglican establishment, and his defense of the right and obligation of an oppressed people to resist their rulers, caused contemporaries and later historians to regard him as one of the earliest spokesmen for American revolutionary principles. Mayhew was, in fact, no more a popular democrat than Gay, but that did not lessen the revolutionary impact of his passionate defense of intellectual liberty. Ebenezer Gay had a very close relationship with this extraordinary young man, but the precise nature of that relationship remains a matter of controversy. Nevertheless, it is possible to shed some light on the friendship that subsisted between these two leading figures of the Arminian movement.[30]

The Reverend Experience Mayhew, Jonathan's father, may well have suggested to his son that he seek out Gay. Alden Bradford, Mayhew's first biographer, suggested that Gay's "character

was well known to the father of Dr. Mayhew." This is hardly surprising, since the theological evolutions of Experience Mayhew and
Ebenezer Gay were strikingly parallel, even though Mayhew was a
generation older. Experience Mayhew had spent his life as a missionary to the Indians on Martha's Vineyard. As with most missionaries, his preaching was simple, practical, and intensely evangelical.
Consequently, like Gay, he became impatient with those elements
of Calvinist doctrine that impeded his efforts and complicated his
message. In the pre-Awakening decade he began to read books that
"embrace or incline to the *Arminian Hypothesis*." In 1744 he published *Grace Defended*, an effort to reconcile his Calvinist heritage
with his day-to-day ministry. Like Gay, he concluded that it was not
*total* depravity that rendered men unable to come to Christ, but
rather their state of corruption and ignorance—conditions that
could be corrected by human endeavor. He admitted quite frankly
that the doctrine of election made no sense to him, and yet, at the
age of seventy-one, the elder Mayhew was not prepared formally to
reject the Westminster Confession. He declared that he was "fully
persuaded of the Truth of the Doctrine of God's Decrees of *Election*
and *Reprobation*." Gay and Experience Mayhew had traveled essentially the same route up to a point, but Gay, as we have seen, resolutely pushed ahead, shedding his Calvinist integument once and
for all. What a perfect counselor for young Jonathan! Here was an
older man who had raised the same theological questions as his
father, but who was in the process of resolving those questions
through the application of reason and the techniques of scriptural
criticism.[31]

Jonathan Mayhew apparently did not study theology with
Gay on a formal basis. The Harvard Overseers' Records indicate
that, from the fall of 1744 after his graduation, until shortly before
his ordination in 1747, Mayhew was in residence at the college.
Furthermore, there is no evidence that Mayhew ever taught school
in Hingham, preached for Gay, or joined the Old Ship Church.
Nevertheless, he apparently did form a very close and enduring relationship with Gay during these years. Alden Bradford declared
that "Dr. Mayhew was very intimate in the family of Dr. Gay, from
the time he entered college," and that "Dr. Gay was the most
confidential friend Dr. Mayhew had, without excepting even Dr.
Chauncy." Gay himself, at Mayhew's ordination, remarked "I have
been pleased, Sir, in frequent Conversation with you, to observe
your Thirst after Knowledge, and inquisitive Disposition to find

Truth." The correspondence in the Gay-Otis papers bears out Bradford's assertion that Mayhew was a close friend of the family; Gay's son Martin, for instance, was quite devoted to him. Gay maintained a consistent interest in Mayhew's career over the years, and he mourned the young man's untimely death in 1766 more than he did that of his own son the year before. One may reasonably infer from all this that Mayhew did, somehow, spend more time in the Hingham parsonage than, as his recent biographer put it, "an occasional overnight lodging on trips to and from Martha's Vineyard."[32]

While Alden Bradford's unsupported assertion that Gay was principally responsible for sending Mayhew down the Arminian road is an exaggeration, it should be noted that Gay and Mayhew did share a notably similar interest in certain authors. Mayhew, for instance, was quite familiar with Hugo Grotius, adopting the Grotian concept of the meaning of Christ's atonement—that Christ's death was not intrinsically necessary for man's salvation, but served more as an example to sinners of the obedience due God's government. Unlike Gay, however, Mayhew was clearly unimpressed with Grotius's advocacy of absolute submission to rulers, whether they be good or bad. Mayhew and Gay both admired the physico-theologians such as Thomas Burnet and John Ray. They believed passionately that the scientific investigation of the universe would lead to a fuller understanding of God's Truth. Perhaps Mayhew rekindled Gay's interest in science since, around 1747, Gay acquired Gravesande's *Mathematical Elements of Natural Philosophy*. Indeed, in the subtle intellectual interplay that always occurs between mentor and pupil, Gay, rather than Mayhew, may have been the chief beneficiary. Gay's instinctive caution may have been at least partly overcome by young Mayhew's ardent temperament and "inquisitive Disposition to find Truth."[33]

In 1747, after a discouraging rejection by the church in Worcester, Mayhew received a unanimous call to settle in Cohasset. Gay's affection and admiration for Mayhew was apparently shared by the people of Cohasset Parish. Mayhew hesitated to accept the invitation of the Cohasset Church, perhaps because he knew he was being considered for the vacant pulpit at Boston's West Church. This ninth church of Boston had been organized in 1737 to meet the needs of the growing population of West Boston. A hitherto sparsely settled part of town, it began to fill up quickly in the 1720s and 1730s with rising young merchants anxious to escape the congestion of the North End. In West Boston they had room to build the "Large and substantial residences" that reflected their prosperity. These young entrepreneurs wanted their own neighborhood church, together with a minister who would not make them feel uncomfortable about their social aspirations. They had found such a one in William Hooper, an eloquent Scottish clergyman and a mild Arminian who occasionally sniped at the Calvinist doctrines of grace. The conservative religious establishment of Boston regarded the popular young Scotsman with understandable suspicion. Consequently, they were outraged, but probably not very surprised, when they learned that Hooper had accepted the rectorship of Boston's Trinity Church. Hooper's defection to the Anglicans was a devastating blow to his supporters and admirers. Gay expressed their sense of betrayal when he declared, "had it been possible, ye would have almost plucked out your own Eyes, rather than have parted with him." Four months after William Hooper's departure, on March 6, 1747, the West Church congregation voted to replace him with Jonathan Mayhew. An ambitious young man such as Mayhew probably had little difficulty in choosing a promising Boston pulpit over the small country parish of Cohasset. Gay may have lost a vigorous ally on the South Shore, but his influence in Boston's religious politics was greatly enhanced by Mayhew's new position.[34]

Mayhew wasted no time in alienating most of the Boston clergy. In 1747, the Boston Association was still dominated by Cotton Mather's disciples, now known as the "old guard"—Foxcroft, Sewall, Prince, Gee, Checkly, and Webb. If Mayhew should choose to preach the Arminian gospel in Boston, he could expect only the quiet support of Charles Chauncy at First Church, the friendship of Samuel Cooper, junior minister at Brattle Street, and the neutrality of old Benjamin Colman, Cooper's senior and the dean of the Boston clergy. Consequently, Mayhew failed to invite any of the "old guard" to participate in his ordination—a serious blunder. Brattle Street and First Church were the only Boston churches that received an invitation. The ordaining council was to be completed by the three men whom he regarded as his theological mentors— Ebenezer Gay, Nathaniel Appleton, and, of course, Experience Mayhew. Benjamin Colman at Brattle Street was greatly disturbed at West Church's failure to invite the other churches "in our Neighborhood," and, after painful deliberation, advised his church not to send any delegates. Thomas Foxcroft, the senior minister at the

First Church, smoothly outmaneuvered Charles Chauncy, his junior colleague, ensuring that their church would send no delegates.
Consequently, on May 20, Gay arrived in Boston for the ordination
and was surprised to find that his old friend, Nathaniel Appleton,
was the only other council member present. Experience Mayhew
had been delayed in travel, so they lacked the majority necessary to
proceed with the ceremony. Gay and Appleton advised the congregation to postpone the ordination, then settled down with Mayhew and his people to consume the lavish feast that had been
prepared.[35]

Gay was incensed at the behavior of the ministers at Brattle
Street and First Church, and may well have had a hand in deter-
mining the next step that the West Church leaders took. They set
June 17 as the new date for Mayhew's ordination. This time invitations were sent to fifteen country churches, pointedly ignoring all
the Boston congregations. Mayhew received no challenges to his
orthodoxy from the eleven ministers who responded to the invitation. The list ranged from Gay and Lemuel Briant of Braintree,
who were more or less open in their Arminianism, to Appleton,
Benjamin Prescott of Salem, and old John Hancock of Lexington,
none of whom were especially inhibited by the Calvinist doctrines
of grace. Mayhew had asked Gay to preach the ordination sermon, another mark of their close relationship, and Gay was only
too happy to comply. He stood in the classically handsome West
Church pulpit, and, with stirring eloquence, sent Mayhew out to do
battle with the "Powers of Darkness."[36]

Gay's sermon, which he titled *The Alienation of Affection from
Ministers*, was really a declaration of theological liberation; a ringing call to arms for the Arminian movement. He declared that "It
is the great and indispensable Duty of Ministers, to tell People
the *Truth*." Gay later defined this truth as "pure, unadulterated,
Scripture-Truths; . . . Not precarious Opinions, dark and intricate
Schemes, abstract metaphysical Notions." The people must free
themselves from the encumbrances of creeds, doctrines, and confessions, and exercise what Mayhew later called "the right and duty
of private judgement." Gay told his audience that the truth which
Paul preached to the Galatians was "that of Christian Freedom
from the Servitude of the *Mosaic Yoke*, the Bondage of the Cere-
monial Law. He thoroughly understood, and boldly asserted the
*Christian Liberty*." When Gay used the phrase "Mosaic Yoke," he was
clearly referring to Calvinist dogma, and his audience understood

this. One year later, in a well-known lecture series published as *Seven Sermons*, Mayhew echoed Gay's words when he said, "Let us all stand fast in the liberty wherewith Christ has made us free; and not suffer ourselves to be intangled with any yoke of bondage. . . . It is not yet too late to assert our liberty, and free ourselves from an ignominious slavery to the dictates of men."[37]

Gay did not spare from criticism the ministers of the Boston Association who had decided to ostracize Mayhew: "Should one Workman malign another, that helpeth him to do his Master's Work? Alas!" He then pointedly condemned "any Endeavors, if not open and notorious, yet sly and plausible, to disgrace, and supplant one another!" Gay also warned Mayhew, however, not to allow the opposition of the old guard to push him into a more radical theology: "'Tis a foolish gratifying the Jealousies of others concerning him, for a Man to depart from the Faith, that he may be at a greater Distance from them: and to verge toward Scepticism that he may appear the more free from Bigotry."[38]

Although Gay was anxious to encourage Mayhew to provide a strong voice in Boston for the "true," uncorrupted gospel, he clearly recognized Mayhew's weaknesses—a tendency to be intolerant, impatient, and belligerent. Gay urged the candidate to use restraint and discretion while preaching the truth of the gospel to his congregation. He should "teach according to People's Need and Ability to learn. It is better for [a minister] to stoop too low, then to soar too high: to feed Men with Milk, then to choke Children with *Strong Meat*." The instinctively cautious Gay was urging the naturally impetuous Mayhew to move slowly, and to hold back controversial new insights when his congregation "cannot bear them as yet." Gay spoke volumes about himself and other Leverett men such as Appleton and Chauncy when he declared that it was often necessary for a minister "to be content with the silent Enjoyment of his own Thoughts." Gay's concern with Mayhew's lack of inhibition was shared by Charles Chauncy. During the 1750s, Chauncy was engaged in the diligent biblical study that would lead him to conclude that his benevolent god ultimately intended the salvation of all men. Chauncy shared his unorthodox reflections with Gay but not with Mayhew, since the latter could not "keep a secret." Chauncy told Gay that if Mayhew ever saw the draft of his works, "such is his frankness that all the world will soon know it."[39]

Having reminded Mayhew of the virtues of pastoral discretion, Gay concluded his sermon in the same militant spirit in which it was begun. He ended with his customary scriptural play on the candidate's name, but this time it was not merely an affectionate jest. This time he was defiantly sending Mayhew into battle with the hostile religious establishment of Boston: "Be valiant for the Truth against all Opposition from the Lusts of Men, and Powers of Darkness. . . . So that from the Blood of the uncircumcised Slain, the Bow of *Jonathan* turn not back empty!"[40]

Gay returned to Hingham, well content with having helped install this bold spokesman for enlightened Christianity in an important new Boston pulpit. The vexing problem of the vacant Cohasset pulpit, however, still remained. Once again, Gay turned to Nathaniel Appleton, who recommended another member of the same circle of Harvard postgraduates that had produced Mayhew and other "Arminian heretics." John Brown, the young man in question, was one of Mayhew's closest friends. After Mayhew's death, Brown spoke of the "intimate acquaintance contracted in youth, and which I have had the honor to maintain with this great and good man." Brown also happened to be the son of Gay's old classmate, the late Reverend John Brown of Haverhill. Like his father, young Brown was not the most energetic scholar, but he was handsome, eloquent, and shrewd. Like his friend Mayhew, Brown was an outspoken defender of intellectual freedom, but he did not share Mayhew's crusading drive. He looked forward to the quiet, congenial, and intellectually supportive world of Gay's Hingham. Brown also had that capacity for making "society innocently cheerful" which Gay valued in his associates, again unlike Mayhew who "was rather grave than gay in his deportment." When, for example, the Cohasset Church called Brown to their pulpit, there was one dissenting vote. The story goes that when Brown visited his opponent, the man told him forthrightly, "'I like your person and manners . . . but your preaching, sir, I disapprove.' 'Then,' said Brown, 'we are agreed. My preaching I do not like very well myself; but how great the folly for you and I to set up our opinion against that of the whole parish.'" This story may also reflect some lingering New Light sympathy in the parish, despite the opposition of Deacon John Jacob and the Cohasset establishment.[41]

Gay was apparently successful in allaying any suspicions that Nathaniel Eels (still the potentate of the South Shore) and the other more conservative ministers in the area might have entertained about Brown's orthodoxy. The ordination council that met on

September 2, 1747, was composed predominantly of moderate Calvinists; Daniel Shute of South Hingham was the only Arminian present, since Gay had been "detained by bodily Disorders." The ministers in attendance were less concerned about Brown's theology than whether he shared their conception of the ministerial office—a well-educated, pragmatic, parish patriarch who would mesh comfortably with the South Shore's presbyterian religious establishment. Having satisfied himself that Brown was such a man, Nathaniel Eels laid his hands on the candidate and said, "we ordain you Bishop." "Bishop" seems a curious word for non-Anglican ministers to use, but it had particular significance for clergymen who were trying to elevate and professionalize their office as the post-Awakening attacks on the ministry intensified. Nathaniel Eels defined precisely what was meant by the term: "a Bishop is one that is regularly introduced into the Pastoral office of a single Church." In other words, a "Bishop" was a minister who had acquired the right professional credentials and did not go wandering about the countryside. John Brown was frequently referred to as "the Bishop" throughout the rest of his ministry.[42]

Brown did not disappoint Gay, either in his preaching or in his pastoral administration. He firmly supported all the major tenets of the new Arminian "orthodoxy." He viewed Christianity primarily as an ethical and moral system "wisely calculated to regulate our sentiments, to set bounds to our passions, and influence us to a regular course of behavior." He was anti-credal: "Let all human creeds, and confessions of faith be considered in a diminutive light in comparison with the word of God. Call no man Master." Brown's theology was also reflected in his administration of the Cohasset Church. The question of discipline, for instance, was handled with the urbanity one might expect of a South Shore liberal. In 1749, Prince Joy and Stephen Stodder, Jr. confessed to the church that they were guilty of "the continued Sin of Drunkeness." In their written confession, they acknowledged "That Rational Beings should properly confess & bewail their Miscarriage in order to conciliate the Favours both of God and Men." There was no groveling at Hingham's Second Parish.[43]

John Brown soon became the staunch third member of that clerical triumvirate that dominated Hingham and Cohasset for nearly forty years. Gay, Shute, and Brown made Hingham the Arminian bedrock for South Shore liberalism. John Brown was an

independent, forceful preacher yet, like Daniel Shute, he acknowledged Gay as his intellectual and spiritual superior, following him
into council after council in defense of ministers accused of Arminianism. Gay now had an effective power base in Hingham from
which he could slowly build a new and more liberal association of
ministers on the South Shore.[44]

# CHAPTER VIII

# A Benevolent Planet with His Satellites

Although Gay had many friends among the South Shore ministers, in early 1748 there were only two clerics outside of Hingham that shared his commitment to a rational, non-Calvinist faith—William Rand of Kingston and Lemuel Briant of Braintree. In February of that year, however, Gay had an opportunity to add another member to the fold. The residents of the western part of Pembroke, a section with the curious name of Tunk, had recently organized as the Second Precinct of Pembroke, and had called Gad Hitchcock to be their first minister. Hitchcock had come to Harvard from Springfield, where he had probably been fitted for the college by that old Arminian heretic, Robert Breck. After his graduation in 1743, he remained in residence at the college while preparing to take his second degree. While living in Cambridge, Hitchcock became yet another member of that same group of young scholars (Mayhew, Brown, etc.) that Gay was so anxious to settle in South Shore pulpits. Hitchcock also came under the direct supervision of Nathaniel Appleton by virtue of his post-graduate residency. Could Appleton (with the backing of Gay and Chauncy) have been the principal agent responsible for discreetly nursing and placing this brood of young Arminians? While Hitchcock was debating whether or not to accept the call to Tunk, he informed the members of that church that he "desired my Friends at College and other Gentlemen to assist me" in coming to a decision. This collective decision was affirmative and, after some hard financial bargaining, Hitchcock settled into Pembroke's Tunk Parish.[1]

Gad Hitchcock's ordination council was not composed of men whose presence would reassure neighboring Plymouth County

145

conservatives. Gay, Appleton, William Smith, William Rand, and Robert Breck accounted for five of the eleven delegates. Hitchcock went on to become one of the most active and well-liked men in the Hingham Association. He was a tall, robust young man who had a plain-spoken Connecticut Valley wit that delighted everyone. His bluff humor, however, tended to obscure the fact that he was the most thorough-going rationalist in the Association. Hitchcock was not guilty of the "High Arianism" with which some have charged him, but his complete faith in reason was evident when he discussed the importance of natural religion: "The . . . greater and the most extensive our knowledge is of natural [truths], the greater may it be of moral truths. The more we know of the latter, the more we may love and embrace them. . . . This is natural religion. From this happiness results."[2]

With the addition of Gad Hitchcock in 1749, the South Shore ministry was quickly acquiring a distinctly Arminian temper. Up to that point, the Arminians had maintained a slightly uneasy alliance with the old and moderate Calvinists, as all three sought to reaffirm order and clerical authority in the face of the New Light threat. The younger ministers had been circumspect and not obnoxiously anti-Calvinist. In 1749, however, the Reverend Lemuel Briant of Braintree shattered the peace with one highly controversial sermon entitled *The Absurdity and Blasphemy of Depretiating Moral Virtue*. Briant was a South Shore boy. He was born and raised in South Scituate, growing up under the spiritual and educational nurture of Nathaniel Eels. After graduating from Harvard in 1739, he returned to the college to take his second degree, and fell in with the Mayhew-Brown coterie. Mayhew and Briant had a good deal in common. The Reverend Experience Mayhew, Jonathan's father and mentor, had walked on the edge of Arminianism for years, without feeling a very great need to reconcile his practice with his Calvinist heritage; Nathaniel Eels had provided Briant with the same equivocal example. Like Mayhew, Briant resolved to purify his theology by discarding what remained of his Calvinist inheritance in favor of enlightened rationalism. Briant reinforced his liberal theology by extensive reading in the works of the English liberal dissenters. He was quite familiar with John Taylor's *Scripture Doctrine of Original Sin*, and, after his settlement in Braintree, he even had the temerity to recommend it to "the prayerful Perusal of some of his Brethren."[3]

In 1745, Briant received a unanimous call from the congregation of Braintree's First Church, that pulpit having stood empty since the death of John Hancock, Jr., the year before. Nathaniel Eels ordained his protégé, with the assistance and blessings of Gay. Briant soon became an active member of Gay's circle, but unlike most of these gentlemen, he insisted (like Mayhew) on trumpeting his Arminianism from the pulpit. In 1749, this rather impulsive young man felt moved to compose and deliver the most disputatious Arminian sermon of the century. Gay's 1746 Convention Sermon, and Mayhew's *Seven Sermons* (1747) had openly delineated the framework of Arminian theology, but Briant's *Absurdity and Blasphemy* was a deliberately provocative blast at the neo-Calvinists. Briant fervently believed, with Mayhew, that "Christianity is principally an institution of life and manners; designed to teach us to be good men, and to show us the necessity of becoming so." Consequently, he finally lost all patience with New Light ministers who dismissed personal righteousness as, in St. Paul's words, "filthy rags." The intensity of Briant's attack is a bit surprising, although he was not a patient man, and, by 1749, his natural irritability was compounded by failing health, a strained financial situation, and marital difficulties. Whatever the provocation, Briant was determined to condemn the antinomian Calvinism that the "unthinking Multitude" believed "allows them the Practice of their Vices, tho' every Article be a downright Affront to common Sense."[4]

Briant spent the greater part of his sermon in attacking and satirizing the Calvinist doctrines of grace, declaring that uneducated laymen, "when they hear of our being *saved by Grace* . . . conceive of it so as to destroy all moral Agency, and set themselves down with this vain Thought, that nothing on their Part is necessary to Salvation, but if they are designed for it, they shall *irresistably* be driven into Heaven, whether they will or not." Although Briant showed his contempt for Original Sin, Election, and the other principal Calvinist tenets, he did not attack directly the great Reformation principle that men are ultimately justified by grace: "the Righteousness of the Saints," Briant said, "renders them amiable in God's Sight," it does not save them. He later responded to a critic by challenging him to single out any passage in his sermon "where the Doctrine of Justification by the *merit* of Man's *personal* righteousness is asserted." The Arminians continued to be quite sensitive about the very natural charge that they were substituting men's righteousness for Christ's atonement. They denied that they believed in justification by merit, but their denial was unconvincing; it was the same sort of lip service that moderate Calvinists paid to the Westminster Catechism while they quietly ignored it. In neither case were the ministers consciously duplicitous; they simply were not ready to recognize the disparity between their practice and their sacred Reformation heritage.[5]

The unusual candor and consequences-be-damned attitude that Briant maintained in his sermon were even more disturbing to his supporters than to his foes. He acknowledged, for instance, the intellectual elitism inherent in the Liberals' support of the right of private judgement: "There always was and always will be some in the world (alas that Number is so few) that have sense eno' and dare trust their own Faculties so far as to judge in Themselves what is right." Gay fully shared the view that not everyone could read the book of nature, but he had the good sense rarely to express it. Briant seemed determined to justify every suspicion that conservatives entertained about the Arminian movement. Weren't the Arminians reducing Christianity to a system of ethics? How could they doubt it when Briant praised "The Pure and perfect Religion of Jesus which contains the most refined System of Morality the World was ever blessed with." How strongly Briant's language evokes the words of Thomas Jefferson, written over sixty years later, when he described the teachings of Jesus as "a system of the most sublime morality which has ever fallen from the lips of man." One of Briant's critics, a moderate New Light, remarked that he had never read "a more *bare-faced* Piece of *Arminianism*, or worse, than Mr. *Briant's* Sermon is." That observation summed it up nicely.[6]

There is no question that Briant had deliberately set out to draw blood from the New Lights and the old Calvinist establishment. He virtually became an Arminian itinerant, delivering his sermon from every friendly pulpit he could find (one wonders if his Braintree congregation ever heard it). He preached his *Absurdity and Blasphemy* from Gay's Old Ship pulpit and in Boston at Jonathan Mayhew's West Church. After Briant's performance at the West Church, Thomas Foxcroft bewailed the "Growth of *Arminianism* and loose Principles in Religion," and further declared that Mayhew and Briant had formed a new sect whose chief tenet was "That Christ always preached the Law, and never the Gospel." Briant had opened the campaign from the pulpit of his boyhood mentor, Nathaniel Eels of Scituate. According to one tradition, the seventy-two-year-old patriarch was dumbfounded, and reprimanded Briant after the service saying, "'Alas! Sir, you have undone today, all that I have been doing for forty years.'" Briant replied, "'Sir, you do me too much honor in saying, that I could undo in one sermon, the labours of your long and useful life.'" The old man who told this story sixty years later went on to say that Eels preached a series of sermons in an effort to repair the damage, but "it was not easy . . . to discern much difference between his doctrine and that of Mr. Bryant." This anecdote was told in a humorous vein, but it really tells a rather poignant tale. Eels, unlike Gay, had been unwilling to face the extent to which his practical theology had diverged from Calvinist orthodoxy. Now his young protégé was holding up a mirror in which Eels could see an unrefracted image of his own Arminianism. His rather pathetic attempts to reaffirm the old orthodoxy were met only with amusement.[7]

The gauntlet that Briant cast down was taken up by John Porter, the minister of North Bridgewater, and one of the leading New Lights in Plymouth County. Porter's reply to Briant was entitled *The Absurdity and Blasphemy of Substituting the Personal Righteousness of Men in the Room of the Surety-Righteousness of Christ*. This unambiguous pamphlet, which defended "the *good old Calvinistical Way* of preaching up Justification by Faith," was attested by five of the leading members of the Plymouth Association. Briant was actively supported by Gay, John Brown, and other South Shore liberals, and so the Weymouth and Plymouth Associations were arrayed against each other once again. The Reverend John Porter proved to be an able controversialist, and Briant entered into a pamphlet war that lasted two years during the course of which Briant backed down considerably. One observer noted that when Briant "can't fairly grapple with an Argument, he knows how to shuffle and *evade*." In 1752, Porter welcomed a new ally into the struggle— seventy-eight-year-old Samuel Niles, pastor of the South Braintree Church, and the senior minister on the South Shore. Unlike Porter, Niles had fiercely opposed the Awakening, but he had remained a strict Calvinist. He had always been suspicious of his young neighbor, and finally entered the lists with the most widely read response to Briant—*A Vindication of Divers Important Gospel-Doctrines*. It is significant that Niles, an Old Light Calvinist, had closed ranks with the New Light Calvinists. He had apparently decided that the threat of Arminianism posed by Briant and his supporters now outweighed the threat to ecclesiastical order posed by the New Lights.[8]

Old Samuel Niles now moved quickly to rid Braintree of the troublesome Briant. The anti-Briant faction of Braintree's North

Church called two ecclesiastical councils, both of which Briant refused to acknowledge. Niles served as moderator of the second council, which met on January 9, 1753 at the house of Deacon John Adams. Niles had assembled a group of "inland" South Shore ministers who shared his rigid Calvinism and were eager to make an example of Briant. This council condemned Briant for his now famous *Absurdity and Blasphemy* sermon, for various moral offenses, and for his "Denial of the Doctrine of divine Decrees, which he calls a Doctrine bordering upon Blasphemy, and in his Denial of the Imputation of the Guilt of Adam's Sin to his Posterity." He was also charged with renouncing the Westminster Assembly's catechism and recommending "Mr. Pierce's" in its place. "Mr. Pierce" was Thomas Pierce, once Dean of Salisbury, who, in 1655, vigorously attacked the Calvinist doctrine that men were totally depraved. The council concluded by urging Briant to repent and reform for the good of all concerned.[9]

Briant's supporters in Braintree and elsewhere rallied to the cause as best they could. Gay conferred with him as often as possible during the height of the crisis. Richard Cranch, a former member of Mayhew's West Church in Boston, had recently moved to Braintree, and wrote to his former pastor asking for a dismission because "it has been thought best by some of the friends of Christian liberty that we should be incorporated with this Church as soon as might conveniently be." A majority of the North Church congregation supported Briant. In March of 1753 they organized a church committee that completely exonerated their pastor from the charges leveled by the Niles Council. The committee struck a blow for the right of private judgement by declaring "we cannot but commend our Pastor for the pains he takes to promote a free and impartial examination into all articles of our holy religion, so that all may judge, even of themselves, what is right." Briant's vindication came too late. His wife had left him and, according to one tradition, he had retreated from Braintree in broken health and was living at Gay's parsonage in Hingham. On October 10, 1753 Briant asked to be dismissed from his pastorate because of ill health and, within a year, he was dead and buried with his fathers in Scituate.[10]

Lemuel Briant had succeeded in bringing the growing debate over Arminianism onto center stage. William Balch had challenged some of the Calvinist doctrines of grace in 1744, but most clergymen were still too preoccupied with preserving ecclesiastical order to pay much attention. In the years following, 1744–1750, the theological challenge of the Arminian party to a newly revived Calvinism assumed more and more importance. By 1750, Briant and Mayhew were leading a bold Arminian assault on Puritan orthodoxy. Gay's coterie of young Arminians suddenly took on an ominous character to orthodox ministers like Samuel Niles, who warned that the churches were "in danger of being corrupted by *Arminian Errors*, or worse . . . propagated by several . . . lately introduced into the *Pastoral* Charge." This old Puritan lamented that he now had to describe himself as "Calvinistical," a necessary "Note of Distinction . . . occasioned very much by the late Growth and Discovery of *Arminianism*."[11]

The furor over the Briant controversy reached into every corner of New England. The Reverend Edward Billings, a New Light who was preaching out in the Green River section of Deerfield, anxiously sent his copy of "Niles against Bryant" to a friend in Belchertown. During the height of the controversy, Jonathan Edwards reminded his Northampton congregation of the Arminian scare in the mid–1730s: "You were many of you, as I well remember, much alarmed, with the apprehension of the danger of these corrupt principles, near sixteen years ago. But the danger then was small, in comparison with what it appears now." While Briant's attack on Calvinism helped to unify the orthodox party, his sudden death made him a kind of martyr for enlightened Christianity to the Arminians. They were more determined than ever to free themselves from the fetters of Calvinist dogma.[12]

Lemuel Briant's stormy career may be contrasted with that of a less abrasive Arminian, the Reverend Job Cushing of Shrewsbury. Cushing, a classmate of Gay's and a native Hinghamite, had traveled essentially the same road to a rational, Arminian theology as had his old friend. Unlike Gay, however, Cushing preached an Arminian gospel in a rural region that was still largely Calvinist. The greater part of his Shrewsbury congregation was apparently restive under Cushing's liberalism, but he was so discreet and commanded such respect that he was never openly opposed. In 1749, however, as the Arminian movement became more militant, even Cushing received a strong warning from worried Calvinists in his church and in the Marlborough Association. Dr. Joshua Smith, a well-educated young parishioner of Cushing's, had taken seriously the Arminians' insistence that intelligent men should search the scriptures for themselves, and exercise their own judgement. Smith did just that, and soon found himself "in ye dark" on the question of original sin and "ye depravation of humane Nature." He soon began to attack publicly these doctrines and, in no time at all, the Marlborough Association had called a council at Shrewsbury to deal with the matter. The Reverend Israel Loring of Sudbury, moderator of the council, told Smith that the question of "How far Christians must be agreed" was still a matter for debate. Nevertheless, Adam's apostasy and mankind's resultant depravity as "exhibited in ye confession of faith received in our Chhs, is a Doctrine of great weight & Importance," and Dr. Smith's remarks had been "inconsistent with & Subversive of ye s^d Doctrine."[13]

The young physician was not without his defenders on the council, as two members "dissented from the rest." William Balch, the outspoken Arminian pastor of Bradford's Second Church, "was observed to turn Advocate for Dr. Smith." The next morning, Balch continued to defend Smith's intellectual liberty, with the able assistance of one other council member—Ebenezer Gay. The Marlborough Association, however, had clearly determined to reprove Dr. Smith. Balch gave up after the morning session, leaving Gay to argue Smith's case alone, a task that he apparently performed with great energy and determination. One of the clergymen present noted that the ministers were "Hard at it—all Day—the Result was read by Candle Light." Gay, in frustration, "drew off" before the council voted, and was not present to hear Dr. Smith receive his formal reprimand. The council then turned to Pastor Cushing. After manifesting their respect and regard, they expressed the hope that "it will be his faithful care still to preach ye great Doctrines of our Holy Religion." Job Cushing had never received such a thinly veiled threat, not even when he had helped defend Benjamin Kent during the first Arminian scare fifteen years before. However, unlike his arrogant, younger colleague Briant, Job Cushing's pastoral tenure was never directly challenged.[14]

As his extraordinary performance at the Shrewsbury council suggests, Gay was now fully committed to the defense of what he and his friends called "the Christian Liberty," a phrase which in those years meant freedom from the doctrinal bondage of Original Sin. Gay was now emerging as the central intellectual and ecclesiastical figure on the South Shore, transforming the Old Light Weymouth Association into the Arminian Hingham Association. If a single event could serve to mark this transition, it would be the death, in August 1750, of seventy-three-year-old Nathaniel Eels, until recently the preeminent figure among the South Shore clergy. Knowing that he was seriously ill, Eels "took a very solemn farewell" of the ministers in the region. Afterwards, he and Gay discussed the state of religion and the ministry as it appeared to them at mid-century. Eels (Harvard, 1699) was nearly a generation older than Gay and was one of the last of that breed of ministers—one could call them the Colman generation—who could breathe the air of the early enlightenment without corrupting their Calvinist heritage (though this was probably less a feat of intellect than of habit). Gay admired these old gentlemen whose philosophical composure was untroubled by the challenges of Samuel Clarke and John Taylor, and he was particularly fond of this imposing old patriarch of Scituate. As Gay assumed the mantle of leadership among the South Shore pastors, he paid tribute to Nathaniel Eels and, in so doing, eloquently defined the ecclesiastical role he wished to assume:

> There never was in this County, if in the Christian World, a Minister so frequently sought to as your late deceased Pastor, when the Churches wanted Light and Peace: And his coming to their Help, in the way of Ecclesiastical Counsel, wherein he, for the most part moderated, might seem as . . . the kindly Aspect of a benevolent Planet with his Satellites.[15]

The first act that Gay performed after Eels's death was to place one of his own students in Eels's vacant pulpit. Jonathan Dorby, the man in question, was a lively, pleasant youth, rather compact in appearance. After graduating from Harvard in 1747, Dorby spent the next two years teaching school in Hingham and studying theology with Gay. On December 6, 1747, Gay admitted him into the fellowship of the First Parish. Despite the paternal affection that Gay felt for most of his students, and particularly for young Dorby of whom he was quite proud, he could be a rigorous and intimidating preceptor. One of the many anecdotes about Gay tells of a young theology student (probably Dorby) who, having preached his first sermon in Gay's pulpit, asked his mentor for an evaluation: "Tell me seriously what you think of this first effort of mine." Gay replied, "I think it sensible and well written, but another text would have been more appropriate." "What would you have selected, sir?" "When you preach it again, I would advise you to prefix this text, 'Alas, master, for it was borrowed.'" Gay also frequently teased Dorby about his "moderate stature." Dorby apparently endured this sort of thing with good grace, and, having completed his preparatory studies, earned this encomium from Gay: "I can, from intimate Acquaintance, bear this young Man witness . . . that he hath taken laudable Pains to be thoroughly furnished unto the good but arduous Work he designed for."[16]

In July 1751, Dorby was called to the South Parish of Scituate, a post that he obtained primarily through the influence of Gay. Gay was in high spirits as he rode down to Scituate on November 13 to install his protégé in that important pulpit. Jonathan Dorby's ordination was the one bright spot for Gay during what seemed to be a period of sustained attack on the authority of ministers, particularly Arminian ministers such as Lemuel Briant. Gay chose this occasion to respond, by defending the preeminence of ministers in a sermon entitled *The Mystery of the Seven Stars in Christ's Right Hand*. Gay quickly explained the mystery. The seven stars mystically represented the angels of the seven Asian churches; those angels, of course, were ministers of the gospel. Twenty-six years before, in his first published sermon, Gay went to some length to demonstrate that ministers were "Men of like Passions with others"; now he characterized them as "Angels by Office." In very uncongregational terms, Gay portrayed the minister as a priest, a sanctified intermediary, one of God's "more immediate Attendants." Clergymen "approach his Person in religious Addresses, and are the People's Mouth to God by Prayer, as well as God's Mouth to them by Preaching."[17]

Gay was implicitly acknowledging the change that had taken place in the status of the clergy since the early days of his own ministry. In the early 1700s, as the more organic, corporate community of the seventeenth century began to crumble, the relationship between minister and town became more contractual in nature. The ministers themselves, following the lead of Cotton Mather, abetted their growing estrangement by reinvigorating clerical associations which would promote the professional interests of ministers, often at the expense of local interests. The general derangement caused by the Great Awakening accelerated these trends on both sides. Towns began to feel less guilty about dissolving their contract with their pastor and shopping around for one who would better suit them. The ministers responded by strengthening their associations and relying even more on those professional distinctions that separated them from, as Gay put it, "Teachers that, in respect of Ability for the Work, are like Jereboam's Priests, of the lowest of the People." Painfully aware of the growing distance between pastor and congregation, Gay insisted that a minister should "spend his Time and Pains in the continual Instruction, Visitation, and Consolation of his People; not being diverted therefrom by the vain Amusements of Pleasure and Company. . . . He must not be a *Runagate*, nor a *Non-Resident*." This kind of devotion would then be appreciated by the minister's flock, who would realize that a permanently settled minister "by long Acquaintance with them, best knows their State, and most naturally cares for it; and between whom and them there is, by the Means, a mutual strong Endearment. The causeless forsaking him, or *putting him away*, as we vulgarly express it, and this when he is old, may be little to their spiritual Advantage." [18]

Although Gay clearly understood most of the reasons that had put such a distance between the shepherd and his flock, he finally became convinced that the breach could not really be healed. The only choice was to preserve and protect the ministry by relying increasingly on higher professional standards, and strengthening those institutions that buttressed clerical authority. Let no one, he urged, disparage the vocation of the gospel ministry. Gay declared that "Divinity is the Queen of Sciences: a Profession in itself, and in the Estimation of all that are wise, the most noble." As for the power of the clergy, Gay thundered that "Ministerial Authority is not to be despised as an empty Name, an insignificant Power, a Shadow without Substance, because there is no external Force to abet it, or to avenge Disobedience to it." Gay, of course, was working hard to back up this rhetoric by fashioning a South Shore association that would provide just such an "external Force." At association meetings, fast lectures, and other occasions, he traveled about the South Shore urging area ministers to govern their flocks with firmness. [19]

In addition to the support of a strong association, ministers must individually master the "right Use of the Key of Government." They must understand how to administer discipline without provoking rebellion: "Discipline is an Edge-Tool, and mad Work is often made with it by angry Ecclesiasticks." The proper use of the Key also included "admitting to and excluding from Sacraments, executing of Censures, and administering all Things which belong to the Order of the Gospel, the due Regulation of christian Worship and Society." If all the "bishops" of the South Shore could exercise this priestly authority as Gay had done for so many years in Hingham, then an orderly social and spiritual hierarchy could be re-established. Gay, who was deeply interested in astronomy (he even flirted a bit with astrology), pictured this ideal religious establishment in heavenly terms: "There is exquisite Order among the Stars: They keep in their proper Orbs, move in their proper Spheres, accomplish their appointed Courses, perform their constant Revolutions with the greatest Certainty and Exactness."[20]

In addition to elevating the status of the minister, Gay also stepped up his attack on the dogmas and creeds of Calvinist orthodoxy. He told young Dorby "'tis pity any Man, at his Entrance into the Ministry, should, in his Ordination Vows, get a Snare to his Soul, by subscribing, or any ways engaging to preach according to another Rule of Faith, Creed or Confession, which is merely of human Prescription and Imposition." Consequently, Gay advised Dorby, according to the dictum of John Locke, that his doctrine should contain nothing "but what is agreeable to the Nature and Reason of Things, and the Oracles of God." Using classic Lockean epistemology, Gay exhorted Dorby to "Open your Eyes to the Light, and yield to the Evidence of Truth, and receive the Impression of it." Gay cautioned, however, that "the Light of Natural Reason . . . is so universally obscured by the Prevalence of moral Corruption, that those Places may well be called Regions of Darkness, where the Light of the glorious Gospel doth not shine." Thus, in 1751, Gay was mapping out the via media of the Arminian ministry—that natural reason, without revelation, was insufficient to guide men towards an apprehension of God's Truth.[21]

Jonathan Dorby was, alas, not destined to play a significant part in Gay's association. On April 13, 1754, Dorby was published to Mary Cushing of Scituate, an excellent match, and a few days later went to Hingham to preach a lecture for Gay. While staying at the home of Colonel Benjamin Lincoln, Dorby was seized "with a Pleurisy Fever of which he died," a "most Shocking providence" to Colonel Lincoln, and a great blow to Gay. The most that could be salvaged from Dorby's untimely departure was the subsequent marriage of Miss Cushing to Gay's nephew, the Reverend Ebenezer Gay, Jr. of Suffield.[22]

The South Parish of Scituate was not long deprived of the benefits of an enlightened, rational gospel. On August 15, 1754, four months after Dorby's death, the church called Mr. David Barnes (Harvard, 1752) to be their pastor. Barnes had received four other calls, most of which were more remunerative, but he appears to have chosen Scituate chiefly because of its proximity to Gay and his liberal associates. He often mentioned his admiration for Gay, and he consciously modeled his preaching style on that of the Hingham patriarch. Yet Barnes was far from being another of Gay's alter egos. He was a thin, red-faced, sharp-featured little man, a stubbornly original thinker, and altogether the most eccentric preacher in the Hingham Association. Barnes was immensely fond of delivering sermons in a voice that was "by no means remarkable for its melody, nor could he be said to manage it with any uncommon skill." Like his colleagues, Barnes was a thoroughgoing rationalist and an implacable foe of Calvinists, particularly New Light Calvinists. Once, in describing Jesus and his apostles, Barnes vigorously asserted that "They were not *enthusiasts.* . . . We may indeed as well suppose that S$^r$ Isaac Newton was an idiot . . . as we can suppose a set of flaming enthusiasts, strangely infatuated, should be the authors of such a system of religion and morality as is contained in the gospels." Barnes's ministry illustrates nicely the observation of religious historian Joseph Haroutunian that "the conflict between Calvinism and the sentiments of the new age can be epitomized as a conflict between the conceptions 'Almighty God' and 'our compassionate heavenly father.'" Barnes once told his parishioners, with that complacence and extraordinary self-confidence one finds only in the eighteenth century, "If we would be ye friends of god, we must cultivate not only an acquaintance, but a likeness to him in his moral perfections."[23]

In the following year, 1755, two more Arminians were added to the Association; one was militant, the other extremely circumspect. The first, Charles Turner, was installed at Duxbury on July 23. Turner, who had nearly become a lawyer, rejected (as Alden Bradford put it) "the peculiar tenets of the Calvinistic creed." Certain ministers from the conservative Plymouth Association attempted to prevent his ordination, but Gay and William Rand of neighboring Kingston defended him and installed him safely in the Duxbury pulpit. Turner quickly became an active member of Gay's Arminian brotherhood and, together with William Rand, helped make the northern Plymouth seacoast a stronghold of rational Christianity. In February of that same year, Gay had traveled up to Braintree to join Nathaniel Appleton in ordaining a successor to the unfortunate Lemuel Briant. Anthony Wibird, the young man in question, would profit from Briant's mistakes, avoiding theological controversy like the plague. Briant's theme, moral virtue, was the subject of Wibird's sermons more often than not, but he preached in such a bland and inoffensive way that no one partic-

ularly cared. John Adams wrote that Wibird's "soul is lost in a dron-
ish effeminancy." Nevertheless, this colorless young cleric became a
loyal, if quiet, supporter of Gay's Association.[24]

By 1760, there was a member of Gay's Arminian party in at
least one church in every South Shore town from Braintree to
Kingston (with the exception of Hull). The Arminian gospel was
flourishing in these bustling, little commercial ports, most of which
were prospering with the growth of the fishing industry. The popu-
larity of Arminian preachers dropped dramatically, however, as
one moved inland. The second tier of parishes could claim only
two Arminians, Daniel Shute of South Hingham, and David Barnes
of South Scituate; Gad Hitchcock was virtually isolated in West
Pembroke (see Appendix 2). At some point, during the 1750s, the
old Weymouth Association became known as the Hingham Association, quite properly reflecting the new order. Ebenezer Gay stood
at the center of this Arminian band, and his influence tended
to extend in the direction of Plymouth, rather than Boston. The
inner circle of Gay's Hingham Association was composed of six
men—William Smith, Daniel Shute, John Brown, Gad Hitchcock,
David Barnes, and William Rand. The impact of this rather small
Arminian regiment in the religious battles of the 1750s was disproportionately great, in large part because of their captain. Gay
was apparently never perceived as a radical by most of the pro-
Calvinist ministry, although extreme New Lights and Baptists such
as Isaac Backus were naturally antagonistic towards him. His great
dignity, now enhanced by his sixty years, his reputation as a scholar,
and his general accessibility caused him to be respected and well-
liked throughout the province. The orthodox Reverend Ebenezer
Parkman of Westborough, for instance, clearly admired Gay, while
he grumbled about Charles Chauncy's "coarseness and unhand-
some conduct." Consequently, Gay was always welcome in the parishes of many ministers who could not tolerate the presence of the
outspoken Jonathan Mayhew or the often abrasive Chauncy.[25]

John Adams once described South Hingham's Daniel Shute as
a man who "loves to laugh . . . delights in banter, but yet reasons
well." The same might be said for nearly every member of the
Hingham Association. When these gentlemen convened in the comfortable parlor of Gay's home, or in William Smith's handsome parsonage in Weymouth, the pipes were lit, the wine and cider flowed,
and the repartee, while not always brilliant, provided a welcome
escape from the pressures of the ministry. One of their colleagues

(not in the Association) confessed in his diary that when he met "in Company with my Brethren in the Ministry," he was inclined to "give an indulgence to innocent and Civil Mirth as an antidote against Melancholy to which I am inclined." The young clerics of the Hingham Association saw no impiety in this sort of levity, though they did try to maintain a more decorous mein in public. Some, such as Lemuel Briant, overstepped the bounds of propriety, causing even a sympathetic parishioner like young John Adams to criticize him for being too "jocular and liberal, . . . too gay and light, if not immoral." John Brown's nineteenth-century successor in the Cohasset pulpit noted disapprovingly that Brown "would sometimes . . . descend to that jesting, which an Apostle has told us, is not convenient."[26]

Glimmerings of what passed for wit in Gay's circle occasionally surface in sermons and correspondence, but most of this humor has survived in anecdotal form, drained of its original vitality by local, Victorian historians. Still, one can try to summon up the shades of these old Arminians and have them once again regale each other with their various tales. Gad Hitchcock, the minister in Pembroke's "Tunk" Parish, had a homespun sort of wit that was intended to elicit guffaws rather than sardonic grins. He told a story once about a sailor he met while he was walking about Boston. The sailor wanted to know his name and place of residence, to which he replied "'My name is Gad Hitchcock, and I belong to Tunk.' . . . The sailor repeated the three names, and cried out, 'Three of the [damndest] names I ever heard.'" David Barnes, the eccentric little minister of Scituate's South Parish even had the temerity to match wits with Gay himself. On one occasion, after Barnes had preached for Gay, the latter criticized Barnes for drawing out his words so much "that you put nearly all my people to sleep." Stung by this rebuke, Barnes got his revenge when he preached the afternoon sermon. He drawlingly recited his sermon text, from Exodus 4 : 11, "Then the Lord said to him, 'Who has made man's mouth?'" The Old Ship congregation was greatly amused at this obvious reference to Gay's enormously wide mouth.[27]

David Barnes satirized Gay at his peril, for Gay, as we have seen, had a quick, sharp wit that could humble any of his colleagues. His talent for the cutting retort is epitomized in one particular anecdote. Gay and a friend were riding along the neck into Boston, when they passed the gallows with the noose of the halter swaying in the wind. This sight prompted his friend to ask Gay where he would be now if the gallows had its due. Gay immediately replied, "Riding alone to Boston." [28]

Another example of Gay's penchant for devastating retorts may be found in an encounter with the Reverend Samuel Dunbar of Stoughton's First Church. Dunbar was a strict Old Light Calvinist who had studied divinity with Cotton Mather. As advancing years began to slow the pace of Samuel Niles, the task of defending the old New England Way (uncorrupted by New Light enthusiasm) on the South Shore fell increasingly to Dunbar. Gay seemed to admire this man, about his own age, who had managed to remain intellectually loyal to the Calvinist heritage they had both shared. Dunbar was a careful scholar, a vigorous preacher, and probably the only Calvinist ever asked to preach from the Old Ship pulpit after the Awakening. He apparently continued to attend Association meetings, but grew increasingly frustrated as Gay and his followers moved into open opposition to Calvinist dogma. On one occasion, when it was his turn to preach at the Association meeting, Dunbar decided to defend the old cause with all his vigor. He ran through each of the Five Points of the Synod of Dort, from total depravity to perseverance of the saints, and after "improving" each point, he pounded his fist on the desk, exclaiming "'This is the gospel.'" Afterwards, each minister had an opportunity to criticize Dunbar's sermon, and when Gay's turn came, he said "'The sermon reminded me of the earliest efforts at painting. When the art was in its infancy, and the first rude drawings were made, they wrote the name of an animal under the figure which was drawn, so that the people could be sure to identify it. Under one rude figure you would see written, "This is a horse"; under another, "This is an ox"; and so on. When the art is perfected a little, this becomes unnecessary, and the animal is recognized without the underscript. I am greatly obliged to my brother Dunbar, in this infancy of the art, that he helped me in this way to identify the gospel. As I followed him through the five figures which he sketched for us, I must confess that unless he had written under each of them, in large letters, "This is the gospel!" I never should have known it.'" This story has obviously been refined in the telling, but it has the ring of truth, vividly reflecting what is known of the character and theological positions of both men. [29]

Gay thoroughly enjoyed this kind of banter, but he drew a sharper line between private and public behavior than did some of his younger colleagues. He was particularly irritated by the unseemly exuberance and intemperate indulgence that accompanied ordinations. In 1759, the Annual Ministers' Convention passed a resolution against "Feasting, Jollity and Revelling at Ordinations." Gay fully concurred with the resolution, and spoke out on the subject in September of that year. The occasion was the ordination of yet another of his protégés into the South Shore ministry. Thomas Brown was the younger brother of the Reverend John Brown of Cohasset. After the death in 1742 of their father, the Reverend John Brown of Haverhill (Gay's Harvard classmate), Gay seemed to have assumed a special responsibility for the careers of both men. After his graduation in 1752, Thomas came to Hingham to study with Gay and prepare for his second degree. Like his brother John, Thomas Brown was openly Arminian, and Gay was able to settle him in the recently vacated Marshfield pulpit. Joseph Green, Jr., the former minister, had been an active member of the Hingham Association, but his promising career at Marshfield had ended abruptly when he was dismissed for getting drunk at a husking bee. Consequently, when Gay gave "The Right Hand of Fellowship" to Thomas Brown, the subject of intemperate behavior was on his mind. He asked the Marshfield congregation if it was "becoming Men and Christians, that the Day of a Gospel-Minister's Separation to the Holy Office, should be made a Play-Day with them; and the Evening and most of the Nights following, be spent in Revelings and Banquetings, in Chambering and Wantonness . . . ? Is it not a Pity, and a Shame, that the Ordination of Christ's Ministers should, in these Things, symbolize with the Consecration of the Priests of Bacchus?"[30]

Gay's fatherly concern for the welfare of young clerics often extended beyond the issue of their theological affiliation. In the 1750s, for instance, he became involved with Grindall Rawson, one of the strangest men who ever donned the black robe and Geneva bands. In 1754 Rawson (Harvard, 1741) left the isolated village of Ware (in central Massachusetts), where he had ministered for over six years, because of the inability of the parish to support him. A year later, he received a call to the First Church of Yarmouth, on Cape Cod. That congregation had just dismissed their minister, the Reverend Thomas Smith, at his own request "for want of support." Consequently, the installation of Grindall Rawson at Yarmouth had, as Clifford Shipton has put it, "something of the air of the marriage of divorced persons." Ebenezer Gay, for reasons that are unclear, was chosen to preach the sermon on this occasion (he may have become acquainted with Rawson during the latter's youth in Milton).[31]

Since the saints at Yarmouth were becoming infamous for losing ministers through their tight-fistedness, Gay's sermon, which he delivered on December 10, 1755, came right to the point. He entitled it *The Levite Not to be Forsaken*, and, lest any of the Yarmouthians miss the point, he made his analogy quite clear: "People should take heed to themselves, that they forsake not the Levite, their Minister, by a parsimonious withholding of due Maintenance from him." Gay bluntly told the congregation how often he had "seen here the Mischief of Strife with a Pastor, so often issuing in the Dissolution of [the pastoral] Relation." Their last minister, Thomas Smith, was an eloquent Old Light preacher whom Gay admired greatly, frequently inviting him to preach from the Old Ship pulpit. Smith's dismissal, he told them, "was wondered at and regretted by us at a Distance." After reminding the Yarmouth flock of their obligations, he warned Rawson, who had already displayed signs of being temperamentally unsuited for the ministry, that "it is now incumbent on you, to take heed unto your self, that you forsake not this People, by any straying Steps in the Course of your Ministry."[32]

Gay's advice was quickly forgotten, and within two years Grindall Rawson had personally alienated nearly every member of his congregation; by 1760 his ministry in Yarmouth had been terminated. Before he left town, this tall, ungainly man had married Desire Thacher, the daughter of a prominent citizen of Yarmouth. After his dismissal, Grindall and Desire went to live with his parents in Milton, and the marriage began to fall somewhat short of complete connubial bliss. In January of 1767 a neighbor saw Desire running out of the house with Rawson's father, Peletiah, in close pursuit. She fell in the snow where he "over took her and Called her many bad names, and told her She Should Go back with him, but She declared She would not, but would go to Mr. Gays, but the Said Rawson took her under his arm and dragged her home. And . . . Grindal Rawson Stood at the Door of the House lookin out." Obviously Gay had kept in close touch with this troubled young couple. The Rawson clan's abusive treatment of Desire intensified until, four years later, she left them and was eventually granted a divorce on grounds of cruelty. Rawson spent the remainder of his life keeping school and preaching in temporarily vacated pulpits in Massachusetts and New Hampshire. Wherever he went, "Old

Grin" quickly made enemies; one of them remarked that Rawson could get "no employment as a preacher, but where you are un-known, (and it seldom takes more than two Sabbaths to know you)." In 1793, the year before this curious, unpleasant man died, he published an edition of *The Levite Not to be Forsaken*, prefixed with a very moving account of Gay's death. Ebenezer Gay was, per-haps, the only stable and reassuring presence in Grindall Rawson's long and unhappy life.[33]

Gay's involvement in the life of Grindall Rawson serves as a necessary reminder that his interest in ecclesiastical affairs was not confined to the great struggle between Arminianism and revived Calvinism. Nevertheless, Gay's most significant achievement in the period from 1745 to 1760 was the transformation of the Old Light Weymouth Association into the Arminian Hingham Association. By 1760, there can be very little doubt that the Hingham Associa-tion was perceived, throughout New England, as a major force in promoting and defending the Arminian ministry. The Association, as we have seen, was not exclusively Arminian, including as it did Old Calvinists such as Stoughton's Samuel Dunbar, and moderate Calvinists such as the inoffensive Shearjashub Bourne of Scituate's First Church. Under Gay's leadership, the Association continued its traditional function of assisting and advising local pastors, main-taining discipline in South Shore parishes, adjusting ecclesiastical grievances, and so on. Within the Association, however, there was an inner group of ministers who were enthusiastically engaged in a reformation formulated on enlightened principles. Gay, Shute, Brown, Rand, and Hitchcock may not have been as outspoken as Jonathan Mayhew or Lemuel Briant, but they shared the same con-tempt for those Calvinist creeds and dogmas that seemed to have no scriptural or rational basis. They were trying to liberate New Englanders from, as Gay put it, "their prejudicate Opinions" and "any religious Principles which they received, with their vain Con-versation, by Traditions from their Fathers."[34]

As the religious conflicts of the 1750s intensified, the mem-bers of the Hingham Association received calls to participate in councils in western Massachusetts, Connecticut, or wherever an Arminian minister and his faction needed support. Gay usually led these delegations and when he could not come he frequently dis-patched one of his lieutenants. John Brown of Cohasset, for in-stance, traveled all the way to Wallingford, Connecticut, to help defend their newly installed pastor, the Reverend James Dana.

Dana's open contempt for Calvinist orthodoxy had offended the members of the powerful, New Light-dominated New Haven Consociation. "Bishop" Brown, ironically, invoked the principle of congregational autonomy in Dana's defense. Clearly, consociations and associations throughout New England had now largely become tools of the various religious factions.[35]

The greatest battle between Gay's Arminians and the forces of orthodoxy occurred in 1757, in the small, newly settled village of Leominster, a frontier settlement located in the rugged wilderness north of Worcester. For fourteen years, the minister of Leominster, the Reverend John Rogers, had been preaching a mild sort of Arminian gospel to his congregation. As the doctrinal debate over original sin sharpened in the 1750s, a fair number of his parishioners became "dissatisfyed with his Doctrine" (Rogers believed that outside agitators were responsible). The aggrieved brethren called an ecclesiastical council, which accused him, in so many words, of Arminian heresy, and the Rogers case quickly came to the attention of most of the major theological combatants of mid-century Massachusetts. John Rogers was the clerical John Scopes of his day, though his celebrity has understandably dimmed over the years. Clifford K. Shipton has been virtually alone among recent historians in fully appreciating the impact of the Leominster controversy.[36]

Rogers had been ordained over the new church at Leominster in 1743 by the Reverend Daniel Rogers of Littleton, one of Gay's first theology students. During the 1750s, John apparently began reading the works of Clarke, Whitby, and Taylor, or he absorbed them indirectly through their American champions. He made the mistake of endorsing the theology of the English liberals in four sermons published in 1756 and 1757. The last of these, entitled *The Nature and Necessity of Spiritual Conversion*, brought his neighbor, the Reverend Elisha Marsh of Westminster, to grief simply for recommending it. Rogers declared unequivocally in that sermon that "'the Voice of Reason' was 'the Voice of God.'" Cotton Mather had written precisely the same thing in 1711, but such sentiments were near blasphemous to post-Awakening Calvinists. The dissident faction in Rogers's church asked him to join with them in calling a council to investigate his theology, but he adamantly refused. He argued, rightly, that ecclesiastical councils had become instruments for intellectual oppression. Rogers reportedly said that "it was not the business of Councils to Determin Matters of faith . . . and besides he knew it was moraly imposable at ye present to get a council of honist men." These remarks accord with a letter that he later wrote, protesting the plans of the dissidents to summon a council. He asked how "the Vote of any Council under Heaven" could presume to determine religious truth for "a sober rational Creature . . . For every man is Commended by the Scripture to Study the whole if it himself and to Judge for himself comparing all Doctrines with that." Allowing a council to intrude upon this right of private judgement, Rogers declared "is directly opposite to the . . . principles of Protestants." Here was a man fully caught up in the Arminian reformation.[37]

The aggrieved brethren, unimpressed with Rogers's arguments, proceeded to call a council of fifteen churches to meet on July 26, 1757. The council, as Rogers had anticipated, was far from being an impartial body. The leading member was that zealous Edwardsean and Presbyterian, Ebenezer Pemberton, pastor at Boston's New Brick Church. Pemberton had recently taken up arms against Jonathan Mayhew, in response to the latter's criticism of the Athanasian Trinity. This latest heresy of Mayhew's was still fresh in the delegates' minds. The council also included Samuel Dunbar of Stoughton, Gay's antagonist in the Hingham Association, and Nathan Stone of Southborough, a merciless stalker of Arminians. With the important exception of Pemberton, however, the council was not composed of Calvinist radicals; they were moderate, Old Light Calvinists who had now come to fear the deistical drift of Arminianism more than they feared the disruptive behavior of the New Lights. The Reverend Peter Clark of Danvers, for instance, was no Edwardsean, but he was in the middle of a pamphlet war with the Reverend Samuel Webster, in which Clark was defending the doctrine of original sin. Clark was not at all happy that John Rogers had just given, in print, "his full approbation and Recommendation" of Webster's pamphlet, *A Winter Evening's Conversation*, a piece that assailed the doctrines of imputed guilt and total depravity. This conservative assembly "with the utmost Regret," charged Rogers with denying the doctrine of original sin, with preaching Arminian views on the nature of conversion, and with casting "most indecent and unchristian reflection on the shorter Catechism." They even suggested that he was flirting with Socinianism (a theology that denied the divinity of Christ). All forty-one delegates on the council accepted this guilty verdict, and recommended that the Leominster Church give Rogers three months to reform before reconvening the council.[38]

John Rogers had no intention of retracting what the council had defined as "Doctrinal Errors." The council reconvened on November 9, only to find Rogers and his supporters resolutely determined to resist their recommendations. The council now voted, again with unanimity, that Rogers should be suspended for two months and, if he did not retract his errors in that time, the pastoral relation should be dissolved. The Leominster Parish voted to act on this advice, but Rogers refused to acknowledge their action, trying to force his way into the pulpit on three successive Sundays. Samuel Dunbar, an equally vigorous combatant, was one of two pastors who preached in his place. Losing all patience with Rogers, the aggrieved brethren moved to recall the council in three days, instead of two months, for the purpose of dismissing their pastor. Accordingly, the exhausted delegates assembled once again, but this time they admonished the members of the anti-Rogers faction for their unseemly haste, advising them that a permanent separation could only be brought about by a mutual council. Interestingly, Jonathan Mayhew suddenly appeared as the scribe of the last session. The Arminians were starting to rally to Rogers's defense.[39]

Rogers's supporters decided to fight fire with fire, and, instead of agreeing to a mutual council, they called in a council of their own. In December, the Arminian heavy artillery began to roll into town. Ebenezer Gay with his South Shore elite corps—John Brown, Daniel Shute, and William Rand, together with Charles Chauncy and Jonathan Mayhew, all convened in Leominster to defend the cause of intellectual liberty and rational religion. They proceeded, as a member of the first council put it, to make "a loud Complaint . . . against the proceedings of the aggrieved Brethren of the Church in Leominster and our Councils, in abetting them & condemning Mr. Rogers." No direct record of the proceedings of this second council has survived, but they apparently decided to contest the legality of the actions already taken against Rogers. One of Rogers's clerical opponents declared that "a principal Article in the Protestation of Mr. Gay, Rand, Mayhew, &c . . . against the Result of the Council there was without grounds; nay it was opposite to the Truths."[40]

Besides protesting the unfair treatment accorded Rogers, Gay and Mayhew may well have suggested the next move that the pro-Rogers faction made. They laid a petition before the Province Council urging that Leominster be divided into two parishes—in effect a denominational action establishing a liberal church and an orthodox church in this small village. The town of Leominster was understandably reluctant to agree to this division, and the pro-Rogers group finally took the matter to court. By 1759, the scene of the Rogers controversy had shifted from Leominster to the Superior Court sitting at Worcester. The great clergymen of the day gave place to the great lawyers of the day. Instead of being defended by Gay, Mayhew, and Chauncy, Rogers now relied on James Otis and Robert Auchmuty, with Jeremy Gridley and Oxenbridge Thacher representing the town. After several reverses, John Rogers and his supporters prevailed, and, on February 18, 1762, the Second Parish of Leominster was officially created.[41]

By the late 1750s, the more radical Arminian clergy in New England had formed a religious party that was every bit as coherent as any of the post-Awakening New Light factions. The adherents of this party were men like Gay who had tired of trying to adjust their Calvinist heritage to the world of their real intellectual allegiance—the world of Locke, Newton, and a rational, benevolent deity; there were also the younger men such as Mayhew and Briant who did not even feel the need to attempt the reconciliation. With the zeal of true reformers, the Arminians had set about trying to free New England's Church from the bondage of Calvinist theology by appealing directly to the scriptures and to the practices of the primitive Christian church. They were happily convinced, as David Barnes of Scituate put it, that Christ and his apostles "were not enthusiasts." Nowhere did the adherents of this Arminian gospel, which Yale President Thomas Clap called the "New Scheme of Divinity," flourish more vigorously than on the South Shore. Under Ebenezer Gay's leadership, the Hingham Association had become a center for the advancement and defense of rational religion. Gay's achievement became all the more important since Boston was still dominated by the orthodox Old Guard, men who were determined to stamp out the Arminian heresy before it led the ministers of the province into Arianism, deism, or worse. Mayhew and Chauncy, then, were forced to look for support in the country, and Gay's association provided that support.[42]

By the time of the Rogers controversy, the Arminian clergy had completely and publicly broken with their more orthodox Old Light allies. Gay was no longer pleading for unity, as he had done

in his 1746 Convention Sermon. The cause of truth, as both orthodox and Arminian factions understood that truth, had become
more important than outward displays of clerical solidarity. Gay
had clearly been more interested in vindicating John Rogers and
championing the cause of rational Christianity in central Massachusetts, than in attempting to restore peace and religious order to
the divided little town of Leominster. Ebenezer Gay had organized
and rallied a strong Arminian force; it now remained for him to
define more precisely the cause for which it was fighting.

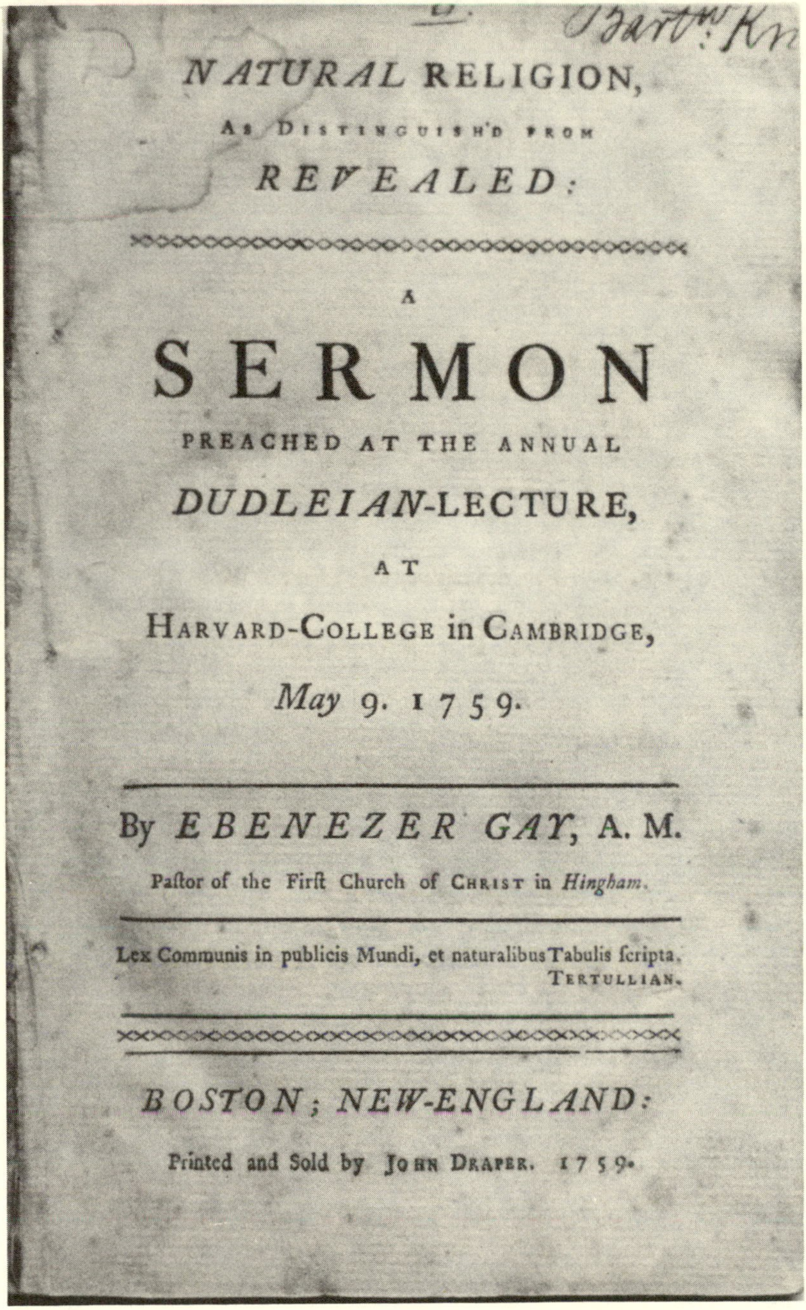

*NATURAL* RELIGION,

As Distinguish'd from

*REVEALED*:

A

# SERMON

PREACHED AT THE ANNUAL

*DUDLEIAN*-LECTURE,

AT

HARVARD-COLLEGE in CAMBRIDGE,

*May* 9. 1 7 5 9.

By *EBENEZER GAY*, A. M.

Paſtor of the Firſt Church of CHRIST in *Hingham.*

Lex Communis in publicis Mundi, et naturalibus Tabulis ſcripta.
TERTULLIAN.

*BOSTON; NEW-ENGLAND*:

Printed and Sold by JOHN DRAPER. 1 7 5 9.

The title page of Ebenezer Gay's Dudleian Lecture on Natural Religion, printed in 1759 (courtesy of Mr. Ebenezer Gay of Hingham).

Portrait of Martin Gay, Boston coppersmith, son of Ebenezer Gay; a copy of an original by an unknown artist (courtesy of Mr. Ebenezer Gay of Hingham).

Portrait of Charles Chauncy, minister of Boston's First Church (1727–87), painted by an unknown artist (Massachusetts Historical Society, Boston).

Portrait of Jonathan Mayhew, minister of Boston's West Church (1747–66), painted between 1747 and 1752 by John Greenwood (Congregational Library, Boston).

# CHAPTER IX

# The Father of Lights

Under Gay's leadership, the Hingham Association became the ecclesiastical center of the Arminian movement, but outside the safe harbor of the South Shore, Arminianism encountered heavier seas. In the immediate post-Awakening years, the great debate between Arminians and Calvinists centered on the role that human initiative played in justifying men before God. The character of the debate did not really change in the 1750s, but rather it intensified, generating some brilliant and impassioned controversial literature concerning the doctrines of grace. There were some occasional flurries of alarm over more exotic heresies. Jonathan Mayhew created a great uproar with a volume of sermons published in 1755 in which he criticized those who rigidly adhered to the Athanasian doctrine of the Trinity. The furor occasioned by Mayhew's observations reached all the way to the Indian mission at Stockbridge where Jonathan Edwards fretted about "Dr. Mayhew's late book, . . . wherein he ridicules the doctrine of the Trinity." Mayhew, however, had not published that collection of sermons with the purpose of launching an attack on the Trinity. Instead his intent had been to carry on the crusade begun by his "martyred" friend Lemuel Briant—a vigorous insistence upon the importance of moral virtue in obtaining salvation.[1]

By 1757 the Arminian-Calvinist debate was back on track, fueled by a new attack on the doctrine of original sin—a tract published anonymously by the Reverend Samuel Webster of Salisbury entitled *A Winter Evening's Conversation*. Webster had relied heavily on John Taylor's *Scripture Doctrine of Original Sin* (1738). Taylor's work, as we have seen, had become the basic text for every clergy-

169

man who could not accept the Calvinist teaching that men were totally depraved. Therefore, when neo-Calvinism's great champion,
Jonathan Edwards, responded to Webster's tract, he directed his reply to "*the Objections and Arguings of Dr. John Taylor.*" Edwards's brilliant *The Great Christian Doctrine of Original Sin Defended* (1758) laid
bare the heart of the differing world views that separated Arminians and Calvinists. Arminian theology revolved around the individual. Each man was capable of influencing his spiritual destiny,
unconstrained by imputed guilt from Adam's sin, or by a totally
corrupt bias that impelled men by necessity to do evil; guilt was entirely a personal matter. Each individual had his own separate covenant with God, and salvation was essentially a matter of fulfilling
the terms of the contract. The terms of man's justification were
clearly laid down in the Scriptures so that, as Jonathan Mayhew put
it, "those who comply therewith, are justified of course, upon such
completion." The Arminian image of the self-reliant pilgrim striving for salvation stands in marked contrast to Edwards's portrait of
a soul, merged in the corporate depravity of all souls, whose destiny is entirely dependent on God's sovereign pleasure. In his book,
Edwards defended the imputation of Adam's guilt to his posterity,
by advancing the theory (based on Locke) that God, who arbitrarily
sustains the identity of things through successive moments in time,
decreed that the human race should be as one. Adam and his
posterity were one complex person. Intellectual historian John
Herman Randall called Calvinism "the most medieval of all the
Protestant systems," and certainly, as Jonathan Edwards interpreted its dogmas, it was not a system that encouraged a modern
sense of individuality.[2]

   Edwards and Mayhew were not only clarifying the great
points of disagreement between the Arminians and the Calvinists,
they were also (with the help of a great many other controversial-
ists) laying down party platforms—partisan ideologies that would
serve, to quote Perry Miller, as "the instrument of a group, or of an
interest." The annual convention of ministers in Boston had become a political battleground between these two great factions and
the smaller groups that gravitated toward one or the other. The
leadership of the Calvinist faction at the convention, however, was
not entrusted to Edwards or his disciples, but to that old Puritan,
Joseph Sewall, senior minister at Boston's Old South Church. Unlike Gay, his friend of former years, the venerable Dr. Sewall had
remained faithful to the spirit of his mentor, Cotton Mather. To-

gether with his zealous comrade Ebenezer Pemberton of Boston's New Brick Church, Sewall sought to defend the orthodox cause from the machinations of Mayhew, Chauncy, and Gay.[3]

The Reverend Ebenezer Parkman, a moderate Calvinist from Westborough, kept an exceptionally detailed diary that allows us an occasional behind-the-scenes look at the convention battles. At the 1756 convention we find the two parties squabbling over the choice of the Clerk of the Convention. According to Parkman, "Mr. Pemberton was thought to be chose, but upon Second Trial it appeared otherwise. Then Dr. Mayhew was nominated by Mr. Williams of Sandwich [Abraham Williams, who once argued that a religion that taught the doctrine of original sin could hardly be rational] and though it was opposed by some, & Dr. Sewall particularly bore his Testimony against it, yet he was the man." At the 1758 convention Parkman observed Chauncy and Gay conferring together. He then takes us into the home of Pemberton where Samuel Wigglesworth, John Chipman, and Nathan Stone, three veteran and implacable foes of Arminianism "are projecting to have the ministers of the orthodox Side (as we speak) to meet the day after Commencement to See if nothing can be done for support of the Truth, against the ill-boding aspects of the present Day."[4]

The Arminian party had an effective, though publicly discreet, chairman in Charles Chauncy, and a vigorous polemicist in Jonathan Mayhew, but they lacked a philosopher like Edwards—a respected intellectual who could provide them with a coherent sense of purpose and theological identity. Chauncy was certainly capable of the task, as the works he published late in life indicate, but he had not yet produced a systematic exposition of rational, Arminian Christianity. Mayhew had come much closer to providing a complete theological framework in his *Seven Sermons* (1749) and *On Hearing the Word* (1755), but he was considered too radical to be accepted as a sober, responsible theologian. In 1759, Ebenezer Gay was given a splendid opportunity to provide the Arminians with a platform on which to stand, and he made the most of it. Although he certainly lacked the intellectual creativity of Edwards (the Arminians never did find a champion equal to him), Gay was about to become the philosopher of Massachusetts rationalism.

The forum for Gay's *tour de force* was the fifth annual Dudleian Lecture at Harvard. Paul Dudley, the Chief Justice of the Province (the same aristocratic, young Attorney-General who had attended Gay's ordination) had died in 1751, leaving a foundation

for a series of lectures on theology. He had stipulated that the subjects be: Natural Religion; Revealed Religion; the Errors of Popery;
and the Validity of Non-Episcopal Ordination. Each was to be expounded in an annual rotation. With some early exceptions, the
Dudleian lectures tended to be assigned to men of liberal, catholic
views. The Trustees of the Lecture soon came under fire from the
"orthodox party" for their liberal bias. Consequently, in 1759, they
rather disingenuously asked the Reverend Dr. Joseph Sewall to deliver the second Lecture on Natural Religion, a subject in which
that rigid Old Calvinist had never exhibited the least interest.
Sewall, not surprisingly, refused to have anything to do with the
lecture, and so the Trustees were free to find a speaker to whom
the topic would be more congenial. Charles Chauncy, who had
been in Hingham recently, may have sounded out Gay on delivering the next Lecture, and certainly for two of the Trustees, President Holyoke and Nathaniel Appleton, Gay would have seemed a
perfect choice. On February 7, 1759 the Trustees voted "That in
case Dr. Sewall upon further application to him, shall still refuse to
preach the above said lecture, the Reverend Mr. Gay of Hingham
be, & at this meeting was unanimously chosen to preach the next
Dudleian Lecture." Gay was so notified and, within two weeks,
wrote to President Holyoke to accept the honor.[5]

So it was that Gay returned to Harvard College on May 9,
1759, to deliver what James W. Jones, in his *Shattered Synthesis*, has
called a *locus classicus* of liberalism. The rationalism that Gay had
imbibed at Leverett's Harvard forty-five years before had since
been purified by his reading in the works of English liberals such as
Samuel Clarke and John Taylor. While these had confirmed him in
his rationalist rejection of Calvinism, the Great Awakening of the
1740s had persuaded him that his tendency to separate the rational
faculties from the emotions was entirely correct. From that point
on he was determined that Reason, "man's original excellence, the
most eminent distinction and glory of his nature," must never "be
subjected to the Sway of brutish Appetites and blind Passions."
There was no role for the emotions in understanding God. Now
the sixty-three-year-old parson from Hingham was about to sum
up his theological and ethical convictions in a lecture that itself was
a model of rational clarity, though not devoid of eloquence, wit,
and even some passion.[6]

Gay made his purpose clear at the outset of the lecture: "The
Belief of GOD's Existence . . . having been at the first of the Dud-

leian Lectures established; the moral Obligation which it induceth upon the Nature of Man, may be the Subject of our present Inquiry." This was to be a lecture about Arminianism and its relationship to rational religion. Indeed, Gay defined natural religion in Arminian terms: "The Religion which is possible to be discover'd by the Light, and practis'd by the Power of Nature, consists in rend'ring all those inward and outward Acts of Respect, Worship and Obedience unto God, which are suitable to the Excellence of his all-perfect Nature.[7]

The first step in the path to Arminian enlightenment was to be convinced "of the Existence and Attributes of God." This, however, was no great problem, for "The Characters of the Deity are plainly legible in the whole Creation around us." One had but to exercise their reason, the highest "Faculty of the human Soul . . . in the Contemplation of the universal Frame of Nature." If one would simply reflect upon the "exquisite Order among the Stars," one would have "a clear and incontestable Proof of One original Being, the divine Architect and Ruler of the Universe." Gay believed that this *a posteriori* argument for God's existence and perfection was more comprehensible and more convincing to "the Bulk of Mankind" than the *a priori* argument from first cause. Indeed, nothing had buttressed Gay's own faith quite so much as his readings in the works of the English "physico-theologians," William Derham, John Ray, and William Whiston, all of which upheld the argument from design. One did not, according to Gay, have to be a Harvard-trained scholar to appreciate the force of this evidence, for it was "plain to the lowest Capacity of those who, with a little Attention, survey the Works of God, that he is a Being of such Perfection."[8]

The argument from design, though it did not especially tax one's intellectual resources, was nevertheless a rational way of apprehending God's existence. The Understanding, as always, was Gay's starting point in approaching the Divine, and by the Understanding he meant the rational, cognitive faculties of the mind and not what Jonathan Edwards would call the Affections. It was not through the emotions (which Gay, unlike Edwards, defined narrowly as passions) but rather through Reason that man "was fitted to contemplate the perfections, and celebrate the praises of his . . . almighty maker; and in which he resembled God, who is the supreme and most perfect reason." Reason enabled the better minds not only to infer the existence of God, but also to deduce the difference between right and wrong that was inherent "in the Nature

and Relations of Things." Gay declared that "There is an essential
Difference between Good and Evil, Right and Wrong . . . which the
Understanding (if made use of) cannot but discern." In short, God
"publishes [his Law] to rational Creatures . . . in making them capable to learn from his Works, what is good and what is required of
them."[9]

In proposing that man could distinguish between right and
wrong through the use of his reason, Gay was directly echoing
Locke and Samuel Clarke. The Arminians' debt to rational, Lockean psychology was explicitly affirmed by Gay's colleague and disciple, Gad Hitchcock of Pembroke, in his own Dudleian Lecture
delivered in 1779: "The opinion of innate ideas and principles,
which prevailed for so long a time, is now, almost, universally given
up; and that of the human mind receiving them afterwards distinct
and simple . . . is adapted in its room, as the original of knowledge." The truth was, however, that the Arminians had not entirely
given up the "opinion of innate ideas and principles," but instead
believed that rationality had another, deeper dimension than
Locke's empirical understanding. Gay spoke of it at the outset of
his sermon when he was describing the ways in which men acquire
knowledge of their spiritual obligations: "And if we open the Volume of our own Nature, and look within, we find there a Law written;—a Rule of virtuous practice prescribed." This innate moral
sense lay closer to the core of Gay's faith in natural religion than
even the deductive powers of the rational faculties. He declared
that in "the due Exercise of their natural Faculties, Men are capable
of attaining some Knowledge of God's Will, and their Duty, . . .
as if it were written in legible Characters on the Tables of their
Hearts." Gay's introductory scripture text for the lecture was a passage from Romans in which St. Paul makes the case for natural religion: "For when the Gentiles, which have not the Law, do by
Nature the Things contained in the Law; these having not the Law,
are a Law unto themselves: Which shew the Work of the Law written in their Hearts."[10]

The concept of the inner moral sense was certainly not a new
one. In 1716, John Norton, Gay's predecessor in the Hingham
pulpit, had spoken of the moral law which "is written in the hearts
or natures of all the children of men." Benjamin Colman and
Solomon Stoddard, prominent New England ministers in Gay's
younger days, had also acknowledged this moral sense, badly cor-

rupted though they believed it to be. The moral faculty was the foundation of the ethical theory of Anthony Ashley Cooper, third Earl of Shaftesbury (1671–1713), a stylish, proto-deistic writer of the early century. Shaftesbury's opinions were too radical for the New England clergy to digest directly (even Mayhew thought he was an atheist) but his teachings were carried on and modified by Francis Hutcheson (1694–1746), a Scottish philosopher who was far more palatable to New Englanders. Charles Chauncy cited Hutcheson in one of his sermons, and it was clear that Gay and Mayhew were heavily indebted to him. Hutcheson attempted to interpret the moral sense in Lockean terms, but these two forms of rationalism did not quite mix. Gay's fellow clergyman, Gad Hitchcock, showed his confusion when, in one lecture he declared that: (1) "We can have no conception of knowledge in man . . . but that which is made up of ideas gradually admitted, and properly ordered by the understanding." (Lockean epistemology.) (2) "I am inclined to think that natural religion is . . . properly defined . . . that which reason sees to be right, and feels the force of when it is known." (The Shaftesburian moral sense.) Jonathan Mayhew, on the other hand, clearly separated the two faculties: "Our Creator, besides endowing us with reason to distinguish betwixt moral good and evil, has moreover given us another faculty, which is sometimes called a moral sense."[11]

This inner moral sense, a rough equivalent of Freud's "superego," has been described as a sort of innate rationalism, and yet it transcended reason. The concept received its first full expression in the works of the Cambridge Platonists, a group of Restoration latitudinarians who were trying to anchor the Church of England firmly between radical Protestant "enthusiasm" and Roman Catholic "superstition." They referred to this innate rationality as the "candle of the Lord," a concept which was at once Platonic in conveying a belief in an abstract, ideal reason, and also mystic, suggesting a divine, inner presence. One of the Platonists, Henry More, wrote in his *Enchiridion Ethicum* (required reading when Gay was at Harvard) that Nature's law is "a whisper of the divine law. . . . The ideas of good and evil, which Reason approves but did not create, are immutable, and in logical order prior even to God. They become God's thoughts, and man's knowledge of them comes from participation in His Mind." Here was an inner light for the Arminians, rational and unchanging. Indeed, this moral sense provided "an inward Spring of Motion and Action, when Reason alone would not give sufficient Quickness and Vigour in pursuing its Dictates."[12]

Gay advanced his interpretation of the moral sense in the context of the Newtonian universe, and the result was a passage of cosmic imagery:

> There may be something in the intelligent moral World analogous to Attraction in the material System—something that inclines and draws Men toward God, the Centre of their Perfection, and consummate Object of their Happiness; and which, if its Energy were not obstructed, would as certainly procure such Regularity in the States and Actions of all intelligent Beings in the spiritual World, as that of Attraction doth in the Positions and Motions of all the Bodies in the material World.

Here was a fascinating blend of Newtonian science, social attitudes, and an almost oriental mysticism. The forces of gravity and magnetism became, for Gay, metaphors for the transcendence and unity of God, the "SUPREME INFINITE." He specifically acknowledged the source of that particular name for the deity: "Created intelligent Beings (says Dr. Cheyne) are images of the SUPREME INFINITE, as he calleth God." George Cheyne (1671–1743) was a Scottish physician and mathematician whose *Philosophical Principles of Religion: Natural and Revealed* (1715) was widely read in New England. The work, on one level, was simply another production of the physico-theology school, but Cheyne had a mystic bent that permeated his thought. His sense of the infinite was based on mathematical principles, allying him with a tradition that has extended from Pythagoras to Einstein, although Sir Leslie Stephen, the fastidious Victorian editor of the *Dictionary of National Biography*, described Cheyne's mingling of theology and mathematics as "too fantastic to bear exposition." Far from finding it fantastic, Gay was clearly moved and inspired by Cheyne's vision.[13]

Gay's close friend and colleague, Daniel Shute of South Hingham, described the moral sense as "The instinct, or propensity, implanted in the human species leading them, as it were mechanically, to *that* to which they are morally obliged." How much more eloquent was Gay's description of our "Attraction" toward God:

> An intelligent Being, coming out of the Hands of infinite Perfection, with an Aversion, or even Indifferency, to be reunited with its Author, the Source of its utmost Felicity, is such a Shock, and Deformity

in the beautiful Analogy of Things, such a Breach and Gap in the harmonious Uniformity, observable in all the Works of the Almighty . . . as is not consistent with finite Wisdom and Perfection, much less with the supremely infinite Wisdom of the ALL-PERFECT.[14]

Having expressed this enlightened vision of a benevolent, merciful, rational deity whose spirit was implanted in the breasts of all intelligent beings, Gay angrily denounced those irrational doctrines which obscured that vision. He argued, using Locke's postulate, that any principle of religion that was clearly contrary to reason must be rejected. He admitted that those who believed in irrational creeds and dogmas usually pointed to the scriptures as their inspiration. This, said Gay, did not mean that Holy Writ was irrational, but rather that its interpreters, either through "Ignorance or Misapprehension of Things hard to be understood in . . . the holy Bible," had erred. He insisted that "Absurdities and Contradictions (from which few human schemes are entirely free) are not to be obtruded upon our Faith. No Pretence of Revelation can be sufficient for the Admission of them." Then, in a thinly veiled attack on the Calvinists, Gay declared:

> To say, in Defence of any religious Tenets, reduced to Absurdity, that the Perfections of God, his Holiness, Justice, Goodness, are quite different Things in Him, from what, in an infinitely lower Degree, they are in Men, is to overthrow all Religion both natural and revealed; and make our Faith, as well as Reason vain. For, if we have no right Notions of the Deity, (as 'tis certain, upon this Supposition we have none,) as we worship, so we believe, we know not what or why.[15]

If Gay was to make the Arminian case effectively, he had to do more than snipe at the irrationality of Calvinist dogma; he had to grapple, at least in passing, with the arguments of Arminianism's most articulate foe, Jonathan Edwards. The heart of the Arminian gospel might be stated thus: Men are naturally capable not only of knowing what their moral duties are, but are also capable of performing them. They are able to choose between one course of action and another and, given sufficient rational persuasion, they will choose the right course.

Jonathan Edwards, on the other hand, argued in his *Freedom of the Will* (1754) that the rational faculties were so irreparably corrupt that the unregenerate man would always go astray. This was what incensed the Arminians generally, and Gay was no exception. Moral accountability was the keystone of his preaching, and he had always insisted that men must be free to choose; he could hardly exhort his flock to behave virtuously if they were capable only of doing evil. Therefore he eagerly challenged Edwards's attack on freedom of choice by declaring that the existence of individual initiative was self-evident. He also, characteristically, evaded the philosophical sticking points:

> Man is not merely so much lumpish Matter, or a *mechanical* Engine, that moves only by the Direction of an impelling Force; but [here Gay borrows directly from Samuel Clarke] he hath a Principle of Action within himself, and is an Agent in the Strict and proper Sense of the Word. The special Endowment of his Nature, which constitutes him such, is the Power of Self-determination, or Freedom of Choice; his being possessed of which is as self-evident, as the Explanation of the Manner of its operating is difficult.[16]

Clearly, said Gay, Man "feels himself free to act one Way, or another: And as he is capable of distinguishing between Actions of the moral Kind; so he is likewise of chusing which he will do, and which leave undone." Thus far Gay sounded as though he were in agreement with the English rationalist, Daniel Whitby, who wrote that men were free "from Necessity, or a Determination to one, i.e. to Good or Evil only." Gay, however, went a half step beyond Whitby's principle of innate moral neutrality, declaring that men had an inherent inclination to virtue: "human Nature . . . was designed and framed for the Practice of Virtue." Although men had complete freedom of choice, Gay said, "Further to qualify our Nature for Virtuous or religious Practice (which must necessarily be of Choice) the Author of it hath annexed a secret Joy or Complacence of Mind to such Practice, and as sensible a Pain or Displicence to the contrary." The failure to perform acts of "human Kindness" or to attend divine worship was "a painful Restraint upon Nature; and to do the contrary, is thwarting its Inclination, and wresting it from its bent." Gay was not reversing the Edwardsean position by declaring that men were free only to do good, but he made it very clear that most men and women were gravitating toward God and not toward the devil.[17]

Man's salvation, according to Gay, begins with this natural bent toward holiness. The "Impression of the divine Image and Law" still existed in human nature, and "Even in its lapsed Estate: There are still in it . . . 'some *legible Characters*, *Out-lines*, and *Lineaments* of its Beauty; some *magnificent Ruins*, which shew what it had been.'" In Gay's soteriology, the justifying grace made available to men through Christ's atonement was only the final step. As Gay put it, God's formation of men "qualifys them, in a measure, for religious Practice, as his Regeneration, or Renovation of them doth more so." The key word here is "Renovation." James W. Jones, in *The Shattered Synthesis*, has correctly observed that "where the Calvinists saw a gap between nature and grace, the liberals saw only continuity." Gay described Christ's spirit as "helping the Infirmities of our Nature," rather like a booster shot into eternal life. In a later sermon he explained that "The grace of God . . . doth not obliterate, but exceedingly brightens, what remains of the natural image of God, since the fall." Using an educational metaphor borrowed from Hugo Grotius, Gay declared that "The Law of Nature, like that of *Moses*, may be serviceable unto Men, *as a SchoolMaster to bring them to Christ*, for higher Instruction." Although Gay admitted that men cannot yield perfect obedience to the Law, and that it "is only by Grace that sinful Men can be saved," yet he thought it nonsense to assert that "whatever Improvement and Progress man made in natural Religion, he was not a Step nearer the Kingdom of God."[18]

Gay and his fellow Arminians could simply not abide the idea that decent, well-educated New England gentlemen were utterly incapable of winning at least a slight smile of approval from God. In Gay's theology, salvation was offered to all men, but on an individual, competitive basis. The exercise of virtue, said Gay, should not be dismissed as filthy rags, for it "makes an important difference among men. 'The righteous is more excellent than his neighbors.'" Gay, then, in rejecting Calvinistic election, was not substituting a universal salvation that guaranteed sweet, heavenly immortality to all, but rather insisting that there was universal access to heaven for those with the intellectual and moral stamina to make it.[19]

This new "Elect," the men who could win God's favor through their own natural ability, was in many respects a more exclusive club than the Calvinist elect. Conrad Wright has argued that the Arminian elect was roughly coterminous with the financial elite of Massachusetts, and that their standards for membership resembled those of a fraternal society of Boston merchants. In 1779 the Reverend Simeon Howard, Gay's student and Mayhew's successor at Boston West, described the form of this society: "Is it not proper that persons should in a public, formal manner be initiated into the society of Christians; and that after they are members, they should by some significant rite distinguishing them from other persons, commemorate the love and goodness of their *founder*?" If Howard tended to confuse the church of Christ with Boston's select Wednesday Evening Club, he was only following in the spirit of Gay, his mentor. In 1766, Gay had asked the aspiring young merchants of Mayhew's church, "How amiable and honorable a society should the church of Christ . . . appear to us? Who may not be ambitious of joining to it, and being counted a member of it?"[20]

Although Gay's Arminian elect was composed of men with a great measure of natural ability, it cannot be exactly equated with Jefferson's "natural aristocracy of talent and virtue"; still less can it be closely compared to the egalitarian, Jacksonian faith in the virtue of the common man. All three, of course, are related, but they reflect different stages of social evolution. Gay was still too much a part of the eighteenth-century world of well-defined social hierarchies to concede that equal capabilities might exist in all classes. His friend Mayhew was quite candid on this point, declaring that he did not believe "that all men have *equal abilities* for judging what is true and right. . . . Those of the the lower class can get but a little ways in their inquiries into the natural and moral constitutions of the world." The perfect philosophical expression of the eighteenth-century social order was the "Great Chain of Being." In his Dudleian Lecture, Gay made it clear that the God of nature, "by creating and establishing a World of Beings in such Order, as he hath done," had limited the capacity of those beings to understand Him and His Law, according to their place on the chain. His South Hingham colleague, Daniel Shute, made it clear that the chain did not merely rank different species, but it also included "somewhat similar gradation in the same species, arising from their make, their connections, and the circumstances they are placed in."[21]

Among the various gradations of humanity, successful merchants occupied a fairly high place, but even they took a back seat to the scholar. The logic here is fairly straightforward. All men were prompted toward virtue by their moral sense, but a clear understanding of God and His Law, natural and revealed, could only be acquired by those who could read and evaluate the Scriptures or Newton's *Principia*. Gad Hitchcock noted simply that all men do not have "the same quantity of reason, and therefore could not all have the same quantity of natural religion." The New England Arminians seemed tacitly to assume that the educated clergy stood just below the angels in the order of creation. Alan Heimert has described the heaven of Charles Chauncy as "a sort of glorified Harvard graduate school," but even Chauncy did not approach the explicit intellectual elitism which permeated Gay's description of the various degrees of sanctification:

> Largeness of understanding, quickness of apprehension, soundness of judgement, depth and compass of learning are embellishments of a sanctified soul, and make a great difference between the subjects of regeneration. . . . So far as a man's intellectual abilities and attainments are superior to others, he may, upon his receiving of grace, out-strip them, as a disciple of Jesus, and be advanced to a higher form in the school of Christ.[22]

Arminian theology rested on the assumption that men were capable of self-improvement, a concept that implied such a continuous progress in knowledge and virtue that perfection could be approached. Gad Hitchcock described this process in intellectual terms: "the larger the stock of science in any mind, the better it is able to advance; the farther it goes, the farther it may go . . . and the progress might be endless." Gay himself expressed the Arminians' sanguine vision of man's prospects on several occasions, always reiterating his belief that sanctification was a continuous process. Gay's optimism may have been ancestral to nineteenth-century perfectionism, but it was not the same. He may have pictured mankind confidently striding toward perfection, but he never assumed that their arrival would be imminent.[23]

Having argued for the validity and, indeed, the primacy of natural religion, Gay concluded his Dudleian Lecture on a cautionary note. He urged his young listeners "To form a just Estimate of Natural Religion; and guard against the dangerous Extremes in our Regards to it—Not to have a debasing, nor a too exalted Notion of it." Gay's warning to hold to this middle verity was by no means a new one. Ever since 1702, when the English deist, John Toland, published his *Christianity not Mysterious*, both the orthodox and the liberal religious parties in New England had been nervously on their guard against deism. The orthodox ministers suspected the liberal-Arminians of drifting into deism, and the Arminians themselves worried that perhaps they were doing just that. Roland Stromberg, in his *Religious Liberalism in Eighteenth-Century England*, notes that, in fact, Toland's deistic ideas were "taken up and exploited by a very few men, who succeeded in making a noise out of all proportion to their numbers and even their talents." In mid-eighteenth-century New England, an actual deist was a *rara avis*, though John Adams claimed to have found a few in Worcester in 1755. The fear of deism was based not on a present reality, but on what the Arminian drift seemed to portend.[24]

In order to confute the deists, who argued that natural religion was sufficient, the Arminians had to establish the need for supernatural revelation. Gay argued that there were two reasons why God had vouchsafed man a divine revelation. The first reason was, simply put, that God needed to get Adam off on the right foot; therefore, Gay argued, Adam had the benefit of revelation from the beginning:

> Had Man, with all his natural Endowments in their perfect Order and Strength, been placed in this World, and no Notice given him of its Maker, might he not have stood wondering some Time at the amazing Fabrick, before he would have thence, by Deductions of Reason, argued an invisible Being of eternal Power, Wisdom, and Goodness, to be the Author of it and him; to whom he was therefore obliged to pay all Regards suitable to such glorious Excellencies? Would he so soon and easily have made those Discoveries, which are necessary to the Perfection of natural Religion . . .?

Adam, then, needed a revelation to hasten his discovery of his duties and obligations, but why did revelation continue to be necessary? The reason was that Adam's fall and, as David Barnes of Scituate put it, "that universal corruption of manners which took place soon after," dimmed the light of nature and the divine image in the soul of man. Adam's fall from grace, said Gay, "greatly alter'd the Case, with respect to him, and his Posterity, and made Revelation a necessary Supplement . . . for the Discovery and Performance of acceptable and available Religion." Our rational nature was so "disorder'd and debilitated" by Adam's apostasy that, without the help of revelation, the generality of men would know little more than "*natural brute Beasts.*"[25]

In this same vein, Gay argued that the ethical and moral philosophy of the deists owed less to the religion of nature than to the very scriptures their philosophy disparaged:

> The Gospel of Christ hath to be sure been a *Light to lighten the* modern deistical *Gentiles*: For the juster Notions they have of the divine Attributes, and moral Duties than the ancients, they are greatly indebted to that Revelation which they decry. Not to say any Thing of

those heavenly Truths and important Duties, which are taught only in the Bible; 'tis there we learn the Religion of Nature in its greatest Purity; . . . It is in the Light of Revelation, added to that of Nature, that Things are so plain and easy to our discerning, as that we are ready to think bare Reason must discover them to all Mankind.

Gay even twitted the self-conceit of the deists by comparing them to "the simple *Rustick*, who thought the World has little Benefit by the Light of the Sun, 'Because it shin'd in the Day-time.'" This simile so amused young John Adams that he copied it in his diary, remarking in characteristic Adams fashion, "Oh the stupidity, not to see that the sun was the Cause of the day light."[26]

At the same time that Gay argued against the deists in favor of the "inestimable Benefit of Revelation," he condemned the Calvinists for their ignorance in dismissing "natural Religion as mere Paganism." Men should not regard them "as if they were two opposite Religions [that] could no more stand together in the same Temple than Dagon and the Ark of God. . . . They subsist harmoniously together, and mutually strengthen and confirm each other. . . . Both are *good Gifts*,—Rays from the *Father of Lights* to *enlighten* every Man." Despite the appearance of maintaining a strict balance between reason and revelation, Gay clearly regarded revelation as secondary—necessary but secondary. He declared that "Revelation gives us the same (tho' clearer) Ideas of the Attributes of God, which we have from Nature and Reason." Seventy years earlier, Archbishop Tillotson, the great seventeenth-century Latitudinarian, wrote, "Natural religion is the foundation of all revealed religion, and revelation is designed simply to establish its duties." Gay's summation of the relationship between natural and revealed religion points out his indebtedness to Tillotson and the Latitudinarian tradition: "Revealed Religion is an *Additional* to Natural; built not on the Ruins, but on the strong and everlasting Foundations of it."[27]

Clearly the idea of Holy Writ being a supplement to natural religion was not new, but for that matter there was little else really new in Gay's Dudleian Lecture. Indeed, if a well-informed scholar at Leverett's Harvard, circa 1720, had read the lecture, he would not have encountered a single unfamiliar idea. What gave the lecture its special impact was not its substance, but the polarized religious atmosphere of the time. Gay unfolded his rational, Arminian creed in an explicitly anti-Calvinist context, a thing he would not have done in 1720. He knew that his lecture was not just an academic exercise, but part of the effort to build a comprehensive ideology for the Arminian party. Gay performed this task while acting as the party's elder statesman, a role he performed with a grace and a calm dignity that unfailingly impressed his contemporaries. For these reasons, *Natural Religion* had a significant contemporary impact on New England theology. Alan Heimert was probably correct in characterizing it as "the manifesto of Congregational Liberalism."[28]

Gay's 1759 Dudleian Lecture heralded the beginning of the Arminians' triumphal decade—the 1760s. The success of the movement, admittedly, did not extend much beyond the commercial communities of Boston and the South and North Shores (though there were many Arminian ministers in isolated pockets inland). The Arminian emphasis on individual aspiration meshed perfectly with the changing values of these communities. The movement was also furthered by the organizational efforts of specific men who occupied important pulpits—Chauncy and Mayhew in Boston; Gay on the South Shore; Thomas Barnard (Salem First) and John Tucker (Newbury First) on the North Shore. Interestingly, as the Arminian ministry on the East Coast became increasingly entrenched, the opposition became less clamorous. One of the reasons for this partial truce in New England's religious warfare had to do with the mounting fear that the Church of England, with the help of the British government, intended to establish an episcopate in the colonies. The Arminians, under the leadership of Jonathan Mayhew, proved to be the most forward among the clerical opponents of episcopacy. The vigor of their opposition helped to identify them in the minds of their suspicious orthodox brethren with the Puritan Errand. Mayhew, for instance, was no longer completely outside the pale of the Boston Association. Congregational Arminians were finally disentangling themselves from identification with Anglican Arminians.[29]

The Arminians did not adopt their anti-Anglican stand purely as a matter of expedience. They were quite sincere, for instance, in their allegiance to the dissenting traditions of their fathers. John Brown of Cohasset described Mayhew as being "uncommonly intent upon inculcating the faith once delivered to the saints." Because of their admiration for the primitive church, the Arminians fully shared the Puritans' aversion for the elaborate episcopal hierarchy and a mode of worship that was, as Mayhew put it, totally distinct "from the simplicity of the Gospel and the apostolic times." The

Arminian cry, "Call no man Father upon Earth," animated much of their resistance to the Church of England. There was also another factor that kindled Arminian antagonism toward the Anglicans—competition. Jonathan Mayhew began his attack on Episcopacy as early as 1750, several years before most of his colleagues began to fret about an American bishop. Mayhew's biographer, Charles W. Akers, put his finger on the probable cause of Mayhew's agitation (which was otherwise something of a puzzle): "By the 1750's Boston high society centered in Anglican drawing rooms, where more and more the younger generations of sons of the old Puritan families were beginning to feel at ease." The Arminians and the Anglicans, in short, were competing for the same constituency. In 1759, when the Anglican Society for the Propagation of the Gospel (S.P.G.) had the temerity to establish a mission church in Cambridge, Mayhew and Chauncy publicly responded in the same way they had to the New Light itinerants—that the Church of Christ was well-established in Boston and settled ministers were capably ministering to their flocks; therefore missionaries to convert the heathen were distinctly superfluous.[30]

The fear of all dissenting ministers that Anglican bishops might be established in the colonies was certainly not unfounded. In 1758, Thomas Secker, a long-time advocate of an American bishopric, became Archbishop of Canterbury and soon began working cautiously but assiduously toward that end. The Anglican Church and its Society for the Propagation of the Gospel soon came to be regarded, by colonists and the British government alike, as a useful tool in extending imperial control over the colonies. Mayhew even raised the specter of a tax levied by Parliament intended for the support of American bishops, a charge that seemed increasingly plausible in the wake of the 1765 Stamp Act.[31]

Ebenezer Gay closely followed Mayhew's crusade for civil and ecclesiastical liberty. He requested copies of Mayhew's attack on the S.P.G. and of his subsequent pamphlet exchange with Archbishop Secker. During the early years of the Mayhew-Church of England controversy, we do not know whether Gay watched the activities of his impetuous young colleague with approval, disapproval, or bemusement. Some of his actions made it clear that Gay did not share Mayhew's fierce antipathy to the English Church, but then he did not have to share his Hingham parish with an Anglican rector. By 1768, however, Gay was convinced that there was an Anglican plot, abetted by certain British ministers, which threatened New

England's religious establishment. On October 12, 1768, just a few days after General Gage had billeted British troops in Boston, Gay acknowledged:

> The present times, it must be confessed, are evil: The days are gloomy. There may be many adversaries, bearing ill-will to our Zion, maliciously, craftily, and eagerly seeking to subvert our constitution and deprive us of our privileges, civil and ecclesiastical. . . . But tho' the Lord gives his people the bread of adversity, and the water of affliction, yet their eyes still see *their teachers*—teachers of their own choosing. In which liberty may these churches always stand firm and unshaken.[32]

On July 9, 1766, Jonathan Mayhew died of a stroke suffered two weeks earlier. Only forty-five years of age, he was struck down while in the thick of his battle for, in Gay's words, "the cause of truth, liberty, and religion." The news of his death came as a tremendous blow to Gay, even though the latter was familiar with the precarious state of Mayhew's health. Martin Gay expressed the feelings of the whole family when he wrote to his brother that "Doctor Mayhew's death is truly a melancholy providence." On the Friday following Mayhew's death, an extremely hot day, Gay sat in the West Church listening to his friend Chauncy pray for Mayhew's soul (thus breaking an old Puritan taboo). Afterwards, it seemed that the greater part of Boston was assembled outside for the long funeral procession. The seventy-year-old Hingham patriarch joined the five other clerical pallbearers, and wearily carried his beloved young friend to the grave.[33]

On the morning of July 27, three Sundays after Mayhew's death, Gay stood in that same West Church pulpit where, just nineteen years before, he had preached Mayhew's ordination sermon. His eulogy for Mayhew was far more impassioned and moving than even that which Charles Chauncy had delivered two weeks before. Like Chauncy, Gay did find it necessary to apologize for some of Mayhew's excesses: "If he was mistaken in any points of the christian doctrine . . . yet none have cause to impute this to his want of love of the truth." Nevertheless, Gay had not come to exculpate, but to mourn and to defend. He set the tone by describing the relationship between Jesus and John, the beloved disciple. He declared that Jesus "treated them all as friends, but John as his bosom friend, with peculiar endearment of affection and intimacy." Later on, Gay burst out "he is absent from us: Alas! is dead, and gone; and hath left us sorrowing deeply that we shall see his face no more."[34]

Gay preached a second eulogy on the evening of that same day, and this time the tone changed from one of mourning to one of defiance. He had ordained Mayhew in the teeth of a hostile clerical establishment in Boston, and now the "orthodox party" were grumbling that Mayhew's death would serve the cause of the Arian interests. (The term "Arminian" was apparently losing its sting, and the liberals were now frequently tarred with the brush of Arianism—the belief that Christ was divine, but yet inferior to and not one with God.) Gay answered the conservatives, urging the West Church congregation never to forget their "late excellent minister, who was set for the defence of the gospel, and so valiant for the truth, bold in his God, and powerful to withstand and repel the adversaries to it, and zealous to promote in this, and in all our churches, whatever he thought belonged to pure and undefiled religion." There were no more apologies as Gay portrayed Mayhew as a champion, leading the victorious forces of enlightened Christianity against its foes:

> Our eyes, at a distance, were struck with the magnitude and brightness of [Mayhew's ministry] as it arose here, and shone with increasing splendor, and prevailing strength against all attempts to darken it, and *cast it to the earth*. . . . The light of it is gone forth into the world, dispelling the darkness of ignorance, error, and sin: illuminating and clearing the minds of all that are not shut and barred with prejudice against it.

Gay here used the metaphor of light to describe the irresistible triumph of rational religion. Fifty-five years later, Thomas Jefferson compared it to a cleansing wind: "The breeze begins to be felt which precedes the storm; and fanaticism is all in a bustle, shutting its doors and windows to keep it out."[35]

After preaching these eulogies at West Church, Gay returned to Hingham in a state of physical exhaustion. His fatigue was soon compounded by a bad, lingering cold. Nevertheless, he was not finished with his exertions on behalf of the West Church congregation. He feared, and not without some reason, that the West Church might collapse following Mayhew's death. Boston West had never been simply a "neighborhood" church, but instead had drawn its strength from the congregation's loyalty to a particular personality—first William Hooper, then Mayhew. Now that Mayhew was gone, his rather well-to-do parishioners might easily decide to transfer their membership to King's Chapel, Christ Church, Brattle Street, or elsewhere. Gay had, in fact, pleaded directly with the West Church people not to desert their church, for God, as he put it, "can make another man." During Gay's illness, John Brown of Cohasset traveled to Boston to boost the morale of the West Church parishioners, and to reinforce Gay's message: "Although some of you have statedly come from the uttermost parts of the town to hear the wisdom of your late pastor, and may now be ready to think that you may with propriety worship elsewhere, from an apprehension that there is no prospect that your loss can be fully repaired; yet I beseech you to consider, my Brethren, that . . . you may yet unite in one to be set over the Congregation."[36]

These were not empty reassurances that Gay and Brown had given to the West Church people, because they both knew that God had, in fact, "made another man." His name was Simeon Howard. Though there is some question about the extent of Gay's influence on Mayhew, there is none about the Gay-Howard relationship. Simeon Howard was Gay's protégé entirely. Howard had been raised in the West Bridgewater parish of Gay's Old Light ally, the Reverend Daniel Perkins. He took his first degree at Harvard in 1758 and, late in 1759, came to Hingham to keep school and study theology with Gay. Howard served as Hingham's schoolmaster for two years, during which time he boarded with the Gays. He was charming, unassuming, a bit awkward, and an excellent scholar; he might have served, physically at least, as a model for Washington Irving's Ichabod Crane. Ungainly though he was, he apparently captured the heart of Gay's twenty-four-year-old daughter, Jerusha. On September 6, 1761, Howard was admitted into full membership in Hingham's First Church. He occasionally preached for Gay, but in order to provide him with a more complete pastoral experience, Gay arranged for him to supply the pulpit at Cumberland, Nova Scotia, a settlement in which his son, Jotham Gay, was a proprietor. The Cumberland grantees were apparently delighted with Howard and extended a call, but Simeon was no frontiersman and he returned to the Bay.[37]

Howard was serving as a Tutor at Harvard, when Mayhew's death opened up the West Church pulpit. Parsons Gay and John Brown vigorously promoted the young scholar, and Howard's own pleasing personality did the rest; on February 10, 1767, he was given a unanimous call. The theological climate in Boston was not very different from what it had been twenty years before when Mayhew was ordained. Two of Cotton Mather's "old guard," Joseph Sewall and Samuel Checkley, were still alive and, together with Ebenezer Pemberton, carefully tended the orthodox flame. Old Sewall suspected that Simeon Howard would prove to be every bit the Arian and Arminian that Mayhew had been. Therefore, most of the Boston churches sent no delegates to Howard's very elegant ordination, and for the next seventeen years he endured much the same sort of ostracism that Mayhew had experienced, though with better grace.[38]

A familiar old trio presided at Howard's ordination service— Charles Chauncy preached; Ebenezer Gay gave the Charge; Nathaniel Appleton gave the Right Hand of Fellowship. Almost all the major figures in the Hingham Association were present—Daniel Shute, John Brown, Gad Hitchcock, and William Smith. All these men were determined to insure that Boston would still hear a strong voice preaching a rational, enlightened gospel. At one point in his sermon, Chauncy turned to Howard and said, "You possess the intellectual powers in too great a degree to be in danger of turning them [his congregation] off with loose, unconnected, empty harangues, which, if they should give heat, can convey little or no light; nor would they be easy under such preaching: They have been too much used to another and more excellent way to be so." In his Charge to the candidate, Gay also reminded his former student that he had some very large shoes to fill, and that he would "reap that whereon [he] bestowed not Labour." The "Father of Lights," said Gay, as "furnished you, Mr. Simeon Howard, with ministerial Gifts, and opened to you a Door, great and effectual [we hope] for the useful Improvement of them." Gay gave his customary injunction not to teach "the Doctrines, Commandments, and Inventions of Men," and he further charged Howard to "Give no offence in any Thing." Howard followed that last bit of advice so faithfully that he was able finally to bring the West Church out of isolation and into the mainstream of Boston's religious life.[39]

Simeon Howard was an excellent representative of the third generation of Arminian ministers. The first generation, men like Gay and Chauncy, tended to move away from their Calvinist heritage quietly and with great caution. The second generation included men like Mayhew and Lemuel Briant who defiantly flung their beliefs in the teeth of orthodoxy. Simeon Howard, however, was so serenely confident in the ultimate triumph of rational religion that he felt no need to engage in apologetics of any kind. His toleration seemed boundless. On one occasion, when he felt obliged to warn his congregation against reposing trust in deists, his criticisms sounded like praise by faint damnation. How could a parishioner take seriously his attacks on "the accute and subtle Hume, or that universal apostle of infidelity, the gay and sprightly Voltaire?" The casual way in which he referred to Jesus as "the greatest and most honorable character that ever appeared upon earth" puts Howard much closer than Gay, or even Mayhew, to the world of the nineteenth-century Unitarians. Perhaps Howard's easy confidence arose, in part, from the conviction that the rational, humanistic faith that he preached was the wave of the future. In 1801, a visiting minister attended Boston's Thursday Lecture where, he recorded, "old Dr. Howard delivered a downright Arian sermon; not in a controversial way, but just as if all agreed with him. Indeed at that time all controversy was proscribed by the liberal party."[40]

With the settlement of Simeon Howard, Gay's ties to Boston's West Church were firmly knotted. One of his most devoted students was in the pulpit and, in 1773, his son Martin was elected deacon. Gay also may have expected to welcome Howard into the family as his son-in-law, but any understanding that Simeon may have formed with Jerusha Gay was forgotten as soon as he met Mayhew's widow. Betsy Clarke Mayhew was still considered one of the loveliest women in Boston, and, after rejecting several distinguished suitors, she married her late husband's successor in 1771. Their marriage was brief, ending only six years later when Betsy died of childbirth complications. Finally, after thirteen years had passed, Parson Howard was married again on November 29, 1790. His bride was none other than his old friend, Jerusha Gay, now fifty-five years old. Thus Ebenezer Gay's last link with West Church was forged posthumously, three years after his death.[41]

By the year 1770, Gay seemed to provide living proof that a benevolent deity did indeed reward the virtuous man. After his 1759 Dudleian Lecture, he had emerged as the *eminence grise* of the Arminian party. Charles Chauncy certainly equalled Gay in learning and intellect, and was a more original thinker, but Gay's great dignity and judicious, deliberate style had earned him the kind of respect that had not yet been fully accorded his Boston colleague. At the age of seventy-four, Gay was more than ever sought after as a postgraduate mentor for Harvard's annual crop of would-be ministers. One might have expected a certain intellectual stagnation at this point in his life, but his theology continued to evolve. In an ordination sermon delivered in 1768, Gay made a passing remark that indicates he had reached the extremes of Arminianism. He told the candidate that if he was to help save any of his parishioners, "there must be on their part, compliance, and concurrent endeavors; without which almighty grace doth not, I might say, cannot help and save them." The role of human initiative in the process of salvation could be taken no further, unless one were to dispense with the need for saving grace altogether. Gay never went that far, but he came perilously close at times.[42]

# CHAPTER X

# Family and Community: The Arminian Patriarch in Changing Times

<hr>

In the early 1750s, no section of Hingham Town was as alive and bustling as the waterfront at the harbor. Drawing from a few scattered references, one can easily improvise a scene down at the wharves on a spring morning in 1753. Preparations are being made to receive the coasting vessel of Captain John Cushing, which is threading its way through the fishing shallops in the small harbor. One or two other merchant vessels are riding at anchor, though perhaps not as many as one would find in Cohasset Harbor down the coast. Two men are approaching the old tide-water gristmill that stood at the head of the harbor, making their way through a maze of barrels full of packed mackerel, cod, and hake. One of these men, dressed in fine, black broadcloth, his penetrating gray eyes peering out from under his wide-brimmed hat, is unmistakenly Parson Gay. Gay's companion is Hezekiah Leavitt, a prosperous merchant who owns one of the largest warehouses on the harbor. Both men hold shares in the gristmill, and Gay is explaining to Leavitt his proposal for building a new wharf thirty feet out from the old mill wharf in order to better protect their property.[1]

Hezekiah Leavitt was one of a number of Hingham gentlemen who, in the 1750s, were making or augmenting their fortunes in the rapid growth of the fishing industry. Hezekiah and his cousin Elisha Leavitt, along with Captain John Thaxter, Doctor Ezekiel Hersey, Deacon Solomon Cushing, and Captain Francis Barker, had formed a fishing company in March 1752. They were all

192

entrepreneurs whose capital was invested principally in nonagricultural pursuits, though four of the six were also landed gentlemen, each owning over one hundred acres of land (in 1754 the average acreage held in Hingham was thirty-one). The Leavitts were merchants, Deacon Cushing was a tanner, Hersey was a physician, and Thaxter was a magistrate and an important figure in the Provincial militia (Hersey and Thaxter were also Harvard graduates). Captain Barker, "master shipwright," was a newcomer. He had moved to Hingham from Pembroke sometime in the early 1740s and, within ten years, had established a shipyard near the foot of the harbor. Barker, an intensely energetic and ambitious man, seemed to be the driving force behind Hingham's booming fishing industry. These six members of the "fishing company," together with Benjamin Lincoln, Esq., comprised the heart and soul of Hingham's commercial establishment at mid-century. It was no coincidence that Gay drew his closest friends in town from among these gentlemen, and that they looked to him for guidance in matters both spiritual and secular. They were well-educated, urbane men whose wealth and exemplary piety made them the natural leaders of Hingham society. According to the precepts of Gay's Arminian gospel, these six men were clearly numbered among the elect.[2]

Commercial enterprise was not a novelty in Hingham. As early as 1650, the town had been shipping timber, planks, and masts to Boston, and there had been some commercial fishing in the area since the days of the Bare Cove settlement. The commercialization of Hingham in the eighteenth century was, then, a matter of degree. A fairly rapid population growth in the first half of the century was accompanied by the growth of shipping (spurred by the expansion of the West Indian trade) and of the fishing industry. In 1737, property assessors recorded two hundred and forty-five tons of shipping in vessels owned by Hingham merchants. By 1749, the amount had grown to four hundred and sixty-three tons, two hundred and forty of which were "engaged in foreign trade." In 1752, the town recognized the growing importance of Hingham's fishing fleet by expanding the number of town offices to include "Packers of Mackerel" and a "Culler of Fish."[3]

The expansion of the mercantile sector in Hingham's economy was joined by a less conspicuous but no less significant phenomenon—the growth of local industries. By 1750, Hingham could boast six gristmills, three sawmills, one fulling-mill, and two iron works; furthermore, the town's famous coopering industry seemed to be developing at a rapid pace. By the 1780s Hingham was indeed a very prosperous community. According to one recent study, Hingham ranked eleventh in commercial wealth among the 343 towns of Massachusetts in the mid-1780s.[4]

In the years between 1700 and 1750, Hingham had moved steadily away from a condition of comparative economic equality towards one of economic stratification. The old oligarchy that had unobtrusively dominated Hingham for so long, consciously eschewing ostentation, was now becoming an increasingly visible social elite. Daniel Scott Smith, in his demographic study of Hingham, has shown that as the population grew, the town's wealth became increasingly concentrated. Between 1711 and 1749, the total wealth held by the richest 30 percent of the townsmen increased by 10.7 percent, while, at the same time, the total wealth of the poorest declined 7 percent. The inequality in land distribution in those same years was even more striking. By 1754 the top 10 percent of Hingham landowners held 35 percent of the land (and the most profitable land as well), the top 20 percent owned 58 percent, while the bottom 60 percent owned only 12 percent of the available land. In the First Parish, this disparity was even more pronounced than in Cohasset·or South Hingham. The number of propertyless males over twenty-one had risen steadily during the first half of the eighteenth century and, by 1754, the bottom 20 percent of rateable polls in all three parishes were landless (see Appendix 4).[5]

Gay's old friend, Deacon Thomas Andrews, was typical of Hingham's economic elite. By 1765 Andrews, who had served as Town Treasurer from 1727 to 1763, was the wealthiest man in the First Parish. He owned one hundred and eighty-one acres of land, nine acres of salt marsh, an apple orchard, and one-half of a sawmill. He had just built a handsome house, known to all as "The Mansion House," just a bit west of Gay's house on Town Street, and he owned another house in South Hingham. When Andrews died in 1784, his entire estate was appraised at £4522.12.8, a princely sum. For all that, Deacon Andrews, who was one of Hingham's old, landed oligarchs, tended to be less self-indulgent than many of those men who were making their fortunes in trade. As wealth became more conspicuously concentrated in the upper levels of Hingham society, the bottom levels were becoming pauperized. By 1747, the number of destitute people in Hingham had risen to such an alarming extent that the Town Meeting voted to create the office of "Overseers of the Poor." In the following year, the town voted for the first time that Treasurer Andrews "be directed to pay for the present Relief of the poor a sum not Exceeding one Hundred and fifty pounds old Tenor." The expenditures for poor relief increased steadily and, in 1785, a "House for the poor of the Town" was erected.[6]

Political participation in Hingham's town government reflected the highly stratified condition of that community in the mid-eighteenth century. The responsibility for governing Hingham had been shared among the various families of the old East Anglian oligarchy for over a century, but the leadership pool had become even smaller as political power became concentrated in the hands of a few long-term office holders. Between 1745 and 1765, fully 80 percent of all the selectmen's terms were served by three families—the Cushings, Lincolns, and Thaxters. The five selectmen who were serving in 1764 (one Thaxter, one Lincoln, and three Cushings) had already served an average of ten terms in that office, even though they were fairly young, ranging in age from thirty-nine to forty-five.[7]

The tenure of most of the selectmen, long as it was, seemed positively ephemeral when compared with some of the other major town offices. Deacon Thomas Andrews had succeeded to the office of Town Treasurer in 1727 upon the death of his father, Lieutenant Thomas Andrews. Deacon Andrews then held the post from 1727 until 1763, when he relinquished it in favor of his good friend and neighbor, Colonel John Thaxter. Six years later, the office reverted to the custody of the Andrews family, when the deacon's nephew, Joseph Andrews, succeeded Thaxter. Similarly, the office of Town Clerk had been part of the Lincoln family patrimony since 1721, when Benjamin Lincoln, "maltster," was elected. At his death in 1727, he was succeeded by his son, Colonel Benjamin Lincoln. That worthy magistrate, in turn, bequeathed the office in 1758 to his son, Benjamin Lincoln, Jr. (the future general). Not incidentally, young Benjamin assumed this important office without ever having served in a lower political capacity. His case was not atypical. The privileged members of the younger Hingham gentry no longer felt obliged to ascend the *cursus honorum* of town offices.[8]

Although the commercialization that was transforming Hingham's economy was creating new social problems, it also provided the means for defusing social tension. Daniel Scott Smith has shown that, from 1721 to 1760, the rate of outmigration from Hingham became increasingly less related to the land inheritance mechanism. Clearly, nonagricultural pursuits were becoming the dominant force in Hingham's economy. The young men who stayed had economic alternatives to farming. The new commercial wealth even expanded the opportunities for the younger members of Hingham's oligarchy to serve in political office. In the years from 1750 to 1767, eight new town office positions were created, all concerned with regulating the harbor commerce.[9]

The social and economic changes in Hingham were faithfully mirrored in the First Church, which was still the focal point of community identity. The leadership of the church was drawn from the upper economic ranks of the town. The 1765 property valuation places the four deacons of the church among the ten wealthiest landowners in the First Parish. By the 1750s, these church leaders began to feel that their rather antiquated meetinghouse, now over seventy years old, did not adequately reflect the growing prosperity of the town. Furthermore, church attendance had increased as the population had expanded, and Sunday services were becoming increasingly cramped and disorderly. There was some brief debate over the wisdom of tearing down the old building and erecting a new structure, but Hingham's fundamental conservatism prevailed, and the parish voted to enlarge and modernize the existing meetinghouse. During the summer of 1755 a west wing, fourteen feet in length, was added in perfect conformity to the existing, late seventeenth-century architectural style. The interior, however, was substantially altered. One of the major changes involved the relocation of the pulpit from the east side to the north side, so that it would now stand at the center of the expanded meetinghouse. The old pulpit apparently did not harmonize with its new location and, after some indecision, the parish voted on October 10 to build a new one. The new "sacred desk" was worthy of the dignity of its occupant. The carpenters erected an elevated, modified "wine glass" pulpit with matching sounding board, set into a box carved with fielded panels. Two handsome arched windows provided a backdrop. Gay's first sermon in his new pulpit was taken from Nehemiah 8:4: "And Ezra the scribe stood upon a pulpit made of wood, which they had made for the purpose" (the scriptural context was the rebuilding of the Temple at Jerusalem).[10]

The other major interior alteration was the installation of box pews. This was a matter of far greater consequence than the new pulpit, the re-glazed windows, or the expanded galleries. Just as the original seating of the meetinghouse in 1681 provided an accurate social portrait of the community, so the introduction of box pews reflected the socioeconomic changes that had occurred in the intervening years. The First Parish leaders, always anxious to preserve Hingham's delicate balance between hierarchy and collective identity, had approached the question of pewing the church very cautiously. The idea of selling box pews to the highest bidder, in order to raise money for improvements to the building, had been broached as early as 1725, but the parish apparently felt that funds for enlarging the meetinghouse could be raised without so radical a measure. About four years later, while the Ship Church was, in fact, being enlarged, a group of gentlemen, headed by Colonel Samuel Thaxter, petitioned the parish to reconsider the idea. They stressed the importance of completing the repairs to the building "in order to make it Convenient & Honourable," and suggested that the costs could be defrayed "by Such Persons as may have the Liberty of Erecting Pews . . . for themselves and Families." Once again, however, a majority in the First Parish felt that the erection of box pews would introduce a jarringly ostentatious note into the carefully composed social harmony of the meetinghouse.[11]

During the next thirty years, the process of social stratification in Hingham continued, and by the 1750s, all resistance to the pressure for box pews crumbled. Hingham's new entrepreneurial personality, typified by Captain Francis Barker, the shipwright, would have its way. In 1756, fifty-six pews were drawn out by lot and put up for bid. One might have expected the results to confirm the emergence of wealth and estate as the primary criteria for privilege in seating. In fact, this was not entirely the case. Twenty-four of the fifty-six pews bid for were transferred to another party. The transference of pews or bidding in partnership was, in many cases, merely a matter of convenience, but it also was a way of insuring that Hingham's intricate social tapestry would not be entirely unraveled by the new, mercantile wealth. Certainly the mere existence of the box pews reflected a major change in Hingham's social structure. Families of pew owners were now grouped together and physically isolated from other worshipers. Pew ownership was a clear mark of social distinction. Nevertheless, the Hingham oligarchs had no intention of allowing seating privileges to become commercialized. Newcomer Francis Barker, for instance, did not occupy a place of distinction even though he was one of the most successful businessmen in the town. The meetinghouse was now "Convenient & Honourable" for prospering merchants, but the seating reflected Hingham's continuing commitment to ascribed status and a stable, social hierarchy whose roots extended well back into the previous century.[12]

Now that the interior of the Old Ship had been modernized in a way more suited to the genteel aspirations of Hingham's economic elite, Parson Gay was anxious to bring the church music and psalmodies up to date. He was determined to end the cacophonous old practice of "lining out" in which a precentor, usually a deacon, sang the tune to each line of the psalm, to be followed by the congregation. Gay wanted his music, which he dearly loved, to be as orderly and harmonious as his Creator's universe. He intended to establish a regular choir, and to introduce the controversial Tate & Brady's *Whole Book of Psalms* (1696). Although Tate & Brady, with its diamond-shaped notes for melody and bass, had appeared in New England by 1700, it still had not supplanted such older collections as the *Bay Psalm Book* (1640) and the *Ainsworth Psalter* (1612). The more orthodox regarded Tate & Brady as a corrupting, Anglican, High Church innovation, and so the use of that psalmody acquired political overtones. Any minister who urged the adoption of Tate & Brady was clearly a liberal with little commitment to the old New England Way, and a man to be viewed with suspicion. After the Great Awakening, many of the Arminian ministers adopted Tate & Brady as a defiant symbol of their break with the past.[13]

Gay moved very cautiously in his efforts to introduce the new psalmody. John Brown had persuaded his Cohasset parish to adopt Tate & Brady as early as 1749, but he apparently had used high-pressure tactics that embittered some members. The Reverend David Barnes was not able to persuade the South Scituate church to use Tate & Brady until 1764. When that church finally came around, they also voted that "a Portion of Scripture should be publickly read on ye Lord's Day," another practice that smacked of "popery" to conservatives. Gay apparently helped to prepare his church for the change by gently poking fun at the old system. Young John Adams recorded in his diary an anecdote he had heard from Gay (probably in the late 1750s):

> . . . at some ordination, a certain Indian, who had never seen a public assembly before, seated himself in the Alley, very near the Deacon's seat. He sat in Silence with the rest while the Priests were

at Prayer, but when the Psalm was named, and the Deacon rose up [to] set the tune, he began to stare and grow angry at the Deacon, but when the Deacon had read a Line and the whole Congregation broke out with him, the Indian grew quite mad and rushing up to the Deacon, layed upon him most unmercifully. "'Tis you," says he "are the Cause of all this plaguey Rout."

In 1763, Gay established the rudiments of a choir, by persuading the church to allow three singers seated "behind the Deacon's to strike first in singing." By 1768, Gay had not only introduced Tate & Brady's psalmody to the Old Ship's devotions, but even had the congregation singing some of Isaac Watts's hymns.[14]

The ecclesiastical and theological message of Gay and his Arminian colleagues meshed in very positive ways with the changing norms and values of mid-eighteenth-century New England. As the commercial centers became more socially stratified, the ideals of the most influential citizens centered on a social model where hierarchical values became dominant. Gay's vision of church polity, which he expressed in 1753, was certainly not inconsistent with that model. He spoke of Christians as "members of the Spiritual Corporation, or Republick, of which Christ is the Head and Governour." This "Corporation," said Gay, "hath different Degrees of Persons in it . . . united to one another in the Bonds of ecclesiastical Polity and Christian Charity; and all disposed in proper Order." One must point out, however, that there was room for upward mobility in Gay's spiritual corporation, just as there was in Hingham's commercial establishment. As Richard E. Sykes, in his study of Massachusetts Unitarianism, has observed: "the values emphasized by the Arminians appealed to the upwardly mobile and to those with a favorable self-image." Gay earnestly encouraged those with "superior abilities and attainments" to "out-strip" their fellow Christians.[15]

Despite the growing socioeconomic stratification in mid-century Hingham, Gay remained the pastor of all his flock. He was the father of the town, the self-conscious symbol of community solidarity. Although he was clearly an important member of Hingham's ruling inner circle, Gay remained, as he described his good friend, Dr. Ezekiel Hersey, "ever as ready to serve the Poor as the Rich." He frequented the wharves and shipyards, and took a great delight in talking with the sailors, mariners, and mechanics who lived and worked in fairly close proximity to his home. He was careful to avoid ostentation. In 1764, when Adino Paddock, a Boston chaise-maker, offered to let the parson have "a very good bargain in a chaise," Gay responded that his "old chaise will do well enough for . . . an old man." Gay's constant attention, even with advancing age, to potential sources of friction in his parish, coupled with sermons that repeatedly emphasized the rewards of moral virtue, proved to be a successful formula. Hingham's economic and population growth had eroded the external forms of social control that a more cohesive community had once exerted. The new personal autonomy and room for individual self-expression posed a threat to social stability. Gay's Arminian gospel could hardly have been more perfectly adapted to meet this challenge. If external controls were collapsing, then the assumption of personal moral responsibility became crucial, and this was precisely what Gay preached. He taught his parishioners that they were directly responsible to God and man for the consequences of their actions; that the state of their immortal soul was dependent on their good behavior.[16]

During the early 1750s, Gay preached a series of sermons to his people in which he dwelt on the omnipresence of the Lord. Gay's god was far more actively involved in His creation than was the "prime mover" of the deists or even the majestic "first author" and "last end" of Jonathan Edwards. The Arminian deity was a watchful, benevolent patriarch who could nevertheless, when the occasion warranted, be terrible in his judgements. At least, this was the portrait of God that the Arminians painted for their congregations. Like many of his Arminian colleagues, Gay seized the opportunity of the 1755 Lisbon earthquake to remind his auditors of the future judgement. In November he preached from Psalms 33:8— "Let all the earth fear the Lord; let all the inhabitants of the world stand in awe of him." He so terrified the usually placid Hinghamites, that he reaped a harvest of twenty-nine souls (including his daughters Abigail and Jerusha) during the following year, a record broken only during the earthquake of 1727 (see Appendix 1). Gay, Chauncy, and Mayhew all understood that nothing could dampen the potentially disruptive "enthusiasm" of the multitude like a good, sobering jeremiad.[17]

Gay's old formula of powerful preaching coupled with Arminian theology worked exceedingly well in the 1750s and 1760s. In 1768, the Reverend Ezra Stiles, eminent pastor of the Second Congregational Church in Newport, Rhode Island, came to preach for Gay. He found the seventy-two-year-old parson in the midst of a major revival (see Appendix 1). Stiles was enormously impressed. He decided that Hingham's First Parish, along with Andover's South Church, "are in the best State of any _____ & nearly as perfect as this World will admit. They are . . . generally bapt[ized] & as many Comun as can be expected." Stiles described the citizens of Hingham as "sober, industrious, don't go to Taverns, generally pray in families & a great number hopefully pious & truly religious." (Hingham's spirited and nearly unanimous resistance to the 1754 Massachusetts Excise Tax Bill on liquor privately consumed may help one understand why they didn't go to taverns.) After Stiles preached from the Old Ship pulpit in June of 1768, he estimated that there were six hundred in the congregation, four hundred below and two hundred in the galleries. Hingham had become such an outwardly peaceable kingdom that, in 1768, the number of tythingmen, that most visible symbol of external social control, was reduced from three to one.[18]

Gay seems to have ruled his household in much the same way that he governed his parish—as a benevolent autocrat. However, the patriarchal style that worked so well for him in the church and community was decidedly less successful in his role as pater-familias. As soon as they were able, his three eldest sons (after the deceased Samuel) left home to seek their fortune. Gay apparently impressed his boys with the conviction that farming was a slightly demeaning occupation for the sons of a gospel minister. This feeling that they should aspire to something higher, coupled with the lack of any significant landed inheritance in Hingham, caused all three to leave the nest as quickly as they could. Their anxiety to leave home, however, was also due to their need to escape the dominating presence of their father. Martin and Calvin entered into trade and commerce, and Jotham had visions of a distinguished military career.

Martin, Gay's second eldest son (b. 1726) was, on the whole, the most successful of the three boys. Sometime during the early 1740s, he was apprenticed to the trade of copper smithing, and by 1748 he was practicing his vocation in Boston. His mother, Jerusha, had inherited some buildings and land on Boston's Union Street, which she and Ebenezer sold to Martin in 1760 for £30. He quickly converted the main building into a brass foundry and a very comfortable apartment. Martin was the secular embodiment of Gay's

Arminian spirit. He was a shrewd, ambitious, and remarkably successful businessman. Handsome, imperious, though a bit hot-tempered, Martin quickly insinuated himself into the most fashionable Boston society. He became a deacon in Jonathan Mayhew's West Church, and captain of the Ancient and Honorable Artillery Company. He soon had shipping interests that proved just as lucrative as the foundry. Among other ventures, he carried on a brisk trade with a community of settlers in Cumberland (now Amherst), Nova Scotia. With his brother Jotham as a factor there, Martin shipped livestock, furniture, utensils, copper sheets, and parts for stills from his foundry in exchange for furs and dairy produce.[19]

Martin's father valued his advice and judgement, and was always solicitous of his welfare, but there was a certain distance between the two. Martin was a very capable businessman, but he had little interest in, or aptitude for, higher learning. Even his business letters written in the period before he could afford an amanuensis were grammatical and orthographic disasters. Furthermore, Martin's piety was something short of exemplary in his father's eyes. The latter frequently urged his son to let "no cares of this life, nor multiplicity of worldly business thrust family religion out of your house." The fact is the two men had very little in common. One also feels that Ebenezer's emotional restraint, the hallmark of a Harvard gentleman, must have been difficult to endure at times. He visited his son in the fall of 1764 to console him after Martin's first wife, Mary Pinckney Gay, had died of childbirth complications. Mary had not, apparently, met the "King of Terrors" with equanimity, and the whole experience had left Martin quite shaken. Gay left his son "in mournful Tears" and, after returning to Hingham, wrote Martin warning him to "indulge not to excessive Grief. My Son, despise not the Chastening of the Lord." Nine years later when Pinckney, the child born of Mary's mortal travail, died, Ebenezer again wrote to Martin, "You may have need to guard against excess in Mourning, as well as to take care that you despise not the Chastening of the Lord." The rest of Gay's letter on this occasion was a rehash of a sermon that he had delivered two years before on God's benevolence.[20]

Of his three surviving sons, Gay was clearly most attached to Jotham, the youngest (b. 1733). Jotham had inherited his father's intelligence, wit, and even, alas, his looks. He was highly literate, and kept the Hingham school for a year, a post usually reserved for Gay's theology students or exceptionally competent young men such as Cotton Tufts. Jotham, however, was a restless young man, eager for adventure and travel, and so he became a soldier. As early as 1753, just as Anglo-French hostilities were starting to re-kindle, Jotham was sent to Grand Pre in Nova Scotia (a fort that the English had held since 1747). He quickly wrote home to inform the family that "This is the Finest Country that Ever I saw." From that point on, Jotham's military career became secondary to his am-bition to make a name for himself in Nova Scotia. Nevertheless, he acquitted himself with distinction as a soldier, rising rapidly under the patronage of his father's friend, Colonel Benjamin Lincoln.[21]

In 1758 Jotham commanded a company of Hingham men during Admiral Boscawen's and General Amherst's successful siege of Louisbourg. After this glorious victory, Captain Gay's company was sent to Halifax to help form part of the garrison there. Jotham apparently shared his father's perception of the military as the apotheosis of the orderly society. On May 14, 1759, he wrote from Halifax, "Here is everything in nature which tends to make any so-ciety happy—under proper regulation." Even before completing his tour of duty at Halifax, Jotham was ambitiously arranging a place for himself in postwar Nova Scotia. He wrote to Martin that a friend "has promised me to speak to the Governor concerning my having an interest in the settlement of the Province. I have pre-sumed to be answerable for a sufficient number to settle a town-ship." Jotham soon went into the shipping business in partnership with a well-connected friend, Joshua Winslow. They exported live-stock and dairy products (trading heavily with Martin Gay in Boston), and acquired extensive agricultural interests. By 1777, Jotham was vigorously enforcing the British Acts of Trade as a cus-toms collector at Fort Cumberland.[22]

Despite Jotham's success, his father ceaselessly worried about the welfare of his bachelor son. He wrote imploring Jotham "to preserve a good moral Character in a place of dangerous Tempta-tion." He wanted his son to come home, and constantly applied pressure to that end. In 1774 his brother Martin wrote that, while he was "disappointed in not seeing you here last fall, father seemed to be *much* affected with it." A year later his sister Jerusha wrote, "father wants you to come home very much. He wants to build a barn and he says that Jotham may do it as he pleases for he can't take the trouble." Ebenezer himself was not above writing letters calculated to arouse guilt feelings in his wandering son, as in an epistle sent in 1761: "I am not so well of late, as when you left me;

and it will be no wonder if I should be gone into the World of Spirits, before you return to your Father's house."[23]

Father Gay, on the whole, took a great deal of pride in the accomplishments of both Martin and Jotham, but his eldest surviving son, Calvin, was an unmitigated disappointment. Perhaps Calvin was predestined to failure. He was the first of the boys to go to Nova Scotia. As early as 1751, he was living in Halifax, acting as an agent for goods consigned to him by his brother Martin. For nearly ten years he traveled from Louisbourg to Halifax to Chignecto Bay, attempting to fetch the best price for the rum, cattle, and stills that Martin shipped from Boston. He did return to the South Shore long enough to become involved with one Mary Smith of Sandwich. They were married in April 1752 and seven months later their daughter, Christiana, was born. Calvin quickly returned to his mercantile activities in Nova Scotia, leaving his wife and child in the care of his parents. In 1760 Calvin apparently received an admonitory letter from his father. The young man's response speaks volumes about his character:

> You inform me that the state of my family was no better than when I left it. I could not expect any favorable account. I rejoice to hear that my wife is so well composed and resigned to the will of God, in her long sickness. . . . If it should please God to take away my wife before my return, I should be glad that one of my sisters would keep house till I return.[21]

Calvin had apparently enlisted in his Majesty's Service, but in November 1759 he wrote a letter to Martin from Louisbourg that detailed his rather desperate efforts to get his discharge. His requests were denied, and a reluctant Calvin Gay was sent to join the forces of Brigadier James Murray that were defending the captured city of Quebec against any attempts on the part of the French to retake it. By August of 1760, Calvin was writing to his father that "This is the best part of the world that I ever yet see. A fine navigable river and the best of land." He decided to settle in Quebec, and persuaded Martin to extend his shipping trade (wine for furs, etc.) to that city. With his scarlet, laced jacket and nankeen coat, Calvin must have cut quite a figure in Quebec, but he proved to be no businessman. He extended credit to the point where he ruined himself and very nearly brought Martin under as well. In 1765 Calvin was seized by "a violent distemper" and died in Quebec at the age of forty. Upon hearing of his death, his brother Martin was something less than distraught, writing to a friend, "This time twelve months, I advanced and shipped goods to him amounting very near to a thousand Pound [?] Money for which I have received but a trifle, besides the loss of so dear a brother." Martin also wrote to another acquaintance, declaring in his blunt way that "I hope he is happy in the other and better world, though fear that there is no just grounds for such a hope."[25]

The most poignant and unsparing reaction to Calvin's death, however, came from his father. In May 1765, a sermon was preached "by Mr. Gay, after the death of his son, Calvin," from 1 Samuel 3:14. Placed in context with the verse preceding, the text reads: "For I have told him that I will judge his home for ever for the iniquity which he knoweth; because his sons made themselves vile, and he restrained them not. And therefore I have sworn unto the house of Eli, that the iniquity of Eli's house shall not be purged with sacrifice nor offering for ever." In 1 Samuel 2:12, Eli's sons are described as "sons of Belial; they knew not the Lord." We can never know whether Gay really lived with the insupportable guilt that this text seems to suggest, or whether he improved this scriptural passage in a way that was less personally damning.[26]

Calvin was gone, but he left behind one very tangible reminder of his unhappy life—his daughter Christiana. Cryssa, as she was called, has allowed us an intimate glimpse of the way in which Gay attempted to regulate the behavior of his children and grandchildren. Gay seemed to have raised his children in the manner one might expect of an enlightened, Arminian clergyman. They were not young colts to be subdued, but rather tender young plants to be nourished. Gay combined this approach with an absolute, patriarchal authority, and the two proved a devastating combination. As we have seen, his sons tried to escape, though they were never completely free of his influence. His daughters, however, could not flee from his authority so easily. Of the three girls that survived to adulthood, only Jerusha married, and she only did so when she was fifty-five years old, three years after her father's death. Gay's granddaughter Christiana, however, came from a different mold.[27]

Cryssa was not a tender young plant. By her mid-teens she had been virtually abandoned by her father, and had watched her mother die a painful, lingering death. Calvin had entrusted her to the care of her Grandfather Gay, and the old man tried to do his best with this bitter and unhappy young girl. In 1773, as she ap-

proached the age of twenty-one, she rebelled by declaring her intention to marry one Bartholomew Jones, a young man of distinctly
inferior social caste (in the eyes of both the Gays and her mother's
family). Her Aunt Jerusha beautifully described the ensuing confrontation between Cryssa and the seventy-seven-year-old patriarch in a letter to Jotham Gay:

> We have had a very troublesome scene with Cryssa. She is published
> to one Jones, a brother of Joseph Jones who you know. . . . We did all
> we could and so did everybody else. You would be amazed to hear
> with what fury and will she behaved to us all. Her grandfather sent
> for [her] to come to him. He said everything to move her. I believe,
> of her age, the only person on earth that would not have fallen on
> their knees before him to have heard such commands, such advice
> and entreaties with tears and promising what he would do for her if
> she obeyed him. . . . She was resolute to proceed for what reason she
> could not tell, but the will and the temper of rebellion in her has
> been almost as shocking as the thing itself. She is an astonishment to
> all who know her. . . . You may judge how improper the proceeding
> must be in her. Her grandfather cast her in a formal manner, tears
> streaming from his aged eyes. . . . We have not seen her since the
> January. She is not married yet. The man is so poor he does not
> know what to do about it.

The willful Christiana defied them all and married Bartholomew
on June 19, 1774. Her Aunt Jerusha again wrote to Jotham to
inform him that "Cryssa was married last June and went away
to a place called Wells at the Eastward, and I fear is very poor."
The postscript to the story of Gay's rebellious granddaughter may
be found in the old man's will, drawn up in 1783. The only specific bequest of money that he made was "sixty pounds for my
Grandaughter Christiana Jones which I give unto her." He may
have "cast her in a formal manner," but Arminians were always uncomfortable with the notion of eternal damnation.[28]

Cryssa's "temper of rebellion" was not unique. Robert A.
Gross, in his study of Concord during the Revolutionary period,
has found that "many women chafed at paternal restraints regard-
ing when and whom they could wed." Their independent behavior
was based, at least in part, on the increasing inability of their
fathers to be able to promise a secure future for them if they
accepted parental guidance. Young men, of course, shared this
rather uneasy sense of freedom, and Cryssa's stubborn independence was matched by her cousin Sam. Samuel was the eldest son

of Martin Gay, who pressured the boy into preparing for the ministry in order to please his grandfather. Sam dutifully entered Harvard in 1772, amid general expectations from relatives that he would "make a good scholar and prove a great comfort and blessing . . . to our family." His grandfather presented him with books from his library. Three years later, however, Sam had left Cambridge to go and live with his Uncle Jotham in Nova Scotia, declaring that he intended to become a farmer. Sam's little rebellion was a great blow to the old parson, as well as to his father. Recovering from his disappointment, Martin finally acknowledged that should Sam "incline to be a farmer, it may be the best thing he can do, considering that all the interest I have in the world is in such a precarious state, that poverty appears to approach very near to me."[29]

Gay was clearly discouraged by his inability to maintain order and harmony in his own family sphere. In the quarter century between 1745 and 1770, however, he had not only to deal with the temper of rebellion but, more tragically, with the "King of Terrors." As the population density of the port city of Boston increased, epidemic diseases became more common, and, like pestilent waves, they frequently washed into the surrounding countryside. On February 19, 1749, the Reverend William Smith of Weymouth noted in his diary that he "Preached for Mr. Gay, his daughter Celia Lay dead." Celia, apparently the victim of a diphtheria epidemic, was only eighteen and a great favorite in the family. Two years later, the "throat distemper" (angina ulcusculosa) began ravaging the region. From July through November of 1751, Hinghamites were dying in alarming numbers, and a somber Gay preached a Fast sermon based on the text, "cruel as the grave." No sooner had the throat distemper abated, then the dread smallpox made its appearance. Martin Gay, in Boston, nearly lost his infant daughter Celia (named after his deceased sister) to the epidemic, but she survived. The family back in Hingham, however, was less fortunate. The parson wrote to Martin that, while Joanna, his youngest child, had recovered from the disease, "The beloved Persis Lyeth at the point of Death." Before the end of March 1752, Ebenezer and Jerusha stood on the burial hill that rose up behind the Old Ship Church, and watched the interment of this thirteen-year-old girl. The Gay family tomb now inclosed the remains of the first Abigail, Ebenezer, Jr., Celia, and Persis (Samuel was presumably buried in England).[30]

The Seven Years' War between England and France also

touched the parsonage in Hingham, but the results were less tragic than frustrating for Gay. As we have seen, Gay believed that a rational resistance to an unjust war was the duty of a Christian, but this belief should not lead us to characterize him as a convinced pacifist. He never considered any war against the French and/or the Papacy to be unjust. In his earliest childhood he had heard stories of the French and Indian atrocities at Deerfield and elsewhere, and his hatred and fear of the French had never abated. This abhorrence of the French was matched by his contempt for their religion, which he regarded as a corrupt repository of creeds, dogmas, and irrational superstition. He expressed his anti-Catholicism at the Annual Convention in 1746 when he told his listeners that "in the Papal Apostacy, abominable Doctrines have evidently their Rise from the vile Lusts of the Man of Sin. And the Missionaries of Rome, that spread them, are of the Members of unclean Spirits, which John saw, like Frogs, come out of the Mouth of the Dragon." In this same sermon, which was delivered in the aftermath of King George's War, Gay berated "the general Backwardness in the Ministers of the Lord, to attend his *Ark* into the *Camp*." Gay found it an easy matter "to reconcile with our Profession" the duties of a chaplain, particularly when fighting an enemy that he characterized in such unflattering, amphibian terms.[31]

When England next declared war against France, Gay was nearly sixty and clearly too old to serve in a chaplaincy. He jealously watched the younger members of the Hingham Association go off to succor the troops. John Brown of Cohasset served as chaplain of a provincial regiment at Halifax from March to November of 1759. Gad Hitchcock of "Tunk" and Daniel Shute of South Hingham both marched off to New York in March 1758. Shute served as chaplain to Colonel Joseph Williams's regiment, which participated in Abercrombie's disastrous attempt to take Fort Ticonderoga. He acquired enough anecdotes on that expedition to entertain and bore his friends for years. Back in Hingham, Gay did his best, preaching furious sermons about "the people that delight in war."[32]

Gay even attempted to draft his son Jotham into the chaplaincy. On June 25, 1759 Gay wrote, in his typically dry, sarcastic style, to John Brown, who was ministering to the garrison at Halifax at the same time that Jotham was stationed there: "I wish you may visit Jotham and minister good instruction to him and company, and furnish him with suitable sermons in print, or in your own very legible, if not very intelligible, manuscripts to read to his men, who are without a preacher; in the room of one, constitute Jotham curate." Brown did as he was bid, and a month later an exasperated Captain Jotham Gay wrote to his brother Martin: "If a good opportunity, should be glad you send me some good practical sermons that will be servicable to read to the Company on Sunday. As I have no Chaplain, and father has ordered me to act the part of one myself." The incident is at once amusing and pathetic, as Gay makes a last attempt to cast one of his sons in the role, however tenuous, of a gospel minister.[33]

Gay persevered through all the afflicting dispensations that God meted out to the South Shore in those years. Like most of his fellow liberals, Gay still believed, or at least acted upon the presumption, that the Lord had a special covenant relationship with New England. He believed in the efficacy of Fast Days and in the importance of public thanksgivings. From 1750 to 1770, he preached at least fourteen sermons on Fast Days. His Arminian deity was intimately involved in the world, punishing Massachusetts for her iniquity and rewarding her for her faithfulness. On August 20, 1761, prompted by a severe drought, the churches kept a Fast Day, and Gay's text on that occasion expressed the Arminian faith rather well: "Confess your faults one to another, and pray for one another, that ye may be healed. The effectual fervent prayer of a righteous man availeth much" (James 5:16). This faith in God's essential benevolence and in man's ability to actively court His favor sustained Gay during the difficult times. Furthermore, except for his conviction that he would not live long, Gay was not a morose man. For instance, in the fall of 1761, he became quite seriously ill and was certain that he soon "should be gone into the World of Spirits." He quickly rebounded, however, and his daughter Abigail, who had despaired of his life, was soon able to report to her brother that "Father is charming well." Gay had a great and infectious zest for life that continually broke through his facade of cautious reserve, delighting his family and friends. During 1761, the year of his illness, he preached from one of his favorite texts, Proverbs 15:15: "All the days of the afflicted are evil; but he that is of a merry heart, hath a continual feast."[34]

In 1768 the people of Hingham celebrated the fiftieth anniversary of Gay's ministry at the Old Ship. The aging parson could rejoice that he still commanded the love and devotion of his parish, and he praised his congregation, saying, "Fifty years have I sustained the pastoral relation to a people, and can now bear them the

testimony that I have not been once put on the disagreeable necessity of begging my bread of them." If Gay had been able to appoint
the time of his death, the year 1768 might not have been a bad
choice; but the rational benevolent deity whom he worshiped had
decided to be a little capricious. The old man was destined to live
on through the American Revolution. He and his family would endure hardships and humiliation, and his well-ordered social world
would be buffeted by a storm even more tempestuous than the
Great Awakening.[35]

# CHAPTER XI

# A Rank Tory

In the summer of 1763, George Grenville, the new English Chancellor of the Exchequer, was busy devising schemes to rescue Britain from the crushing burden of debt incurred during the last great war with France. Within the next two years a variety of measures were taken in order to enforce more efficiently the Laws of Trade and Navigation. The powers of the Admiralty Court were enlarged and the jurisdiction of customs officers extended in order to put an end to smuggling. More than this, however, the Grenville ministry began to treat duties on imports to the British colonies as important sources of revenue for the Crown. The Sugar Act of 1764, for instance, was unquestionably a measure designed to tax the American colonists. The strict enforcement of duties, particularly on the importation of foreign molasses, quickly began to pinch New England's mercantile economy. The leading merchants of Hingham were angry and so was Gay and his family. Jotham and Martin Gay began doing their best to smuggle rum into Nova Scotia "to escape paying the duty." Martin complained bitterly about the "heavy duties and taxes imposed on trade. The affects of which is so sensibly felt, together with what is soon to take place [the Stamp Act] that the people in general are much enraged."[1]

Ebenezer Gay himself grew increasingly apprehensive about the consequences of Britain's new and aggressive colonial policy. He opposed the Stamp Act and the right of Parliament to tax the colonies, and condemned those who were "eagerly seeking to subvert our constitution and deprive us of our privileges, civil and ecclesiastical." Gay believed that the rights granted by the old Massachusetts charter were under attack, but he would not counte-

211

nance any form of violence to protest the infringement of those rights. He recoiled in horror after learning about the Stamp Act riot in Boston, and after that event, became more and more determinedly Loyalist in his sympathies. He shared the reaction of his son Martin who wrote: "what the consequences of these horrid outrages committed by a rabble of mad, unreasonable men will be, time can only determine, for my part I wish for peace and good order."[2]

After the riotous summer of 1765, Gay became obsessed with the threat to social order posed by "demagogues" and mob violence. None of the measures of the British government worried him as much as "the Wrath of Men, which is cruel when it breaketh out in mobbish Fury." Gay's fear of the mob and his horror of civil chaos was shared by many of the Arminian clergymen; even Charles Chauncy, soon to become one of Boston's most zealous Whigs, was concerned about the "violent outrages" committed upon property during the Riot. Nevertheless, as British-American relations deteriorated with the subsequent passage of the Townshend Acts, the arrival of British troops in Boston, and the Coercive Acts, most of the Liberal clergy decided that the threat to their civil and religious liberties justified the socially disruptive consequences of resistance. Gay never came to that point, but instead maintained a steadfast loyalty to British authority. His allegiance to the Crown was determined by a multiplicity of factors that included age, temperament, environment, and philosophical conviction. None of these elements were individually determinative, but taken in conjunction they propelled Gay along his lonely Loyalist course.[3]

One of the more obvious factors that influenced Gay's attitude towards the Revolution was his old age. He was nearly seventy years old at the time of the Stamp Act crisis, nine years older than the veteran Chauncy. His advanced age tended to make him less flexible and more imperious than his younger colleagues, but it also revealed him increasingly as a child of the seventeenth century. The younger Arminians, as Alan Heimert has suggested, had difficulty reconciling their faith in human rationality and Divine benevolence with the unrestrained passions of the time. They tended to ignore the increasingly irrational politics of the day, or, like Mayhew, they began to identify their crusade for "Christian Liberty" with the struggle for civil liberty. Like the first group, Gay also avoided dwelling on unpleasant political realities, but when he did confront the issues and events, he tended to fall back into the old covenant rhetoric which stressed God's displeasure with his chosen people. Like Nathaniel Appleton, his contemporary in age, Gay publicly interpreted events such as the Boston Massacre as judgements against an unruly and disobedient people. Calamities like the Massacre were seen as occasions for introspection and repentance rather than as motives for resisting tyranny.[4]

Gay's indifference to the Whig cause was also influenced by his distance from Boston and, of course, by his conservative temperament. He was a conciliator by nature, a latitudinarian who believed that reasonably intelligent men could adjust differences and reach compromise in order to secure a greater good in which they all believed. Living in Hingham, Gay was not confronted with British troops marching along the streets or drilling on the common; he was far removed from the daily provocations of a military occupation. He had no Anglican churches in town to remind him of the threat of "Episcopal tyranny." Consequently, Gay simply found it difficult to understand why his old friend Chauncy, even allowing for the latter's choleric disposition, had thrown in his lot with James Otis and Sam Adams. Gay explicitly compared the Boston mob with the deluded disciples of Whitefield and Davenport, twenty years before. The Sons of Liberty became for him the very incarnation of the unruly passions, and Gay was determined that "Reason may know its divine Right to govern, to maintain its Empire in the Soul, regulating the Passions and affections."[5]

Fear of social disruption, old age, a country parish—all these were constituent elements in Gay's Toryism, but they were not enough to launch this judicious man into active opposition to the Whig party. The justifying principle that seems to have animated and sustained Gay's Loyalism from 1765 on through the Revolution was that of passive obedience to properly constituted authority. Gay's belief in political nonresistance appears to have its source in the writings of Hugo Grotius, the seventeenth-century Dutch philosopher; specifically in Grotius's *De Jure Belli ac Pacis*, the same work that had so inspired him in the early 1730s. Grotius had based his philosophy of absolute submission, even to tyrants, largely on the example of the early church and the New Testament writings of Paul (particularly Rom. 13 : 1–7). Gay, in effect, told his Hingham parishioners that if Paul had advocated submission even to the tyranny of the depraved Roman emperors, then the misguided policies of essentially well-intentioned British ministers should certainly not justify armed rebellion. Buttressed by Grotius and Saint Paul, Gay, as a contemporary observed, "inculcated Submission to Authority in pretty strong Expressions."[6]

Gay publicly expressed his opinion of the Boston riot and the Stamp Act Congress on Thanksgiving Day, 1765. He stood in the pulpit of the Old Ship and pleaded for restraint, reminding his congregation that "the ancient Weapons of the Church were Prayers and Tears, not Clubbs." Passions were still running high, however, and for the first time in his forty-seven-year ministry, Gay found himself clearly out of sympathy with the majority of his parish. The Reverend William Smith of Weymouth related the story to his son-in-law, John Adams, describing the "Uneasiness among the People of Hingham. . . . His People said that Mr. Gay would do very well for a Distributor, and they believed he had the Stamps in his House, and even threatened, &c." Parson Smith himself apparently aggravated the situation. The Sunday after Gay's disastrous Thanksgiving sermon, Smith preached at the Old Ship. While, according to Adams's account, Smith recommended "Obedience to good Rulers," he also urged "a Spirited Opposition to bad Ones, interspersed with a good deal of animated Declamation upon Liberty and the Times." The sermon was widely praised in Hingham and the dissatisfaction with Gay was heightened. This public rebuke from his old friend must have rankled Gay, but the two ministers did not allow their political differences to separate them. During the Revolution, Smith continued to exchange pulpits with Gay, even though the latter's Loyalism caused other Whig ministers to shun him.[7]

Gay's policy of nonresistance had suddenly opened a breach between himself and many of his old acquaintances. He was moving in the opposite political direction not only from Jonathan Mayhew and William Smith, but also from many of the leading citizens of Hingham. One of his closest friends, Dr. Ezekiel Hersey, was the most active Whig in town, organizing town and regional political action committees and constantly urging Hingham down the path of radical opposition. Gay was so convinced of the propriety of his own course, however, that he organized a "Clubb" to promote his views. John Adams recorded the names of some of the club members, and the list suggests that Gay was still supported by many of the most influential members of the Hingham Town establishment. All the members of the club were predisposed to Loyalism, since their careers, their wealth, and much of their influence depended largely on their connections with the Crown. Colonel

Benjamin Lincoln was at that time serving as a member of the Governor's Council, a position he held from 1753 to 1770; Captain Joshua Barker had served as a commissioned officer in His Majesty's Service from 1740 to 1762, and was now supporting his family on his pension (Adams described him as "an half Pay Officer"); Captain Francis Barker, a prosperous shipwright, shared his brother's loyalty to the Crown; Colonel John Thaxter, the powerful, aristocratic grandson of old Colonel Samuel Thaxter, also had military and political connections with the royal establishment. All these gentlemen lived within a few minutes' walk to the parsonage, and they were all related.[8]

The very existence of this club was something remarkable. Loyalists rarely formed organizations to promulgate and defend their views; consequently the Whigs rarely met any coherent opposition. Gay, however, was determined to moderate and subdue the unruly passions in Hingham and so he very quickly formed this network of influential, like-minded citizens. The members met every Sunday evening in Gay's parlor and, again according to John Adams, their principal aim was to promote "Passive Obedience—as the best Way to procure Redress." Adams could not resist adding, "A very absurd Sentiment indeed!" Ebenezer Gay was still marshaling the troops against the forces of enthusiasm; the scene of battle had simply shifted from the religious to the secular arena.[9]

After the repeal of the Stamp Act in 1766, Gay and his party had an easier time of it. Economic prosperity had returned to Hingham and the moderate conservatism of the town reasserted itself. The local merchants, for the most part, were not particularly agitated by the Townshend Acts of 1767. The duties the Acts imposed on enumerated articles may have been politically obnoxious, but they had little real effect on the economy. Consequently, when Sam Adams wrote to the country towns to ask them to join Boston in a boycott of British goods and to encourage domestic industry, Hingham voted not to participate. By the time of the Massachusetts Convention of 1768, Dr. Hersey's Whigs and the Gay-Lincoln faction were agreed on basic political objectives. The convention had been called by Sam Adams to decide how to respond to the British troops that the Ministry was sending to restore order in Boston after the "Liberty Riot." The instructions to the Hingham delegate, drafted principally by Dr. Hersey and Colonel Lincoln, carried the same conservative message of most of the country towns. They urged their representative to "use your Endeavours to preserve peace & good Order in the Province and Loyalty to the King." At the same time, Hingham's delegate was instructed to use "Every Legal & Constitutional method for ye preservation of Our Rights & Libertys" and to urge that citizens be encouraged "to keep up Military Duty whereby they may be in a Capacity to Defend themselves against Foreign Enemies."[10]

In the year 1769, the lull before the Revolutionary storm, Gay was dispirited. He seriously doubted whether his constitution was strong enough to cope with the "ruinous Contentions" that lay ahead. Joseph Thaxter, the young man whom he was currently tutoring in theology, later wrote of Gay, "It was his greatest dread, he often said to his friends, to live beyond his usefulness." This depression was deepened when he learned of the death, on October 18, of his brother Lusher, aged eighty-four. The pious old squire of Clapboard-trees had been, since boyhood, Gay's confidante and trusted advisor. After attending the funeral at Dedham, Gay came to Braintree to preach for Anthony Wibird. John Adams heard the sermon, and has left us this sensitive account:

> The good old Gentleman . . . seemed to be very much affected. He said in his Prayer, that God in the Course of his Providence was admonishing him that he must very soon put off this Tabernacle, and prayed that the Dispensation might be sanctified to him—and he told the People in the Introduction to his Sermon, that this would probably be the last Exhortation they would ever hear from him their old Acquaintance. I have not heard a more affecting, or more rational Entertainment any Sabbath for many Years.[11]

Beginning on March 5, 1770, the "good old Gentleman's" ordeal commenced in earnest. On the evening of that day, a confrontation between the Boston mob and soldiers from His Majesty's Twenty-ninth Regiment resulted in the death of five civilians. News of the "Boston Massacre" turned the tide of public opinion in Hingham back against the British Ministry and their "bloodthirsty" army of occupation. At about this same time the leadership of the Whig party in Hingham was assumed by Benjamin Lincoln, Jr. His Tory father, Colonel Lincoln, was retiring from public affairs due to ill health and the thirty-seven-year-old son quickly emerged as the dominant personality in Hingham's public life. He was, in some respects, even more aristocratic than his father, but he was nevertheless a staunch Whig. On March 19 young Lincoln, in his capacity as Town Clerk, informed the Boston Committee of Merchants of some resolutions that had been approved at the annual town meeting. One involved Hingham's decision to join in the Non-Importation Agreement until the Townshend Duties were repealed. Another resolution expressed Hingham's hearty sympathy "with our brethren of the town of Boston, in the late unhappy destruction of so many of their inhabitants." [12]

Throughout the year 1770, anxiety over the intentions of the British continued to mount in Hingham, and Gay attempted to dispel the fears of his flock. His foremost effort was a sermon entitled *The Devotions of God's People Adjusted to the Dispensations of His Providence* which he delivered on December 6, a day that Governor Hutchinson had appointed for public thanksgiving. Gay's discourse was in part a sermon of thanksgiving, albeit muted thanksgiving, and in part an old-fashioned jeremiad. Both themes met with a chilly reception from his congregation. The thanksgiving portion was embarrassingly strained, and Gay acknowledged that some people thought a public Fast "would have been more seasonable." The blessings that he enumerated included "Peace . . . with foreign Enemies, by his Majesty's Care preserved to all his Dominions"; the absence of "infectious or any epidemical Diseases"; "the good Encrease of our Land (free from Parliamentary Taxation)." [13]

In this thanksgiving sermon, Gay was essentially pleading for perspective. He sought to calm what he perceived as the irrational fear of ministerial plots against colonial liberties by insisting that the situation be assessed dispassionately. Once this were done, the people of Hingham would see that "we continue as yet possessed of the most valuable Liberties and Privileges belonging to Englishmen, and Christians, and do lead our Lives so comfortably as we do. We still have Rulers that will not oppress in themselves, nor, if they can prevent it, suffer others to oppress us." While not specifically denying the right of an oppressed people to throw off tyranny, Gay answered the would-be rebels by vigorously denying that the current governing authorities qualified as despots: "they must be worse Rulers than are Known in *Old England* or *New*, from whose administration People do not receive more Benefits, than they suffer Mischiefs. . . . What the Proportion between these hath been in the late difficult Times, I'm not about to compute." That last admission suggests that Gay understood the weakness of his case; nevertheless, he insisted that his congregation evaluate political events in a balanced way, remembering that "The Condition of a People in this World is not at any Time altogether prosperous nor quite desperate."[14]

After dutifully enumerating the blessings that God and the king had bestowed on the Bay Province, Gay turned to the subject that was on everyone's mind—the Massacre. He simply could not suppress the horror and outrage he felt, and he expressed it in the form of a jeremiad, a style of preaching Gay had skillfully employed throughout his ministry. He told his listeners that "A righteous God hath punished us for our Iniquities." How?

> By leaving us to fall into ruinous Contention among ourselves—into a most unquiet state, in which Men's Minds have been extremely discomposed, and exasperated; their Mouth filled with evil Speeches, bitter Invectives, and horrid Execrations; and their Hands stretched out in base injurious Deeds of Violence—the public Counsels have been divided—friendly and profitable Commerce interrupted—Tumults raised—Outrages committed—Blood shed.

Gay was saying, in effect, that God's punishment was not being administered through the British Ministry or its troops, but rather through the social upheaval created by ranting demagogues and the Boston rabble who followed them. The greatest affliction in the land was the spirit of civil disobedience that was being promoted by Sam Adams and the radical Whigs of Boston.[15]

Gay's call to repentance, indeed his entire thanksgiving sermon, excited great indignation among the Boston radicals. Sam Adams supposedly remarked that Gay was "trimming with the Almighty," and Martin Gay sent a copy to Jotham commenting that "The enclosed Sermon has established father in the minds of some to be a rank Tory." Gay's outspoken Loyalism and the somewhat tepid Whiggism of Hingham both received their share of invective in the Boston papers. Late in 1772, a "Lover of Truth and his Country" compared the patriotic zeal of Hingham with that of Plymouth, and found the former wanting: "if we may judge from their Inactivity at Times, &c., and from the known sentiments of their aged Minister (whose system of Religion and Politicks by the way can never be made to coincide) they are moderate in the extreme." On November 24, Deacon Joshua Hersey defended Gay and the town in the pages of the *Boston Weekly News-Letter*. Hersey had been a deacon of the First Church since 1740 (succeeding his father) and had served as Hingham's Representative since 1758. He wrote:

> The People in our Town are generally moderate Whigs, real Friends to Liberty, which we know can never be maintained except we are under some Form of Government or other. We think that the present Leaders in the Town of Boston are hurting the cause of Liberty as well as the Cause of Government. . . . Our good old Minister is uniform in his Religion and in his Politicks. He has always preached the same Doctrine in both. He tells us that we should let our Reasons and not our Passions govern us in both.[16]

Deacon Hersey and "Lover of Truth" (who may very well have been Sam Adams himself) were fighting the battles of the Great Awakening all over again. "Lover of Truth" developed his charge that Gay's politics did not conform to his theology: "in religious Matters [Gay] carries Liberty to as great an Extent as any Man, but in civil tis said is not so liberal; and so indissoluble is the Connexion between civil and religious Liberty, as will warrant my Assertion." Deacon Hersey, in his turn, made an explicit connection between New Light fervor and revolutionary zeal. In an earlier letter to the editor he wrote: "Your Demosthenes who flourished away in last Monday's Boston Gazette is a Madman. His Rant and Rhapsody puts us in mind of the Ravings of religious Enthusiasm, both being equally calculated to work up the Minds of weak and undiscerning Men to extravagant Undertakings." Martin Gay, a far more virulent Tory than his father, invariably characterized the rebels as demented enthusiasts. Even after the Revolution was accomplished, Martin sarcastically referred to "the United Saints," "this pious country," and "this New Heaven and Earth."[17]

One can certainly argue, as Alan Heimert does, that Arminian ministers such as Gay were not the sort of men one would expect to find in the vanguard of the Revolutionary movement. Like Gay, they were committed to preserving social and ecclesiastical stability, and they were quite naturally repelled by the impassioned, irrational, dogmatic effusions of men like Sam Adams. Yet the fact remains that Gay stood virtually alone among the South Shore liberals in his adamant Toryism. Recognizing this, Heimert has argued, in effect, that Gay was the only man among them to have the courage of his convictions. As an example, Heimert properly cites South Hingham's Daniel Shute as an example of an Arminian pseudo-Whig, whose political principles were much closer to Gay's than they were to the Sons of Liberty. In his 1768 Election Sermon, Shute had warned that "To pour contempt upon rulers . . . is to sow the seeds of libertinism!" Then, revealing his total political kinship with Gay, he advised that, instead of "speaking evil of dignities, and cruelly charging them with the blame of prevailing disorders, we should recriminate ourselves." That Shute did not follow Gay into overt Loyalism was probably due to the politics of his parish. South Hingham had a far more rebellious temper than the Town, and Theophilus Cushing, Jr., the son of Shute's chief patron, was one of the most zealous members of Hingham's Committee of Safety. Shute, consequently, kept his political opinions to himself and became so acceptable to Hingham's Whigs (partly by virtue of contrast with Gay) that they chose him as their representative to the Massachusetts constitutional convention of 1779.[18]

Although the Heimert thesis may account for the behavior of Gay and even Shute, it does not explain the patriotic fervor with which many of the South Shore Arminians were imbued. They spoke passionately about the need for defending American liberties, and they defined those liberties as fundamental rights proceeding from the Law of God and Nature. Gad Hitchcock of "Tunk" delivered an inflammatory Election Sermon in 1774. In the presence of General Gage, the new governor, he spoke of "our groanings that cannot be uttered," and proclaimed: "Our danger is not visionary, but real—Our contention is not about trifles, but about liberty and property; . . . If I am mistaken in supposing plans are formed and executing, subversive of our natural and chartered rights and privileges, and incompatible with every idea of liberty, *all America is mistaken with me.*" Gage was said to have been furious after Hitchcock's sermon because of "the air of defiance that pervaded it." The Election Sermon of the preceding year had been delivered by the Reverend Charles Turner of Duxbury, another South Shore Arminian. He spoke of the right of a people to resist when they believed their constitutional freedom to be imperiled, and dwelt on the close connection between civil and religious liberty. Later in 1773, Turner exhorted a crowd at Plymouth to keep up "A *spirit* of liberty" which he said was "necessary to the preservation of the thing."[19]

Gad Hitchcock and Charles Turner were not alone among the members of the Hingham Association in their defiance of the Crown. Old William Smith's Whiggish sympathies have already

been described, and John Brown of Cohasset was positively militant. Brown was constitutionally hot-tempered, and he became increasingly convinced that the British Ministry, with the connivance
of "Domestick enemies," was conspiring against "our happy Constitution." In a letter to General John Thomas, he described his
course of action after receiving news of the fight at Lexington:

> I instantly repaired to the Meeting house where there was a full Col-
> lection of the Inhabitants of this District upon publick Business. I
> read the News, expatiated upon it, and could plainly perceive an un-
> common Elevation of Spirit in the People.

Seven years later, on November 11, 1782, Brown noted in his diary:
"At Home. Preached on Surrender of Cornwallis, a Devil, at Vir-
ginia." Brown had considered serving as a chaplain, but decided
that his flock would need their shepherd. Gad Hitchcock, on the
other hand, did serve several times during the Revolution as an un-
commissioned chaplain, and so did Joseph Thaxter, Gay's latest
protégé and heir apparent to the Old Ship pulpit. Thaxter, according to tradition, was present during the battle at Concord Bridge,
"armed with a brace of pistols." He later served as chaplain to Colonel Prescott's regiment at the time of Bunker Hill. The social conservatism of the South Shore Arminians clearly did not inhibit
most of them from joining the struggle for liberty with as much enthusiasm as the merchants and mariners in their congregations.[20]

Gay's Arminian associates in Boston, living in the center of
the storm, also embraced the patriot cause. Charles Chauncy became fondly known as "Charles Old-Brick," a prickly and irascible
foe of the royal establishment. In the aftermath of the Boston Massacre, when Gay was inveighing against "mobbish Fury," Chauncy
was demanding vengeance against those "who have murderously
spilt the blood of others!" Simeon Howard, Gay's other Arminian
colleague in Boston, reacted in a far more circumspect way than
Chauncy. Howard was a man who instinctively shunned controversy, and so he tried to remain politically neutral. He was well
aware that inflammatory Whig discourses would have met with a
cool reception at West Church where the lay leadership was comprised of such active Loyalists as Harrison Gray and Martin Gay.
Howard himself has been characterized as a quiet Tory by some
historians, but if he was, he certainly failed to convince the British
of his loyalty. The King's Regulars pulled down the West Church
steeple, assuming that it was being used to communicate with the

rebel troops across the Charles River in Cambridge, after which they commandeered the church for use as a barrack. In June 1775 Howard and some of his congregation attempted to reconstitute themselves in Nova Scotia, but poor Simeon was temporarily clapped in jail by the authorities in Halifax. There is no question that, though Howard's public commitment to political and religious liberty may have been muted during the American Revolution, by the time of the French Revolution he was either more candid or his vision had been enlarged. In 1791 this former student of Ebenezer Gay wrote to Jonathan Mayhew's daughter, declaring:

> Light seems to be now a second time coming into the world, and the great Father of all to be calling his children out of darkness; and for this purpose he will probably raise up Miltons, Lockes, Sidneys, Hoadleys, and Prices, and multiply Paines, Priestlys, &c. . . . I flatter myself that the period is not very far distant when Liberty, the choicest gift of Heaven, will be more fully enjoyed not only in G.B. but in all the other countries of Europe, then it has ever been; however furiously the Burkes may labor to prevent it.[21]

Clearly, a majority of the Arminian clergymen in Boston and the South Shore supported the Whig cause. Some were reluctant rebels and others were extremely zealous. Their revolutionary sympathies were inspired by a variety of factors that included local town and parish politics, family connections, and personal temperament. Most of them feared the prospect of social revolution, but they had an even greater fear of the economic, religious, and political consequences of British ministerial policy. Consequently, Ebenezer Gay, far from being representative of the liberal ministry, was almost alone in his dogged insistence on loyalty and passive obedience. His political views strained relations not only with his colleagues in the Hingham Association, but even with old friends like Chauncy. The breach between Gay and his fellow Arminians was not irreparable—he was too well loved and respected for that—but it was nonetheless painful for him while it lasted. In 1777 his daughter Jerusha wrote to her brother that "Father's differing from most of the ministers in his opinions has deprived him of their company which used to be his greatest pleasure." Gay persisted in his course, however, despite his ostracism. He once declared that a minister should proceed "uniformly in his Work, not changing with the Wind of a vertiginous World."[22]

There may have been a certain distance between Gay and his

children on other matters, but on the question of loyalty to the Crown, the Gay clan was clearly united. After the Boston Tea Party in December 1773, the feelings of Gay and his kin were best expressed by Jotham when he wrote to Martin wondering if the latter could send him "a few pounds of tea (without subjecting yourself to be *tarred and feathered*)." In March 1776 Jotham vigorously asserted his allegiance to Great Britain before the authorities at Halifax. In 1774 Martin became a public enemy to the Whig cause when he signed a farewell letter that thanked the departing Governor Thomas Hutchinson for his capable administration. Many of the principal lawyers, merchants, magistrates, and Episcopal clergymen in the Boston area were among the one hundred and twenty-three signers. Ebenezer Gay's nephew, Colonel Eliphalet Pond of Dedham, joined Martin as one of the "Addressers" to Hutchinson. (Colonel Pond, a wealthy landowner, was the son of Mary Gay Pond, Gay's eldest sister. He was only eight years younger than Gay and the two had been close friends for years.) This Loyalist sentiment also extended to members of Jerusha Gay's family who lived in Hingham. Her nephew, Captain George Lane, was an active member of Hingham's Tory faction. The bitter political atmosphere even affected Gay's daughter, Jerusha, who was normally even-tempered and apolitical. She wrote to Jotham that "the happy time will come when we shall meet in peace and be delivered from this slavery which is falsely called Liberty." [23]

In the years after 1771, Gay was keenly aware that he was alienating the affections of his parish. The Captain still kept his place, but the "crew" of the Old Ship was clearly following the lead of Hingham's most prominent Whig, Deacon Benjamin Lincoln, Jr. Still Gay struggled to re-assert control. He strained the tolerance of his congregation to the limit and beyond, as Sunday after Sunday he urged submission to the Crown. The old man stood in the towering Ship Church pulpit and vividly depicted the terrible consequences of rebellion. The sermons themselves have not survived, but the scripture texts from which he preached were recorded. These skillfully chosen texts provide us with a clear picture of the message that Gay was trying to convey to his flock. On June 12, 1774, he preached from 2 Kings 8:11, 12: "and Hazael said, why weepest my lord? And he answered, Because I know the evil that thou wilt do unto the children of Israel; their strongholds wilt thou set on fire, and their young men wilt thou slay with the sword, and wilt dash their children, and rip up their women with child." Three days later he preached from Acts 12:20: "And Herod was highly displeased with them of Tyre and Sidon; but they came of one accord to him, and . . . desired peace, because their country was nourished by the king's country." By July 26, 1777 he was improving texts such as 1 Samuel 24:5—6: "And it came to pass afterward that David's heart smote him, because he had cut off Saul's skirt. And he said unto his men, The Lord forbid that I should do this thing unto my master, the Lord's anointed."[24]

As the jeremiads and calls to repentance continued to pour forth from the pulpit, the Old Ship congregation and the town itself grew increasingly restive. In 1775 the Church Appropriations Committee reduced Gay's salary from £110 to £100. With the exception of a small revival in 1776, the number of admissions to full communion dwindled to an average of only three persons per year (see Appendix 1). The most overt display of hostility to Gay survives only as a part of Hingham tradition. There is, however, no reason to doubt that the broad outlines of the story are true. The incident was printed as early as 1827 in Solomon Lincoln's *History of Hingham*, and Lincoln, a fairly careful local historian, wrote: "We have this anecdote from an authentic source." During the Revolution, one of the duties of the Committee of Safety was to search the homes of suspected Loyalists and seize any weapons or ammunition which they might find. The members of the Committee decided that, using this as a pretext, they should call on Gay, simply to give him an "official admonition that he held obnoxious sentiments. . . . That the thing to be done was a little aggravating did not take away the zest of doing it." This last comment was particularly true, since four of the five members of the Committee came from outside the First Parish. Here was a perfect opportunity to harass Gay and the Tory-leaning Town establishment with impunity.[25]

The Committee, led by Theophilus Cushing, Jr. of South Hingham (the Cushings were ever a thorn in Gay's side), arrived at the parsonage and Gay received them in his study. Standing before them, the tall, dignified old man calmly asked the purpose of their visit. The leader responded that it was the duty of the Committee to ask about any arms he might have in the house. Then, to quote from the felicitous prose of Solomon Lincoln:

> [Gay] looked at them kindly, perhaps a little reproachfully, for a moment or two before answering, and then said, laying his hand upon a

large Bible on the table by which he stood, "There, my friends, are *my* arms, and I trust to find them ever sufficient for me."

The Committee retired with some precipitation, discomfited by the dignified manner and implied rebuke of Dr. Gay, and the chairman was heard to say to his associates, as they passed out of the yard, "The old gentleman is always ready."[26]

Solomon Lincoln implied that Gay's Loyalism was only a minor irritant in the otherwise harmonious relations between Gay and his people. Although it is true that most of his parishioners forgave him after the Revolution, they apparently felt, at this time, a deep and bitter sense of betrayal by their old pastor. Later, reflecting on the period, Gay remarked that if "an end had been put to our existence, we should have been so far happy as not to have seen the evil of these days of old age; and we may have cause to think it had been well for us not to have lived to them." In March 1777 his daughter Jerusha wrote a letter to Martin Gay which incisively described the atmosphere at the parsonage:

> . . . all this part of the world are so prejudiced against tories—it is dreadful times here. . . . Father has been very ill with a pain in his stomach. He is better. We are in constant expectation of his death. I am afraid you will never see him again. He thinks that all this country will be destroyed, but he says he shall not live to see it—but he is ready and willing to depart. He says he can't write as he thinks it is not safe for him to do anything as he is watched in all he says and does.[27]

It is not surprising that Gay, with his penchant for identifying himself with Old Testament patriarchs, preached increasingly from the Book of Job as the Revolution wore on. Like the biblical Job, Gay, in addition to losing the esteem of many of his former friends, also continued to suffer the torment of watching his children die. Although they saw their sons only infrequently, Ebenezer and Jerusha had been comforted by their three daughters, Abby, Rusha, and Joe (Joanna). However, in 1772, Joanna, Gay's youngest child, became ill. She had always been frail, and had barely survived the 1752 smallpox epidemic that had carried off her sister Persis. Her very fragility had made her the family favorite, and now they helplessly watched the thirty-one-year-old Joe suffer a "long sickness and very hard death."[28]

In May 1775 this "sorrowful providence" was partly ameliorated by the arrival from Boston of John and Celia Boyle and their two children. Celia was the twenty-three-year-old daughter of Martin Gay; she was described as a charming young woman of "lively penetrating Genius." In 1772 she had married John Boyle, a Boston printer who was rising rapidly in his profession. After the rebel militia had encircled Boston, Boyle decided to remove "my Family from Boston to Hingham by Water (where I propose to Reside during the Continuance of our public Difficulties)." A year later, on April 4, 1776, Celia gave birth at the parsonage to Martin Gay Boyle; three days later he was baptized by his proud great-grandfather. A week after the boy was born, however, Celia was suddenly seized by "a violent Fever, which . . . very soon put a period to her Existence." So it was that, twenty-seven years after the death of her aunt and namesake, the second Celia Gay was laid to rest in Hingham. Within the month, a despondent John Boyle had returned to Boston.[29]

Gay also suffered from some of the same infirmities of the flesh that afflicted Job, including a "sore" on his face. He was not constitutionally infirm, but he apparently did have high blood pressure and ulcers. His occasional bouts of illness seemed to be due largely to the stress of the times, and to his reluctance to slacken his pace. For instance, during May and June of 1773, he was utterly incapacitated, and even by late June was barely able to sit through the service which one of his theology students conducted at the meetinghouse. Yet within a month, he felt well enough to ride to Boston and return the next day. In 1775, Gay became so ill that he could not preach from August through November; his daughter wrote that "his death is to be expected daily." On most of these and other occasions, Gay's preaching and pastoral duties fell to Joseph Thaxter, his former student (1768–1770), who was acting as a *de facto* associate pastor. Thaxter, a great-grandson of Colonel Samuel Thaxter, Gay's early patron in Hingham, fully expected to become the fourth minister of Hingham's First Parish. He cherished that hope until 1780 when, after numerous false alarms, he apparently became convinced that the old Tory did not intend either to resign or to die. In later years, Gay himself marveled, "How often hath God healed our diseases, and brought us back from the gates of death, that we might praise him in the land of the living!"[30]

The social ostracism of the family and the tribulations of her children also took their toll on old Jerusha Gay, but like her husband, she was fairly resilient. In May 1775 a granddaughter wrote that "Grandmother . . . has had a very ill turn but is much better, so well as to be at work out of doors; the distress of the times we thought would quite make an end of her." One of the greatest vexations afflicting the old couple during the Revolution was the near impossibility of getting tea. Their daughter Jerusha wrote to Jotham, "If it should be in your power to send us some, I believe it would add to father's and mother's days for they can't live without it and we cannot buy it hear [sic] at the price it is."[31]

Most of the suffering that Ebenezer and Jerusha endured was psychological. Their greatest anxieties concerned the welfare of their sons, Jotham and Martin, whom they despaired of ever seeing again. One would have thought that Jotham, living in Nova Scotia, could not have been better situated to wait out the war in safety. However, he found himself in the middle of the only significant rebel action taken in that province. Jonathan Eddy, one of Jotham's fellow Cumberland grantees, was a zealous Whig who, in the late autumn of 1776, organized a party of Yankees and Acadians to attack and seize Fort Cumberland. His raiders numbered less than two hundred and the attack was repulsed, but he then turned to terrorizing and looting the countryside. Jotham wrote, "I cannot describe to you the horror and misery which he has brought on the county and its inhabitants." He had just offered shelter to three families who had been burnt out by Eddy when the raiders arrived at his own farm. Jotham was disarmed, confined "and threatened with immediate death if I or any person belonging to the family was seen . . . to be one foot off my own land." He survived, however, and soon after, Eddy's forces were surprised in their camp and dispersed by two companies of British marines.[32]

Jonathan Eddy's raid, terrifying as it was, was only a passing incident in the life of Jotham Gay. For his brother Martin, however, the Revolution launched a lifetime of tribulation. On March 17, 1776, this implacable Tory sailed for Halifax with the British when they evacuated Boston. He left his wife Ruth and five-year-old-son Ebenezer in town to try to secure his Union Street property against seizure by the rebels. Within the year, a neighboring shopkeeper named Harbottle Dorr attempted to do just that. He tried to attach the house and copper foundry on the grounds that Martin had looted *his* shop while the British and Tories were still in Boston. Exiled in Halifax, Martin could only deny the charge and fume about "That republican, N[ew] E[ngland] puritanical Harbottle Dorr." Ruth Gay, however, had the wit and courage to keep Dorr and other litigants from seizing the property.[33]

During his eight year exile in Halifax, Martin energetically attempted to establish an export business, but he was thwarted at every turn. At one point, while he was sailing on business across the Bay of Fundy, Martin's ship was accosted by a rebel privateer. The pirates relieved him of all his money, his watch, some new clothes, and left him, as he put it, with "only the rough clothes I had on my back, except one shirt and one pair of stockings. I was confined a prisoner under very disagreeable circumstances for near a fortnight." Failing to get adequate compensation for all his losses from the British government, Martin returned to Boston in September 1784, and, with extraordinary insensitivity, began to demand the repayment of debts owed him, pleading "the protection and privilege of a British subject." His position in Boston quickly became precarious. As he looked about the city he had fled eight years before, he concluded, as did many Loyalists, that this had been a social revolution as well as a war for independence:

> This town and the part of the country I have visited appear as natural to me as formerly, but the sight of the greatest part of the people inhabiting them, together with the change of property the late Revolution has made, is not a little mortifying and occasions no pleasing reflections when compared with former times when the country was under the government of the truly great and venerable.

Martin did manage to survive in Boston but he was never able to reach the level of prosperity he had enjoyed before the Revolution. He remained as embittered at his death in 1809 as he had been in 1789 when he declared, "I cannot feel my prejudice in the least abated, and hope it will be so ordered by a good providence that I may live and die a British subject."[34]

The sufferings of his children and the sullen behavior of disaffected parishioners made the Revolutionary years the bleakest period in Gay's long life. Unlike the patriarch Job, however, old Ebenezer's lot was not entirely devoid of small pleasures. In the summer of 1777, for instance, Gay attended a delightful outing on Langlee Island in Hingham Harbor, accompanied by his former pupil and fellow Loyalist (though a very quiet one), Caleb Gannett. The gentle sea breeze on the island dispelled the oppressive summer heat and the thirty-six "gentlemen and ladies" spent "an agreeable afternoon," even though coffee was served in place of tea. A more interesting diversion was supplied to Gay by the military authorities when they temporarily quartered Colonel Groton, a British prisoner of war, at the parsonage. The colonel was probably interrogated more exhaustively by his host than he had ever been by his captors. Gay's greatest pleasure, however, was his latest and last theology student, Bezaleel Howard.[35]

Bezaleel, like his distant cousin Simeon, came from Bridgewater. He graduated from Harvard in 1781 and came to Hingham in the fall to teach school and study with Gay. Howard fully shared his mentor's Arminian theology and his detestation of the war. Like all of Gay's pupils, as far back as Daniel Rogers in 1729, Howard vowed to base his ministry solely on the scriptures, and not, as he put it, to "warp his mind with any of those human bodies of divinity." Calvinist dogma, in his opinion, was simply irrational, a primitive relic of an earlier age. In 1785, he received a call from the First Parish of Springfield; their pastor, that old Arminian, Robert Breck, had died the year before. Thus, Gay's last theology student found himself occupying the only Arminian pulpit in the Connecticut Valley, the region that Conrad Wright has called "Yale territory."[36]

Even before the Revolution had ended, Gay began to move toward reconciliation with the disaffected members of his parish. The alienation of affection, to use one of Gay's favorite phrases, was certainly not irremediable. Despite his unwavering opposition to the Revolutionary cause, Gay was too practiced a diplomat to antagonize his people needlessly. Even after the hazing, for such it was, by the Committee of Safety, Gay kept his temper and followed his own advice "To keep the spirit quiet and undisturb'd amidst all provocation to wrath, and storms of adversity." At the same time, Gay's loyal friends and supporters, such as Deacons Joshua Hersey and Joseph Thaxter, Sr., worked to persuade the more disgruntled church members to bear with their old minister and not allow his Loyalist sympathies to obscure a lifetime of pastoral devotion. After 1775, the church leaders conscientiously tried to adjust Gay's salary to the horrendous inflation of the paper currency issued by the Continental Congress. In 1777 his salary was raised from £100 to £300, in 1778 to £600, in 1779 to £1600, and in 1780 to £5500. In 1781 the parish gave Gay "twenty cord of wood . . . in consideration of the small salary he had last year." The Levite was not forsaken.[37]

# CHAPTER XII

# The Old Man's Calendar

Gay was, in a sense, reunited with his flock on August 26, 1781, his eighty-fifth birthday. He preached a sermon that day that he later published as *The Old Man's Calendar*. The discourse was at once touching and frightening as it depicted the miseries and travails of old age. It went through several editions (the last in 1846) and, according to the preface of the 1822 edition, "met with so much favor from the public, that it was re-printed not only in this country, but also in England and in Holland, being translated into the Dutch language." Gay began the sermon with the mournful observation that "There is not in this assembly more than one person who can adopt the words of the text, and say, I am this day fourscore and *five years old*." This sort of prose apparently touched the sentimental nerves of nineteenth-century readers, but the sermon was, in fact, a piece of classic eighteenth-century Arminian exposition. As was frequently the case, Gay's sermon had two aims. The more explicit theme was his call to the senior citizens of Hingham to repent while they still had the opportunity. His primary, though less obvious intent, however, was to offer an olive branch to the Old Ship congregation.[1]

*The Old Man's Calendar* was basically designed to show the relevance of the Arminian gospel for the aged. Gay repeatedly made the point that, although old age is attended with "peculiar inconveniences," it was nevertheless a gift from God, since it gave men a kind of last-minute reprieve to put their spiritual house in order. "Length of days," said the old Arminian, "is a real advantage to our improving in virtue, perfecting of holiness, and attaining to high degrees of glory at last." In an implicit rebuttal of that Calvinist doctrine called perseverance of the saints, Gay warned that men must "continue their repentance in old age, and to the end of their days." He declared that "Good men die repenting." In a powerful effort to move the hearts of the old sinners in his congregation, Gay painted an unsparingly grim portrait of old age: "Our breath is corrupt, our vital spirits are wasted, our days are extinct, the graves are ready for us; we are tottering over them, and shall soon tumble into them." This was undiluted terror revivalism, though Gay hoped it would serve as a "rational influence, to bring our hearts unto wisdom."[2]

At length, Gay "put an end to this discourse," and asked his hearers, "young and old," to give "a few minutes attention to the conduct of divine Providence toward their aged Minister." He reminded them that he had ministered in Hingham for sixty-three years, "from fathers to children, and children's children," and that he was only the third minister since the town was founded one hundred and forty-six years before. He consequently observed, with some understatement, that the people of Hingham "have not been given to change, nor with itching ears have heaped to themselves teachers." Gay told them that he had rejoiced in his ministry among them, saying, "I retain a grateful sense of the kindnesses (injuries I remember none) which I Have received from them." He even acknowledged, probably to the astonishment of all, that the people "may feel their great need of one more able in body and mind to serve them in the gospel ministry," and so he strongly urged them to think about hiring an associate pastor. Gay concluded his praise of the First Parish by remarking that "Your fathers despised not my youth for its weakness, nor have you my old age for the infirmities that attend it."[3]

*The Old Man's Calendar* was well received and Gay seemed to acquire a vigorous new lease on life. "The ship," as he metaphorically put it, was "still under sail." Throughout the early 1780s, his friends and family frequently remarked that Gay "remains remarkable well and hearty" or that he "continues to perform his ministerial function to the admiration of all." A surviving manuscript version of *The Old Man's Calendar* shows that Gay's hand was steady and strong. He seemed to be in constant motion, visiting friends or attending meetings from Boston to Kingston. He was now generally driven about by Aaron, a young black servant, but the pace was not diminished. For at least two years after the death in 1783 of his dear old friend, William Smith, Gay frequently traveled to Weymouth to administer the sacrament or baptize infants, while that congregation searched for a new pastor. He still retained his dry sense of humor and his lifelong penchant for wordplay. In 1784, during a visit with relatives in Dedham, Gay had asked the Reverend Peter Thacher of Malden to preach for him in Hingham. He wrote to his daughters asking them to welcome Thacher and give him "suitable Entertablement."[4]

There was, however, another, less pleasant side to Gay's character that emerged during his last years. The benevolent patriarch became less benevolent and more autocratic. For years Gay, like other successful Arminian ministers, had run a tight ship while seeming to stay aloof from church and parish politics. In reality, Gay had controlled church policy as carefully as he regulated the behavior and even the theological opinions of his parish. We have seen, for instance, how Gay continually reminded his congregation of their obligations to search the scriptures for themselves, and to "examine the Grounds of their Belief; open their Minds to Conviction, and yield to Evidence." Woe betide them, however, if the evidence should lead them to theological beliefs radically different from those that Gay preached. He asserted that insofar as any in the congregation "differ in Opinion and Practice from the *Truth*, which he [their minister] tells them, so far do they forsake him, as their spiritual Guide."[5]

Gay communicated the hostility and fear with which he regarded radical religious dissent to his people. In the 1780s, the Baptist revival that was sweeping across New England awakened once again the spirit of enthusiasm. Lay exhorters were once more threatening Hingham's religious homogeneity, but this time they would be given no quarter. Gay opposed the Baptists and Separate-Baptists with all the fervor his Grandfather Eleazer Lusher had exhibited when he was appointed to try "vagabond Quakers" over one hundred years before. In this sense, Gay must be held partly to blame for the disgraceful anti-Baptist riot that took place in Hingham in 1782.[6]

For years certain families in Hingham, such as the Sprague clan, had been restive under the Arminian preaching of Gay and Shute. These families, who seemed to cluster in the vicinity of Hingham Centre, formed the nucleus of a small, underground Baptist community. By 1782 they apparently felt bold enough to declare themselves and, in May, they invited Richard Lee, a gifted Baptist evangelist who had been preaching in Scituate, to come to

Hingham. On the evening of May 28, the dissenters were gathering for the meeting when, to quote from the account of Isaac Backus (a Baptist leader): "a large mob came up, armed with clubs and staves, and warned Lee and his friends to depart out of Hingham immediately, or it would be much worse for them." Lee rather unwisely defied them and the confrontation became ugly. The mob's leader shook a club over Lee's head and threatened to tie him up and whip him thirty times. Lee purportedly replied that Saint Paul had been whipped more severely than that. "What! d—n you," shouted someone in the crowd, "do you compare yourself with Paul!" At that, someone else threw soft cow dung in Lee's face and he was hauled violently out of town. The mob also threatened to burn down the house of anyone who permitted its use for Baptist meetings. More than thirty years passed before the Baptists again attempted to hold open meetings in Hingham.[7]

Gay's increasingly brusque and autocratic behavior was also evident in his administration of the Ship Church itself. He had declared, in *The Old Man's Calendar*, "injuries I remember none," but he clearly did remember and resent them. Now that he had regained control of the church, the old man was determined to hold it. He had once proclaimed that Christians should "be subject to a parental authority in all ecclesiastical administrations of government and discipline . . . and with a child-like temper receive due corrections for their faults." In Gay's last years, this patriarchal approach was transformed into a form of ecclesiastical tyranny. For instance, in the 1781 *Calendar* sermon, Gay had suggested that the Parish Committee should begin searching for an associate minister. He apparently included this advice as a conciliatory afterthought with little expectation that the parish would take him seriously. They quickly seized the opportunity, however, and a parish meeting was called to discuss the need for procuring a colleague for Gay. According to one account, the meeting had barely begun when Gay arose and said, "Gentlemen, I see no reason for this discussion. I dismiss this meeting." The congregation tolerated this querulous imperiousness, assuming, probably, that they would not have to bear it for long.[8]

One of the most keenly felt burdens of Gay's old age was the loss of his friends. This most social of men had, as he put it, "buried the most . . . of our coeval friends, early acquaintances, and dear companions." The list was depressingly long—his brother Lusher, Stephen Williams, Cornelius Nye, Dr. Ezekiel Hersey, John Hancock, Jr., Nathaniel Eels, William Rand, and even some of his students such as Jonathan Dorby and, of course, the beloved Mayhew. His joy, then, was all the greater when, in 1783, he traveled up to Cambridge for a reunion with two old friends who *had* survived— Charles Chauncy and Nathaniel Appleton. These three aged men— Gay was eighty-seven, Chauncy was seventy-eight, and Appleton was ninety—had joined together in more ecclesiastical councils, ordinations, and conflicts with the New Lights, than they could remember. Gay's friendship with Chauncy dated back at least as far as 1740, when they had both attempted to vindicate Samuel Osborn from the charge of Arminian heresy. Gay had known Appleton even longer. Seventy years had passed since the time when they were both undergraduates at Leverett's Harvard.[9]

Gay's grandnephew, Alden Bradford, was an undergraduate at the college when he saw these three "venerable and learned men pass through the college yard to the Library." Gay and Chauncy then accompanied Appleton to the chapel where the latter conducted a service. Bradford observed that the whole event "excited great attention at the time." In a sense these three old men were the corporeal embodiment of the eighteenth-century religious experience in New England. As young men, they had known Increase Mather, one of the last great seventeenth-century Puritan divines. Now, their stately procession to the college chapel was watched by undergraduate Henry Ware who would preside over the liberal theological revolution at Harvard in the early nineteenth century. In an age of heated religious and political debate, these three "Leverett" gentlemen had quietly and unobtrusively presided over the transition of New England theology from Calvinism to Arminianism. Their discretion was legendary and was, perhaps, epitomized by Appleton. He had recently settled yet another church controversy. At the conclusion of the council, a younger minister wrote: "D$^r$ Appleton hath conducted in the matter as he hath done in every other. He never let me, nor anybody else, know whether it was agreeable or disagreeable to him. He is ninety years old!"[10]

Soon after Gay returned to Hingham from this pleasant visit in Cambridge, he was confronted with the most painful separation of all. On August 19, 1783, Jerusha Bradford Gay, his wife of sixty-four years, died "after a lingering indisposition." She had never fully recovered from the turmoil of the Revolution and, as a family member indicated, "this was not a sudden or unlooked for event. . . . father bears it like a Christian, though he feels it like a man."

Jerusha had not only managed the financial and domestic affairs of the parsonage, she had also, in her later years, accompanied her husband on many of his travels to ecclesiastical councils and ordinations. At Jerusha's funeral, Gay expressed his grief by quoting the words used by the patriarch Abraham, after the death of his wife Sarah. After the conclusion of the funeral service, Gay turned to David Barnes and Daniel Shute and whispered, "I thank you, my friends, for burying the poor remains of my wife out of my sight."[11]

The old man's calendar was indeed filled with loneliness, but it was also filled with honors. Despite the testy behavior of his later years, Gay was venerated by the people of Hingham. He was particularly pleased when, in November 1784, he was appointed the first of the Trustees of Derby Academy, a coeducational institution founded and endowed by Madam Sarah Derby. Madam Derby was the widow both of Dr. Ezekiel Hersey, Gay's old friend, and Captain Richard Derby, a wealthy Salem merchant; each had left her with enough money to indulge her philanthropic interests. She had known and admired Gay since the 1720s when she was a young girl living in the property adjoining the parsonage. In 1785, Gay received the most gratifying of all his honors. The Harvard Corporation, prompted perhaps by Board member Simeon Howard, cast a long overdue vote to award Gay the degree of Doctor of Divinity. Consequently on July 20, 1785, the eighty-eight-year-old Hingham parson traveled to Cambridge to attend Commencement for the last time. That the D.D. had been deferred for so long did not dim the pleasure of the old man who received it, or the emotions of the bystanders.[12]

Despite the accolades and honors, which, of course, were really farewells, Gay refused to be embalmed just yet. Instead, he became associated with the anti-Trinitarian movement. The debate over the Athanasian Trinity had flared up in Massachusetts in 1755 after Jonathan Mayhew openly ridiculed the doctrine. From that point on, the seed of doubt grew in the mind of any New England minister who insisted that his faith be rational and scriptural. The anti-Trinitarians relied principally on Samuel Clarke's *Scripture-Doctrine of the Trinity* (1712), a brilliant work in which Clarke persuasively argued that the orthodox doctrine of the trinity had no basis in scripture. Some of the younger ministers turned to Arianism. A very few became Socinians, believing that Christ was a man, though one whom God had created fully perfect in order to fulfill his plan of redemption. In December 1766, one of these Socinians, a recent Harvard graduate named Thomas Fessenden, paid a visit to the orthodox Reverend Ebenezer Parkman of Westborough. Parkman was appalled by Fessenden's opinions and, he records, "I had shewed him *Turrettine* &c ____ but it was of no avail, he would adhere to the Bible." Two years later, a somewhat shaken and puzzled Parkman acknowledged, "I am much employed upon that great mystery of the Trinity—the importance of it, & necessity of believing it: consulting various authors upon it—but confess I make but too little way a Head." [13]

Gay's earliest sermons suggest that he unquestioningly accepted the validity of the trinity doctrine. Speaking of Christ in 1730, he declared: "In him dwelt all the fulness of the infinite Godhead bodily; and from him did it shine forth in the Days of his Flesh, he being the Effulgence of his Father's Glory." By 1742, however, he was praying that "our hearts" might be brought to a full understanding "of the Mystery of GOD, and of the Father, and of Christ." After that, the trinity doctrine completely disappeared from Gay's published sermons. Perhaps he quietly moved into the Arian camp, as did his pupil, Simeon Howard, or he may even have advanced toward Socinianism. The clear affinity between the Arminians and the anti-Trinitarians would not have escaped Gay. Both tended to view Christ's atonement as insufficient, believing that God forgave man and rewarded him primarily on the basis of his own virtue. [14]

Gay's close association with radical anti-Trinitarianism has been inferred from his connection with William Hazlitt (1737–1820), an Irish Socinian minister and disciple of Joseph Priestley, the free-thinking English divine. Parson Hazlitt wandered about England and Ireland for nearly twenty years in search of a congregation that could tolerate both his radical theology and his overbearing personality. Finally, in 1783, he sailed for America with his family, expecting to find religious freedom and acceptance. He spent some time in the Philadelphia area, but when no vacant pulpit appeared, he set off for Boston in the mistaken belief that he was about to be offered the Brattle Street pulpit. Hazlitt was disappointed again, but he nevertheless made an impression in Boston. His acquaintance with Priestley and his enthusiastic expositions of Priestley's ideas fortified and encouraged the two leading New England Socinians—James Freeman of Boston's King's Chapel, and William Bentley of Salem's Second Church. Freeman later wrote that "Before Mr. Hazlitt came to Boston, the Trinitarian doxology was almost universally used. That honest and good man prevailed upon several respectable ministers to omit it." Indeed, many of the Boston ministers, including Chauncy and Simeon Howard, respected Hazlitt's scholarship and his ideas, but "Paddy," as he was derisively called, seemed also to impress them as an opinionated, egotistical bore.[15]

Unable to secure a permanent pulpit, Hazlitt finally, in November 1784, settled his family in the rented home of the late Reverend William Smith of Weymouth. The five Hazlitts spent a rather rugged first winter there; furthermore, because of his radical reputation, the Weymouth First Church deacons were not anxious to have him preach from their pulpit. Hazlitt found solace, however, in the kind reception that he received in Hingham from Ebenezer Gay. David Barnes, Daniel Shute, and other members of the Hingham Association shared Gay's enthusiasm for Hazlitt's preaching. He and his family were introduced into Gay's elite circle of close friends in Hingham—the Thaxters, the Barkers, Madam Derby, and General Benjamin Lincoln. Hazlitt's seventeen-year-old son, John, an aspiring artist, painted portraits of many of these worthies and even induced a reluctant Gay to sit. The early Hingham historian, Solomon Lincoln, remarked judiciously that "if we can judge of [Gay's] features as delineated by the pencil of Hazlitt, they were not particularly handsome." Yet, said Lincoln, "Those who loved him held him in such affection and reverence that they would not admit that Hazlitt's portrait was not a beautiful picture."[16]

That Gay welcomed Hazlitt to Hingham is not in itself particularly surprising, but his motives for allowing Hazlitt to use the Old Ship pulpit for a forum are unclear. The Hazlitts later claimed that William preached in Hingham, before Gay's congregation of over twelve hundred people, on over forty occasions. This claim is partially corroborated by one contemporary journal, which documents eleven occasions on which Hazlitt preached, ranging from November 7, 1784 to June 4, 1786. One may assume that Hazlitt proclaimed the Socinian teachings of Priestley from the influential Hingham pulpit with the same fervor he exhibited elsewhere. Perhaps poor old Gay was simply overwhelmed by the personal force of this Irish Socinian zealot who had invaded the South Shore. Perhaps he was being pressured by supporters of Hazlitt in the First Parish. Certainly Hazlitt had expectations of being appointed associate minister. In fact, he was bitterly disappointed when, having given up on prospects in New England, he learned of Gay's death shortly after he arrived back in England. Hazlitt's daughter remarked, "Had he but staid over that winter [1786–87], it is probable that we should never have left that dear country." [17]

In any case, it is dangerous to assume that Gay, whose mental acuity was slipping rapidly in these last years, was deliberately endorsing the proto-Unitarian movement through his connection with Hazlitt. The transition from Gay's Arminianism to Hazlitt's Socinianism was not, however, too abrupt for the First Parish congregation. There is no evidence that Hazlitt was ever hooted out of the pulpit. Furthermore, Henry Ware, Gay's successor, was able to calmly and resolutely steer the Old Ship into Unitarian waters.

Shortly after William Hazlitt's departure from the scene, Gay became seriously ill. He was unable to preach from September to November of 1786, yet somehow he recovered and continued on. The basis for his incredible tenacity is revealed in this passage from *The Old Man's Calendar*: "while our outward man is perishing, our inward man [should] be renewed day by day. Our diligence should be quickened, our zeal promoted, amidst, and even by, our bodily weaknesses, as they intimate the time of working out our salvation is short." The people of Hingham must have begun to think he was immortal. Young boys in town, as they saw the great white wig approach, ran and hid themselves, "so great was their awe of him." Many of the adults held him in a sort of reverence that was not very different from the fear of the youngsters. One of Gay's more elderly admirers was John Barnes, a sixty-eight-year-old farmer who lived near the harbor. Barnes had been baptized as an infant by Gay, and the old parson very nearly buried him. Daniel Shute, Gay's most intimate friend in his last years, has left this vivid portrait of the ancient cleric:

> . . . when the powers of his mind are, in some degree, impaired by the debility of advanced years, and the very nerves of his soul are relaxed, he still keeps the post assigned to him, and, like Gideon and his men of old, though faint yet persueth. [18]

On March 12, 1787 Gay opened his large record book and entered the death of a young man named William Hobart. The entry was written in a larger script than usual; the handwriting was clear but slightly wavering. One can almost feel the rigid determination to keep the trembling hands steady. Six days after he made that entry, Gay arose on Sunday morning, around seven o'clock, to review his sermon notes for that day's service. He suddenly felt rather ill and so returned to bed. In less than an hour, "his soul, being tired of its house made of clay, took its flight." Gay had made a characteristically decorous exit. Shortly after, the Reverend William Bentley of Salem noted in his diary, "Gay died at last."[19]

Jotham Gay, who had returned from Nova Scotia shortly before, took charge of the funeral details. Jotham, incidentally, elected to stay in Hingham and soon became a man of importance in town and state affairs. The Parish Committee voted "to grant to Rev. Mr. Gay's family £15 to defray the expenses of his funeral." On March 23, Gay was interred in his plot, which was situated on a hill just yards from the meetinghouse where he had preached for sixty-nine years. Daniel Shute preached his funeral sermon, and the tributes and eulogies from his colleagues and former students continued for weeks afterwards. On the Sunday following his burial, Simeon Howard supplied the preaching; the next Sunday it was John Brown; then Gad Hitchcock, David Barnes, and others. The Old Ship congregation heard numerous encomiums such as Gay's "light was so illustrious, that his praise is in all the churches." It was Daniel Shute, however, who clearly sounded the message that Gay wanted his people to hear again and again. Shute told the leaderless flock "to search the Scriptures as the unerring standard of truth, and the undeviating rule of practice." He told them that they were not to "receive for doctrines the commandments of men: You are, in this view, to call no man father on earth—not even a Doctor Gay."[20]

# Notes

---

*Abbreviations to Notes*

HCR   The records of the First Church and Parish in Hingham; deposited with the Massachusetts Historical Society. The material is organized in forty-nine books and boxes, and covers the period from 1635 to 1958.
MHS   The Massachusetts Historical Society.


PROLOGUE

1. Claude M. Newlin, *Philosophy and Religion in Colonial America* (New York, 1962), 140; Charles W. Akers, *Called unto Liberty: A Life of Jonathan Mayhew, 1720–1766* (Cambridge, Mass., 1964), 79.

2. Alan Heimert, *Religion and the American Mind: From the Great Awakening to the Revolution* (Cambridge, Mass., 1966), 209.

3. Charles F. Adams, ed. *The Works of John Adams*, 10 vols. (Boston, 1850–56), 10:287–88; Sydney Howard Gay to Solomon Lincoln, New York, November 7, 1861 (Courtesy of John P. Richardson of Hingham); Samuel A. Eliot, ed., *Heralds of a Liberal Faith* (Boston, 1910), 2; Clifford K. Shipton, ed., *Sibley's Harvard Graduates* (Boston, 1942), 6:62.

4. Ebenezer Gay, *The Mystery of the Seven Stars in Christ's Right Hand* (Boston, 1752), 19.

5. Ebenezer Gay, *A Beloved Disciple of Jesus Christ Characterized* (Boston, 1766), 10–11.

6. Ebenezer Gay, *The Character and Work of a Good Ruler, and the Duty of an Obliged People* (Boston, 1745), 26.

241

CHAPTER I
Dedham

1. Ebenezer Gay, *St. John's Vision of the Woman Cloathed with the Sun* (Boston, 1766), 27–28; Frederick Lewis Gay, *John Gay of Dedham, Massachusetts, and Some of His Descendants* (Boston, 1879), 4.

2. The classic study of the social history of early Dedham is Kenneth A. Lockridge's *A New England Town: The First Hundred Years* (New York, 1970).

3. Frank Smith, *A History of Dedham, Massachusetts* (Dedham, 1936), 169; F. L. Gay, *John Gay*, 4, 5; Don Gleason Hill, ed., *The Early Records of the Town of Dedham, Mass., 1635–1706* (Dedham, 1899), 5:149; Julius H. Tuttle, ed., *Early Records of Dedham, 1706–1736* (Dedham, 1936), 6:188.

4. F. L. Gay, *John Gay*, 4; Estate of Nathaniel Gay, Sr., 1712, Suffolk County Registry of Probate, #3391; Ebenezer Gay to Frederick L. Gay, Boston, February 3, 1879 (New England Historical and Genealogical Society). The name Ebenezer means a stone erected to God in thankfulness for his help. Since the name does not seem to occur in the Gay family before this point, it provides another indication that Nathaniel may have set aside this child from birth as a sort of living tithe.

5. Ebenezer Gay, *A Call from Macedonia* (Boston, 1768), 27. For one assessment of the impact of a major commercial road intruding into a village, see Paul Boyer and Stephen Nissenbaum, *Salem Possessed: The Social Origins of Witchcraft* (Cambridge, Mass., 1974), 100–102.

6. F. L. Gay, *John Gay*, 3; Lockridge, *A New England Town*, 61; Smith, *History of Dedham*, 3–4, 8, 20; Robert C. Anderson, "A Note on the Gay-Borden Families in Early New England," *New England Historical and Genealogical Register* 130 (January 1976): 35–39. John Gay (possibly with a father also named John) arrived in the New World in 1630, settling in Watertown. He was descended from an old Norman family, but the pre-migration genealogy of the Gays is obscure.

7. Middlesex County Court Records, Folder 51–54; Hill, *Early Records of Dedham* 5:161, 230, 237, 250, 286.

8. Burgis Pratt Starr, *A History of the Starr Family* (Hartford, 1879), 6–9; Erastus Worthington, *The History of Dedham: 1635–1827* (Boston, 1827), 42, 49, 50; *Proceedings of the Two Hundred and Fiftieth Anniversary of the Incorporation of the Town of Dedham, Mass.* (Cambridge, Mass., 1887), 64–65; Lockridge, *A New England Town*, 45; Edward Johnson, *Wonder-Working Providence, 1628–1651*, ed. J. Franklin Jameson (New York, 1910), 143. In his will, Eleazer Lusher bequeathed "to Liddia Starre, the daughter of my wife's sister, who hath lived with me from her infancy, £100." See Frederick Lewis Gay, "Lusher Wills," *Dedham Historical Register* 2 (October 1891): 132.

9. Edward M. Cook, Jr., "Social Behavior and Changing Values in Dedham, Massachusetts, 1700–1775," *William and Mary Quarterly*, 3d ser., 27 (1970):562–63; Lusher Gay to Mary Gay Ballantine, Dedham, January 5, 1742 (Kent Memorial Library, Suffield, Conn.); F. L. Gay, *John Gay*, 6, 9.

10. Cook, "Social Behavior in Dedham," 561–63; Will of John Gay, December 18, 1686, *Howe Family Papers* (MHS); Lockridge, *A New England Town*, 103–6, 111–14.

11. Cook, "Social Behavior in Dedham," 559–63; Samuel Dexter Diary (Dedham Historical Society), 300. See also George Willis Cooke, *A History of the Clapboard Trees or Third Parish, Dedham, Massachusetts* (Boston, 1887).

12. Hill, *Early Records of Dedham* 5:238; Smith, *History of Dedham*, 52–55, 384. The house presently known as the Timothy Gay Tavern stands on the old Nathaniel Gay home lot, and a portion of Nathaniel's dwelling may be incorporated in the present structure.

13. Lockridge, *A New England Town*, 86–87; Clifford K. Shipton, ed., *Sibley's Harvard Graduates* (Cambridge, Mass., 1933), 4:28, 29; Cook, "Social Behavior in Dedham," 560.

14. Ebenezer Burgess, ed., *Dedham Pulpit* (Boston, 1840), 167, 169.

15. Shipton, *Sibley's Harvard Graduates* (Boston, 1937), 5:512–14.

16. Ibid., 515.

17. Samuel Eliot Morison, *The Intellectual Life of Colonial New England*, 2d. ed. (New York, 1956), 68, 105–6, 110–11; Estate of Nathaniel Gay, Sr.

CHAPTER II
## Harvard

1. Perry Miller, *The New England Mind: From Colony to Province* (Cambridge, Mass., 1953), 455. The term "Latitudinarian" refers to those English Churchmen who embraced a reasonable faith, avoiding thorny dogmatic questions whenever possible. Led by Archbishop Tillotson in the 1690s, they were concerned principally with virtue and man's moral obligations.

2. For two discussions of the Leverett administration at Harvard, and the various conflicts with the Mathers, see chap. 4, "The Great Leverett" in Samuel Eliot Morison's *Three Centuries of Harvard: 1636–1936* (Cambridge, Mass., 1936), 53–75; also chap. 27, "The Death of an Idea" in Miller's *Colony to Province*, 447–63. Most of the clerical support for Leverett, with the exceptions of Colman and the Reverend Benjamin Wadsworth, came from outside Boston.

3. Cotton Mather, *Magnalia Christi Americana: or, the Ecclesiastical His-*

*tory of New England*, 1st Amer. ed. (Hartford, 1820), vol. 2, bk. 4, pt. 1, 16; Morison, *Harvard*, 31; Benjamin Rand, "Philosophical Instruction in Harvard University from 1636 to 1900," *Harvard Graduates Magazine* 37 (1928–29):32.

4. Clifford K. Shipton, ed., *Sibley's Harvard Graduates* (Cambridge, Mass., 1933), 4:163, 165, 300–303, 533.

5. Morison, *Harvard*, 54, 64.

6. Morison, *Harvard*, 26–27; Shipton, *Sibley's Harvard Graduates* (Boston, 1942), 6:6–7, 59. In Clifford Shipton's introduction to the Class of 1714, he observed that the class ranking "cannot be explained by what we know of the social standing, piety, or intellectual promise of the students."

7. Morison, *Harvard*, 29–30; *Massachusetts Gazette*, March 30, 1787.

8. Morison, *Harvard*, 29–30; Rand, "Philosophical Instruction," 32; Claude M. Newlin, *Philosophy and Religion in Colonial America* (New York, 1962), 6–7; Joseph J. Ellis, *The New England Mind in Transition: Samuel Johnson of Connecticut, 1696–1772* (New Haven, 1973), 56; Perry Miller, in *The New England Mind: The Seventeenth Century* (New York, 1939), discussed the seemingly unlikely affinity of the *Dialecticae* of Petrus Ramus with the world of the Enlightenment. See Miller's chapter on "The Instrument of Reason."

9. Shipton, *Sibley's Harvard Graduates* 4:533; John Locke, *An Essay Concerning Human Understanding* (London, 1690), 4:418.

10. Gerald R. Cragg, *The Church and the Age of Reason: 1648–1789* (Grand Rapids, Mich., 1960), 159.

11. Shipton, *Sibley's Harvard Graduates* 6:38–40, 47, 52, 67–69; Ebenezer Gay, *Ministers Are Men of Like Passions with Others* (Boston, 1725), i; *History of the Town of Hingham*, 3 vols. (Hingham, 1893), vol. 1, pt. 1, 251; Ebenezer Gay to [Stephen Williams], Hadley, June 13, 1715 (Pennsylvania Historical Society).

12. Shipton, *Sibley's Harvard Graduates* 6:25, 28; John Williams, *The Redeemed Captive*, ed. Edward W. Clark (Amherst, Mass., 1976), passim.

13. Morison, *Harvard*, 27; Miller, *Seventeenth Century*, 221; Rand, "Philosophical Instruction," 32. Gay's classmate, Adam Cushing, owned a copy of the *Meletemata*, now held by the American Antiquarian Society.

14. Morison, *Harvard*, 27–28, 59; Elisha Williams to Stephen Williams, Hatfield, March 16, 1712 (Yale University Library).

15. Conrad Wright, *The Beginnings of Unitarianism in America* (Boston, 1955), 57; Louis Leonard Tucker, *Puritan Protagonist: President Thomas Clap of Yale College* (Chapel Hill, 1962), 20–21; Joshua Gee, *Catalogus Librorum Bibliothecae Collegii Harvardini Quad Est Cantabriglae in Nova Anglia* (Boston, 1723).

16. Morison, *Harvard*, 53–55; "John Leverett's Record," 1707–1723 (MS at Harvard University Archives), January 29 and February 23, 1712; Shipton, *Sibley's Harvard Graduates* (Boston, 1937), 5:240–41.

17. "John Leverett's Record," memorandum for 1712; Shipton, *Sibley's Harvard Graduates* 6:8.

18. Morison, *Harvard*, 31; Rand, "Philosophical Instruction," 32; Miller, *Colony to Province*, 440.

19. "John Leverett's Record," September 9, 1712; Morison, *Harvard*, 58; Shipton, *Sibley's Harvard Graduates* 5:241, 267.

20. Cotton Mather, *The Christian Philosopher; A Collection of the Best Discoveries in Nature, with Religious Improvements* (London, 1721), 291.

21. Miller, *Colony to Province*, 440; Newlin, *Philosophy and Religion*, 32; Robert Middlekauf, *The Mathers: Three Generations of Puritan Intellectuals, 1596–1728* (New York, 1971), 285, 296–99; Pershing Vartanian thoughtfully discussed the way in which Cotton Mather's contemplation of a mechanistic universe (with occasional miracles) led to an even more intense piety. See Vartanian's "Cotton Mather and the Puritan Transition into the Enlightenment," *Early American Literature* 8 (Winter 1973).

22. Morison, *Harvard*, 58; Samuel Sewall, "Diary," *Collections of the Massachusetts Historical Society*, 5th ser., vol. 2 of vol. 6 (Boston, 1879), 410; Shipton, *Sibley's Harvard Graduates* 6:36, 43, 67, 71.

23. "John Leverett's Record," September 13, 1713; Morison, *Harvard*, 32–33.

24. Morison, *Harvard*, 33–34; Sewall, "Diary," *Collections of the Massachusetts Historical Society*, 5th ser., vol. 3 of vol. 7 (Boston, 1882), 9; "John Leverett's Record," July 7, 1714.

25. Ebenezer Gay to [Stephen Williams], Hadley, December 30, 1714 (Pennsylvania Historical Society).

26. Julius H. Tuttle, ed., *The Early Records of the Town of Dedham, Mass., 1706–1736* (Dedham, 1936), 6:128; Ebenezer Gay to [Stephen Williams], Hadley, December 30, 1714; Shipton, *Sibley's Harvard Graduates* 6:18–20; Ebenezer Gay to [Stephen Williams], Hadley, June 13, 1715.

27. Shipton, *Sibley's Harvard Graduates* 6:6–7; Justin Winsor, *A History of the Town of Duxbury* (Boston, 1849), 115.

28. Experience Mayhew, *A Discourse Showing That God Dealeth with Men as with Reasonable Creatures* (Boston, 1720), 17.

29. Shipton, *Sibley's Harvard Graduates* 6:8; "Diary of Rev. Stephen Williams" (Typescript from original MS, Storrs Library, Longmeadow, Mass.), February 22, 1716.

30. Shipton, *Sibley's Harvard Graduates* 6:25–26; Sylvester Judd, *History of Hadley* (Springfield, Mass., 1905), 60. Gay was also known to John Partridge of Hadley (1686–1717) who, despite his youth, was one of the most influential of the "River Gods" in the Connecticut Valley. John had served as the Dedham schoolmaster from 1705 to 1707. See Carlos Slafter, *The Schools and Teachers of Dedham, Massachusetts, 1644–1904* (Dedham, 1905), 41 and Shipton, *Sibley's Harvard Graduates* 5:289.

31. Ebenezer Gay to [Stephen Williams], Hadley, December 30, 1714.

32. Isaac Chauncey, *The Faithful Evangelist, or the True Shepherd* (Boston, 1725), 2, 26.

33. Ibid., 5, 19–20. Isaac Chauncey was an ardent disciple of Solomon Stoddard. In defense of Stoddard's practice of open communion, Chauncey wrote, "We can tell who are Visible Saints, but we cannot tell who are Invisible Saints, . . . Besides it stands to Reason that Visible Saints have a right to Visible Priviledges, and Invisible saints to Invisible Priviledges." Lest anyone mistake the source of Chauncey's ideas, he concluded "But I need not Multiply words, for the Reverend Mr. Stoddard by his Excellent and Elaborate Discourses hath brought the Truth to Noonday Light." See Chauncey, *Faithful Evangelist*, 19–20.

34. Judd, *Hadley*, 58; Ebenezer Gay to [Stephen Williams], Hadley, June 13, 1715.

35. Ebenezer Gay to [Stephen Williams], Hadley, June 13, 1715; Chauncey, *Faithful Evangelist*, 20.

36. Thomas F. Waters, *Ipswich in the Massachusetts Bay Colony*, 2 vols. (Ipswich, 1905), 1:426 and 2:277–78.

37. "Diary of Rev. Stephen Williams," bk. 1, April 7, 1716; John Wise, *A Vindication of the Government of New England Churches* (Boston, 1717), 38; George A. Cook, *John Wise: Early American Democrat* (New York, 1952).

38. Wise, *Vindication*, 38; Newlin, *Philosophy and Religion*, 50; Ebenezer Gay, *Natural Religion, as Distinguish'd from Revealed* (Boston, 1759), 11, 31.

39. Mather, *Christian Philosopher*, 291–92; "Diary of Cotton Mather, 1709–1724," *Collections of the Massachusetts Historical Society*, 7th ser. (Boston, 1912), 8:144.

40. Morison, *Harvard*, 34–35; Robert Ward, "Commonplace Book" (MHS), 113.

41. Morison, *Harvard*, 35; Shipton, *Sibley's Harvard Graduates* 6:45, 59; John Langdon Sibley to Solomon Lincoln, Cambridge, November 15, 1861 (Town of Hingham Papers, 1861–1864, MHS). Gay's *Quaestio* in the original Latin reads, "An cuique Animae humanae immediate post mortem sit locus et status proprius a Deo assignatus, prout bene aut male se gesserant in praesante seculo?"

42. Miller, *Colony to Province*, 451–52; Sewall, "Diary," vol. 3 of vol. 7: 186. My association of Gay with Stoddard and Wise is based chiefly on geographical proximity and a subsequent correspondence of some theological and ecclesiastical views.

43. Benjamin Colman to White Kennet, Boston, November 1712 (Colman Papers, MHS).

CHAPTER III
Hingham: The Early Years

1. "Diary of Cotton Mather, 1709–1724," *Collections of the Massachusetts Historical Society*, 7th ser. (Boston, 1912), 8:539; Samuel Sewall, "Diary," *Collections of the Massachusetts Historical Society*, 5th ser., vol. 3 of vol. 7 (Boston, 1882), 186.

2. Perry Miller, *The New England Mind: From Colony to Province* (Cambridge, Mass., 1953), 451; Samuel Eliot Morison, *Three Centuries of Harvard: 1636–1936* (Cambridge, Mass., 1936), 64–66; Clifford K. Shipton, ed., *Sibley's Harvard Graduates* (Cambridge, Mass., 1933), 4:42–54 and (Boston, 1937), 5:376–93. Perry Miller's list of Mather's clerical apostles in Boston includes (with dates of ordination): Thomas Foxcroft at First Church, 1717; Joshua Gee, Mather's colleague at Old North, 1723; Joseph Sewall and Thomas Prince at Old South, 1713 and 1718; William Cooper at Brattle Street (the enemy camp), 1716; John Webb at New North, 1714; Samuel Checkley at New South, 1719.

3. Frederick L. Weis, "Ebenezer Gay," *The Proceedings of the Unitarian Historical Society*, vol. 4, pt. 2 (1936):3.

4. Hingham Town Records, 1657–1720 (Hingham, Mass. Town Hall), 2:61; *History of the Town of Hingham*, 3 vols. Hingham, 1893), vol. 1, pt. 2. General observations about Hingham's physical appearance are based on scattered references in the Hingham town history, particularly Edward T. Bouve's sketch, "Ancient Landmarks," *History of Hingham*, vol. 1, pt. 2, 157–200. In discussing place names and residential locations in eighteenth-century Hingham, I have generally relied on the genealogy section of the town history, as well as the extensive research into Hingham deeds, wills, and conveyances compiled by Julian Loring and John Richardson, both of Hingham.

5. *History of Hingham*, vol. 1, pt. 1, 204–7.

6. *History of Hingham*, vol. 1, pt. 1, 3–5 and pt. 2, 155–80; Commonwealth of Massachusetts, *Historical Data Relating to Counties and Towns in Massachusetts*, by Frederic W. Cook, Secretary of the Commonwealth (1948).

7. John J. Waters, "Hingham, Massachusetts, 1631–1661: An East Anglian Oligarchy in the New World," *Journal of Social History* 1 (1968): 351–70; *History of Hingham*, vol. 1, pt. 1, 201. I support Prof. Waters's thesis that the conservative, oligarchical character of Hingham had its roots in the struggle of the East Anglians to preserve their own identity, which they perceived as threatened by the West Countrymen and the General Court.

8. Waters, "East Anglian Oligarchy," 355–61; *History of Hingham*, vol. 1, pt. 2, 2–3.

9. Waters, "East Anglian Oligarchy," 357, 362–63; Cotton Mather, *Magnalia Christi Americana: or, the Ecclesiastical History of New England*, 1st

Amer. ed. (Hartford, 1820), vol. 1, bk. 3, 498; John Winthrop, *Journal,*
*1630–1649,* ed. James K. Hosmer, 2 vols. (New York, 1908), 2:244.

10. Waters, "East Anglian Oligarchy," 365; Edward Johnson, *Wonder-*
*Working Providence, 1628–1651,* ed. J. Franklin Jameson (New York, 1910),
116; John Coolidge, "Hingham Builds a Meetinghouse," *The New England*
*Quarterly,* 34 (December 1961):438; Winthrop, *Journal,* 2:232, 234–35;
Nathaniel B. Shurtleff et al., eds., *Records of the Governor and Company of the*
*Massachusetts Bay,* 5 vols. (Boston, 1853–54), 2:97, 113.

11. Winthrop, *Journal,* 2:289, 321; Waters, "East Anglian Oligarchy,"
365; Robert G. Pope, *The Half-Way Covenant: Church Membership in Puritan*
*New England* (Princeton, N.J., 1969), 142, 207–8.

12. Waters, "East Anglian Oligarchy," 365–66n., 369–70; Hingham
Town Records, 2, March 7, 1720; Coolidge, "Hingham Builds a Meeting-
house," 441–42; Thomas J. Wertenbaker, *The First Americans, 1607–1690*
(New York, 1929), 184–86.

13. Coolidge, "Hingham Builds a Meetinghouse," 444–51; James
Hawke's Account Book, 1679–1684 (MHS), October 9, 1680.

14. Coolidge, "Hingham Builds a Meetinghouse," 454–59; Daniel
Cushing's copy of the seating list for "the New meeting house in Hingham," seating list prepared in January 1681 (MHS).

15. Johnson, *Wonder-Working Providence,* 117; *History of Hingham,*
vol. 1, pt. 2, 21–22.

16. John Norton, "Sermon preached upon a day of humiliation,"
1678, copied from a contemporary transcription made by Matthew Hawke
(HCR, Box 11), 134–35; John Norton, copy of a MS sermon dated February 19, 1716 (HCR, Box 11), 107–9, 111; John Norton, "Mr. Norton His
Exposition upon 19 chap. of John:vers:1:2," a contemporary transcription of one of Norton's sermons, made by Matthew Hawke, c. 1678–1684
(courtesy of John Richardson of Hingham). See also the excellent discussion of the theology of the elder John Norton in James W. Jones's *The Shat-*
*tered Synthesis: New England Puritanism before the Great Awakening* (New Haven, 1973), 3–31.

17. Jedidiah Andrews to Thomas Andrews, Philadelphia, May 19,
1718 (Town of Hingham Papers, 1637–1749, MHS); Assessors Record of
the First Parish in Hingham, 1718–1816 (HCR), 1; *History of Hingham,*
vol. 1, pt. 2, 22, 24; Shipton, *Sibley's Harvard Graduates* 5:414; Solomon
Lincoln, *History of Hingham* (Hingham, 1827), 25. For comparable salaries
of the period, see J. William T. Youngs, Jr., "God's Messengers: Religious
Leadership in Colonial New England, 1700–1750" (Ph.D. dissertation,
University of California at Berkeley, 1970), 283, n. 26.

18. Samuel A. Eliot, ed., *Heralds of a Liberal Faith* (Boston, 1910), 1;
Hingham Town Records 2:60; "Rev. Ebenezer Gay, D.D.," in "Pulpit
Services, 1681–1891," collected and arranged by Fearing Burr (HCR),
November 28, 1717.

19. Hingham Town Records 2:60–61.

20. *History of Hingham* 2:12, 56, 269, 373; 3:6, 93, 231.

21. Hingham Town Records 2:61; Ebenezer Gay, *Ministers' Insufficiency for Their Important and Difficult Work* (Boston, 1742), 21.

22. Ebenezer Gay, "Record of Births, Marriages, Deaths and Admissions, 1718–1787," (HCR), from remarks entered at the end of the book; *Records of the First Church at Dorchester in New England, 1636–1734* (Boston, 1891), 228; John Langdon Sibley, *Harvard Graduates: Biographical Sketches of Those Who Attended Harvard College* (Cambridge, Mass., 1881) 2:251; Shipton, *Sibley's Harvard Graduates* 5:235; Samuel Deane, *History of Scituate* (Boston, 1831), 197–200.

23. Gay, "Record," from remarks entered at the end of the book; Assessors Record, 1; Mather, "Diary, 1709–1724," 539.

24. Jedidiah Andrews to Thomas Andrews, Philadelphia, May 18, 1718; Ebenezer Gay, a deposition made concerning the Andrews family, August 29, 1785 (Town of Hingham Papers). Jedidiah Andrews, in 1734, denounced his younger assistant, Samuel Hemphill, as a "Deist and Socinian" for presuming to preach virtue and good works from the pulpit. See Alfred O. Aldridge's *Benjamin Franklin and Nature's God* (Durham, N.C., 1967), 87.

25. Ebenezer Gay, MS sermon preached at Hingham, August 24, 1721 (courtesy of the Reverend J. Gorham Smith of Suffield, Conn.). I have seen four other MS sermons preached by Gay, but they are all written in a crabbed and (to me) impenetrable shorthand.

26. Gay, "Record," passim; Daniel Scott Smith, "Underregistration and Bias in Probate Records: An Analysis of Data from Eighteenth-Century Hingham, Massachusetts," *William and Mary Quarterly*, 3d ser., 32 (1975):102–3.

27. Gay, "Record"; Pope, *Half-Way Covenant*, 246–47; Ross W. Beales, Jr., "The Half-Way Covenant and Religious Scrupulosity: The First Church of Dorchester, Massachusetts, as a Test Case," *William and Mary Quarterly*, 3d ser., 31 (1974):479. Twenty-eight percent of the adult baptisms in Hingham were non-whites—three Indians and fourteen blacks. The Sprague clan accounted for fully 20 percent of the unchurched whites. The Spragues were one of the West Country families that had remained in Hingham. Many of them appeared to have been Baptist dissenters, continuing a Baptist tradition in their family that had its roots in the seventeenth century. See Frederick L. Weis, *The Colonial Clergy and the Colonial Churches of New England* (Lancaster, Mass., 1936), 191–92.

28. Franklin B. Dexter, ed., *Itineraries and Correspondence of Ezra Stiles* (New Haven, 1916), 259–60.

29. Dexter, ed., *Itineraries of Ezra Stiles*, 260; Gay, "Record," passim; Richard Cranch to James Freeman (draft), Boston, August 8, 1749 (Christopher P. Cranch Papers, 1749–1799, MHS); Ebenezer Gay, "The

Charge," appended to *A Sermon Preached at the Ordination of The Rev. Simeon Howard*, by Charles Chauncy (Boston, 1767), 46.

30. Burr, "Pulpit Services," March 1720; Assessors Record, 1; Ebenezer Gay to Frederick L. Gay, Boston, February 3, 1879 (New England Historical and Genealogical Society).

31. Ezekiel 9:1–11; Ebenezer Gay, *Ministers Are Men of Like Passions with Others* (Boston, 1725), 9, 13, 33.

32. Ebenezer Gay, *A Discourse on the Transcendent Glory of the Gospel . . . To Which Is Added, a Pillar of Salt, To Season a Corrupt Age* (Boston, 1728), i; J. William T. Youngs, Jr., "Congregational Clericalism: New England Ordinations before the Great Awakening," *William and Mary Quarterly*, 3d ser., 31 (1974):486–87, 490; Gay, *Like Passions*, 11, 14, 22, 23, 31; Gay, *The Mystery of the Seven Stars in Christ's Right Hand* (Boston, 1752), 26.

33. Ebenezer Gay, *The True Spirit of a Gospel-Minister Represented and Urged* (Boston, 1746), 28; Gay, "The Charge," 45; Pope, *Half-Way Covenant*, 272–73.

34. Gay, *Transcendent Glory*, 14, 31; Gay, *Like Passions*, 8, 9, 15; Cedric B. Cowing, *The Great Awakening and the American Revolution: Colonial Thought in the 18th Century* (Chicago, 1971), 67–68; Gay, "Record," admissions for 1719, 1723, and 1728. Fifteen were admitted to full communion in 1719 (66 percent were women); nineteen in 1723 (63 percent were women); thirty-four in 1728 (44 percent were women).

35. Parish Records of the Hingham First Church, vol. 1, 1720–1806, transcription by Arthur D. Marble (HCR), 12–50; Assessors Record, 7–16; *Boston Weekly News-Letter*, June 24 to July 1, 1731; Gay, *Transcendent Glory*, iii; Weis, "Ebenezer Gay," 10.

36. Justin Winsor, *A History of the Town of Duxbury* (Boston, 1849), 115; Frederick Lewis Gay, *John Gay of Dedham, Massachusetts, and Some of His Descendants* (Boston, 1879), 6; John Boyle to Martin Gay, Boston, September 29, 1783 (Courtesy of Mr. William O. Gay of Dedham); Joshua Winslow to Jotham Gay, Marshfield, Mass., April 26, 1774 (William O. Gay).

37. *History of Hingham* 3:93–94; F. L. Gay, *John Gay*, 6–7; Gay, "Record," entry under "Deaths" for April 26, 1744. After the marriage of Capt. Norton's widow, the house and lands were inherited by John Norton III who was only seven at the time.

38. Suffolk County Registry of Deeds, 41: 166; "The Hobart Journal," *New England Historical and Genealogical Register*, 121 (January 1967): 15; Notebooks of Julian Loring (Hingham Historical Society, microfilm copy at the Hingham Town Library). The information concerning the architecture and interior decoration of the Gay House is based primarily on the research of the present Mr. Ebenezer Gay of Hingham. I have accepted Julian Loring's date (1728) for the construction of the house.

39. *History of Hingham*, vol. 1, pt. 2, 30–31.

40. Ebenezer Gay to [Stephen Williams], Hadley, June 13, 1715

(Pennsylvania Historical Society); "Rev. Nehemiah Hobart Record" in *Copy of Early Ministers' Records* by Arthur D. Marble (HCR), 234, 236; Weis, *Colonial Clergy*, 107–8.

41. "Nehemiah Hobart Record," 235; *History of Hingham* 2 : 373–74.

42. Hingham Town Clerk's Records, vol. 3, 1720–1762 (Hingham Town Hall), October 2, 1719, April 27, 1722, March 4, 1723, May 6, 1728, November 19, 1731, May 15, and August 24, 1732; Daniel Scott Smith, "Population, Family, and Society in Hingham, Massachusetts, 1635–1880" Ph.D. dissertation, University of California at Berkeley, 1973), 91, 93; Samuel Freeman, *The Town Officer* (Boston, 1793), 103–5.

43. Hingham Town Clerk's Records, 3, March 7, 1720—December 30, 1729.

44. Hingham Parish Records, 1, "Moderators," 1–21 and "South Hingham Church and Parish," 13.

45. Hingham Parish Records, 1, "Moderators," 14 and "Pews," 15–16; *History of Hingham* 2 : 12 and 3 : 6.

46. Hingham Town Records, 2, March 3, 1718—March 2, 1719; Hingham Town Clerk's Records, 3, March 7, 1720—March 5, 1729.

47. Hingham Parish Records, 1, "Assessors," 10 and "Appropriations," 25–32; "Earliest records located at Parish House of Hingham First Church," (Hingham First Church), 1 : 1.

48. Gerald R. Cragg, *The Church and the Age of Reason: 1648–1789* (Grand Rapids, Mich., 1960), 72; Gay, *Like Passions*, 36; Burr, "Pulpit Services," March, 1721 and September 3, 1727.

49. Roland N. Stromberg, *Religious Liberalism in Eighteenth-Century England* (London, 1954), 116; Benjamin Colman, *God Deals with Us as Rational Creatures* (Boston, 1723), 8.

50. Shipton, *Sibley's Harvard Graduates* (Boston, 1942), 6 : 385, 388; Donald G. Trayser, *Barnstable: Three Centuries of a Cape Cod Town* (Hyannis, Mass., 1939), 56; Ebenezer Gay to Joseph Green, Hingham, May 20, 1725 (Foxcroft Papers, Mugar Library, Boston University); Gay, *Like Passions*, i, ii; Claude M. Newlin, *Philosophy and Religion in Colonial America* (New York, 1962), 58; Gay, *Transcendent Glory*, i; Gay, *Mystery of the Seven Stars*, 19.

51. Gay, *Like Passions*, 11, 17. The basic intellectual foundations of the Arminian movement are described in Conrad Wright's *The Beginnings of Unitarianism in America* (Boston, 1955).

52. Gay, *Like Passions*, 32; Gay, *Transcendent Glory*, 14, 18. Gay, in this 1725 sermon, expressed his sense of man's innate virtue when he declared that "Humane virtue consists in acting agreeably to the Humane Nature in its primitive constitution." *Like Passions*, 10.

53. Gay, *Like Passions*, 21; *The Dictionary of National Biography*, ed. Sir Leslie Stephen and Sir Sidney Lee, 22 vols. (London, 1885–1901), 6 : 539–41; *The Diary of Ebenezer Parkman, 1703–1782*, ed. Francis G. Walett (Worcester, Mass., 1974), 27; Henry F. May, *The Enlightenment in America*

(New York, 1976), 38. Gay was citing John Edwards's *The Whole Concern of Man—What he ought to know and do in order to Eternal Salvation*, 2d ed. (Boston, 1725).

54. Joseph J. Ellis, *The New England Mind in Transition: Samuel Johnson of Connecticut, 1696–1772* (New Haven, 1973), 125; Norman Pettit, *The Heart Prepared: Grace and Conversion in Puritan Spiritual Life* (New Haven, 1966), 205; Patricia J. Tracy, *Jonathan Edwards, Pastor: Religion and Society in Eighteenth-Century Northampton* (New York, 1980), 32–34.

55. Wright, *Beginnings of Unitarianism*, 18; Gerald J. Goodwin, "The Myth of 'Arminian-Calvinism' in Eighteenth-Century New England," *The New England Quarterly* 41 (June 1968):230; Alan Heimert, *Religion and the American Mind: From the Great Awakening to the Revolution* (Cambridge, Mass., 1966), 169.

56. Gay, *Like Passions*, 37–38.

57. "Nehemiah Hobart Record," 300; Gay, *Transcendent Glory*, ii, 39, 64.

58. Gay, *Transcendent Glory*, ii, 22; Paul R. Lucas, *Valley of Discord: Church and Society along the Connecticut River, 1636–1725* (Hanover, N.H., 1976), 196–200.

59. Gay, *Transcendent Glory*, 55, 58.

60. Ibid., 51–53, 63.

61. Burr, "Pulpit Services," September 3, 1727; Ebenezer Gay, *Zechariah's Vision of Christ's Martial Glory* (Boston, 1728), 9, 14, 27, 31, 26. Gay's references to angels were always intended to be understood literally. He believed in their existence both as a supernatural rationalist who refused to reject the miraculous, and more importantly, as an essential link in the great chain of being.

62. *Massachusetts Gazette*, March 30, 1787; Gay, *Zechariah's Vision*, 32.

63. John Gorham Palfrey, *History of New England*, 5 vols. (Boston, 1858–90), 4:498; Charles W. Elliott, *The New England History*, 2 vols. (New York, 1857), 2:32; John Eliot, *A Biographical Dictionary . . . of the First Settlers, and Other Eminent Characters . . . in New England* (Boston, 1809), 212; Diaries of Reverend William Smith of Weymouth, 1728–1763 (MHS), entries on fly leaf for 1741, 1749, and 1755.

64. Shipton, *Sibley's Harvard Graduates*, 6:60 and (Boston, 1945), 7:561–63; Eliot, *Biographical Dictionary*, 412n; George Willis Cooke, *Unitarianism in America: A History of Its Origin and Development* (Boston, 1910), 59.

65. Ebenezer Gay, *The Duty of People to Pray for and Praise Their Rulers* (Boston, 1730).

66. Ibid., 16, 18, 19, 28, 34–35.

67. Gay, *Duty of People*, 33; *History of Hingham*, vol. 1, pt. 1, 251; "An Account of the time and Expense of the Gentlemen . . . who attended his

Excellency the Governour . . . at Falmouth" (Alfred H. Hersey Collection, Hingham Historical Society), 71.

68. *A Conference of His Excellency Jonathan Belcher, Esq.; . . . with Edawakenk Chief Sachem of the Penobscot Tribe . . . at Falmouth in Casco-Bay* (Boston, 1732), 1, 7; William D. Williamson, *The History of the State of Maine*, 2 vols. Hallowell, Me., 1932), 2:175–76.

CHAPTER IV
The Great Noise About Arminianism

1. The Hobart Diary, 1635–1780 (MHS), September 18, 1735; Ebenezer Gay, *Ministers Are Men of Like Passions with Others* (Boston, 1725), 30–31.

2. *History of the Town of Hingham*, 3 vols. (Hingham, Mass., 1893), 2:336, 414; Suffolk County Registry of Deeds, vol. 54:64, vol. 59:57, vol. 67:194; F. E. Oliver, ed., *The Diaries of Benjamin Lynde and of Benjamin Lynde, Jr.* (Boston, 1880), 69; Colonel John Thaxter Daybook, 1764–1767 (Thaxter Family Papers, Hingham Historical Society), August 2, 1766.

3. Gay, *Like Passions*, 31; Frederick Lewis Gay, *John Gay, of Dedham Massachusetts, and Some of His Descendants* (Boston, 1879), 6–7; *History of Hingham*, vol. 1, pt. 2, 111.

4. John White, *New England's Lamentations* (Boston, 1734), 17.

5. C. C. Goen, ed., *The Great Awakening*, vol. 4 of *The Works of Jonathan Edwards*, ed. John E. Smith (New Haven, 1972), 7, 148; White, *Lamentations*, 16; Cotton Mather, *Ratio Disciplinae Fratrum Nov-Anglorum* (Boston, 1726), 5. Francis A. Christie in "The Beginnings of Arminianism in New England," *Papers of the American Society of Church History*, 2d ser., 3 (1912):153–72, argued that the anti-Arminian rhetoric of the 1730s reflected chiefly a fear of Anglican gains, and that the spread of Arminian views among the Congregational clergy was largely a myth fostered by George Whitefield. This thesis was championed most recently by Gerald J. Goodwin who portrayed the New England ministry as a Gibraltar of Calvinist orthodoxy. See his "The Myth of 'Arminian Calvinism' in Eighteenth-Century New England," *New England Quarterly* 41 (June 1968), 213–37. The alternative view, that Arminianism was real enough, and that its roots were to be found in the preparationism of Covenant theology, is most forcefully expressed in Conrad Wright's chapter "Arminianism Before the Great Awakening," in his *The Beginnings of Unitarianism in America* (Boston, 1955). See also Cedric B. Cowing, *The Great Awakening and the American Revolution: Colonial Thought in the 18th Century* (Chicago, 1971), 29, and C. C. Goen's introduction to *The Great Awakening*, cited above.

6. Clifford K. Shipton, *Sibley's Harvard Graduates* (Boston, 1945),

7:502–4 and (Cambridge, Mass., 1952), 8:221–22. Ammi Cutter had roomed at Harvard with Gay's first theology student, Daniel Rogers, Jr.

7. "Diary of Reverend Stephen Williams," bk. 3, November 18, 1734; Goen, *Great Awakening*, 17–18.

8. Shipton, *Sibley's Harvard Graduates* 8:663, 673–75; *A Narrative of the Proceedings of Those Ministers of the County of Hampshire &c* . . . (Boston, 1736), 28; Louis Leonard Tucker, *Puritan Protagonist: President Thomas Clap of Yale College* (Chapel Hill, 1962), 52; *An Examination of and Some Answers to a Pamphlet, Intitled, A Narrative and Defence of the Ministers of Hampshire* . . . (Boston, 1736), 59; William Cooper, *The Work of Ministers Represented under the Figure of Sowers . . . and Appended The Confession of Faith, Which Mr. Breck Gave In to the Council, and Was Publickly Deliver'd by Him at His Ordination* (Boston, 1736), 20–21.

9. Wright, *Beginnings of Unitarianism*, 280–88.

10. Roland N. Stromberg, *Religious Liberalism in Eighteenth-Century England* (London, 1954), 24–25; Perry Miller, *The New England Mind: From Colony to Province* (Cambridge, Mass., 1953), 462; Norman Pettit, *The Heart Prepared: Grace and Conversion in Puritan Spiritual Life* (New Haven, 1966), 117–24.

11. White, *Lamentations*, 26; Cowing, *Great Awakening and the American Revolution*, 28; Joseph J. Ellis, *The New England Mind in Transition: Samuel Johnson of Connecticut, 1696–1772* (New Haven, 1973), 36; Joshua Gee, *Catalogus Librorum Bibliothecae Collegii Harvardini Quad Est Cantabriglae in Nova Anglia* (Boston, 1723).

12. Gerald R. Cragg, *The Church and the Age of Reason: 1648–1789* (Grand Rapids, Mich., 1960), 77–78, 159–60; Stromberg, *Religious Liberalism*, 53–54.

13. Benjamin Colman to William Hooper, Boston, February 15, 1740 (MHS); Shipton, *Sibley's Harvard Graduates* (Cambridge, Mass., 1933), 4:356–65; [Samuel Moody], *A Faithful Narrative of God's Gracious Dealings with a Person Lately Recovered from the Dangerous Errors of Arminius* (Boston, 1737), 1, 7; *The Diary of Ebenezer Parkman, 1703–1782*, ed. Francis G. Walett (Worcester, Mass., 1974), 1:72.

14. [Moody], *Faithful Narrative*, 1, 5.

15. John Bulkley, *The Usefulness of Reveal'd Religion, to Preserve and Improve that which is Natural* (New London, Conn., 1730), 5, 10, 29, 34; Israel Loring, "A journal in which the rules & proper forms of prayer are set forth," 1715 (MHS), 126. I have seen no evidence that Bulkley had a direct influence on other New England liberals. His sermon is mentioned simply as a very early and important exposition of a theme that is central in Gay's mature theology.

16. Claude M. Newlin, *Philosophy and Religion in Colonial America* (New York, 1962), 58; Shipton, *Sibley's Harvard Graduates* (Boston, 1942), 6:52;

Edward Goddard to Nathan Stone, Framingham, July 6, 1736 (Nathan Stone Papers, MHS).

17. Shipton, *Sibley's Harvard Graduates* (Boston, 1970), 15:395; "Richard Baxter," *The Encyclopedia Britannica*, 11th ed. Ebenezer Gay, *The True Spirit of a Gospel-Minister Represented and Urged* (Boston, 1746), 32. A few signed books from Parson Gay's library have survived, and have been made available to me through the courtesy of Mr. Ebenezer Gay of Hingham.

18. Richard Baxter, *Holy Commonwealth* (London, 1659), 274. Norman Brantley Gibbs in "The Problem of Revelation and Reason in the Thought of Charles Chauncy" (Ph.D. dissertation, Duke University, 1953), contends that Baxter exerted a profound influence on Chauncy's thinking.

19. Wright, *Beginnings of Unitarianism*, 56–57; Edward Dumbauld, *The Life and Legal Writings of Hugo Grotius* (Norman, Okla., 1969), 3–19; from the Reverend Ebenezer Gay's signed copy of Hugo Grotius's *The Truths of the Christian Religion in Six Books*, trans. John Clarke, D.D., Dean of Sarum (London, 1729). Gay evidently passed on a portion of his library to his nephew and namesake, the Reverend Ebenezer Gay of Suffield, Conn. These, together with later books acquired by the younger Gay, are now the property of Suffield Academy.

20. Gay, *Like Passions*, 18; Joan D. Tooke, *The Just War in Aquinas and Grotius* (London, 1965), 199; Grotius, *Truths of the Christian Religion* (London, 1729), v, vii.

21. Tooke, *The Just War*, 206, 221.

22. Ebenezer Gay, *Well-Accomplish'd Soldiers, a Glory to Their King, and a Defence to Their Country* (Boston, 1738), 5–6, 7–8, 11; Hugo Grotius, *De Jure Belli Ac Pacis*, trans. Francis W. Kelsey, 2 vols. (London, 1925), 2:592.

23. Gay, *Well-Accomplish'd Soldiers*, 15, 17, 18, 26.

24. J. William T. Youngs, Jr., *God's Messengers: Religious Leadership in Colonial New England, 1700–1750* (Baltimore, 1976), 78–80, 86; Gay, *True Spirit*, 32.

25. Shipton, *Sibley's Harvard Graduates* 8:220–23; Wright, *Beginnings of Unitarianism*, 23.

26. *At a Council of Ten Churches Convened at Marlborough on February 4, 1734* (Boston, 1734); *New England Weekly Journal*, February 10, 1735; Shipton, *Sibley's Harvard Graduates* (Boston, 1956), 9:179–80; "Exchanges and Occasional" in "Pulpit Services, 1681–1891," collected and arranged by Fearing Burr (HCR).

27. Edward M. Griffin, *Old Brick: Charles Chauncy of Boston, 1705–1787* (Minneapolis, 1980), 50–51.

28. Frederick Lewis Gay, *John Gay*, 7; Daniel Scott Smith, "Population, Family, and Society in Hingham, Massachusetts, 1635–1880" (Ph.D. dissertation, University of California at Berkeley, 1973), 233; Parish Records

of the Hingham First Church, vol. 1, 1720–1806, trans. Arthur D. Marble (HCR), 46; Diaries of Reverend William Smith of Weymouth, 1728–1763 (MHS), September 4, 1738. Franklin B. Dexter claimed that at the time of the appointment of Thomas Clap as Rector in 1739, "the Trustees were prevailingly, if not exclusively, Arminian." See Richard Warch, *School of the Prophets: Yale College, 1701–1740* (New Haven, 1973) and Franklin B. Dexter, "Thomas Clap and His Writings," *Papers of the New Haven Colony Historical Society* (New Haven, 1899), 5:253.

29. The Osborn-Stone controversy with all its ramifications is fully discussed in John M. Bumstead's "The Pilgrims' Progress: The Ecclesiastical History of the Old Colony, 1620–1775" (Ph.D. dissertation, Brown University, 1965), 105–49; Gustavus Swift Paine, "Ungodly Carriages on Cape Cod," *New England Quarterly* 25 (1952):190; Samuel Osborn, *The Case and Complaint of Mr. Samuel Osborn, Late of Eastham* (Boston, 1743), 4, 5–6, 9.

30. Osborn, *Case and Complaint*, 14; "Diary of Rev. Ebenezer Gay of Suffield, 1738–1792" (Kent Memorial Library, Suffield, Conn.), entries for December 16 and 19, 1738; Bumstead, "Pilgrims' Progress," 187–88; Samuel Deane, *History of Scituate* (Boston, 1831), 198–99.

31. Osborn, *Case and Complaint*, 14–15. Benjamin Prescott, minister of Salem's Third Church, was a champion of ministerial authority, and later, a vigorous opponent of Whitefield. See Shipton, *Sibley's Harvard Graduates* (Boston, 1937), 5:488.

32. Osborn, *Case and Complaint*, 23; Griffin, *Old Brick*, 48–50.

33. Osborn, *Case and Complaint*, 6, 22–23.

34. White, *Lamentations*, 18.

35. Cooper, *The Work of Ministers*, 20; Shipton, *Sibley's Harvard Graduates* 8:220; [Moody], *Faithful Narrative*, 2; "David Brainerd: Memoirs, 1732–1741," in *The Great Awakening at Yale College*, ed. Stephen Nissenbaum (Belmont, Cal., 1972), 44.

36. Isaac Chauncey, *The Faithful Evangelist, or the True Shepherd* (Boston, 1725), 35; Theophilus Lindsey, *An Historical View of the Unitarian Doctrine and Worship from the Reformation to Our Own Times* (London, 1783), 260.

37. "Diary of Rev. Stephen Williams" (Typescript from original MS, Storrs Library, Longmeadow, Mass.), May 1, 1735.

CHAPTER V
## The Great Awakening: The Noisy Passions A-Float

1. "Diary of Rev. Ebenezer Gay of Suffield, 1738–1792" (Kent Memorial Library, Suffield, Conn.), entries for February 22, March 31, and December 16, 1738 and August 28, November 4, and November 30, 1740; "Harvard College Records, pt. 2," *Collections of the Colonial Society of Mas-*

*sachusetts* (Boston, 1925), 16:675, 683; Frederick Lewis Gay, *John Gay of Dedham, Massachusetts, and Some of His Descendants* (Boston, 1879), 6. Samuel Gay's interest in medicine is not surprising, given his father's reputation for skill in the healing arts. That Gay, like many other New England ministers, was familiar with medicine is attested by his frequent use of medical metaphors in sermons. The following example shows, for instance, that he was well-acquainted with placebos: The preaching of the gospel minister is "not like those innocent medicinal Prescriptions, which, if they do no Good, are sure to do no Hurt." See Ebenezer Gay, *Ministers' Insufficiency for Their Important and Difficult Work* (Boston, 1742), 6, and J. William T. Youngs, Jr., *God's Messengers: Religious Leadership in Colonial New England, 1700–1750* (Baltimore, 1976), 44–45.

2. Joseph Lathrop, *A Funeral Sermon* (Hartford, [1796]), 15; Clifford K. Shipton, *Sibley's Harvard Graduates* (Boston, 1958), 10:171–72; "Harvard College Records, Pt. II," 687, 692, "Diary of Ebenezer Gay of Suffield," March 31, 1738; *History of the Town of Hingham*, 3 vols. (Hingham, Mass., 1893), vol. 1, pt. 2, 38–39.

3. F. L. Gay, *John Gay*, 6–7; Ebenezer Gay to [Martin Gay], Hingham, March 24, 1752 (Gay-Otis Papers, Columbia University); Assessors Record of the First Parish in Hingham, 1718–1816 (HCR, Box 36), 13–15.

4. *History of Hingham*, vol. 1, pt. 2, 34, vol. 2, 12, 157, 302, and vol. 3, 231; Real Property Valuation for 1754 (Hingham, Mass. Town Hall); Hingham Town Clerk's Records, vol. 3, 1720–1762 (Hingham, Mass. Town Hall); "South Hingham Church and Parish," Parish Records of the Hingham First Church, 1720–1806, transcription by Arthur D. Marble (HCR), 1:44.

5. *History of Hingham*, vol. 1, pt. 2, 25.

6. "Copy of the Reverend Nehemiah Hobart's Journal," transcription by James Savage (MHS), May 17, 1738.

7. Shipton, *Sibley's Harvard Graduates* (Boston, 1942), 6:68, 265; Ezekiel Goldthwait to the Hingham Selectmen, Boston, June 12, 1744, in *The Benjamin Lincoln Papers*, ed. Frederick S. Allis, Jr. (MHS, 1967); Notebooks of Julian Loring (Hingham Town Library).

8. The theology, ecclesiology, and pastoral style of Gay and his colleagues were very similar to those of the moderate wing of the Presbyterian Church in Scotland. See Henry F. May, *The Enlightenment in America* (New York, 1976), 342–43.

9. Ebenezer Gay, "The Right Hand of Fellowship Given to the Rev. Mr. Thomas Browne," appended to *Gospel Ministers to Preach Christ to Their People*, by John Cushing (Boston, 1759), ii & vi; John Jacob et al. to William Smith, Hingham, December 7, 1741 (Weymouth First Church); David D. Hall, *The Faithful Shepherd: A History of the New England Ministry in the Seventeenth Century* (Chapel Hill, 1972), 118–19; Alan Heimert, *Religion and the*

*American Mind: From the Great Awakening to the Revolution* (Cambridge, Mass., 1966), 361n.

10. Williston Walker, *The Creeds and Platforms of Congregationalism* (New York, 1893), 470–71, 486–94; "Plymouth Association Book, 1722" (Congregational Library), August 29 and October 24, 1722, October 28, 1724, and July 24, 1725.

11. Hingham Town Clerk's Records, vol. 3, November 21, 1726; *The Acts and Resolves of the Province of Massachusetts Bay* (Boston, 1903), 11:512; "Plymouth Association Book," October 24, 1722.

12. John Langdon Sibley, *Harvard Graduates: Biographical Sketches of Those Who Attended Harvard College* (Cambridge, Mass., 1885), 3:437; Walker, *Creeds and Platforms*, 484, 490; Shipton, *Sibley's Harvard Graduates* 6:317 and (Boston, 1945), 7:312–13; Diaries of Reverend William Smith of Weymouth, 1728–1763 (MHS), July 28, 1739. John Danforth of Dorchester was a mainstay in the old Weymouth Association, and his successor, Jonathan Bowman, at first remained active in the revived association. After the Awakening, however, the center of the association shifted towards the south, and the Dorchester Church seems to have fallen into the orbit of Boston.

13. Shipton, *Sibley's Harvard Graduates* 6:316–18; Ebenezer Gay, *The Untimely Death of a Man of God Lamented* (Boston, 1744), 22, 23.

14. Shipton, *Sibley's Harvard Graduates* 7:588–89; Diaries of Reverend William Smith, entry on fly leaf for 1739 and entry for July 28, 1739; Ebenezer Gay to William Smith, Hingham, March 17, 1745 (Weymouth First Church).

15. Edwin S. Gaustad, *The Great Awakening in New England* (New York, 1957), 24–29, 31–32; Edward M. Griffin, "A Biography of Charles Chauncy (1705–1787)" (Ph.D. dissertation, Stanford University, 1966), 147; "Diary of Rev. Ebenezer Gay of Suffield," September 24, 1740; Charles W. Akers, *Called unto Liberty: A Life of Jonathan Mayhew, 1720–1766* (Cambridge, Mass., 1964), 31, 34.

16. Gaustad, *Great Awakening*, 32–33.

17. Gaustad, *Great Awakening*, 33; Leonard J. Trinterud, *The Forming of an American Tradition: A Re-examination of Colonial Presbyterianism* (Philadelphia, 1949), 57–58.

18. Gay, *Ministers' Insufficiency*, 31–32. By June of 1741, Charles Chauncy was already condemning itinerancy and the censoriousness of the revival party. Chauncy's emergence as the leading opponent of the Awakening in New England is nicely treated in Chaps. 2 and 3 of Edward M. Griffin's *Old Brick: Charles Chauncy of Boston, 1705–1787* (Minneapolis, 1980).

19. Sydney E. Ahlstrom, *A Religious History of the American People* (New Haven, 1972), 271; Gay, *Ministers' Insufficiency*, 22.

20. John Hancock, *The Examiner, or Gilbert against Tennent* (Boston,

1743), 8; Ebenezer Gay, "Record of Births, Marriages, Deaths, and Admissions, 1718–1787" (HCR), back of front cover; Ephesians 5:14, John 3:3; Thomas Prince, *The Christian History* (Boston, 1744), 314.

21. Gay, "Record," admissions for April 5, 1741; *History of Hingham* 3:134, 232.

22. Gay, "Record," admissions for 1741–42; Cedric B. Cowing, "Sex and Preaching in the Great Awakening," *American Quarterly*, Fall 1968, 632; Gaustad, *Great Awakening*, 53.

23. Gay, *Ministers' Insufficiency*, 17, 18.

24. James A. Henretta, *The Evolution of American Society, 1700–1815: An Interdisciplinary Analysis* (Lexington, Mass., 1973), 131–33; Gaustad, *Great Awakening*, 42–43.

25. Daniel Scott Smith, "Population, Family, and Society in Hingham, Massachusetts, 1635–1880" (Ph.D. dissertation, University of California at Berkeley, 1973), 93–94, 104; Hingham Town Clerk's Records, 3, July 2 and August 5, 1741.

26. Smith, "Population," 55, 244–45, 286; Philip J. Greven, Jr., "Youth, Maturity, and Religious Conversion: A Note on the Ages of Converts in Andover, Massachusetts, 1711–1749," *Essex Institute Historical Collections* 108 (1972):119–34. In "Religion, Finance, and Democracy in Massachusetts: The Town of Norton as a Case Study," *Journal of American History* 57 (1971):817–31, John M. Bumstead suggests that the Awakening was particularly vigorous in areas of economic unrest and land hunger.

27. Cowing, "Sex and Preaching," 632 and passim; Ebenezer Gay, *The True Spirit of a Gospel-Minister Represented and Urged* (Boston, 1746), 16.

28. Cowing, "Sex and Preaching," 629, n. 16; Smith, "Population," 272–73.

29. Mary Catherine Foster, "Hampshire County, Massachusetts, 1729–1754: A Covenant Society in Transition" (Ph.D. dissertation, University of Michigan, 1967), 107, 111, 115, 121, 123–24; "Diary of Rev. Stephen Williams" (Typescript from original MS, Storrs Library, Longmeadow, Mass.), July 5, 1741; Gay, *Ministers' Insufficiency*, 36.

30. Shipton, *Sibley's Harvard Graduates* 10:171–73; Robert H. Alcorn, *The Biography of a Town: Suffield, Connecticut 1670–1970* (Suffield, 1970), 49–51; Ebenezer Gay to Stephen Williams, Suffield, December 30, 1741 (Pennsylvania Historical Society). The Reverend John Ballantine was no enthusiast. While his brother-in-law was contending with the ferocious New Lights of Suffield, John was carefully reading "Dr. Watts' Disc° on ye abuse of ye passions in religion." See "Diary of the Rev. John Ballantine" (Typescript copy at the Atheneum, Westfield, Mass.), May 1743.

31. "Diary of Rev. Ebenezer Gay of Suffield," January 11, 1742; Ebenezer Gay to Stephen Williams, Suffield, December 30, 1741; "Diary of Rev. Stephen Williams," January 12 and June 11, 1742; Ebenezer Gay to Stephen Williams, Hingham, March 12, 1742 (MHS).

32. Gay, *Ministers' Insufficiency*, 17, 30, 31; Foster, "Hampshire County," 115.

33. Griffin, *Old Brick*, 69–70.

34. Gay, *Ministers' Insufficiency*, 23–24, 26–27.

35. Ibid., 25, 27, 36. If Gay's sermon had about it a slightly Arminian tone, the Reverend Stephen Williams rather pointedly set things straight in his charge to the candidate, repeatedly emphasizing "Justification by the free Grace of God."

36. Ebenezer Gay to Ebenezer Gay, Hingham, December 6, 1742 (Pennsylvania Historical Society); "Diary of Rev. Stephen Williams," March 19, 1742.

37. *Boston Evening-Post*, July 5, 1742; Joseph Tracy, *The Great Awakening: A History of the Revival of Religion in the Time of Edwards and Whitefield* (Boston, 1845), 209, 230–55.

38. Alcorn, *Suffield*, 51–53; Foster, "Hampshire County," 123; Ebenezer Gay to Ebenezer Gay, Hingham, December 6, 1742. Gay's letter to his nephew dealt with very practical questions of pastoral strategy. He even referred the young man to useful legal precedents enacted by the General Court that dealt with the problem of disruption of a parish by "outside agitators" (Suffield's New Light West Parish was continuing to harass young Gay's First Parish).

39. *The Dictionary of National Biography*, ed. Sir Leslie Stephen and Sir Sidney Lee, 63 vols. (London, 1885–1901), 26:173–80 and 32:236–40; Diaries of Reverend William Smith, entry on fly leaf for 1741; Gay, *Ministers' Insufficiency*, 27.

40. Ebenezer Gay to Ebenezer Gay, Hingham, December 6, 1742; Shipton, *Sibley's Harvard Graduates*, 6:293–94; *George Whitefield's Journals* (London, 1960), 535; "Plymouth Association Book," August 3, 1763.

41. Leonard W. Labaree, "The Conservative Attitude Toward the Great Awakening," *William and Mary Quarterly*, 3d ser., 1 (1944):339–42; Griffin, *Old Brick*, 76; Conrad Wright, *The Beginnings of Unitarianism in America* (Boston, 1955), 44.

CHAPTER VI

## The Great Awakening: The Captain Kept His Place

1. Edward M. Griffin, *Old Brick: Charles Chauncy of Boston, 1705–1787* (Minneapolis, 1980), 75–76; "The Diary of Ebenezer Parkman," *Proceedings of the American Antiquarian Society*, vol. 72, pt. 1 (1961), 150.

2. Joseph Tracy, *The Great Awakening: A History of the Revival of Religion in the Time of Edwards and Whitefield* (Boston, 1845), 286–94.

3. *The Testimony of the Pastors of the Churches in the Province of Massachusetts-Bay in New England at Their Annual Convention in Boston, May 25, 1743*

(Boston, 1743); John Hancock, *An Expostulary and Pacifick Letter* (Boston, 1743), 10; Griffin, *Old Brick*, 76.

4. Tracy, *The Great Awakening*, 294–95.

5. Tracy, *The Great Awakening*, 296, 298, 299–302; Thomas Prince, *The Christian History* (Boston, 1744), 157–66. On the day proclaimed for the second convention, Gay did travel to Cambridge, but his journey was prompted by personal business: his son, Samuel Gay, was receiving his master's degree at the Harvard Commencement. The Overseers voted Samuel's degree even though he was "absent upon a *forrein* Voyage." See Harvard Corporation Records, 1, 1707–1743 (Harvard University Archives), 221, 738.

6. Perry Miller, *Jonathan Edwards* (New York, 1949), 176; Charles Chauncy, *Seasonable Thoughts on the State of Religion in New-England* (Boston, 1743), 422.

7. The South Shore ministers who subscribed for *Seasonable Thoughts* were: Benjamin Bass (Hanover); Shearjashub Bourne (North Scituate); Jonathan Bowman (Dorchester); Philip Curtis (South Stoughton); Samuel Dunbar (North Stoughton); Nathaniel Eels (South Scituate); John Fowle (Cohasset); Ebenezer Gay (Hingham); John Hancock (North Braintree); Daniel Lewis (Pembroke); Thaddeus Maccarty (Kingston); Samuel Niles (South Braintree); William Smith (North Weymouth); John Taylor (Milton); possibly Samuel Hill (Marshfield). See Chauncy, *Seasonable Thoughts*, 1–18.

8. John M. Bumstead, "The Pilgrims' Progress: The Ecclesiastical History of the Old Colony, 1620–1775" (Ph.D. dissertation, Brown University, 1965), 216–17, 301.

9. Clifford K. Shipton, ed., *Sibley's Harvard Graduates* (Boston, 1942), 6:373–75; "Copy of the Hull Church Records, 1725–1746 & 1753–1767," transcription by C. F. Binney in 1847 (New England Historical and Genealogical Society), 6; Bumstead, "Pilgrims' Progress," 163.

10. *The Boston Weekly News-Letter*, March 8, 1744; "Hull Church Records," 5; Harold Field Worthley, "An Inventory of the Records of the Particular (Congregational) Churches of Massachusetts Gathered 1620–1805," *Harvard Theological Studies* 25 (1970):301; Bumstead, "Pilgrims' Progress," 216–20.

11. David R. Proper, *History of the First Congregational Church, Keene, New Hampshire* (Keene, N.H., 1973), 15–17, 19–20; Ebenezer Gay, *Jesus Christ the Wise Master-Builder of His Church* (Boston, 1753), ii, 1, 22. On this occasion, Gay's customary word play with the candidate's name provided the theme for the entire sermon—*Jesus Christ the Wise Master-Builder of His Church*.

12. Samuel Brown et al. to the First Church in Weymouth, Abington, August 10, 1749 (Dyer Memorial Library, Abington, Mass.); Benjamin

Hobart, *History of the Town of Abington* (Boston, 1866), 93, 94; Samuel Brown to "Rev$^d$ Sir," Abington, June 30, 1744 (Dyer Memorial Library).

13. Hobart, *Abington*, 93–94; Bumstead, "Pilgrims' Progress," 259, 410, n. 23; Shipton, *Sibley's Harvard Graduates* (Boston, 1937), 5:481; Samuel Brown to "ye Dissatisfied Brethren," Abington, August 4, 1749 (Dyer Memorial Library); Numbers 16:1–35. On September 13, 1744, immediately after Gay and Eels had tried to help Samuel Brown, they met in council in Duxbury to try to adjudicate another controversy, this one in Middleborough. This complex affair involved a struggle between the church and the precinct over the choice of a successor to their recently deceased pastor, Peter Thacher. Aside from the various legal questions, the church wanted to settle a pro-revivalist, the Reverend Sylvanus Conant, and the precinct wanted an opposer. One of the precinct committeemen declared that "He had rather have a Papist settled among them, than a New-Light." Each side called a sympathetic council, and the anti-revival precinct chose a group that was headed by Nathaniel Eels and Ebenezer Gay. This council supported the primacy of the precinct or parish over the church in the matter of calling a minister; a decision which, they hoped, would also prevent the settlement of a popular New Light minister in Middleborough. See Bumstead, "Pilgrims' Progress," 204–15; Isaac Backus, "Pamphlet 10: A Door Opened for Christian Liberty," in *Isaac Backus on Church, State, and Calvinism: Pamphlets, 1754–1789*, ed. William G. McLoughlin (Cambridge, Mass., 1968), 433–34.

14. Ebenezer Gay, *The Untimely Death of a Man of God Lamented* (Boston, 1744), 18, 24; Frederick Lewis Gay, *John Gay of Dedham, Massachusetts, and Some of His Descendants* (Boston, 1879), 4. Gay resorted to the metaphor of minister as pilot and church as ship with great regularity. When he preached his nephew's ordination sermon, he used it again: "Parishes (saith one) are holy Ships, whose Ministers are the Pilots, and Eternity the Port they must guide them to." See Ebenezer Gay, *Ministers' Insufficiency for Their Important and Difficult Work* (Boston, 1742), 24–25.

15. *George Whitefield's Journals* (London, 1960), 469; Conrad Wright, *The Beginnings of Unitarianism in America* (Boston, 1955), 41; Samuel Niles, *Tristitiae Ecclesiarum* (Boston, 1745), 6.

16. Tracy, *The Great Awakening*, 340–47.

17. *George Whitefield's Journals*, 535; Nathaniel Eels, *A Letter to the Second Church and Congregation in Scituate* (Boston, 1745), 7, 9, 10, 14.

18. George Lincoln, *Hingham Journal*, March 13, 1891. The story suggests that Gay may have taken ship for England in 1744 to visit his son, Samuel, but no documents have survived that in any way support this allusion to an Atlantic crossing. There is also the possibility that Gay visited England in order to settle affairs after the death of his son in March, 1746, the same year that Whitefield commenced a third tour of New England.

See John Gillies, ed., *Memoirs and Sermons of Rev. George Whitefield* (Philadelphia, 1854), 181.

19. Alan Heimert and Perry Miller, eds., *The Great Awakening: Documents Illustrating the Crisis and Its Consequences* (Indianapolis, 1967), 341, 347–48.

20. Ebenezer Gay to William Smith, Hingham, December 31, 1744 (Weymouth First Church).

21. Bumstead, "Pilgrims' Progress," 275; Samuel Niles et al., *The Sentiments and Resolutions of an Association of Ministers (convened) at Weymouth, Jan. 15, 1744/5* (Boston, 1745), 4.

22. Niles et al., *Sentiments and Resolutions*, 3, 4.

23. Ibid., 5, 10–11. The Weymouth testimony was signed by Samuel Niles (South Braintree); Samuel Brown (Abington); Nathaniel Eels (South Scituate); Ebenezer Gay (Hingham); Daniel Perkins (West Bridgewater); John Angier (East Bridgewater); John Taylor (Milton); Samuel Dunbar (North Stoughton); Jonathan Bowman (Dorchester); William Smith (North Weymouth); John Fowle (Cohasset); Philip Curtis (South Stoughton).

24. Bumstead, "Pilgrims' Progress," 212.

25. *History of the Town of Hingham*, 3 vols. (Hingham, 1893), vol. 1, pt. 2 and vol. 2, 156; Real Property Valuation for 1754.

26. "The First Book of Records of the Third Parish in Hingham," 1742–1865 (South Hingham Church), 1 (hereafter cited as South Hingham Parish Records); Hingham Town Clerk's Record, vol. 3, 1720–1762 (Hingham Town Hall), 1737–1758; *History of Hingham*, vol. 1, pt. 2, 156, vol. 2, 158 and vol. 3, 31–32.

27. "South Hingham Church and Parish," Parish Records of the Hingham First Church, trans. Arthur D. Marble (HCR), 1:44, 54–57; Hingham Town Clerk's Record, 3, October 3, 1743 and March 5, 1744; "Appropriations," Hingham Parish Records 1:57; *The Acts and Resolves of the Province of Massachusetts Bay* (Boston, 1905), 13:385–86, 562.

28. "South Hingham Church and Parish," 60–61; *Acts and Resolves* 13:386; "A Book of Records Belonging to the Third Church in Hingham," 1746–1844 (South Hingham Church), January 13 and January 25, 1747 (hereafter referred to as South Hingham Church Records).

29. John Gorham Palfrey, *Dr. Palfrey's Discourse on the Life and Character of Dr. Ware* (Cambridge, Mass., 1845), 13; Ebenezer Gay to "ye 3ᵈ Chh of Christ in Hingham," Hingham, December 9, 1746 (South Hingham Church).

30. South Hingham Parish Records, 2; South Hingham Church Records, 10. For a more extended discussion of the formation of the South Hingham Parish, see Robert J. Wilson III, "Ebenezer Gay, New England's Arminian Patriarch: 1696–1787" (Ph.D. dissertation, University of Massachusetts, 1980), 243–55.

31. Shipton, *Sibley's Harvard Graduates* (Boston, 1960), 11:304; *History of Hingham*, vol. 1, pt. 2, 43; South Hingham Parish Records, 12; Daniel Shute to "the Inhabitants of the 3rd Parish in Hingham," Malden, September 13, 1746 (South Hingham Church); Daniel Shute to "the Inhabitants of ye 3rd Parish in Hingham," Hingham, March 9, 1752 (South Hingham Church).

32. "The Report of a committee of Hingham First Parish, chaired by Solomon Lincoln on the question of pulpit exchange with the other religious societies of Hingham," March 6, 1846 (Town of Hingham Papers, MHS); *History of Hingham*, vol. 1, pt. 2, 44; Daniel Shute, "The Charge," appended to *A Sermon Delivered December 10, 1788* by Timothy Hilliard (Newburyport, 1789), 39; Shipton, *Sibley's Harvard Graduates* 11:304.

33. Daniel Shute, *A Sermon Delivered . . . at the Interment of the Rev. Ebenezer Gay, D.D.* (Salem, 1787), 28; "Exchanges and Occasional" in "Pulpit Services, 1681–1891," collected and arranged by Fearing Burr (HCR). Shute quickly became a part of the South Hingham establishment when he married Captain Abel Cushing's daughter, Mary. By 1752, he felt secure enough in his position to demand that the parish raise his salary from £40 to at least £70. He told them plainly that he was "determined not to suffer for want of Bread in this Place So long as it is in my Power to avoid it." The Third Parish voted the raise he requested and thereafter Shute came gradually to exercise the same strong influence in South Hingham that Gay enjoyed in the Town. Shipton, *Sibley's Harvard Graduates* 11:305; *History of Hingham*, vol. 1, pt. 2, 44; Daniel Shute to "the Inhabitants of ye 3rd Parish in Hingham," Hingham, March 9, 1752; South Hingham Parish Records, 12.

34. Ebenezer Gay, *The Character and Work of a Good Ruler, and the Duty of an Obliged People* (Boston, 1745), 30.

35. Michael Zuckerman, "The Fabrication of Identity in Early America," *William and Mary Quarterly*, 3d ser., 34 (April 1977):200–204.


CHAPTER VII
## Pure and Undefiled Religion

1. *Journals of the House of Representatives* (Boston, 1946), 21:239; Ebenezer Gay, *The Character and Work of a Good Ruler, and the Duty of an Obliged People* (Boston, 1745), 21.

2. Bernard Bailyn, *The Ideological Origins of the American Revolution* (Cambridge, Mass., 1967), 32.

3. Benjamin Walker Diary (MHS), May 29, 1745; Gay, *Character and Work*, 18.

4. Gay, *Character and Work*, 3, 5, 18, 30.

5. Howard H. Peckham, *The Colonial Wars, 1639–1762* (Chicago,

1964), 99, 101–4; Robert Zemsky, *Merchants, Farmers and River Gods: An Essay on Eighteenth-Century American Politics* (Boston, 1971), 129–56; Ebenezer Gay, *The Levite Not to Be Forsaken* (Boston, 1756), 16; Gay, *Character and Work*, 18, 19–20, 25, 29; James A. Henretta, *The Evolution of American Society, 1700–1815: An Interdisciplinary Analysis* (Lexington, Mass., 1973), 132; Zemsky, *Merchants*, 129–56. The themes of Election Sermons had changed in the years immediately preceding 1745, and Gay's sermon fully reflected those changes. Since 1734, the "Errand" motif, which contrasted recent apostasy with the intentions of the first settlers, had virtually disappeared from Election Sermons. The ministers were now much more likely to address specific issues such as oppressive taxes or depreciating currency. See A. W. Plumstead, ed., *The Wall and the Garden: Selected Massachusetts Election Sermons, 1660–1775* (Minneapolis, 1968), 283–84.

6. Gay, *Character and Work*, 11, 13.

7. Ibid., 25–26.

8. *The Diary of Ebenezer Parkman, 1703–1782*, ed. Francis G. Walett (Worcester, Mass., 1974), 121; *Massachusetts Gazette*, March 30, 1787. Gay's sermon text was 1 Samuel 14:6.

9. Charles Chauncy, *Seasonable Thoughts on the State of Religion in New-England* (Boston, 1743), 12. The best summary of the Maccarty affair may be found in John M. Bumstead's "The Pilgrims' Progress: The Ecclesiastical History of the Old Colony, 1620–1775" (Ph.D. dissertation, Brown University, 1965), 191–96.

10. Bumstead, "Pilgrims' Progress," 194–95.

11. Bumstead, "Pilgrims' Progress," 195; "A Council of Three Churches Mutually chosen by the Pastor and Church at Kingston met There October 22, 1745" (Weymouth First Church).

12. Clifford K. Shipton, *Sibley's Harvard Graduates* (Boston, 1942), 6:550–52; C. C. Goen, ed., *The Great Awakening*, vol. 4 of *The Works of Jonathan Edwards*, ed. John E. Smith (New Haven, 1972), 17–18.

13. Diaries of Reverend William Smith of Weymouth, 1728–1763 (MHS), August 14, 1754, February 19, and June 18, 1755; "Plymouth Association Book, 1722" (Congregational Library), August 12, 1761, August 3, 1763, and November 7, 1764.

14. Ebenezer Gay, *The True Spirit of a Gospel-Minister Represented and Urged* (Boston, 1746), 9, 10, 19; Ebenezer Gay, *The Alienation of Affection from Ministers Consider'd and Improv'd* (Boston, 1747), 11.

15. Roland N. Stromberg, *Religious Liberalism in Eighteenth-Century England* (London, 1954), 43; Gerald R. Cragg, *The Church and the Age of Reason: 1648–1789* (Grand Rapids, Mich., 1960), 158. Clarke's *Being and Attributes of God* (1704) was delivered as one of the Boyle Lectures, a series of lectures endowed by the great English chemist, Robert Boyle. Their purpose was to reconcile the Christian tradition with post-Newtonian rationalism.

16. Stromberg, *Religious Liberalism*, 43, 44–46; Conrad Wright, *The Beginnings of Unitarianism in America* (Boston, 1955), 77.

17. Wright, *Beginnings of Unitarianism*, 76–80, 137.

18. Wright, *Beginnings of Unitarianism*, 76–78; Stromberg, *Religious Liberalism*, 116; Edward M. Griffin, "A Biography of Charles Chauncy (1705–1787)" (Ph.D. dissertation, Stanford University, 1966), 210; Henry Ware's Reading List for Divinity Students, 1806 (MHS).

19. Goen, *Great Awakening*, 10; Wright, *Beginnings of Unitarianism*, 60–62.

20. Gay, *True Spirit*, 27, 28.

21. Gay, *True Spirit*, 6; David D. Hall, *The Faithful Shepherd: A History of the New England Ministry in the Seventeenth Century* (Chapel Hill, 1972), 93–120.

22. Gay, *True Spirit*, 28, 30, 31, 32, 33.

23. Ibid., 10, 26–27.

24. Gay, *True Spirit*, 19; Wright, *Beginnings of Unitarianism*, 225. William Rand, minister at Kingston and an active member of the Hingham Association, also viewed the consequences of private interpretation from a latitudinarian perspective: "Therefore we ought to be willing that every one of our brethren should approve himself to God . . . and not be over-much solicitous to please us by conforming to our particular opinions." See Shipton, *Sibley's Harvard Graduates* 6:550.

25. Gay, *True Spirit*, 11.

26. Gay, Ibid., 10.

27. *Diary of Ebenezer Parkman*, 137; Gay, *True Spirit*, 33.

28. *History of the Town of Hingham*, 3 vols. (Hingham, 1893), vol. 1, pt. 2, 39; Shipton, *Sibley's Harvard Graduates* (Boston, 1956), 9:152–53; John Fowle to William Smith, Cohasset, December 24, 1745 (Weymouth First Church).

29. Charles W. Akers, *Called unto Liberty: A Life of Jonathan Mayhew, 1720–1766* (Cambridge, Mass., 1964), 23, 40; Jonathan Mayhew to Experience Mayhew, Boston, October 1, 1747 (Mayhew Papers, Boston University).

30. Alan Heimert in his *Religion and the American Mind: From the Great Awakening to the Revolution* (Cambridge, Mass., 1966), 290–93, is foremost among those who have challenged the myth that has glorified Mayhew as a herald of American democracy. Mayhew, like Gay, was clearly a social conservative who believed that the majority of the populace was incapable of exercising the right of private judgement.

31. Alden Bradford, *Memoir of the Life and Writings of Rev. Jonathan Mayhew, D.D.* (Boston, 1838), 483; Akers, *Called unto Liberty*, 63–65.

32. Akers, *Called unto Liberty*, 39–41; Bradford, *Memoir*, 21, 483; Gay, *Alienation of Affection*, 26; Jotham Gay to Martin Gay, Hingham, July 17, 1764 (Gay-Otis Papers, Special Collections, Columbia University); Jotham

Gay to Martin Gay, Cumberland, N.S., September 16, 1766 (Gay-Otis Papers); Abigail Gay to Jotham Gay, Hingham, August 22, 1766 (Gay-Otis Papers). The credibility of Alden Bradford's comments on the Gay-Mayhew relationship is enhanced by Bradford's kinship with the Gays. Jerusha Bradford Gay was Alden's grandaunt. See *The New England Historical and Genealogical Register* 4 (1850): 240.

33. Bradford, *Memoir*, 483; Akers, *Called unto Liberty*, 29, 32–41; Wright, *Beginnings of Unitarianism*, 218–19; Gay, *Alienation of Affection*, 26. Gay's copy of William Gravesande's *Mathematical Elements of Natural Philosophy*, trans. John T. Desaguliers (London, 1747), was made available through the courtesy of Mr. Ebenezer Gay of Hingham. Charles W. Akers, in his biography of Mayhew, puts Gay's influence on the young man in perspective. Akers shows that, after Mayhew's brief flirtation with the New Light in 1741, he was sobered up by a multiplicity of agencies—the liberal Harvard curriculum, his circle of skeptical friends, and his father.

34. Akers, *Called unto Liberty*, 41–43, 44–48, 53–55; John Brown, *A Discourse Delivered at the West Church in Boston* (Boston, 1766), 13; Gay, *Alienation of Affection*, 2.

35. Akers, *Called unto Liberty*, 48–51; Wright, *Beginnings of Unitarianism*, 65–66.

36. Akers, *Called unto Liberty*, 46, 51–52; Wright, *Beginnings of Unitarianism*, 66; Gay, *Alienation of Affection*, 27; Ebenezer Gay, *Jesus Christ the Wise Master-Builder of His Church* (Boston, 1753), 20–21.

37. Gay, *Alienation of Affection*, 10, 21, 26; Akers, *Called unto Liberty*, 66, 68–69, 71. Gay's admiration for St. Paul was shared by Mayhew, who characterized him as "a reasonable, catholick man, and a friend to the rights of private judgement." See Akers, 71.

38. Gay, *Alienation of Affection*, 19, 26.

39. Gay, *Alienation of Affection*, 21; Gay, *True Spirit*, 15; Charles H. Lippy, *Seasonable Revolutionary: The Mind of Charles Chauncy* (Chicago, 1981), 109.

40. Gay, *Alienation of Affection*, 27.

41. Brown, *A Discourse*, 12; Shipton, *Sibley's Harvard Graduates* (Boston, 1960), 11:12–13; Harrison Gray to Thomas Hollis, Boston, July 27, 1766 (MHS).

42. Cohasset Church Records, 1747–1796 (First Parish Church of Cohasset). September 2, 1747; Bradford, *Memoir*, 27n.; Nathaniel Eels, *The Evangelical Bishop* (New London, Conn., 1734), 10.

43. Brown, *A Discourse*, 8–9; Shipton, *Sibley's Harvard Graduates* 11: 13; Cohasset Church Meeting Records, 1748–1785 (First Parish Church of Cohasset), September 28, 1749.

44. Brown, *A Discourse*, 12; Shipton, *Sibley's Harvard Graduates* 11:14.

CHAPTER VIII
A Benevolent Planet with His Satellites

1. Clifford K. Shipton, *Sibley's Harvard Graduates* (Boston, 1960), 11:231; "Book of Records of the Second Precinct in Pembroke" (owned and held by the Congregational Church of Hanson, Mass.), 7; Gad Hitchcock to "The Inhabitants of a New Precinct," Cambridge, March 28, 1748 (Congregational Church of Hanson). William Smith of Weymouth continued to be a mainstay in the association, even after it came to be dominated by Gay and his Arminian associates, but his continued support may reflect no more than a close friendship with Gay, and a delight in the congenial company of Gay's circle.

2. "Records of Second Precinct in Pembroke," 9; Shipton, *Sibley's Harvard Graduates* 11:232–33; Gad Hitchcock, *Natural Religion Aided by Revelation and Perfected in Christianity* (Boston, 1779), 18.

3. Shipton, *Sibley's Harvard Graduates* (Boston, 1958), 10:341–42, 344; Charles W. Akers, *Called unto Liberty: A Life of Jonathan Mayhew, 1720–1766* (Cambridge, Mass., 1964), 23; [Samuel Niles et al.], *The Result of a Late Ecclesiastical Council* (Boston, 1753), 3. While Briant and Mayhew were reading the recently introduced works of Taylor, Foster, etc., Gay was still turning to the works of seventeenth-century divines to sanction and inspire his Arminian theology. In 1749, he was reading the latitudinarian *Fifteen Sermons* by John Sharp (1645–1714), Archbishop of York. See Diaries of the Reverend William Smith of Weymouth, 1728–1763 (MHS), fly leaf entry for 1749; *The Dictionary of National Biography*, ed. Sir Leslie Stephen and Sir Sidney Lee, 63 vols. (London, 1885–1901), 51:408–12.

4. Peter Adams et al. to William Smith, Braintree, November 18, 1745 (Weymouth First Church); Akers, *Called unto Liberty*, 74; Shipton, *Sibley's Harvard Graduates* 10:342, 345, 347; Lemuel Briant, *The Absurdity and Blasphemy of Depretiating Moral Virtue* (Boston, 1749), 23.

5. Briant, *Absurdity and Blasphemy*, 7, 20; Conrad Wright, *The Beginnings of Unitarianism in America* (Boston, 1955), 69.

6. Briant, *Absurdity and Blasphemy*, 16, 23; Saul K. Padover, ed., *A Jefferson Profile: As Revealed in His Letters* (New York, 1956), 307; Wright, *Beginnings of Unitarianism*, 69–70.

7. Akers, *Called unto Liberty*, 78; Colonel Benjamin Lincoln Diary (Benjamin Lincoln Papers, MHS), January 28, 1750; Samuel Deane, *History of Scituate* (Boston, 1831), 199.

8. Wright, *Beginnings of Unitarianism*, 69–70; Shipton, *Sibley's Harvard Graduates* 10:344; Akers, *Called unto Liberty*, 79; Claude M. Newlin, *Philosophy and Religion in Colonial America* (New York, 1962), 140.

9. Shipton, *Sibley's Harvard Graduates* 10:345–46; [Niles et al.], *The Result*, 2, 3, 4, 6; *Dictionary of National Biography* 45:260.

10. Journal of Joseph Andrews, 1752–1787 (MHS), May 24, 1752;

Richard Cranch to Jonathan Mayhew, Braintree, June 10, 1752 (Christopher P. Cranch Papers, MHS); Shipton, *Sibley's Harvard Graduates* 10:347; Charles Francis Adams, *Three Episodes of Massachusetts History*, 2 vols. (Boston, 1892), 2:64.

11. Newlin, *Philosophy and Religion*, 141–43.

12. Diary of Reverend Edward Billings of Belchertown and Greenfield, 1743–1756 (Pocumtuck Valley Memorial Association), April 25, 1753.

13. "A Council of Six Chhs convened at Shrewsbury Oct. 11, 1749" (Nathan Stone Papers, MHS); Andrew H. Ward, *Family Register of the Inhabitants of the Town of Shrewsbury, Mass.* (Boston, 1847), 228.

14. *The Diary of Ebenezer Parkman, 1703–1782*, ed. Francis G. Walett, (Worcester, Mass., 1974), 1:204; "A Council of Six Chhs at Shrewsbury."

15. Shipton, *Sibley's Harvard Graduates* (Cambridge, Mass., 1933), 4:470; Ebenezer Gay, *The Mystery of the Seven Stars in Christ's Right Hand* (Boston, 1752), 29.

16. Shipton, *Sibley's Harvard Graduates* (Boston, 1962), 12:126, 127; *History of the Town of Hingham*, 3 vols. (Hingham, 1893), vol. 1, pt. 2, 28, 111; Ebenezer Gay, "Record of Births, Marriages, Deaths, and Admissions, 1718–1787" (HCR), December 6, 1747; "Rev. Ebenezer Gay, D.D.," in "Pulpit Services, 1681–1891," collected and arranged by Fearing Burr (HCR), November 13, 1751; Gay, *Mystery*, 30.

17. Gay, *Mystery*, 7.

18. Ebenezer Gay, *The Levite Not to Be Forsaken* (Boston, 1756), 18, 19, 20, 21. For an excellent discussion of the rise of professionalism in colonial and early national America, see Daniel H. Calhoun, *Professional Lives in America: Structure and Aspiration, 1750–1850* (Cambridge, Mass., 1965). The ways in which the New England ministers organized as a professional group are nicely described in Chapter 4, "Congregational Clericalism," in J. William T. Youngs, Jr., *God's Messengers: Religious Leadership in Colonial New England, 1700–1750* (Baltimore, 1976).

19. Gay, *Mystery*, 7, 10, 11–12.

20. Ebenezer Gay, *The True Spirit of a Gospel-Minister Represented and Urged* (Boston, 1746), 17, 18; Diaries of Reverend William Smith, June 5, 1754; Gay, *Mystery*, 12.

21. Gay, *Mystery*, 17, 18, 19, 30.

22. Shipton, *Sibley's Harvard Graduates* 12:127; Colonel Benjamin Lincoln Diary, April 27, 1754.

23. Shipton, *Sibley's Harvard Graduates* (Boston, 1965), 13:189–91; Deane, *Scituate*, 204–5, 206–7; Samuel A. Eliot, ed., *Heralds of a Liberal Faith* (Boston, 1910), 12–13; David Barnes, "Revealed Religion," 1780 (MS sermon at Harvard University Archives), 13, 15; Joseph Haroutunian, *Piety Versus Moralism: The Passing of the New England Theology* (New York, 1932), 24; David Barnes, "He was called the Friend of God" (MS sermon at Houghton Library, Harvard University), last page.

24. Shipton, *Sibley's Harvard Graduates* 13:293–95; Diaries of Reverend William Smith, entry under "Minister Meeting," 1763; D. M. Wilson, ed., *The "Chappel of Ease" and Church of Statesmen* (Quincy, Mass., 1890), 58. Gay gave the "charge" at Charles Turner's ordination, according to information supplied to me by the Town Historian of Duxbury.

25. Diaries of Reverend William Smith, February 19, 1755 and March 7, 1759; Ebenezer Parkman Diary, January 1756–May 1761 (American Antiquarian Society), May 26 and June 3, 1760.

26. Lyman H. Butterfield, ed., *Diary and Autobiography of John Adams*, 4 vols. (Cambridge, Mass., 1961), 1:278; Israel Loring Diary, bk. 2, 16–17; Shipton, *Sibley's Harvard Graduates* 10:347 and (Boston, 1956), 11:13.

27. Eliot, *Heralds*, 15; *History of Hingham*, vol. 1, pt. 2, 28.

28. Frederick L. Weis, "Ebenezer Gay," *The Proceedings of the Unitarian Historical Society*, vol. 4, pt. 2 (1936): 10.

29. Shipton, *Sibley's Harvard Graduates* (Boston, 1945), 7:166–70; "Exchanges and Occasional" in "Pulpit Services, 1681–1891," collected and arranged by Fearing Burr (HCR); *History of Hingham*, vol. 1, pt. 2, 28–29.

30. Akers, *Called unto Liberty*, 128; Shipton, *Sibley's Harvard Graduates* 12:29 and 13:204–5; *History of Hingham*, vol. 1, pt. 2, 111; Diaries of Reverend William Smith, February 19, 1755; Ebenezer Gay, "The Right Hand of Fellowship," in John Cushing's *Gospel-Ministers to Preach Christ to Their People* (Boston, 1759), iv, v.

31. Shipton, *Sibley's Harvard Graduates* 7:586–87 and 11:58–61.

32. Gay, *The Levite*, 9, 11, 23, 26; Burr, "Exchanges and Occasional"; Shipton, *Sibley's Harvard Graduates* 11:59.

33. Shipton, *Sibley's Harvard Graduates* 11:61–64; Grindall Rawson, the "Advertisement" prefixed to Ebenezer Gay's *The Levite Not to be Forsaken* (Dover, N.H., 1793).

34. Diaries of Reverend William Smith, June 5, 1754; Gay, *The Levite*, 14.

35. For the most complete account of the "Wallingford Controversy," see Charles H. S. Davis, *History of Wallingford* (Meriden, Conn., 1870), 164–88.

36. Shipton, *Sibley's Harvard Graduates* 11:189–91.

37. Shipton, *Sibley's Harvard Graduates* 11:190–92; William S. Heywood, *History of Westminster* (Lowell, Mass., 1893), 120; "Diary of Cotton Mather, 1709–1724," *Collections of the Massachusetts Historical Society*, 7th ser. (Boston, 1912), 8:144; Suffolk County, Massachusetts Court File and Early Records, 1629–1799, #81,153.

38. Shipton, *Sibley's Harvard Graduates* 11:192–93; Suffolk Court File, #77,354; Wright, *Beginnings of Unitarianism*, 82.

39. Shipton, *Sibley's Harvard Graduates*, 11:193–94.

40. Ebenezer Parkman Diary, January 1756–May 1761 (American Antiquarian Society), December 7 and 17, 1757.

41. Shipton, *Sibley's Harvard Graduates* 11:194–97.

42. Barnes, "Revealed Religion," 13; Richard L. Bushman, *From Puritan to Yankee: Character and the Social Order in Connecticut, 1690–1765* (Cambridge, Mass., 1967), 247.

CHAPTER IX
## The Father of Lights

1. Charles W. Akers, *Called unto Liberty: A Life of Jonathan Mayhew, 1720–1766* (Cambridge, Mass., 1964), 117–23.

2. Clarence H. Faust and Thomas H. Johnson, eds., *Jonathan Edwards* (New York, 1935), lxvi–lxxi; Conrad Wright, *The Beginnings of Unitarianism in America* (Boston, 1955), 83–85, 122; John Herman Randall, *The Making of the Modern Mind* (Boston, 1926), 283. John Taylor's basic position was that Adam had not been created as a perfectly righteous man. Instead, he was simply a primitive, who was unable to attain the high standards of morality that God required. Furthermore, Adam's failure and his guilt were his alone; sin and guilt were personal matters and could not be imputed or transferred. It should be noted, however, that although they acknowledged his influence, neither Gay nor Chauncy nor Mayhew were slavish followers of Taylor's doctrine.

3. Perry Miller, "The Insecurity of Nature. Being the Dudleian Lecture for the Academic Year 1952–1953," *Harvard Divinity School Bulletin: Annual Lectures and Book Reviews* (1954):31.

4. Ebenezer Parkman Diary, January 1756–May 1761 (American Antiquarian Society), May 26, 1756, May 31, 1758, and June 1, 1958; Akers, *Called unto Liberty*, 59.

5. Conrad Wright, *The Liberal Christians: Essays on American Unitarian History* (Boston, 1970), 7–8; Harvard Corporation Records, 1750–1778 (Harvard University Archives), 2:117–18; Journal of Joseph Andrews, 1752–1787 (MHS), July 16, 1758.

6. James W. Jones, *The Shattered Synthesis: New England Puritanism before the Great Awakening* (New Haven, 1973), 133; Ebenezer Gay, *A Beloved Disciple of Jesus Christ Characterized* (Boston, 1766), 10; Ebenezer Gay, *Natural Religion, as Distinguish'd from Revealed* (Boston, 1759), 10.

7. Gay, *Natural Religion*, 5, 7.

8. Gay, *Natural Religion*, 6, 8–9; Ebenezer Gay, *The Mystery of the Seven Stars in Christ's Right Hand* (Boston, 1752), 12.

9. Gay, *A Beloved Disciple*, 10; Gay, *Natural Religion*, 10–11.

10. Wright, *Beginnings of Unitarianism*, 142–43; Gad Hitchcock, *Natu-*

*ral Religion Aided by Revelation and Perfected in Christianity* (Boston, 1779), 20; Gay, *Natural Religion*, 5, 6, 11.

11. John Norton, copy of a MS sermon dated February 19, 1716 (HCR), 108; Roland N. Stromberg, *Religious Liberalism in Eighteenth-Century England* (London, 1954), 84–85; Wright, *Beginnings of Unitarianism*, 144; Hitchcock, *Natural Religion*, 11, 15.

12. Stromberg, *Religious Liberalism*, 19–20; G. P. H. Pawson, *The Cambridge Platonists and Their Place in Religious Thought* (London, 1930), 58, 59; Gay, *Natural Religion*, 13.

13. Gay, *Natural Religion*, 13–14; Herbert M. Morais, *Deism in Eighteenth Century America* (New York, 1934), 35–36; *The Dictionary of National Biography*, ed. Sir Leslie Stephen and Sir Sidney Lee, 22 vols. (London, 1885–1901), 4:217–19.

14. Daniel Shute, *A Sermon Preached before His Excellency Francis Bernard* (Boston, 1768), 9; Gay, *Natural Religion*, 14.

15. Randall, *Modern Mind*, 288; Gay, *Natural Religion*, 21–22.

16. Wright, *Beginnings of Unitarianism*, 103–4; Gay, *Natural Religion*, 12.

17. Gay, *Natural Religion*, 12, 14, 15; Wright, *Beginnings of Unitarianism*, 96–97.

18. Gay, *Natural Religion*, 16, 17, 20, 21, 27; Jones, *Shattered Synthesis*, 141; Gay, *A Beloved Disciple*, 10.

19. Ebenezer Gay, *St. John's Vision of the Woman Cloathed with the Sun* (Boston, 1766), 27.

20. Wright, *Beginnings of Unitarianism*, 153; Gay, *St. John's Vision*, 22.

21. Alan Heimert, *Religion and the American Mind: From the Great Awakening to the Revolution* (Cambridge, Mass., 1966), 47; Gay, *Natural Religion*, 10; Shute, *A Sermon Preached*, 6.

22. Hitchcock, *Natural Religion*, 17; Heimert, *Religion and the American Mind*, 47; Gay, *A Beloved Disciple*, 10–11.

23. Hitchcock, *Natural Religion*, 19; Gay, *St. John's Vision*, 27–28.

24. Gay, *Natural Religion*, 19; Stromberg, *Religious Liberalism*, 53; Wright, *Beginnings of Unitarianism*, 149.

25. Wright, *Liberal Christians*, 10–11; David Barnes, "Revealed Religion," 1780 (MS sermon at Harvard University Archives), 3; Gay, *Natural Religion*, 24, 25, 27.

26. Gay, *Natural Religion*, 30–31; Lyman H. Butterfield, ed., *Diary and Autobiography of John Adams*, 4 vols. (Cambridge, Mass., 1961), 1:120.

27. Gay, *Natural Religion*, 19–20, 23, 30–31; Randall, *Modern Mind*, 289. The phrase beginning "Both are good Gifts . . ." echoes the opening words of Samuel Willard's *Brief Directions to a Young Scholar Designing the Ministry* (1735). Here was a work that Gay might profitably have assigned to any of his theology students whom he suspected of succumbing to the

lure of deism. See J. William T. Youngs, Jr., *God's Messengers: Religious Leadership in Colonial New England, 1700–1750* (Baltimore, 1976), 19–20.

28. Heimert, *Religion and the American Mind*, 5–6.

29. Wright, *Beginnings of Unitarianism*, 6–8.

30. John Brown, *A Discourse Delivered at the West Church in Boston* (Boston, 1766), 10; Bernard Bailyn, *The Ideological Origins of the American Revolution* (Cambridge, Mass., 1967), 254–56; Akers, *Called unto Liberty*, 82–83.

31. Akers, *Called unto Liberty*, 171–72; Bailyn, *Ideological Origins*, 256.

32. Akers, *Called unto Liberty*, 240; Ebenezer Gay, *A Call from Macedonia* (Boston, 1768), 32. Gay urged his son Martin in Boston to send him "the Bishop of London's answer to Doctor Mayhew as we hear it is published." See Jotham Gay to Martin Gay, Hingham, April 16, 1764 (Gay-Otis Papers, Special Collections, Columbia University).

33. Akers, *Called unto Liberty*, 221–23; Gay, *A Beloved Disciple*, 25; Martin Gay to Jotham Gay, Boston, August 26, 1766 (Gay-Otis Papers).

34. Akers, *Called unto Liberty*, 221–22; Gay, *A Beloved Disciple*, 7, 24, 26.

35. Akers, *Called unto Liberty*, 222; Gay, *St. John's Vision*, 36, 39; William D. Gould, "The Religious Opinions of Thomas Jefferson," *The Mississippi Valley Historical Review* 20 (September 1933): 200.

36. Abigail Gay to Jotham Gay, Hingham, August 22, 1766 (Gay-Otis Papers); Gay, *St. John's Vision*, 39; Brown, *A Discourse*, 17.

37. Shipton, *Sibley's Harvard Graduates* (Boston, 1968), 14:279; Assessors Record of the First Parish in Hingham, 1718–1816 (HCR), 25–26; *History of the Town of Hingham*, 3 vols., (Hingham, 1893), vol. 1, pt. 2, 111; Ebenezer Gay, "Record of Births, Marriages, Deaths, and Admissions, 1718–1787" (HCR), September 6, 1761; Journal of Joseph Andrews, November 7, 1762, June 19, 1763, and August 11, 1765. Gay tried to settle yet another of his students in the impoverished Nova Scotian town of Cumberland. Caleb Gannett (Harvard, 1763), a rather pompous young man with his eye on the main chance, had no great desire to bury himself in the Maritimes. Despite Parson Gay's solemn charge to "go forth and preach Christ in a distant part of our American world," and despite Jotham Gay's offer of five hundred acres of land for his support, Gannett was most reluctant. His mentor finally declared that he must go "immediately . . . without any hesitation, excuse, or delay." Gannett, who had no other prospects, obeyed. He was not well received by the Cumberland Society, however, and soon lost his parish to a well-funded S.P.G. missionary. See Robert J. Wilson III, "Ebenezer Gay: New England's Arminian Patriarch, 1696–1787" (Ph.D. dissertation, University of Massachusetts, 1980), 403–7.

38. Shipton, *Sibley's Harvard Graduates* 14:279–81.

39. Ibid., 280; Thomas Foster, et al. to William Smith, Boston, April 13, 1767 (Weymouth First Church); Charles Chauncy, *Sermon Preached . . . at the Ordination of the Rev. Simeon Howard* (Boston, 1767), 36, 44, 46, 48.

40. Simeon Howard, *Christians No Cause to Be Ashamed of Their Religion* (Boston, 1779), 21, 33; James Alexander, *Life of Archibald Alexander* (New York, 1854), 251.

41. Harold Field Worthley, "An Inventory of the Records of the Particular (Congregational) Churches of Massachusetts Gathered 1620–1805," *Harvard Theological Studies* 25 (1970):84; Shipton, *Sibley's Harvard Graduates* 14:282, 284; Ruth Atkins Gay to Martin Gay, Boston, February 3, 1791 (Courtesy of William O. Gay).

42. Gay, *A Call from Macedonia*, 14.

CHAPTER X
Family and Community: The Arminian
Patriarch in Changing Times

1. *History of the Town of Hingham*, 3 vols. (Hingham, 1893), vol. 1, pt. 2, 170–71; Jotham Gay to Martin Gay, Cumberland, N.S., July 1, 1771 (Gay-Otis Papers, Columbia University); Real Property Valuation for 1754 (Hingham Town Hall); Hingham Town Clerk's Records, vol. 3, 1720–1762 (Hingham Town Hall), May 24, 1753.

2. *History of Hingham*, vol. 1, pt. 2, 171 and vol. 2, 22, 431; Real Property Valuation for 1754. Gay himself was not behind-hand in improving his temporal lot in his later years. Between 1767 and 1774, he bought thirty-eight acres of land in Cohasset, and seventeen acres divided between Squirrel Hill and Otis Hill. The hill land may have simply provided additional grazing for his cattle and swine, though there were brick kilns at the foot of Squirrel Hill, and the property also abutted the major highway to Boston. See Suffolk County Registry of Deeds, 111:32, 33 and 125:50; Estate Inventory of the Reverend Ebenezer Gay, Suffolk County Registry of Probate, #18,890; *History of Hingham*, vol. 1, pt. 1, 180.

3. Edward Johnson, *Wonder-Working Providence, 1628–1651*, ed. J. Franklin Jameson (New York, 1910), 116; *History of Hingham*, vol. 1, pt. 2, 170–71; Hingham Town Clerk's Records, 3, March 2, 1752.

4. *History of Hingham*, vol. 1, pt. 2, 155–80; Van Beck Hall, *Politics without Parties: Massachusetts, 1780–1791* (Pittsburgh, 1972), A-1. Hall constructed his commercial index from four items on the state property valuation lists—stock in trade, silver, money lent at interest, and vessel tonnage. For his methodology, see Hall, *Politics without Parties*, 4–5. Among the other towns represented in the Hingham Association, Scituate ranked twelfth, Braintree eighteenth, Weymouth twenty-second, Marshfield twenty-ninth,

Kingston thirty-fourth, Pembroke forty-sixth, and Cohasset (by then a separate town) forty-seventh.

5. Daniel Scott Smith, "Population, Family, and Society in Hingham,
Massachusetts, 1635–1800" (Ph.D. dissertation, University of California at
Berkeley, 1973), 90, 93, 95, 96, 97; Real Property Valuation for 1754.

6. Smith, "Population," 104; Real Property Valuation for 1765
(Hingham Town Hall); Inventory of Estate of Deacon Thomas Andrews
(Town of Hingham Papers, 1637–1799, MHS); Hingham Town Clerk's
Records, 3, March 2, 1747 and May 12, 1748; *History of Hingham*, vol. 1,
pt. 2, 380–81.

7. Hingham Town Clerk's Records, vols. 3 and 4, 1762–1813 (Hingham Town Hall).

8. Hingham's political leadership provided a classic example of what
Edward M. Cook, Jr. has called a highly stratified, major country town,
having a fairly narrow leadership pool, significant family continuity, a con-
centration of power in long-servers, and a high rate of average service. See
his "Local Leadership and the Typology of New England Towns, 1700–
1785," *Political Science Quarterly* 86 (December 1971):586–609.

9. Smith, "Population," 248, 250; Hingham Town Clerk's Records,
vols. 3 and 4. Hingham's growing commercial wealth is reflected in the one
thousand pound Province Tax assessment. In 1735 Hingham ranked nineteenth in assessments, in 1742 the town ranked fifteenth, and in 1751,
fourteenth. See *Journals of the House of Representatives of Massachusetts* (Boston, 1932), 13:242 and (Boston, 1952), 20:217.

10. Real Property Valuation for 1765; *History of Hingham*, vol. 1,
pt. 2, 34–35; Parish Records of the Hingham First Church, vol. 1, 1720–
1806, transcription by Arthur D. Marble (HCR), 75, 77, 86; "Rev. Ebenezer Gay, D.D.," in "Pulpit Services, 1681–1891," collected and arranged by
Fearing Burr (HCR), sermon text in 1755. The four First Church deacons
in 1765 were Solomon Cushing, Thomas Andrews, Josiah Lincoln, and
Joshua Hersey.

11. Hingham First Parish Records 1:8, 21; Samuel Thaxter, et al.,
to "the Committee Appointed to Call Meetings in the first precinct in
Hingham," n.d. [c. 1729–30] (Aurelia Fearing Collection, Hingham Historical Society).

12. Hingham First Parish Records 1:76; Reconstructed seating chart
and copy of "Names of owners of square pews, 1756," in "Earliest Records," vol. 1 (Parish House of Hingham First Church). A brief but sensitive discussion of the eighteenth-century changes of criteria in seating
patterns and the impact of box pews may be found in Patricia J. Tracy's
*Jonathan Edwards, Pastor: Religion and Society in Eighteenth-Century North-
ampton* (New York, 1979), 126–28.

13. Hamilton C. MacDougall, *Early New England Psalmody: An Historical Appreciation, 1620–1820* (Brattleboro, Vt., 1940), 28.

14. Cohasset Church Meeting Records, 1748–1785 (First Parish Church of Cohasset), September 28 and November 24, 1749; Norwell Church Records, vol. 2, "The Church Book" (First Parish, Norwell, Mass.), 51; Lyman H. Butterfield, ed., *Diary and Autobiography of John Adams*, 4 vols. (Cambridge, Mass., 1961), 1:120; Hingham First Parish Records, 1:91; Franklin B. Dexter, ed., *Itineraries and Correspondence of Ezra Stiles* (New Haven, 1916), 260.

15. Richard D. Brown, "Modernization and the Modern Personality in America, 1600–1865: A Sketch of a Synthesis," *Journal of Interdisciplinary History* 2 (Winter 1972):212; Ebenezer Gay, *Jesus Christ the Wise Master-Builder of His Church* (Boston, 1753), 4, 25; Richard E. Sykes, "Massachusetts Unitarianism and Social Change: A Religious Social System in Transition, 1780–1870" (Ph.D. dissertation, University of Minnesota, 1966), 14; Ebenezer Gay, *A Beloved Disciple of Jesus Christ Characterized* (Boston, 1766), 10–11.

16. Daniel H. Calhoun, *Professional Lives in America: Structure and Aspiration, 1750–1850* (Cambridge, Mass., 1965), 92; *Boston Post-Boy*, December 24, 1770, 2; Jotham Gay to Martin Gay, Hingham, July 17, 1764 (Gay-Otis Papers); James A. Henretta, *The Evolution of American Society, 1700–1815: An Interdisciplinary Analysis* (Lexington, Mass., 1973), 100–102.

17. "Pulpit Services," sermon texts for 1752 and November, 1755; Ebenezer Gay, "Record of Births, Marriages, Deaths, and Admissions, 1718–1787" (HCR), March 7, 1756; Alan Heimert, *Religion and the American Mind: From the Great Awakening to the Revolution* (Cambridge, Mass., 1966), 77.

18. Ezra Stiles Itinerary, 1762–1769 (Beinecke Manuscript Library, Yale University), 360; Dexter, ed., *Itineraries of Ezra Stiles*, 236, 260; Hingham Town Clerk's Records, 3, October 16, 1754 and March 21, 1768.

19. Jotham Gay to Martin Gay, Hingham, May 19, 1748 (Gay-Otis Papers); Suffolk County Registry of Deeds, 95:198; *History of Hingham* 2: 265; Martin Gay to William Allan, Boston, August 13, 1764 (Gay-Otis Papers).

20. Jotham Gay to Martin Gay, Hingham, October 10, 1752 (Gay-Otis Papers); Ebenezer Gay to [Martin Gay], Hingham, November 22, 1764 (Gay-Otis Papers); Martin Gay to William Allan, Boston, November 27, 1764 (Gay-Otis Papers); *History of Hingham* 2:265; Ebenezer Gay to Martin and Ruth Atkins Gay, Hingham, May 1, 1773 (Gay-Otis Papers).

21. Sydney Howard Gay to Solomon Lincoln, New York, November 7, 1861 (Courtesy of John Richardson of Hingham); *History of Hingham*, vol. 1, pt. 2, 111; Jotham Gay to [Calvin Gay?], Grand Pre, Nova Scotia, August 29, 1753 (Gay-Otis Papers); Howard H. Peckham, *The Colonial Wars, 1689–1762* (Chicago, 1964), 111–12; Ebenezer Gay to Jotham Gay, Hingham, October 19, 1761 (Gay-Otis Papers).

22. *History of Hingham*, vol. 1, pt. 1, 255, 257, 264, 266; Peckham, *Co-*

*lonial Wars*, 141–43; Jotham Gay to Martin Gay, Fort Edward, Nova Scotia, May 14, 1759 (Gay-Otis Papers); Jotham Gay to Martin Gay, Fort Edward, Nova Scotia, July 23, 1759 (Gay-Otis Papers); Jotham Gay, "Business Papers," 1773–1786 (Gay-Otis Papers); Jotham Gay to Jonathan Binney—Collector of the Customs at Halifax, Cumberland, Nova Scotia, July 29, 1777 (Gay-Otis Papers).

23. Ebenezer Gay to Jotham Gay, Hingham, October 19, 1761; Martin Gay to Jotham Gay, Boston, February 7, 1774 (Gay-Otis Papers); Jerusha Gay to Jotham Gay, Hingham, January 21, 1775 (Gay-Otis Papers).

24. Calvin Gay to Martin Gay, Halifax, July 8, 1751 (Gay-Otis Papers); Calvin Gay to Martin Gay, Louisbourg, September 8, 1758 (Gay-Otis Papers); *History of Hingham* 2 : 265; Frederick Lewis Gay, *John Gay of Dedham, Massachusetts, and Some of His Descendants* (Boston, 1879), 6; Calvin Gay to Ebenezer Gay, Quebec, August 28, 1760 (Gay-Otis Papers).

25. Calvin Gay to Martin Gay, Louisbourg, November 9, 1759 (Gay-Otis Papers); Peckham, *Colonial Wars*, 193, 197; Calvin Gay to Martin Gay, Quebec, February 16, 1762 (Gay-Otis Papers); Martin Gay to Calvin Gay, Boston, August 14, 1762 (Gay-Otis Papers); Jotham Gay to Martin Gay, Quebec, June 15, 1765 (Gay-Otis Papers); Martin Gay to William Allan, Boston, May 16, 1765 (Gay-Otis Papers); Martin Gay to Jonas Clarke Minot, Boston, May 6, 1765 (Gay-Otis Papers); Estate Administration of Calvin Gay, Inventory, Suffolk County Registry of Probate, #13,626. It is interesting to note that "Mayhews Sermons in Octavo" appeared among the items listed in Calvin's estate inventory.

26. "Pulpit Services," sermon text for May 1765; 1 Samuel 3 : 13–14 and 1 Samuel 2 : 12.

27. Philip Greven, *The Protestant Temperament: Patterns of Child-Rearing, Religious Experience, and the Self in Early America* (New York, 1977), 170, 175; *History of Hingham* 2 : 265.

28. Calvin Gay to Ebenezer Gay, Quebec, August 28, 1760; Jerusha Gay to Jotham Gay, Hingham, April 7, 1773 (Gay-Otis Papers); F. L. Gay, *John Gay*, 6; Jerusha Gay to Jotham Gay, Hingham, January 21, 1775 (Gay-Otis Papers); Estate of Ebenezer Gay of Hingham, Will, Suffolk County Registry of Probate, #18,890.

29. Robert A. Gross, *The Minutemen and Their World* (New York, 1976), 100; *History of Hingham* 2 : 265; Jotham Gay to Martin Gay, Cumberland, N.S., June 1, 1772 (Gay-Otis Papers); Martin Gay to Jotham Gay, Boston, May 7, 1775 (Gay-Otis Papers).

30. Henretta, *Evolution of American Society*, 13–15; Diaries of Reverend William Smith of Weymouth, 1728–1763 (MHS), February 19, 1749, and scattered entries from July–November 1751; *History of Hingham* 2 : 265; "Pulpit Services," sermon text for December, 1751; Ebenezer Gay to [Martin Gay], Hingham, March 2, 1752 (Gay-Otis Papers).

31. Ebenezer Gay, *The True Spirit of a Gospel-Minister Represented and Urged* (Boston, 1746), 10, 24.

32. Clifford K. Shipton, ed., *Sibley's Harvard Graduates* (Boston, 1960), 11:14, 233, 305–6; "Pulpit Services," sermon text for 1755.

33. E. Victor Bigelow, *A Narrative History of the Town of Cohasset* (Cohasset, 1898), 280–81; Jotham Gay to Martin Gay, Fort Edward, Nova Scotia, July 23, 1759 (Gay-Otis Papers).

34. "Pulpit Services," sermon texts from March 1751 to 1769; Diaries of Reverend William Smith, August 20, 1761; Ebenezer Gay to Jotham Gay, Hingham, October 19, 1761; Jerusha Gay to Jotham Gay, Hingham, November 1, 1766 (Gay-Otis Papers). Gay preached very frequently from the Book of James. This particular epistle is distinguished among the apostolic works for its emphasis on ethics, practical Christianity, and the importance of "works." In the second chapter of James, the author insists that God will judge men according to their compliance with the Law, concluding, "Ye see then how that by works a man is justified, and not by faith only." Needless to say, James was never very popular with evangelicals in the Reformed Tradition.

35. Ebenezer Gay, *A Call from Macedonia* (Boston, 1768), 22.


CHAPTER XI
## A Rank Tory

1. Martin Gay to Jotham Gay, Boston, August 26, 1765 (Gay-Otis Papers, Columbia University Library); Jotham Gay to Martin Gay, Cumberland, N.S., February 1, 1774 (Gay-Otis Papers).

2. Ebenezer Gay, *A Call from Macedonia* (Boston, 1768), 32; Martin Gay to George Smith, Boston, September 9, 1765 (Gay-Otis Papers).

3. Ebenezer Gay, *The Devotions of God's People Adjusted to the Dispensations of His Providence* (Boston, 1771), 18; Edward M. Griffin, *Old Brick: Charles Chauncy of Boston, 1705–1787* (Minneapolis, 1980), 141.

4. Alan Heimert, *Religion and the American Mind: From the Great Awakening to the Revolution* (Cambridge, Mass., 1966), 413–16, 425–60.

5. Boston Weekly News-Letter, November 26, 1772; Ebenezer Gay, *Natural Religion, as Distinguish'd from Revealed* (Boston, 1759), 10.

6. Joan D. Tooke, *The Just War in Aquinas and Grotius* (London, 1965), 199; Lyman H. Butterfield, ed., *Diary and Autobiography of John Adams*, 4 vols. (Cambridge, Mass., 1961), 1:279. Gay's insistence on passive obedience ran directly counter to the argument advanced by his friend Jonathan Mayhew in the latter's *Discourse Concerning Unlimited Submission* (1750). Mayhew argued that those nations which did *not* resist tyranny and oppression "would receive to themselves damnation." See Charles W.

Akers, *Called unto Liberty: A Life of Jonathan Mayhew, 1720–1766* (Cambridge, Mass., 1964), 83–86.

7. *Diary of John Adams* 1:279; Diaries of Reverend William Smith of Weymouth (MHS), March 22, April 26, and July 19, 1778.

8. Clifford K. Shipton, ed., *Sibley's Harvard Graduates* (Boston, 1951), 8:434; *Diary of John Adams* 1:279; *History of the Town of Hingham*, 3 vols. (Hingham, 1893), vol. 1, pt. 2, 315–16, vol. 2, 21, 22, and vol. 3, 8, 232. Gay's neighbor Elisha Leavitt (later Hingham's most notorious Tory) was almost certainly a member of the group, though Adams does not directly name him. For a useful sketch of the socioeconomic characteristics of most American Loyalists, see Chapter 1: "The Roots of Loyalty" in William H. Nelson's *The American Tory* (New York, 1961).

9. *Diary of John Adams* 1:279.

10. John C. Miller, *Sam Adams: Pioneer in Propaganda* (Stanford, Cal., 1936), 134–65, 193–97; Hingham Town Clerk's Records, vol. 4, 1762–1813 (Hingham Town Hall), December 29, 1767 and September 21, 1768.

11. Gay, *A Call from Macedonia*, 32; Gay, *Devotions of God's People*, 21; *Massachusetts Gazette*, March 30, 1787; Frederick Lewis Gay, *John Gay, of Dedham Massachusetts, and Some of His Descendants* (Boston, 1879), 4; *Diary of John Adams* 1:344–45.

12. Miller, *Sam Adams*, 178–82; *History of Hingham*, vol. 1, pt. 1, 272 and vol. 3, 8, 9.

13. Gay, *Devotions of God's People*, 16, 17; Heimert, *Religion and the American Mind*, 426.

14. Gay, *Devotions of God's People*, 7, 20–21.

15. Ibid., 21.

16. Shipton, *Sibley's Harvard Graduates* (Boston, 1942), 6:63; Martin Gay to Jotham Gay, Boston, February 11, 1771 (Gay-Otis Papers); *Boston Weekly News-Letter*, January 14, 1773 and November 26, 1772; *History of Hingham*, vol. 1, pt. 2, 34 and vol. 2, 302.

17. *Boston Weekly News-Letter*, March 4, 1773 and November 26, 1772; Martin Gay to Winckworth Allen, Boston, July 29, 1785 (Gay-Otis Papers).

18. Heimert, *Religion and the American Mind*, 414–15; Shipton, *Sibley's Harvard Graduates* (Boston, 1960), 11:306–7; *History of Hingham*, vol. 1, pt. 1, 302 and vol. 2, 161.

19. Heimert, *Religion and the American Mind*, 436–38; Alice M. Baldwin, *The New England Clergy and the American Revolution* (Durham, N.C., 1928), 119, 43n., 181.

20. Shipton, *Sibley's Harvard Graduates* 11:15, 235; John Brown to John Thomas, Cohasset, May 1, 1775 (Thomas Papers, 1746–1776, MHS); E. Victor Bigelow, *A Narrative History of the Town of Cohasset* (Cohasset, 1898), 312; *History of Hingham*, vol. 1, pt. 1, 281.

21. Griffin, Old Brick, 149; Gay, *Devotions of God's People*, 18; Shipton,

*Sibley's Harvard Graduates* (Boston, 1968), 14:282–83; Heimert, *Religion and the American Mind*, 418–19; Simeon Howard to Betsy Mayhew, Boston, August 2, 1791 (General MSS Collection, Columbia University Library).

22. Jerusha Gay to Martin Gay, Hingham, March 5, 1777 (Gay-Otis Papers); Ebenezer Gay, *The True Spirit of a Gospel-Minister Represented and Urged* (Boston, 1746), 12.

23. Jotham Gay to Martin Gay, Cumberland, N.S., May 11, 1774 (Gay-Otis Papers); Jotham Gay to William Allan, Cumberland, N.S., March 9, 1776 (Gay-Otis Papers); *Proceedings of the Massachusetts Historical Society, 1869–1870* (Boston, 1871), 393, 395; Edward D. Harris, *A Genealogical Record of Daniel Pond, and His Descendants* (Boston, 1873), 909; Jerusha Gay to Jotham Gay, Hingham, January 21, 1775 (Gay-Otis Papers); Jerusha Gay to Jotham Gay, Hingham, October 8, 1777 (Gay-Otis Papers).

24. "Rev. Ebenezer Gay, D.D.," in "Pulpit Services, 1681–1891," collected and arranged by Fearing Burr (HCR), sermon texts for June 12 and June 15, 1774; [Anon.], Day Book, "The Texts of Ebenezer Gay, A.M.," 1772–1787 (Courtesy of John P. Richardson), sermon text for July 26, 1777.

25. Assessors Record of the First Parish in Hingham, 1718–1816 (HCR), 33; *History of Hingham*, vol. 1, pt. 1, 302 and pt. 2, 26, 334–36. From 1823 to 1826, Solomon Lincoln studied in the law office of the "Hon. Ebenezer Gay of Hingham," grandson of Parson Gay.

26. *History of Hingham*, vol. 1, pt. 1, 302 and pt. 2, 26–27.

27. Ebenezer Gay, *The Old Man's Calendar* (Boston, 1781), 8; Jerusha Gay to Martin Gay, Hingham, March 5, 1777.

28. "Texts of Ebenezer Gay," 1777–1780, passim; Jotham Gay to Martin Gay, Cumberland, N.S., October 8, 1772 (Gay-Otis Papers).

29. Martin Gay to Jotham Gay, Boston, July 23, 1772 (Gay-Otis Papers); John Boyle, "Journal of Occurrences in Boston &c," 1759–1778 (New England Historical and Genealogical Society), March 12, 1772, May 9, 1775, April 11, and May 1, 1776; Ebenezer Gay to Frederick L. Gay, Boston, February 3, 1879 (Gay Letters, New England Historical and Genealogical Society), 9.

30. Ruth Atkins Gay to Martin Gay, Boston, May 23, 1786 (Gay-Otis Papers); Journal of Joseph Andrews, 1752–1787 (MHS), passim; Joshua Winslow to Jotham Gay, Boston, June 23, 1773 (Courtesy of William O. Gay); Martin Gay to Jotham Gay, Boston, July 27, 1773 (Gay-Otis Papers); Jerusha Gay to Jotham Gay, Hingham, January 21, 1775 (Gay-Otis Papers); Gay, *Old Man's Calendar*, 6. In 1780 Joseph Thaxter was finally settled at Edgartown on Martha's Vineyard, the island of the Mayhews. See *History of Hingham*, vol. 1, pt. 2, 111, 351–52.

31. Mary Gay to Jotham Gay, Boston, May 15, 1775 (Gay-Otis Papers); Jerusha Gay to Jotham Gay, Hingham, October 8, 1777 (Gay-Otis Papers).

32. Jerusha Gay to Jotham Gay, Hingham, October 6, 1777 (Gay-Otis Papers); John B. Brebner, *The Neutral Yankees of Nova Scotia: A Marginal Colony during the Revolutionary Years* (New York, 1937), 323–24; Jotham Gay to Martin Gay, Cumberland, N.S., January 21, 1777 (Gay-Otis Papers). Jotham's reference to "the family" concerned Mary and Samuel Gay, two of Martin's children, who were staying with him at that time.

33. Martin Gay to John Joy, Boston, December 9, 1784 (Courtesy of William O. Gay); Martin Gay to _____, Cumberland, N.S., May 14, 1777 (Gay-Otis Papers). For the history of the disputed Union Street property, see Edward Wheelwright, "Three Letters Written by an American Loyalist and His Wife, 1775–1788," *Publications of the Colonial Society of Massachusetts* (*Transactions*, 1895–1897), 3 : 379–400.

34. Martin Gay to Ruth Atkins Gay, Halifax, July 8, 1780 (Gay-Otis Papers); Martin Gay to William Allan, Boston, November 17, 1784 (Gay-Otis Papers); Martin Gay to Benjamin DeWolf, Boston, September 12, 1784 (Gay-Otis Papers); Martin Gay to John Joy, Boston, December 9, 1789 (Gay-Otis Papers).

35. "Diary of Caleb Gannett, Esq. of Cambridge," 1777–1782 (Houghton Library, Harvard University), August 8, 1777; Ruth Atkins Gay to Martin Gay, Boston, July, 1782 (Gay-Otis Papers).

36. *History of Hingham*, vol. 1, pt. 2, 111; Bezaleel Howard, *A Sermon Delivered at the Ordination of the Rev. Antipas Steward* (Springfield, Mass., 1794), 8; S. W. Edson, et al., *Sketches of The Churches and Pastors in Hampden County, Mass.* (Westfield, Mass., 1854), 105–6; Conrad Wright, *The Beginnings of Unitarianism in America* (Boston, 1955), 255, 286. Howard's Toryism is reflected in a note he wrote to his father at the outbreak of Shays' Rebellion: "The old spirit of 1775 seems to have reared his ghastly head again—but I hope his reign will be short." See Bezaleel Howard to Nathan Howard, Springfield, September 16, 1786 (MS at Springfield Public Library). In later years, Howard formally aligned himself with the Unitarians.

37. Ebenezer Gay, *A Beloved Disciple of Jesus Christ Characterized* (Boston, 1766), 17; Assessors Record, 34–37.


CHAPTER XII
## The Old Man's Calendar

1. Ebenezer Gay, *The Old Man's Calendar* (Boston, 1781), 2, 3.
2. Ibid., 8, 9, 11–12, 13.
3. Ibid., 25, 26, 27.
4. Gay, *Old Man's Calendar*, 20; Martin Gay to John Joy, Boston, August 6, 1785 (Gay-Otis Papers, Columbia University Library); John Boyle to Martin Gay, Boston, September 29, 1783 (Courtesy of William O. Gay); Weymouth First Church Records (Tufts Library, Weymouth), Au-

gust 22, 1784; Ebenezer Gay to "Dear Children," Dedham, June 19, 1784 (Gay-Otis Papers). A MS version of *The Old Man's Calendar* is held by the Massachusetts Historical Society.

5. Ebenezer Gay, *The Levite Not to Be Forsaken* (Boston, 1756), 14.

6. Frank Smith, *A History of Dedham, Massachusetts* (Dedham, 1936), 29.

7. Isaac Backus, *A Door Opened for Christian Liberty* (Boston, 1783), Pamphlet 10 in *Isaac Backus on Church, State, and Calvinism: Pamphlets, 1754–1789*, ed. William G. McLoughlin (Cambridge, Mass., 1968), 434–35; *History of the Town of Hingham*, 3 vols. (Hingham, 1893), vol. 1, pt. 2, 57.

8. Gay, *Old Man's Calendar*, 25, 26; Ebenezer Gay, *St. John's Vision of the Woman Cloathed with the Sun* (Boston, 1766), 30; Frederick L. Weis, "Ebenezer Gay," *The Proceedings of the Unitarian Historical Society*, vol. 4, pt. 2 (1936):11.

9. Gay, *Old Man's Calendar*, 19.

10. Weis, "Ebenezer Gay," 9; "Jeremy Belknap Papers," *Collections of the Massachusetts Historical Society*, 6th ser., (Boston, 1891), 4:244. The last meeting of Chauncy and Gay may have occurred in 1786 when Chauncy presented the old man with a copy of *The Benevolence of the Deity* (1784), his classic summation of rational Christianity in the eighteenth century.

11. John Boyle to Martin Gay, Boston, September 29, 1783 (Courtesy of William O. Gay); Ruth Atkins Gay to Martin Gay, Boston, October 16, 1783 (Gay-Otis Papers); *The Diary of Ebenezer Parkman, 1703–1782*, ed. Francis G. Walett (Worcester, Mass., 1974), 245; Samuel Deane, *History of Scituate* (Boston, 1831), 207.

12. *History of Hingham*, vol. 1, pt. 2, 115–16, 119, 123; Clifford K. Shipton, ed., *Sibley's Harvard Graduates* (Boston, 1951), 8:435–36; Harvard Corporation Records, 1778–1795 (Harvard University Archives), 3:237–39. Gay was an active supporter of the newly established American Academy of Arts and Sciences. In 1781, he was cheerfully providing useful demographic data culled from his church records for a study being conducted by Professor Edward Wigglesworth on longevity in New England. Wigglesworth considered Gay's Record of Births, Marriages, Deaths, and Admissions "very serviceable . . . possibly more so than any others that can be obtained." See Ebenezer Gay to Benjamin Lincoln, Hingham, December 25, 1781 (Houghton Library, Harvard University); American Academy of Arts and Sciences, *Memoirs* (Boston, 1783), 1:565–68.

13. Conrad Wright, *The Beginnings of Unitarianism in America* (Boston, 1955), 201–5; Ebenezer Parkman Diary, June 1764–June 1769 (MSS at American Antiquarian Society), December 16, 1766 and May 25, 1768.

14. Ebenezer Gay, *The Duty of People to Pray for and Praise Their Rulers* (Boston, 1730), 7; Ebenezer Gay, *Ministers' Insufficiency for Their Important*

*and Difficult Work* (Boston, 1742), 7; Roland N. Stromberg, *Religious Liberalism in Eighteenth-Century England* (London, 1954), 38.

15. Stromberg, *Religious Liberalism*, 48; Wright, *Beginnings of Unitarianism*, 213–14; Thomas Belsham, ed., *Memoirs of the Late Reverend Theophilus Lindsay*, (2d ed. London, 1820), 179; William Hazlitt to James Freeman, Norwich, England, January 18, 1787 (Pennsylvania Historical Society).

16. Ralph M. Wardle, *Hazlitt* (Lincoln, Neb., 1971), 16–19; *The Journal of Margaret Hazlitt: Recollections of England, Ireland, and America*, ed. Ernest J. Moyne (Lawrence, Kan., 1967), 17–19, 70–71, 120–21; *History of Hingham*, vol. 1, pt. 2, 24–25. Peggy Hazlitt, the minister's daughter, was enchanted by Gay, "a very pleasant old man above 90 years of age." In her journal she related the following anecdote:

> He was fond of a good story, and used to tell with great glee how he cured a man of the propensity to steal. It seems this man was in the habit of making free with his pastor's hay, which, Mr. Gay suspecting, he one evening took his pipe in his mouth and, standing behind the stable door, softly shook out the ashes of his pipe on the hay the man was carrying away on his back. And as soon as he got out, the fresh air kindled it into a flame, at which the poor fellow was so much terrified that he came the next morning to confess his trespass, saying that fire came down from heaven to consume his stolen hay, and promised never to steal again. . . .

See *Journal of Margaret Hazlitt*, 69–70.

17. Wardle, *Hazlitt*, 17–18; Journal of Joseph Andrews, 1752–1787 (MHS), July 11, 1784—June 4, 1786, passim; *Journal of Margaret Hazlitt*, 81–82.

18. Journal of Joseph Andrews, September 3–November 5, 1786; Gay, *Old Man's Calendar*, 20–21; Sydney Howard Gay to Solomon Lincoln, New York, November 7, 1861 (Courtesy of John P. Richardson); *History of Hingham* 2:24; Daniel Shute, *A Sermon Delivered . . . at the Interment of the Rev. Ebenezer Gay, D.D.* (Salem, 1787).

19. Ebenezer Gay, "Record of Births, Marriages, Deaths, and Admissions, 1718–1787" (HCR), March 12, 1787; Martin Gay to John Joy, Boston, May 25, 1787 (Gay-Otis Papers); Shipton, *Sibley's Harvard Graduates* (Boston, 1942), 6:64; *The Diary of William Bentley, D.D.*, 4 vols. (Salem, 1905–1914), 1:57. Chauncy had died the month before on February 10.

20. *History of Hingham* 2:265; "Funeral Expenses," Hingham First Parish Records, 1720–1806 (HCR), 1:120; "Texts of Ebenezer Gay," March 18, March 23, March 25, April 1, April 8, and April 15, 1787; Shute, *A Sermon*, 20, 27–28.

# Selected Bibliography

## General Reference

The reconstruction of the ecclesiastical world of Ebenezer Gay would have been a far more formidable task without the Herculean labor of Clifford K. Shipton. His continuance of the work begun by John Langdon Sibley—*Biographical Sketches of Those Who Attended Harvard College*, 17 vols. (Boston, The Massachusetts Historical Society, 1873–1975)—generally provided the starting point for my research into the lives of Gay's colleagues and students. Two other works which, when used in conjunction, facilitated the identification of ministers were: Harold Field Worthley, "An Inventory of the Records of the Particular (Congregational) Churches of Massachusetts Gathered 1620–1805," *Harvard Theological Studies* 25 (Cambridge, Mass., 1970) and Frederick L. Weis, *The Colonial Clergy and the Colonial Churches of New England* (Lancaster, Mass., 1936).

## Manuscripts

Gay's manuscript legacy is slender. I have been able to locate only six MS sermons. The most legible of these is a 1721 catechism, held by the First Church of Suffield, Connecticut. Similarly, much of Gay's correspondence has been lost or destroyed. Seven of his letters survive in the Gay-Otis Family Papers, held by Columbia University in the Special Manuscript Collections of the Butler Library. The surviving correspondence of Gay's children, however, is voluminous, and much of it refers to the activities of their father. In addition to the Butler Library collection, eight of Gay's letters are known to be extant. Three of the most important—one written in 1714, one in 1715, and one in 1742—may be found in the Gratz Collection of the Pennsylvania Historical Society.

285

Gay has also discouraged biographers by his failure to leave a diary, but this lacuna can be partially filled by the diaries of his friends and contemporaries. The most useful of these is unquestionably the diary kept by Gay's clerical neighbor, the Reverend William Smith of Weymouth. His entries were recorded from 1728 to 1763 in a series of interleaved almanacs held by the Massachusetts Historical Society.

The Hingham First Church and Parish Records are deposited with the Massachusetts Historical Society. Gay's original, and meticulously kept, record of births, marriages, deaths, and admissions to church membership (1718–1787) may be found in Box 8 of the collection. Unfortunately, most of the eighteenth-century church and parish records are available only as photostats of copies made by Mr. Arthur D. Marble of Hingham, probably in 1928. Marble organized his copies according to categories such as "Appropriations," "Moderators," "Singers," "Pews," and so on. The problem here, transcriptional accuracy aside, is the possibility of omission, intentional or otherwise. There are, for instance, no records of any disciplinary actions taken by the church.

The South Hingham Parish Records (1742–1865) and the South Hingham Church Records (1746–1844) are held by that church, along with a letter by Gay and several by the Reverend Daniel Shute. The Cohasset Church Records (1747–1796) are held by the First Parish Church of Cohasset. The Cohasset records kept by the Reverends Nehemiah Hobart and John Fowle (1721–1747) may be found in Box 10 of the Hingham First records at the Massachusetts Historical Society.

For students of South Shore ecclesiastical history, there is a small but excellent collection of original manuscripts, relating to ecclesiastical councils and ordinations, which is housed in the First Church of Weymouth. The Reverend William Smith seems to have served as a sort of secretary for the Hingham Association, and most of the documents date from the time of his ministry.

The Hingham Town Records for the eighteenth century are quite extensive and are kept in excellent condition at the Hingham Town Hall. I have used "The Select Men's Second Book of Records" (1717–1785), and the Town Clerk's Records, vol. 3 (1720–1762) and vol. 4 (1762–1813). Real Property Valuations, kept in the lower safe of the Town Hall, are extant for the years 1754, 1757, 1765, 1767, 1772, 1779, 1788, and 1790.

*Other Manuscripts:*

Andrews, Joseph. Journal, 1752–1787. Massachusetts Historical Society.
Barnes, David. "Mr. Barnes's Sermon on Revealed Religion," 1780. Harvard University Archives.
"Diary of Caleb Gannet, Esq. of Cambridge," 1777–1782. Houghton Library, Harvard University.

"Diary of Rev. Ebenezer Gay of Suffield, 1738–1792." Kent Memorial Library, Suffield.

The Hobart Diary. Massachusetts Historical Society.

"John Leverett's Record," 1707–1723. MS at Harvard University Archives.

Loring, Julian. Notebooks. Hingham Historical Society; microfilm copy at the Hingham Town Library.

Parkman, Ebenezer. Diary. Roughly the first chronological half (1719–1755) of Parkman's enormous manuscript diary has been published as *The Diary of Ebenezer Parkman, 1703–1782*, ed. Francis G. Walett (American Antiquarian Society, Worcester, Mass., 1974). The manuscripts for the years 1755 to 1782 are available at the Massachusetts Historical Society either in the original or in reproduced form.

"Plymouth Association Book." Congregational Library, Boston.

Williams, Stephen. Diary. Typescript from original MS at the Storrs Library, Longmeadow, Mass.

## Primary Sources: Printed

Most of the eighteenth-century works mentioned here, and the great number that have not been included in the bibliography, are available on microcard, catalogued in Clifford K. Shipton and James E. Mooney, eds., *National Index of American Imprints through 1800: The Short-Title Evans* (American Antiquarian Society, Worcester, Mass., 1969).

Briant, Lemuel. *The Absurdity and Blasphemy of Depretiating Moral Virtue*. Boston, 1749.

Brown, John. *A Discourse Delivered at the West Church in Boston*. Boston, 1766.

Bulkley, John. *The Usefulness of Reveal'd Religion, to Preserve and Improve that which is Natural*. New London, Conn., 1730.

Butterfield, Lyman H., ed. *Diary and Autobiography of John Adams*. 4 vols. Cambridge, Mass., 1961.

Chauncey, Isaac. *The Faithful Evangelist, or the True Shepherd*. Boston, 1725.

Chauncy, Charles. *Seasonable Thoughts on the State of Religion in New-England*. Boston, 1743.

Dexter, Franklin B., ed. *Itineraries and Correspondence of Ezra Stiles*. New Haven, 1916.

Faust, Clarence H. and Johnson, Thomas H., eds. *Jonathan Edwards*. New York, 1935.

Hill, Don Gleason, ed. *The Early Records of the Town of Dedham, Mass., 1635–1706*. 5 vols. Dedham, 1886–1889.

Hitchcock, Gad. *Natural Religion Aided by Revelation and Perfected in Christianity*. Boston, 1779.

"Diary of Cotton Mather, 1709–1724." *Collections of the Massachusetts Historical Society*. 7th ser., no. 8. Boston, 1912.

[Moody, Samuel]. *A Faithful Narrative of God's Gracious Dealings with a Person Lately Recovered from the Dangerous Errors of Arminius*. Boston, 1737.

Osborn, Samuel. *The Case and Complaint of Mr. Samuel Osborn, Late of Eastham*. Boston, 1743.

Shute, Daniel. *A Sermon Delivered . . . at the Interment of the Rev. Ebenezer Gay, D.D.* Salem, 1787.

Tracy, Joseph. *The Great Awakening: A History of the Revival of Religion in the Time of Edwards and Whitefield*. Boston, 1845.

Walker, Williston. *The Creeds and Platforms of Congregationalism*. New York, 1893.

White, John. *New England's Lamentations*. Boston, 1734.

Wise, John. *A Vindication of the Government of New England Churches*. Boston, 1717.

*The Printed Sermons of Ebenezer Gay*

Ministers are Men of Like Passions with Others. A Sermon Preached at Barnstable, May 12, 1725. The Day on Which a Church was Gathered . . . and Joseph Green was Ordained Pastor of It. Boston: Printed by B. Green. 1725.

A Discourse on the Transcendent Glory of the Gospel . . . at Hingham. To Which is Added, A Pillar of Salt, to Season a Corrupt Age. A Sermon to Bring Lot's Wife to Remembrance . . . Boston: Printed for D. Henchman. 1728.

Zechariah's Vision of Christ's Martial Glory. . . . In a Sermon Preached at the Desire of the Honourable Artillery-Company in Boston, June 3, 1728. . . . Boston: Printed for J. Eliot, J. Phillips, and B. Love. 1728.

The Duty of People to Pray for and Praise Their Rulers. A Sermon at the Lecture in Hingham, August 12, 1730, on Occasion of the Arrival of His Excellency Jonathan Belcher, Esq.; To His Government . . . Published at the Desire of His Hearers. Boston: Printed by Thomas Fleet, in Pudding-Lane, near the Town-House. 1730.

Well-Accomplish'd Soldiers, a Glory to Their King, and a Defence to Their Country. A Sermon Preached at Hingham, on a Training-Day There, May 16, 1738. In the Audience of Four Military Companies, and Now Published, at the Desire of Their Officers. . . . Boston: Printed by T. Fleet, for Daniel Henchman, over-against the Brick Meeting House in Cornhill. 1738.

Ministers' Insufficiency for Their Important and Difficult Work, Argued from the Opposite Eternal Events of It. A Sermon Preach'd at the Ordination of the Rev. Ebenezer Gay, Junior, in Suffield, Jan. 13, 1741. 2. And Published at the Desire of the People There. . . . Boston: Printed by D. Fowle for S. Eliot in Cornhill. 1742.

The Untimely Death of a Man of God Lamented. In a Sermon Preach'd at the Funeral of the Reverend Mr. John Hancock, Pastor of the First

Church of Christ in Braintree; Who Died May 7th, 1744. Aetatis Suae 42. . . . Boston: Printed by S. Kneeland and T. Green in Queen-Street. 1744.

The Character and Work of a Good Ruler, and the Duty of an Obliged People. A Sermon Preached before His Excellency William Shirley, Esq.; The Honorable His Majesty's Council, and House of Representatives of the Province of Massachusetts-Bay in New England, May 29th, 1745. Being the Anniversary for the Election of His Majesty's Council for the Province. . . . Boston: Printed for Daniel Gookin in Marlborough-Street over against the Old South-Meeting-House. 1745.

The True Spirit of a Gospel-Minister Represented and Urged. A Sermon Preach'd before the Ministers of the Province of Massachusetts-Bay in New England, at their Annual Convention in Boston; May 29, 1746. . . . Boston: Printed by Daniel Gookin, in Marlborough-Street, over against the Old South-Meeting-House. 1746.

The Alienation of Affection from Ministers Consider'd and Improv'd. Preached at the Ordination of the Reverend Mr. Jonathan Mayhew to . . . the West Church in Boston, June 17, 1747. Boston: 1747.

The Mystery of the Seven Stars in Christ's Right Hand; Open'd and Apply'd in a Sermon Preached at the Ordination of the Reverend Mr. Jonathan Dorby, to the Pastoral Care of the Second Church in Scituate: November 13, 1751. . . . Boston: Printed and Sold by J. Draper, in Cornhill. 1752.

Jesus Christ the Wise Master-Builder of His Church. A Sermon Preached at the Installment of the Reverend Ezra Carpenter to the Pastoral Care of the People in Keene and Swanzey in the Province of New-Hampshire, October 4th, 1753. . . . Boston: Printed and Sold by S. Kneeland in Queen Street. 1753.

The Levite Not to Be Forsaken. A Sermon Preach'd at the Installment of the Rev. Mr. Grindall Rawson, in the Pastoral Charge of the First Church of Christ in Yarmouth; December 10th, 1755. . . . Boston: Printed in the Year 1756.

Natural Religion, as Distinguish'd from Revealed: A Sermon Preached at the Annual Dudleian-Lecture, at Harvard College in Cambridge, May 7th, 1759. . . . Boston: Printed and Sold by John Draper. 1759.

A Beloved Disciple of Jesus Christ Characterized. In a Sermon Preached at the West-Church in Boston, July 27, A.M. 1766. The Third Lord's Day from the Decease of the Reverend Pastor Jonathan Mayhew, D.D. . . . Boston: Printed by R. and S. Draper, T. and J. Fleet, and Edes and Gill. 1766.

St. John's Vision of the Woman Cloathed with the Sun &c. in Rev. XII. 1–5. Explained and Improved in a Discourse Had at the West Church of Christ in Boston, July 27th, P.M. 1766. The Third Lord's Day after the Decease of the Reverend Pastor Jonathan Mayhew,

D.D. . . . Boston: Printed by R. and S. Draper, in Newbury Street; and T. and J. Fleet in Cornhill. 1766.

A Call from Macedonia. A Sermon Preached at Hingham, in New England, October 12th, 1768, at the Ordination of the Reverend Mr. Caleb Gannett to the Work of the Ministry, and Pastoral Care of a Society of Protestant Christians in the town of Cumberland, and Province of Nova-Scotia. . . . Boston: Printed by Richard Draper and Thomas and John Fleet. 1768.

The Devotions of God's People Adjusted to the Dispensations of His Providence. A Sermon Preached in the First Parish of Hingham, December 6, 1770. The Day Observed Throughout the Province as a Day of Public Thanksgiving and Prayer. . . . Boston: Printed by Richard Draper. 1771.

The Old Man's Calendar. A Discourse . . . Delivered in the First Parish of Hingham, on the Lord's Day, August 26, 1781, the Birthday of the Author, Ebenezer Gay. Boston: Printed by John Boyle. 1781.


## Secondary Sources: Books


Akers, Charles W. *Called unto Liberty: A Life of Jonathan Mayhew, 1720–1766.* Cambridge, Mass., 1964.

Bradford, Alden. *Memoir of the Life and Writings of Rev. Jonathan Mayhew, D.D.* Boston, 1838.

Bushman, Richard L. *From Puritan to Yankee: Character and the Social Order in Connecticut, 1690–1765.* Cambridge, Mass., 1967.

Cooke, George Willis. *Unitarianism in America: A History of Its Origin and Development.* Boston, 1910.

Cragg, Gerald R. *The Church and the Age of Reason: 1648–1789.* Grand Rapids, Mich., 1960.

Deane, Samuel. *History of Scituate.* Boston, 1831.

Eliot, Samuel A., ed. *Heralds of a Liberal Faith.* Boston, 1910.

Ellis, Joseph J. *The New England Mind in Transition: Samuel Johnson of Connecticut, 1696–1772.* New Haven, 1973.

Gaustad, Edwin S. *The Great Awakening in New England.* New York, 1957.

Gay, Frederick Lewis. *John Gay, of Dedham Massachusetts, and Some of His Descendants.* Boston, 1879.

Griffin, Edward M. *Old Brick: Charles Chauncy of Boston, 1705–1787.* Minneapolis, 1980.

Heimert, Alan. *Religion and the American Mind: From the Great Awakening to the Revolution.* Cambridge, Mass., 1966.

Henretta, James A. *The Evolution of American Society, 1700–1815: An Interdisciplinary Analysis.* Lexington, Mass., 1973.

*History of the Town of Hingham.* 3 vols. Hingham, 1893.

Jones, James W. *The Shattered Synthesis: New England Puritanism before the Great Awakening*. New Haven, 1973.

Lockridge, Kenneth A. *A New England Town: The First Hundred Years*. New York, 1970.

May, Henry F. *The Enlightenment in America*. New York, 1976.

Miller, Perry. *The New England Mind: From Colony to Province*. Cambridge, Mass., 1953.

Morison, Samuel Eliot. *Three Centuries of Harvard: 1636–1936*. Cambridge, Mass., 1936.

Newlin, Claude M. *Philosophy and Religion in Colonial America*. New York, 1962.

Pawson, G. P. H. *The Cambridge Platonists and Their Place in Religious Thought*. London, 1930.

Pope, Robert G. *The Half-Way Covenant: Church Membership in Puritan New England*. Princeton, N.J., 1969.

Randall, John Herman. *The Making of the Modern Mind*. Boston, 1926.

Smith, Frank. *A History of Dedham, Massachusetts*. Dedham, 1936.

Stromberg, Roland N. *Religious Liberalism in Eighteenth-Century England*. London, 1954.

Tooke, Joan D. *The Just War in Aquinas and Grotius*. London, 1965.

Wright, Conrad. *The Beginnings of Unitarianism in America*. Boston, 1955.

Youngs, J. William T., Jr. *God's Messengers: Religious Leadership in Colonial New England, 1700–1750*. Baltimore, 1976.

## Secondary Sources: Articles

Brown, Richard D. "Modernization and the Modern Personality in America, 1600–1865: A Sketch of a Synthesis." *Journal of Interdisciplinary History* 2 (Winter 1972).

Bumsted, John M. "Religion, Finance, and Democracy in Massachusetts: The Town of Norton as a Case Study." *Journal of American History* 57 (1971).

Cook, Edward M., Jr. "Local Leadership and the Typology of New England Towns, 1700–1785." *Political Science Quarterly* 86 (December 1971):586–608.

Cook, Edward M., Jr. "Social Behavior and Changing Values in Dedham, Massachusetts, 1700–1775." *William and Mary Quarterly*, 3d ser., 27 (1970):546–80.

Coolidge, John. "Hingham Builds a Meetinghouse." *The New England Quarterly* 34 (December 1961):435–61.

Cowing, Cedric B. "Sex and Preaching in the Great Awakening." *American Quarterly* (Fall 1968):624–44.

Howe, Daniel Walker. "The Decline of Calvinism: An Approach to Its

Study." *Comparative Studies in Society and History* 14 (June 1972): 306–27.

Rand, Benjamin. "Philosophical Instruction in Harvard University from 1636 to 1900." *Harvard Graduates Magazine* 37 (1928–29): 29–37.

Shipton, Clifford K. "Ebenezer Gay." *Sibley's Harvard Graduates*, vol. 6 (Boston, 1942): 59–66.

Waters, John J. "Hingham, Massachusetts, 1631–1661: An East Anglian Oligarchy in the New World." *Journal of Social History* 1 (1968): 351–70.

Weis, Frederick L. "Ebenezer Gay." *The Proceedings of the Unitarian Historical Society*, vol. 4, pt. 2, (1936): 1–23.

Youngs, J. William T., Jr. "Congregational Clericalism: New England Ordinations before the Great Awakening." *William and Mary Quarterly*, 3d ser. 31 (1974): 481–90.

## Secondary Sources: Ph.D. Dissertations

Bumsted, John M. "The Pilgrims' Progress: The Ecclesiastical History of the Old Colony, 1620–1775." Ph.D. dissertation, Brown University, 1965.

Foster, Mary Catherine. "Hampshire County, Massachusetts, 1729–1754: A Covenant Society in Transition." Ph.D. dissertation, University of Michigan, 1967.

Smith, Daniel Scott. "Population, Family, and Society in Hingham Massachusetts, 1635–1880." Ph.D. dissertation, University of California at Berkeley, 1973.

# APPENDIX I

# Admissions to Full Communion in Hingham from 1718–1787

APPENDIX IA. First Church Members Admitted to Full Communion—1718–1787

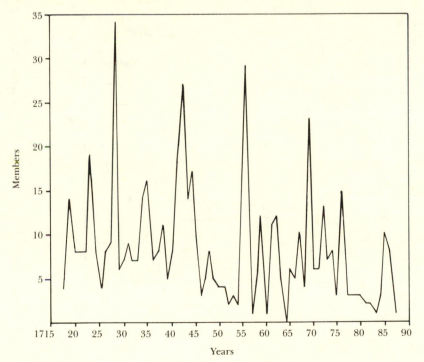

APPENDIX 1B. Members Admitted to Full Communion in the Cohasset and South Hingham Churches—1722–1769

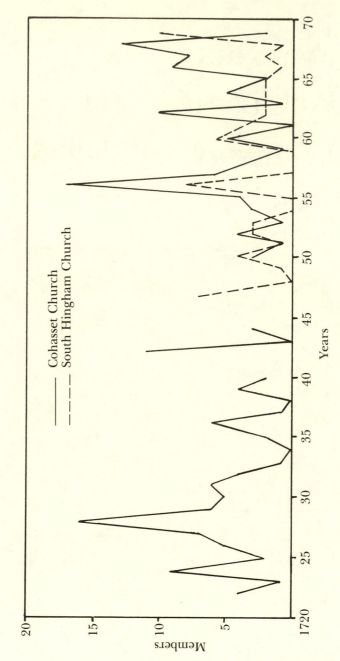

NOTE: The Cohasset Church was embodied in 1721 with 19 members. Cohasset Church records are unavailable for 1745–49. There was no minister in 1741. The South Hingham Church was embodied in 1746 with 65 members.

# APPENDIX II
# South Shore Maps

APPENDIX 2A. Hingham 1750

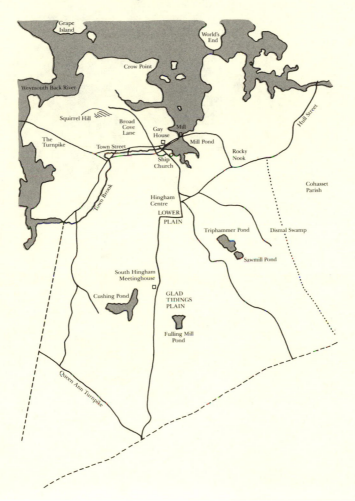

Grape Island

World's End

Crow Point

Weymouth Back River

Squirrel Hill

Broad Cove Lane

Gay House

Mill

Mill Pond

The Turnpike

Town Street

Ship Church

Rocky Nook

Hull Street

Cohasset Parish

Town Brook

Hingham Centre

LOWER PLAIN

Triphammer Pond

Dismal Swamp

Sawmill Pond

South Hingham Meetinghouse

Cushing Pond

GLAD TIDINGS PLAIN

Fulling Mill Pond

Queen Ann Turnpike

NOTE: The parish lines are only very approximate reflections of the actual precinct bounds.

Plymouth's Third Church was formed by Old Light secessionists from the First Church, and so it was not fundamentally a territorial parish.

The stippled areas represent the parishes of the Arminian clergy in the Hingham Association.

# APPENDIX III

# South Shore Clergymen

*A List, by Town and Parish, of the South Shore Clergymen Referred to in This Work, and Their Tenure in Office*

Abington. Samuel Brown (1714–1749).
Braintree:
    North Parish. John Hancock, Jr. (1726–1744).
                Lemuel Briant (1745–1753).
                Anthony Wibird (1755–1800).
    South Parish. Samuel Niles (1711–1762).
Bridgewater:
    East Parish. John Angier (1724–1787).
    North Parish. John Porter (1740–1802).
    West Bridgewater. Daniel Perkins (1721–1782).
Dorchester. John Danforth (ca. 1681–1729).
          Jonathan Bowman (ca. 1729–1773).
Duxbury. Samuel Veazie (1739–1750).
          Charles Turner (1755–1775).
Hingham:
    First Parish. Ebenezer Gay (1718–1787).
    Second Parish (Cohasset). Nehemiah Hobart (1721–1740).
                    John Fowle (1741–1746).
                    John Brown (1747–1791).
    South Parish. Daniel Shute (1746–1802).
Hanover. Benjamin Bass (ca. 1728–1756).
Hull. Zechariah Whitman (1670–1726).
    Ezra Carpenter (1725–1746).
    Samuel Veazie (1753–1767).
Kingston. Thaddeus Maccarty (1742–1745).
          William Rand (1746–1779).
Marshfield:
    First Parish. Joseph Green, Jr. (1753–1758).
              Thomas Brown (1759–1763).

Middleborough:
    First Parish. Peter Thacher (1709–1744).
                 Thomas Weld (1745–1749).
                 Sylvanus Conant (1748–1777).
    North Parish (Titicut). Isaac Backus (1748–1756).
Milton. John Taylor (1728–1750).
Pembroke:
    First Parish. Daniel Lewis (1712–1753).
                 Thomas Smith (1754–1788).
    West Parish (Tunk). Gad Hitchcock (1748–1803).
Plymouth:
    First Parish. Nathaniel Leonard (1724–1760).
Scituate:
    First Parish. Nathaniel Pitcher (1707–1723).
                 Shearjashub Bourne (1724–1761).
    South Parish. Nathaniel Eels (1704–1750).
                 Jonathan Dorby (1751–1754).
                 David Barnes (1754–1811).
Stoughton:
    First Parish. Samuel Dunbar (1727–1783).
Weymouth:
    First Parish. William Smith (1734–1783).
    South Parish. James Bayley (1723–1766).

# APPENDIX IV

# A Partial Genealogy of the Gay Family

1. John Gay emigrated to America about 1630. He was one of the original proprietors of Dedham and settled there about 1636. He married the widow Joanna Borden. He died March 4, 1688; she died August 14, 1691. His children were:

    i. Samuel, b. March 10, 1639; d. April 15, 1718.

    ii. Hezekiah, b. July 3, 1640; d. November 28, 1669.

2.  iii. Nathaniel, b. January 11, 1643; d. February 20, 1712.

    iv. Joanna, b. March 23, 1645; married, first, Nathaniel Whiting, Jr.; married, second, John Ware, of Wrentham, January 1680.

    v. Eleazer, b. June 25, 1647; d. April 13, 1726.

    vi. Abiel, b. April 23, 1649; married Daniel Hawes, February 23, 1677.

    vii. Judith, b. April 23, 1649 (twin); married John Fuller, February 8, 1672.

    viii. John, b. May 6, 1651; d. November 19, 1731.

    ix. Jonathan, b. August 1, 1654; date of death uncertain.

    x. Hannah, b. October 16, 1656; d. February 26, 1660.

2. Nathaniel, b. January 11, 1643. He married Lydia, the daughter of John and Martha Bunker Starr. In her infancy, Lydia was, in effect, adopted by Eleazer and Mary Bunker Lusher. Nathaniel died February 20, 1712. His wife Lydia died August 6, 1744, aged 92. They had:

    i. Benjamin, b. May 3, 1675; d. August 1, 1675.

    ii. Nathaniel, b. April 17, 1676; d. May 1, 1676.

    iii. Mary, b. March 30, 1677; married Jabez Pond, January 11, 1699. They had: Eliphalet Pond, b. May 17, 1704; d. January 19, 1795.

    iv. Lydia, b. August 12, 1679; married Thomas Eaton, October 15, 1697.

    v. Nathaniel, b. April 2, 1682; d. May 25, 1750.

   vi. Lusher, b. September 26, 1685; d. October 18, 1769. He married Mary Ellis. She died October 7, 1780, aged 90. Among their nine children were included:

      2. Ebenezer, b. May 4, 1718; d. March 7, 1796. Minister at Suffield, Conn.

      6. Mary, b. March 31, 1726; married Rev. John Ballantine of Westfield.

      9. Bunker, b. July 31, 1735; d. October 19, 1815. Minister at Hinsdale, N.H.

  vii. Joanna, b. September 3, 1688; married Ephraim Wilson, December 19, 1706.

 viii. Benjamin, b. April 20, 1691; date of death uncertain.

   ix. Abigail, b. February 15, 1694.

3.    x. Ebenezer, b. August 15, 1696; d. March 18, 1787.

3. The Reverend Ebenezer Gay of Hingham was born at Dedham on August 15, 1696. He married Jerusha Bradford, dau. of Samuel and Hannah Rogers Bradford of Duxbury, November 3, 1719. She was born March 10, 1699, and died August 19, 1783. He died March 18, 1787. Their children were:

    i. Samuel, b. January 15, 1721; d. March 26, 1746.

   ii. Abigail, b. September 8, 1722; d. February 8, 1729.

  iii. Calvin, b. September 14, 1724; d. March 11, 1765. He married Mary Smith of Sandwich, April 2, 1752. They had one child:

      1. Christiana, bap. November 26, 1752; married Bartholomew Jones, June 19, 1774.

4.  iv. Martin, b. December 29, 1726; d. February 13, 1809.

    v. Abigail, b. August 20, 1729; d. unm. April 7, 1804.

   vi. Celia, b. August 13, 1731; d. February 18, 1749.

  vii. Jotham, b. April 11, 1733; d. October 16, 1802.

 viii. Jerusha, b. March 17, 1735; married the Rev. Simeon Howard of Boston, November 29, 1790, and d. January 1812.

   ix. Ebenezer, b. March 3, 1737; d. July 3, 1738.

    x. Persis, b. November 2, 1739; d. March 24, 1752.

   xi. Joanna, b. November 23, 1741; d. July 23, 1772.

4. Martin Gay, Boston "brass-founder" and merchant, was born in Hingham on December 29, 1726. He married first, Mary Pinckney, December 13, 1750, and after her death in November 1764, he married Ruth Atkins, October 29, 1765. He died on February 13, 1809. His children by Mary were:

    i. Celia, b. 1751/2; married John Boyle, a printer, of Boston, March 12, 1772, and d. April 11, 1776.

   ii. Mary, b. circa 1753; married the Rev. William Black of Halifax, N.S.

iii. Samuel, b. 1754; d. January 21, 1847.

iv. Martin, b. 1760; d. April 17, 1778.

v. Frances, bap. April 1763; married Dr. Isaac Winslow, January 10, 1805, and d. October 12, 1846.

vi. Pinckney, bap. November 18, 1764; d. April 1773.

His children by Ruth were:

vii. Ebenezer, bap. September 21, 1766; d. soon.

viii. Ebenezer, bap. February 24, 1771; d. February 11, 1842.

ix. Pinckney, bap. July 2, 1775; d. in two weeks.

# Index

303